MW01427006

Howdy! Hola! Bonjour! Guten Tag!

I'm a *very special book*. You see, I'm traveling around the world making new friends. I hope I've met another friend in you. Please go to **www.BookCrossing.com** and enter my BCID number (shown below). You'll discover where I've been and who has read me, and can let them know I'm safe here in your hands. Then... *READ and RELEASE me!*

BCID: 183-13387011

Christian Controversies

15 May 2015

Nada,

Congratulations! May this book help you find the truth.

Christian Controversies:

Seeking the Truth

Scott S. Haraburda, PhD

Spencer, Indiana

Christian Controversies: Seeking the Truth

Copyright © 2013 by Scott S. Haraburda. All rights, including translation, reserved. No part of this book may be used or reproduced, stored in a retrieval system, or transmitted in any form or by any means electronic, mechanical, photocopying, recording, or otherwise, without written permission of the publisher except in the case of brief quotations embodied in critical articles and reviews.

Unless otherwise noted, all images contained in this book are in the public domain because the copyright has expired or because the artist died more than 100 years ago. For some of the images from European Union countries, it is because the artist died more than 70 years ago.

Published by: Meaningful Publications
PO Box 343, 30 S Washington St, Spencer, IN 47460
mp@haraburda.us / www.haraburda.us

Cover design by Scott S. Haraburda.

Publisher's Cataloging-In-Publication Data
(Prepared by The Donohue Group, Inc.)

Haraburda, Scott S.
  Christian controversies : seeking the truth / Scott S. Haraburda.
    p. : ill. ; cm.
  Issued also as an ebook.
  Includes bibliographical references and index.
  ISBN: 978-0-9886072-0-0 (cloth)
  ISBN: 978-0-9886072-1-7 (pbk.)

  1. Christianity--Philosophy. 2. Bible--Evidences, authority, etc. 3. Religion and science. 4. Church and social problems. I. Title.

BR100 .H37 2013
230.01   2012921339

To my wife, Marie, without whose support and assistance, none of this book would have been possible. She is the love of my life and first in my book.

Acknowledgments

No one walks alone on the journey of life. Just where do you start to thank those who have walked beside you and helped you along the way? Throughout my life, those I have met and worked with have shared many insights into the meaning of life, and the true desires of God. So, perhaps this book and its pages will be seen as "thanks" to the thousands who have helped make my life what it is today. Much of what I have learned from the years comes from being a father to five wonderful and delightful children: Ashlee, Beverly, Krystal, Jessica, and Christine, all of whom in their own way, has inspired me, which has contributed a tremendous amount to the content of this book. Moreover, I have to thank my amazing, loving wife, Marie, whose brilliant words and actions over the years have taught me much about myself and the wonderful spiritual ways of life. Both Marie and Krystal helped edit my book and provided me with several constructive suggestions. Finally, it would be incomplete if I failed to acknowledge the numerous military chaplains throughout my long military career who personally mentored me with their thought-provoking insights into Christianity and the true meaning of being a Christian. It's through their teachings, encouragement, and support that I have grown as a Christian. A little bit of each of them is woven in and out of the pages.

Contents

Tables vii

Figures viii

Chapter 1. What's This Book Really About 1

Chapter 2. Wise Christians are Open-Minded 5
    Open-Mindedness. 6
    Data. 12
    Information. 18
    Knowledge. 20
    Understanding. 24
    Wisdom. 28
    Conclusion. 29

Chapter 3. Christian Rules Violate Jesus' Lessons 37
    Secular Ethics. 38
    Ethics of Jesus. 49
    Early Christian Church Ethics. 58
    Modern Age Christian Ethics. 72
    Conclusion. 77

Chapter 4. Bible Can Justify Opposite Claims 87
    Content 88
    Translations and Interpretations 103
    Context 114
    Contradictions and Mistakes 128
    Denominations 142
    Conclusion. 144

Chapter 5. Christian Leaders Defy Jesus' Lessons 159
    Infamous Examples 160
    Infamous Popes 176
    Good Leadership 182
    Christian Leadership 191
    Conclusion. 205

Chapter 6. Many Christians Also Defy Jesus 219

- Group Behavior 220
- Group Dynamics 223
- Group Membership Process – Boot Camp Story 224
- Groupthink 235
- Christian Groupthink. 252
- Christians. 254
- Devil Made Me Do It 260
- The Church 264
- Conclusion. 269

Chapter 7. Additional Christian Controversies 281

- Controversial 'What If' Questions 281
- Probing Questions 325
- Conclusion. 329

Abbreviations 339

Index 341

- Authors, Artists, Groups and Key People 341
- Books and Films 351
- Canonical and non-Canonical Scriptures 352
- Subjects 355

About the Author 359

Tables

Table 1. Discredited Scientific Theories. 8
Table 2. Questions Eliciting False Answers. 15
Table 3. Different People Describing a Movie. 16
Table 4. Symptoms of Post-traumatic Stress. 17
Table 5. Facts Contradicting Popular Misinformation 22
Table 6. Controversies of Percentages. 27
Table 7. Ecumenical Councils. 63
Table 8. Books of the Bible – Old Testament. 90
Table 9: Books of the Bible – New Testament. 92
Table 10. Books of the Bible – Apocrypha. 94
Table 11. Some Books Missing From the Bible. 98
Table 12. Eight Popular Misquotes of the Bible. 111
Table 13. List of Biblical Contradictions. 131
Table 14. Transcription Errors. 136
Table 15. Translation Errors. 140
Table 16. Major Christian Denominations. 145
Table 17. Early Christians Martyrs. 200
Table 18. Methods of Christian Martyrdom. 201
Table 19. List of My Group Memberships 221
Table 20. Individual vs Collective Narcissistic Thinking 225
Table 21. Christian Bumper Stickers 259
Table 22. Women as Weaker Sex in Ancient Documents 307
Table 23. Biblical Rules I Refuse to Follow 309
Table 24. Recent Heroic Individuals 314

Figures

Figure 1. The Atmosphere: Popular Meterology. 11
Figure 2. Christ in Front of Pilate. 23
Figure 3. Different Number of Shelves Image. 29
Figure 4. Plato, Seneca, and Aristotle. 40
Figure 5. Saint Nicholas of Myra Saves Three Innocents from Death.. 52
Figure 6. Curses Against the Pharisees. 57
Figure 7. The Kiss of Judas and Peter Cutting off the Ear of Malchus. 64
Figure 8. Inquisition Scene 66
Figure 9. Joan at the Stake 68
Figure 10. Inquisition Torture Chamber. 70
Figure 11. Jesus and the woman taken in adultery 72
Figure 12. Papyrus 20. 112
Figure 13. Adam and Eve in Worthy Paradise 129
Figure 14. Jim Jones as the Loving Father of the "Rainbow Family" 166
Figure 15. Members of the Westboro Baptist Church 171
Figure 16. Burning of Templars. 175
Figure 17. The Cadaver Synod of 897. 177
Figure 18. The Army of the Second Crusade. 179
Figure 19. Flagellation of Our Lord Jesus Christ. 192
Figure 20. Joseph Interprets Pharoah's Dream. 194
Figure 21. Saul Attempts to Kill David 196
Figure 22. Crucifixion of St. Pete. 198
Figure 23. Parable of the Good Samaritan. 203
Figure 24. Me and My Drill Sergeant. 229
Figure 25. Charge of the Light Brigade. 243
Figure 26. Exhumation of Polish Officers from Katyn Massacre. 246
Figure 27. Space Shuttle Challenger Crewmember Remains. 251

Figure 28. Give us Barabbas. 255
Figure 29. Lamentations of Mary Magdalene on the Body of Christ. 286
Figure 30. Inferno 22. 288
Figure 31. The Birth of Venus. 302
Figure 32. Marriage at Cana. 317
Figure 33. Last Judgment 322

Chapter 1. What's This Book Really About

> *It was the best of Christianity, it was the worst of Christianity, it was the age of Wisdom, it was the age of Ignorance, it was the time of Belief, it was the time of Doubt, it was the season of Light, it was the season of Darkness, it was the spring of Hope, it was the winter of Pessimism, we had everything, we had nothing, we were all going directly to Heaven, we were all going directly to Hell*[1].

Even though this sounds cheesy, this is my Christian translation of Dickens' classic story about two cities, which is very applicable to Christianity today. Think about this.

As you're probably aware, there are millions of books written about Christianity, many of them contradicting one another. As a matter of fact, religious leaders and religious academic experts wrote many of them. For example, I heard many of those so-called leaders preach that we should return to the traditional biblical family values. If you hear this, run the other way. Why? For starters, the Bible is full of rules that describe women as property. They can be forced into marriage without their permission, whether it's their father's demands based upon receipt of payment from the future husband (otherwise known as the bride price[2]), or after being captured in a military battle[3]. Sacred prostitution was also acceptable[4]. These are some of the traditional biblical family values that I do NOT support!

---

[1] This is the famous introduction to this classic Dickens' story, which during every age, people experience the same contradictory struggles, difficulties, and joys. I took the liberty to rewrite this for Christianity instead of for life.
[2] Exodus 22:16-17 and Deuteronomy 22:28-29. Also in Genesis 29. This was probably the reason that Jacob worked two consecutive seven-year terms in order to marry both Leah and Rachel.
[3] Numbers 31:17-18.
[4] Genesis 38 in which Judah paid to have sexual relations with Tamar. As a result, she gave birth to Perez, an ancestor of King David and Jesus. Judah was one of the brothers who sold Joseph into slavery. See also Westenholz 1989.

I'm none of those religious leaders or experts. So, why should you read this book? I'm just a humble servant of the Lord with no formal religious training. Nevertheless, I profess myself to be a Christian, having started my life as a Catholic and having attended a Protestant church throughout most of my adulthood. While as a former Army Brigade commander, I supervised the religious programs for more than 2,000 Soldiers, with a variety of different Christian denominations and different non-Christian religions, such as Wiccan, Judaism, and Muslim faiths. Furthermore, I spent several years teaching Sunday School classes in various non-denominational Christian churches (or chapels), including the United Methodist Church. Moreover, I also served one year as the Sunday School Superintendent while teaching at West Point.

During my life's travels, I experienced life in different regions of the world; and, I read the Bible several times over in my feeble attempt to understand it. Yet, in my extensive scholarly research of the biblical messages, I have come to believe that God wants us to understand the basic theme throughout the Bible, and that involves the Greatest Commandment to love our neighbors. If that is the basic and simple premise behind being a Christian, then why do we have thousands of denominations, each trying to complicate the issues by telling us that the other ones are incorrect? I guess that is the basic Christian controversy. They must be both correct and incorrect, or one correct and the other incorrect. So, what do we need to know? Who do we believe?

Today, we live in a very selfish and terrifying world. It's full of greed and brutality with millions starving, people slaughtered indiscriminately, environmental degradation, widespread ignorance, and insidious prejudices. Franklin Spinney, an expert known for fighting fraud, waste, and abuse inside the Pentagon, described this quite accurately when he wrote that the United States has, "become a fearful nation, a bunkered nation, bogged down in never ending wars abroad accompanied by shrinking civil liberties at home"[5].

---

[5] 2011

What's This Book Really About

No wonder Americans, being fearful of everything, have a difficult time understanding Christianity. They should be fearful, especially about their spiritual well-being. Based upon my understanding of ancient history, specifically about the Athenian Empire, failure to learn from historical failures condemns us to repeat these failures[6]. This ancient empire was very similar to that of the United States. It started off as a democracy, expanded itself by gaining control over other countries, and lost everything when it destroyed itself from the inside out. The same is happening with Christians today. When we become more focused upon controlling what other people and organizations do, we begin to neglect ourselves. Then, eventually, we begin to lose ourselves spiritually and no longer believe in and follow the teachings of Jesus.

Although intended to be ironically humorous, George Carlin's monologue on religion portrays the perceptions that many Christians have regarding their faith, which I paraphrase below[7].

> *The Christian religion requires its members to believe there's an invisible man living in the sky who constantly sees everything we do. And this Voyeur has a bunch of rules for us. If we break any of them, He'll send us to a fiery hot place where we'll suffer forever. What's more, He loves us.*

A Christian should be able to respond to the errors implied within Carlin's monologue, but most of us can't. Largely, this results from lacking the wisdom of our faith, especially when dealing with contemporary controversial issues. As implied by its title, my book addresses many of the modern controversies surrounding the Christian faith and in a philosophical way, discusses different topics such as logic, epistemology, metaphysics, and even science.

---

[6] Santayana 1905-06. A paraphrase of "Those who cannot remember the past are condemned to repeat it."
[7] Dawkins 2006, 317. You can read the entire monologue in this book.

I'll share with you topics such as ethics, leadership, Bible-thumping judgment of each other, a perfect Bible, sex, lying, killing, and women's equality to men (or women's rights), and what we find in the Bible on these subjects.

To illustrate several items graphically, I have included several historical paintings, some that most people have never seen. Ultimately, my book will extend beyond just an academia view of the history of Christianity and enter into the real volatile world of globalization in which people live as they confront modern issues.

So, fasten your seatbelt and put your tray in the upright and locked position, because you're about to take off on a fantastic journey that explores how dealing with these Christian controversies impacts everlasting survival along your life's path.

References.

Dawkins, R. (2006). *The God Delusion.* New York: Bantam Books.

Dickens, C. (1859). *A Tale of Two Cities.* London: Chapman & Hall.

Santayana, G. (1905-06). *Reason in Common Sense, The Life of Reason: The Phases of Human Progress.* Vol. 1. New York: C. Scribner's Son.

Spinney, F.C. (2011, February). "Why is this Handbook Necessary." In Wheeler, Winslow T., Ed. *The Pentagon Labyrinth.* Center for Defense Information, World Security Institute.

Westenholz, J.G. (1989). "Tamar, Qedesa, Qadistu, and Sacred Prostitution in Mesopotamia." The *Harvard Theological Review.* 82(3): 245-65. http://clio.missouristate.edu/mcooper/HST541/Articles/Sacred_Prostitution.pdf. Accessed 31 August 2012.

Chapter 2. Wise Christians are Open-Minded

> *Can wise Christians possess absolute understanding about the teachings of Jesus? This is the Christian wisdom controversy. Only God has complete knowledge about this. Christians, who are mortal humans, should remain open-minded and grow in their faith, even if it means replacement of previous beliefs. Otherwise, faith will be nothing more than blind credulity, retrospective backwardness, and idle superstition. Becoming wise requires us to understand the wisdom hierarchy: data, information, knowledge, understanding, and wisdom. Without this wisdom, Christians risk making numerous defective decisions resulting from misleading experience, misleading prejudgments, inappropriate self-interest, and inappropriate attachments.*

Wisdom is a controversy too and is mentioned first because we need wisdom to fully understand the other controversies. My general hypothesis of this controversy, though, is that most Christians tend to welcome advances in science and technology but fear similar advances in religion. This close-minded faith prevents Christians from becoming wise, making it difficult for them to develop a closer relationship with God. To illustrate my point, I have witnessed many Christians taking full advantage of current technologies while still believing that the world is only five thousand years old, its first human inhabitants were Adam and Eve, the stories contained in the Bible are a completely accurate account of human history, along with the future destination of the condemnation of billions of people today. This same Christian mindset is based upon creeds which represented people living more than 1,500 years ago, even though common sense, reason, technology, and average intelligence have advanced significantly since then[8]. It's no wonder that for more than forty years that some

---

[8] Gulley 2010, 74.

modern theologians argue that God is dead and that we should get along without Him[9]. I totally disagree with this argument of a dead God and challenge all Christians to pursue wisdom in their faith, and not totally abandon it.

Wisdom – what is it? Do we picture a wise person as a white-haired elderly person sitting atop a mountain dishing out advice? Although that's the typical picture of a wise person, I advocate that anyone can be wise, providing that they possess the analytical experience to understand knowledge with an open mind. To be a wise Christian, we must understand our religion. It's more than just a recitation of mere facts or Scripture verses. To illustrate what I mean by wisdom, I offer the analogy of the wisdom hierarchy, which Russell Ackoff presented to the International Society for General Systems Research[10]. According to Ackoff, an organizational systems theorist, the human mind can process data in five progressive categories: data, information, knowledge, understanding, and wisdom. I have added an additional category of open-mindedness in that without it, the human mind can't process data in the other five categories.

Open-Mindedness.

Uncompromising close-minded attitudes have resulted in extreme cruel behavior[11]. Ancient Hebrews stoned their prophets[12]. Religious members demanded the death of Socrates for being an evildoer and not believing in the Athenian gods[13]. Religious leaders murdered one of its own with cries of "Crucify Him, crucify Him!" including "Away with this Man, and release to us Barabbas"[14]. Middle Age Christian leaders frequently tortured and killed both heretics and reformers. It was so bad that these Christian leaders' close-mindedness stood in the way of human progress by forcing Bruno, Galileo, Darwin, Haeckel and other

---

[9] Fuerbringher 1966.
[10] 1989.
[11] Schilpp 1938, 13.
[12] Acts 14:19-20.
[13] See especially Stone 1988.
[14] Luke 23:18-21.

scientists to deny what they knew to be the truth[15]. Religious beliefs became so strict that groups of Christians, many led by Martin Luther and John Wesley, broke away and revised their beliefs without the strict rigid adherence of their time[16].

Today, many historians and scientists identify the faith of many Christians as that of blind credulity, retrospective backwardness, and idle superstition[17]. These same intelligent people also consider much of the Christian beliefs to be emotional in nature with little tolerance for rational analyses and criticisms[18]. As a scientist, I fully understand why scientists have a skeptical opinion of the Christian religion. But, on the other hand, I fully understand that science and its scientific analyses are based upon faith too in that science is fundamentally based upon assumptions. For example, Table 1 lists several scientific theories that were accepted as undisputed facts when developed are no longer valid based upon recently acquired knowledge.

That's the beauty of science – it's willing to correct itself when it finds itself in error. This is because scientists know that we're extremely limited in our ability to understand the true nature of the universe. As a former chemist and a college chemistry instructor, I completely understand the evolution of the atomic theory, an example of science changing its beliefs based upon additional information. The following is a brief chronological development of this theory in which previous beliefs were allowed to change when new knowledge and understanding of atoms were observed.

In 1803, John Dalton published his concept of atomic weights for various substances. In 1897 through his work using cathode rays, J.J. Thomson discovered electrons and developed his "plum pudding model" for the distribution of this electron field[19]. In

---

[15] Schilpp 1938, 133.
[16] See Luther 1958 and Collins 2007.
[17] Schilpp 1938, 142.
[18] Schilpp 138, 150.
[19] 1897 and 1904.

Table 1. Discredited Scientific Theories.

Theory	Truth
Cold Fusion	In 1989, Martin Fleischman and Stanley Pons conducted experiments and reported generation of a low energy nuclear reaction[20]. The media took these reports and raised hopes of a future technology capable of generating cheap and abundant energy supply. Fortunately, other scientists attempted to replicate the experiments and didn't obtain the same results. Soon, this theory was discredited.
Flat Earth	In ancient times, people thought the earth was flat and that going far enough in one direction would result in falling off the earth. This theory persisted until advancements in science challenged it. As early as the sixth century BCE, Pythagoras proposed a mind-boggling theory to people of his day that the earth was round[21]. Nevertheless, after many centuries later of additional significant scientific studies into the matter and acceptance by the educated men of the time validating Pythagoras' theory, several early Christian leaders continued denying that the earth was round by supporting their claim using the Bible as proof[22]. Fortunately, most people living on the planet today don't believe this.
Static Universe	In 1917, Albert Einstein proposed that space is neither expanding nor contracting. In other words, we live in a static universe . However, in 1929, Edwin Hubble made a discovery that the universe isn't static, but expanding. Even Einstein can be wrong too.

---

[20] Simon 2002, 49.

[21] Russell 1997. There is a great debate among scholars and religious leaders between the BC/AD and the BCE/CE systems for representing dates. I'll use the latter system because the other one misrepresents the birth of Jesus by as much as seven years. To illustrate my point, how can Jesus be born in 7 BC (Before Christ)? The BCE represents "Before Common Era" while CE represents "Common Era." Anno Domini (AD) means "In the Year of the Lord," and should be placed before the year and not after it. Of note, the BC/AD system was introduced by Dionysius Exiguus in the sixth century. Regardless, both systems represent the same dates.

[22] 1 Chronicles 16:30, Psalms 93:1, 96:10, 104:5, and Isaiah 45:18.

Table 1. Discredited Scientific Theories (continued).

Theory	Truth
Phrenology	In 1796, German physician Franz Joseph Gall believed that a person's personality, thoughts, and emotions were caused by the different parts of their brain. Several other scientists supported this theory, resulting in the establishment of several phrenological societies and the use of phrenologists as the professional name of these scientists. It was taken seriously and was prevalent within written publications during the nineteenth century. Yet, mainstream academia rejected it since the basis of this theory didn't have valid scientific basis. Throughout the twentieth century, additional experimental data contradicted the items within the theory, causing most scientists to completely abandon it.
Vulcan Planet	In 1860, French mathematician Urbain Jean Joseph Le Verrier announced the discovery of Vulcan, a planet between Mercury and the Sun[23]. Several other observations supported this discovery. Yet, for several decades, many others couldn't find this planet. In 1915 as part of his theory of relativity, Albert Einstein explained that the object discovered by Le Verrier and others was the perihelion shift of Mercury[24]. A perihelion shift involves the concept of curved space and time. On a side note, this was also the name for the fictional planet of the ancestors of the character Spock in the *Star Trek* science fiction shows.

---

[23] Encyclopædia Britannica 1911. His most famous achievement was his prediction in 1846 that Neptune existed, which was later confirmed by Johann Galle and Heinrich d'Arrest about a month later.
[24] Ryden 2003.

Table 1. Discredited Scientific Theories (continued).

Theory	Truth
Luminiferous Aether	In 1704, using information derived from personal scientific experiments, Isaac Newton proposed that light travels on very small particles, called Aether (or ether). More than a hundred years later, James Clerk Maxwell developed a theory of electromagnetic waves that suggested that light didn't require a particle for propagation[25]. Albert Einstein disproved much of the ether theory in 1920, although not completely[26]. Shortly afterwards, the scientific community no longer supported this theory of light travel.
Martian Canals	In 1877, the Italian astronomer Giovanni Schiaparelli observed several dark lines on the planet of Mars and assumed they were canals. For several decades, other astronomers continued to support this theory of canals on Mars. By 1903, Joseph Edward Evans and Edward Maunder conducted experiments to discount the idea that Mars contained canals. Several other scientific studies continued to erode this theory, until it was finally disproved in 1965 with pictures taken by NASA's Mariner IV of the barren landscape[27].

1909, Thomson's former student, Ernest Rutherford, discovered that most of the mass of an atom is concentrated with a positive charge in a very small fraction of the atom in the center and the negative charges are much smaller particles surround the nuclear in a "planetary model"[28]. Unfortunately, this model couldn't explain the problems involving electrons not losing energy from its orbital motion and the presence of different spectra absorption of the atoms. Using the quantum theory developed by Albert Einstein and Max Planck, in 1913, Niels Bohr developed a model describing the electrons orbiting the nucleus in fixed circular

---

[25] 1878 and 1864.
[26] 1922.
[27] Smith et al. 1965.
[28] 1911.

angular momentum and energy[29]. In 1916, Arnold Sommerfield added elliptical orbits to the "Bohr Model" to explain extra spectral emission lines for multi-electron atoms, which are atoms other than hydrogen[30]. In 1926, Erwin Schrödinger used the observation from Louis de Broglie that electrons exhibit wave-like behavior by developing an equation to describe the electron as a wave function[31]. There have been additional significant improvements and changes to atomic theory since 1926, which was very important to me personally in that I used this scientific knowledge and its resulting beliefs (or theories) in my doctoral research for developing a rocket thruster. Yes, I'm a rocket scientist; but, we don't have to be one to become wise Christians and understand information and knowledge that challenges the current Christian beliefs.

Figure 1. The Atmosphere: Popular Meterology.
L'Atmosphere: Météorologie Populaire (1888) by Camille Flammarion.

---

[29] This is known as the "Bohr Model".
[30] Mehra 1982.
[31] This is known as the "Schrödinger Equation".

In my doctoral dissertation describing particle flow through an electric rocket thruster, I used statistical mechanics to describe the thermodynamic properties and chemical reaction mechanisms of atoms at extremely high temperatures near 50,000 degrees Celsius[32]. Statistical mechanics applies probability theory to physics by expanding quantum mechanics down to the microscopic, or atomic, level. I fully believe that my calculated data in this rocket design will be replaced with better data when more advanced measurement instruments are developed to accurately measure these same properties at these extremely high temperatures. This is called evolution of technology. Using the same logic, I believe that evolution should occur with Christian beliefs when better data is discovered that affects those beliefs. Our religious beliefs should evolve continually with better data and not remain static. Faith in our beliefs must be rationally grounded since it's impossible for a rational person to believe in something that he knows definitely isn't true[33]. I firmly believe that a rational God can't expect His followers to think irrationally.

So, what does having an open mind mean to us? In the basic purest sense of its meaning, the adult mind contains numerous facts of events, experiences, and beliefs such that it's virtually impossible to have a "blank slate" or a completely open mind[34]. Instead of this extreme condition, an open mind for should mean that the mind is not "closed" to the introduction of new knowledge and understanding, even though it may contradict previous ideas[35].

Data.

This consists of symbols, such as letters, characters, images, numbers and other outputs. It's raw in that it simply exists and doesn't have any meaning of itself. Data also refers to qualitative or quantitative attributes of a variable or set of variables. For example, the number "7" in the Bible is just a number and doesn't

---

[32] Haraburda 2001.
[33] Schilpp 1938, 157-58.
[34] Schilpp 1938, 8.
[35] Schilpp 1938, 9.

mean anything by itself. Thus, data on its own carries no meaning or value. For it to become information (the next level of wisdom), data must be interpreted and provide meaning. Finally, for data to have useful value to someone, it must be accurate, relevant, and practical[36].

Accurate.

For the data to be accurate, they must be valid and reliable. Valid data refer to data that can be directly related to factors being measured. One aspect of valid data being collected is that of causality. We must take special care to ensure that the data being collected caused the effect to occur. Reliable data refer to data that would be consistent regardless of the data collection technique. An effort should be made to eliminate or minimize errors in data collection due to collector bias, data collection administration, and wording. Another thing to consider is that people's memories should be considered flawed, and data obtained from them as also flawed. During the 24th Army Science Conference in Orlando, Florida, in December 2004, Harvard University psychology professor Daniel Schacter presented his theories of the "seven sins of memory" to the Army's scientific community[37]. In addition to providing a brief description of these memory problems, he effectively demonstrated that I, along with the rest of his audience, exhibited memory problems. If a person's memory isn't accurate, decisions based upon these faulty memories can cause significant problems.

Transience

This is decreasing memory over time. In 1885, German psychologist Hermann Ebbinghaus published his groundbreaking article "Über das Gedchtnis" ("On Memory") in which he described experiments he conducted on himself to describe the process of forgetting. A popular schematic of this problem is the forgetting curve, which illustrated the decline of memory retention over time. The stronger the memory, the longer one retained it. A

---

[36] Haraburda 2003.
[37] Haraburda 2007.

typical graph of the forgetting curve showed that humans tend to halve their memory of newly learned knowledge in a matter of days or weeks unless they consciously review the learned material.

Absent-mindedness

This is forgetting to do things. This is memory loss resulting from failure to pay attention when carrying out an act—putting your keys or glasses down without registering where you're putting them. Schacter's example involved cellist Yo Yo Ma. In October 1999, he left his $2.5 million cello, made in 1733 by Antonio Stradivari, in a New York cab. Apparently, he was preoccupied with other things and forgot to remind himself to ask the cab driver to retrieve his cello from the trunk.

Blocking

This is the tip-of-the-tongue experience. This is characterized by being able to retrieve quite a lot of information about the target word without being able to retrieve the word itself. We may know the meaning of the word, how many syllables the word has, or its initial sound or letter, but you can't retrieve it. The experience is coupled with a strong feeling that you know the word and that it is hovering on the edges of our thought.

Misattribution

This is attributing a memory to an incorrect source, such as hearing something from a friend and thinking that it was heard elsewhere, such as on the radio. An example of this involves Donald Thomson, a memory researcher, who in the 1970s appeared in a television show on the unreliability of eyewitness testimony. Not long after the show aired, the police picked him up because a rape victim had identified him as the rapist. He had an unshakable alibi: the assault had occurred when he was on TV describing how people could improve their ability to remember faces. The victim had been watching Thomson on TV before the attack and had confused her memory of him with her memory of the rapist. I recently conducted a couple of experiments with several senior military leaders. In the first experiment, I asked participants to read a four-line passage orally and count the number of times that a specific letter of the alphabet occurred. No matter how hard they tried, and retried, about half of them were unable to come up with the correct number. This was significant, since several of them were field-grade military officers who possessed graduate degrees and should have been fully capable of identifying their alphabet letters. In the second experiment, I read a list of fifteen words orally to these same leaders to determine their short-term memory retention. Over ninety percent of them claimed hearing a word that wasn't given to them, thus creating a false memory.

Table 2. Questions Eliciting False Answers.

Question	Description
Assumptive Question	This bases the question on an assumption. "How much will the price of gas go down next month?" assumes that the price will go down.
Linked Statement	This links two different items together and doesn't provide the same information for both items. Asking "Would you prefer to live in Detroit or Lansing where the crime rate is high?" doesn't mention anything about the crime rate in Detroit.
Implication Question	This provides a cause and effect result to the answer of the question. "If you stay out late tonight, how will you remain awake at work tomorrow morning?"
Asking for Agreement	This is typically the closed question that requires either a "yes" or "no" answer. "Do you agree that we need to help our church members before helping anyone else?"
Tag Question	These usually involve short phrases that end in a negative question. "You are coming to the very important church meeting, aren't you?"
Coercive Question	The context or tone of the question results in either an implicit or explicit coercion. In the following example, "How can you say that you will not be there?" the questioner conveys negative consequences for not attending.

Suggestibility

This is implanted memory from others. We need to be careful about the way in which we solicit information from others since the way a question is asked may generate false information. Table 2 contains six different types of questions that can elicit a false answer or inaccurate memory.

Bias

This is distortion based upon knowledge, beliefs, and perspective. We need to understand the basis of the information that people provide. If four people observe the same object or event, they will describe it from four different perspectives. Table 3 lists how four people might describe the movie *The Wizard of Oz*.

Table 3. Different People Describing a Movie.

Person	Description
Young Child	Tells the story, listing the sequence of events, but not necessarily in the right order.
Emotional Child	Explains that the movie was very scary with witches and wizards and flying monkeys
Adolescent	Describes the movie's special effects.
Intellectual	Identifies the themes within the movie.

Persistence

This is unwanted memory. Within the military, the most prevalent example of this is Post-traumatic Stress Disorder (PTSD). Audie Murphy, the most decorated American soldier in history at the time of World War II, suffered from PTSD as a result of his experiences. According to his first wife, he suffered terrible nightmares and always slept with a gun under his pillow. Table 4 lists the three symptoms that we must understand.

Table 4. Symptoms of Post-traumatic Stress.

Symptom	Description
Intrusion	Since the sufferer can't process difficult emotions in a normal way, he or she re-experiences the trauma in recurrent nightmares or daytime flashbacks, leading to high anxiety levels.
Hyper-arousal	Characterized by a state of nervousness, the person is in fight-or-flight mode, exhibiting jumpiness in connection with sudden sounds or movements.
Avoidance	The event is so distressing that the person strives to avoid contact with everything and everyone—even his own thoughts—that can arouse memories of the trauma. This leads to isolation.

Relevant.

For the data to be relevant, they must be credible and important. Credible data refer to data that will be believable by the people making the decisions. This is why I included hundreds of footnotes in this book, which provides you with the primary source of my data. As a wise decision maker, we should ensure there is a plan or baseline from which to compare, which should include the goals. Important data refer to data that address the important items associated with the factors being measured. For example, we shouldn't collect data on trivial items just because they are easy to collect and measure, such as the number of Christian members in a church. In this case, a better measurement would be the amount of good work provided by this church to the needy.

Practical.

For the data to be practical, it must be timely, simple, economic, and unchangeable. Timely data refer to data that can be measured in enough time to be effectively used. Simple data refer to data that are easy to understand. Economic data refer to data that can be obtained within the budget constraints for data collection. Unchangeable data refer to data that cannot be easily distorted to provide different information.

Information.

This is a combination of accurate, relevant, and practical data that provides the answers to "who", "what", "where", and "when" questions. The answers to these questions come from a relational connection of data. For example, the number "7" preceding the words "churches today" provides the answers to "who" and "when". Other than that, it doesn't offer any additional meaning. It doesn't provide meaning to how these "7 churches today" will do anything.

Once the information is developed, it should reflect reality. It should be as close to the truth as we can determine. Otherwise, this information could lead to erroneous knowledge, which could result in inappropriate actions. Historically, the Christian church and its members have used erroneous information and created more problems to God's people, especially the needy. For example, the Church and its religious leaders supported evil actions such as supporting slavery and Inquisitions of Medieval Europe as God's will[38]. For centuries, the Church condemned women as second-rate people or as objects owned by men[39]. Religious leaders even stated that diseases were a punishment from God[40]. And, they stated that poverty was another form of divine rejection, usually in an effort to convince a non-Christian to become a Christian and profess the same beliefs and other Christians[41].

Information can also include hypotheses involving the Christian faith, which are really hypotheses of metaphysical speculation[42]. In essence, God isn't an object of empirical data. Often times, many religious leaders insist that positive changes in a person's life are verifiable proofs that God exists. Although these changes prove the person's faith about God, these changes can't prove the actual existence of God or anything about Him[43]. Belief in God is based

---

[38] See Lippy 2007 and Vacandand 1907.
[39] See especially Westerkamp 2007.
[40] See especially Allen 2000.
[41] See especially Hughes 2009.
[42] Schilpp 1938, 167-68.
[43] Schilpp 1938, 170.

Wise Christians are Open-minded

upon faith, not verifiable data. Thus, information about the Christian faith not being the same as information about scientifically verifiable data doesn't mean that this faith-based information is irrelevant. The simple quote from Schilpp expresses this sentiment quite eloquently. "The meaning and significance of religious faith lie in what it is, not in what it is not"[44].

I caution you when you gather information to consider everything available, including information that we know contradicts our preconceived ideas. I almost didn't see one of my favorite movies, the 1986 film, *Heartbreak Ridge*, starring Clint Eastwood in a war film about a Marine. When it first came out, several veterans' groups were actively protesting this movie for its blatant misrepresentation of historical facts. The Battle of Heartbreak Ridge was fought by Army Soldiers in Korea in the fall of 1951[45]. It wasn't fought by Marines as implied by the Eastwood film. Had I refused to watch the movie because of their protests, I wouldn't have seen a very good movie. I also realized that these protesters failed to watch the movie prior to their protests. Had they watched it, they would have discovered that Eastwood was an Army Soldier awarded the Medal of Honor for his duties during the Battle of Heartbreak Ridge and later became a Marine. Instead, the movie wasn't about the actual Battle of Heartbreak Ridge, but about the effects of that battle many years later. It was a good thing that I considered additional information, and wasn't close-minded.

So, what does this have to do with Christianity? Have you considered obtaining information about other religions? How about subjects that dispute the existence of God? On a New York Times' best seller list was the 2006 book, *The God Delusion*, written by Richard Dawkins, a self-proclaimed Atheist. Because this was a best seller, many Christians probably read this book. Why would they? Do they question the existence of God? Are they beginning to lose faith in their religion? Or, are they just searching for additional information. For me, I just wanted to read all information about the same subject from different perspectives.

---

[44] Schilpp 1938, 175.
[45] Second Infantry Division, Korean War Veterans Association 2011.

A wise person would do that, knowing that not all information from one source represents reality or the truth. Failure to consider all sides of a topic could lead to faulty decisions, which I'll describe in several examples later in this book.

When searching for the truth behind information, we should consider science along with faith. Popular evolutionist, Stephen Jay Gould, once wrote, "science covers what the universe is made of and why it works this way", and "religion extends over questions of ultimate meaning and moral value"[46]. Both of these positions should coexist without conflict. We too should be open-minded, accepting that religion and science could both be correct.

Knowledge.

This is the application of both data and information, which answers "how" questions. In essence, this is a collection of information that provides some use to the person. Memorizing Scriptures in the Bible provides a person with knowledge, but it doesn't provide any additional knowledge. As an engineer, I offer the following analogy. In elementary school, I learned the math *times table* through memorization drills. I still remember my tables today in that I can easily tell you that "2 x 3 = 6". But this doesn't provide us with the skills to answer the question of "222 x 333". And, the answer isn't "666", instead correctly being "73,926". The *times table* in itself doesn't provide the answer because these large numbers aren't part of the *times table*. Unfortunately, today, most adults are fully incapable of answering this question without a calculator. They are limited to the knowledge of the *times table* if they can still remember it.

Knowledge may change with new information. For example, I was told as a young adult several decades ago that eating eggs significantly raises cholesterol, which could lead to coronary problems. Today I'm told by experts that eggs don't significantly affect a person's cholesterol levels. Also, I hear many different ideas on weight loss, including the protein diet, no-carb diet, no

---

[46] 2002.

Wise Christians are Open-minded

exercise diet, and input versus output energy balance diet. In almost everything that we do, we can find someone to support one idea and another to support the opposite. What are we to believe? If doing something today is good and later told it's wrong by someone else, why should I believe it's good? How do we determine the correct information and get the correct knowledge? These are good questions. My only advice is for us to continue looking at all of the information available and to keep an open-mind to possible changes. For example, Table 5 contains seven facts that contradicts popular misinformation, and should change the knowledge we have regarding the areas of aviation, communications, science, and the military.

Facts are nothing more than data about the world in which we live. Theories and knowledge are developed that attempt to explain these facts. The facts don't disappear when researchers argue rival theories to explain them. Our interpretation of them changes. For example, Einstein's theory of relativity involving gravity replaced Newton's gravity theory[47]. Gravity didn't change – apples fell from the trees for both Newton and Einstein. From a biblical perspective, even Pontius Pilate understood the need to obtain knowledge when he asked Jesus, "What is truth?" Afterwards, he told the Jews that he didn't find Him guilty[48].

In his book, Dawkins discussed the confusion of the word "God". God can be seen as a superstitious idol to be worshipped, while others represent God as the supreme mystery behind the existence of the natural scientific universe. In my opinion, why can't he be both? Dawkins also described how close-minded religious believers react badly to criticism of their religion. Several times, Dawkins laid out logical arguments against religious theologians and tried to use scientific principles to further justify his theory that God doesn't exist. For example, he attempted to prove evolution over creationism. This didn't answer two questions that I had: why must there be only two possible options to human existence, and

---

[47] 1920.
[48] John 18:38.

Table 5. Facts Contradicting Popular Misinformation.

Person	Description
Charles Lindbergh	He wasn't the first man to cross the Atlantic Ocean by air. He was the first to do it solo, doing it in May 1927[49]. However, it was Captain John Alcock and Lieutenant Arthur Brown who made the first non-stop crossing of the Atlantic Ocean in June 1919[50].
Columbus	He wasn't the first European to discover North America, which was done by Viking Leiv Eiriksson[51].
The Wright Brothers	They weren't the first to fly an airplane. Others, such as Gustav Whitehead, Clément Ader, and Alexander Mozhaiski have valid claims to have done this prior to the Wright Brothers[52].
Alexander Graham Bell	He didn't invent the telephone. Although he was the first to obtain a patent for it. Elisha Gray was the first to create a working telephone[53].
Charles Darwin	He wasn't first to create theory of evolution. It was based upon theories of previous scientists, including Jean-Baptiste Lamarck, Pierre Louis Maupertius, and Erasmus Darwin[54].
Thomas Edison	He didn't invent the light bulb. He just made it better. Others developing it prior to him were Humphrey Davy and Frederick de Moleyns[55].
George Custer	He wasn't a general at the Battle of Little Big Horn, even though he was a general during the Civil War. Following the war as the size of the US Army was reduced, he returned to the permanent rank of lieutenant colonel[56].

---

[49] Smithsonian National Air and Space Museum 2011.
[50] The New York Times 2011.
[51] Ryne 2011.
[52] See Randolf and Phillips 1935, Crouch 2011, and Gray 2011.
[53] Baker 2000, 90-91. The Patent Office quoted that, "while Gray was undoubtedly the first to conceive of and disclose the [variable resistance] invention, as in his caveat of 14 February 1876, his failure to take any action amounting to completion until others had demonstrated the utility of the invention deprives him of the right to have it considered."
[54] Gould 2002, 187; Bowler 2003, 73-75; and Fara 2011.
[55] Lamont-Brown 2004 and Encyclopædia Britannica 2011.
[56] Custer and Custer 1950, 185, 296.

why can't we have creationism through evolution? Also in his book, as a scientist himself, he implied that a real scientist wouldn't value the opinion of someone whose entire system of knowledge is based upon a book of myths. As a scientist myself, Dawkins hasn't proven that the myths weren't real. Dawkins' attempted to disprove God's existence using scientific logic was really nothing more than a word game. In my professional opinion, much of his evidence was based upon misinterpretations of nature or just plainly figments of his imagination. Furthermore, he claimed that almost all true intellectuals are Atheists, including the tendency that the higher a person's education level, the less likely they are to be religious. This does have some element of truth to it since I personally know several intellectual Atheists. But, this still doesn't convince me that God doesn't exist.

Figure 2. Christ in Front of Pilate.
jezus przed pilatem (1881) by Mihály Munkácsy.

In addition to my own self-assessment of his book, I also considered assessments from others, both those supporting Dawkins' theory and those who didn't. With a slight positive view, Jim Holt wrote that, "What Dawkins brings to this approach is a couple of fresh arguments -- no mean achievement, considering how thoroughly these issues have been debated over the centuries -- and a great deal of passion. ... There is lots of good, hard-hitting stuff about the imbecilities of religious fanatics and frauds of all stripes"[57]. Thomas Nagel wrote a negative view with, "Dawkins is convinced that religion is the enemy of science. The book is a very uneven collection of scriptural ridicule, amateur philosophy, historical and contemporary horror stories, anthropological speculations, and cosmological scientific argument"[58].

The Economist briefly described thoughts I had about his book and why all serious Christians should read it. Although he constructed a strong case against religion, "Atheists will love Mr Dawkins' incisive logic and rapier wit and theists will find few better tests of the robustness of their faith. Even Agnostics, who claim to have no opinion on God, may be persuaded that their position is an untenable waffle"[59].

Regrettably, Julius Caesar's words, *homines id quod volunt credunt,* express my concerns about people's search for the knowledge of truth. "Men believe what they want to"[60]. Unfortunately, most Christians would rather argue with someone instead of discussing with them about something they don't already know or believe. Instead, they're more influenced by the simple sound-bites of political talk-show radio rather than in what Jesus really taught[61].

Understanding.

Once we possess knowledge, the next step towards wisdom is to assess the "why" question. Understanding knowledge is a cognitive and analytical process that transforms into new knowledge. Let me provide you an example of this in a situation that happened to me. When I was in college, I had a difficult time learning organic chemistry. I didn't understand the complex

---

[57] 2006.
[58] 2006.
[59] 2006.
[60] Clark 2002, 204.
[61] Collier 2012, 28 and 39.

organic reaction mechanism because it was just a leap of faith for me. In essence, I had to memorize the reaction steps. This was similar to just memorizing the Scriptures in the Bible and not analyzing that information to generate understanding. Reading the Bible and understanding the Bible are completely different.

In a recent poll on religion, the Pew Research Foundation asked over three thousand people in 2010 several questions involving religion in general. According to this survey, they claimed that Atheists and Agnostics knew more about religion than Christians. Unfortunately, this survey was flawed in that it only asked questions requiring facts and some knowledge. It didn't ask questions to assess one's understanding of their own religion. This survey contained questions about the history of Hindu, Buddhist, and Muslim religions. Yet, many theologians and other Christians have quickly used this survey results to validate their claims that Atheists know more than Christians. Maybe they do, but about all religions in general though. I agree that most Christians don't really understand their own religion. I also don't believe Atheists and Agnostics with the same educational level really understand Christianity either. This survey doesn't prove anything to me either.

Let me illustrate another problem many people have in understanding knowledge they hear or read. I'll do this by describing my simple controversy of percentages[62]. This controversy involves a bag containing two types of steel balls, both small and large, totaling one hundred balls. Three different people are asked to calculate the percentage of large balls in this bag with each providing contradictory results: 1%, 50%, and 99%. If I heard this initially, I'd think that two of these had to be wrong, and so would most people. However, in this controversial example, all three answers are correct. You're probably thinking I'm crazy to even imply such an impossible thing, and you might consider nominating me for the fictional absent-minded professor of the year award.

---

[62] Haraburda 2008, 20-21.

Now let me explain this set of contradictory knowledge further. These people represented three different types of professions: accounting, construction, and transportation. The first person was an accountant concerned with the number of balls – 1 large and 99 small, resulting in 1% by number. Now, you must be thinking that this accountant had the real correct answer, with the other two definitely being wrong. The second person was a painter concerned with the surface area of the balls involving the amount of paint to use – the 1 large ball had a surface area of about 600 square inches and the total amount of the surface area of the very small 99 balls had the same cumulative surface area also of 600 square inches, resulting in 50% by area. You are thinking that this must be a trick problem. Finally, the third person was a truck driver concerned with the weight of the balls – the 1 large ball weighing about 396 pounds and all of the 99 small balls together weighing about 4 pounds, resulting in 99% by weight. Most people can't believe this. They would have made a different decision depending upon which percentage they had heard. As we may have been told, probably in math class a long time ago, percentages have no units of measurement, such as length or weight. However, as represented in Table 6, percentages do have units, such as percent by number, percent by area, and percent by weight. No wonder people hate numbers so much. Nevertheless, we should always try to understand the source of these percentages – we may even discover additional knowledge about reality along the way.

So, how does a Christian understand all of the knowledge it receives? As we can see from the controversy of percentages above, understanding something may become counter-intuitive. It may contradict some of our unchangeable beliefs. In our journey to understand this knowledge, we're challenged to understand the difference between empirical knowledge, metaphysical speculation, and Christian faith. As I cautioned you previously, our faith should extend beyond both science and reason and shouldn't be expressed in an equation[63]. Trying to worship God becomes impossible if we can't understand Him. Furthermore, if

---

[63] Schilpp 1938, 158.

rational people are to become and remain Christian, their faith shouldn't contradict scientific facts or reason. To help, we might consider Christianity as simply a collection of emotions and feelings and leave the rest to scientific analyses. As we begin to seriously assess our faith and that of our fellow Christians, we may begin to realize that most Christians care more about things regarding Jesus than following his example. For me, I care more about His message rather than Him as the Messenger from God.

Table 6. Controversies of Percentages.

Profession	Characteristics	Big Ball	Small Ball
Accountant	Number (each)	1	99
	TOTAL NUMBER	1	99
	Percentage	1%	99%
Painter	Area (square in. each)	600	6.06
	TOTAL AREA	600	600
	Percentage	50%	50%
Truck Driver	Weight (pounds each)	396.0000	0.0404
	TOTAL WEIGHT	396	4
	Percentage	99%	1%

Source: Haraburda 2008

Finally, understanding the Christian knowledge is important since Christian theology is really the product of human hands and hearts. Many Christian leaders will try to convince us that everything written in the Bible is completely accurate since it was written through divine intervention. Furthermore, they'll try to convince us that a specific theory or doctrine is accurate as well, since the development of that theory was divinely inspired as well. But, don't believe them. Consider the words of Cicero, *damnant quod non intellegunt*, meaning "they condemn what they do not understand"[64]. Instead, we need to research their theory and attempt to understand why it's both correct and incorrect. As you can tell by now, I'm not going to tell you what you should believe or understand about being a Christian. So, if you think my book is another instruction book on what you need to know, you will be

---

[64] Van Evrie 1864: 8.

very disappointed. I'm not going to do something Jesus never did to His disciples or others. Jesus didn't tell His followers what to do nor what to think, instead making them learn on their own through stories, questions, and parables. Likewise, I challenge all Christian leaders to focus their leadership more upon mentoring other Christians on "how" to think, not "what" to know so that their followers can understand their faith more fully.

Wisdom.

Wisdom provides us the best course of action in a specific situation. Obtaining it comes from an evaluation of knowledge to allow you to respond effectively with the "who", "what", "where," "when", "how", and "why" answers. Wisdom results from a rational extrapolation of existing knowledge to provide us an understanding in areas with little to no knowledge, even in areas where there'll never be concrete definitive empirically based knowledge, such as life after death. Some people might refer to this as philosophical probing[65]. This evaluation allows us to discern the difference between right and wrong actions, good and bad ideas, and the relative value of gray-area information that doesn't fall clearly in a "black" or "white" classification. The process of obtaining wisdom requires us to have a soul since it requires both our heart and our mind.

The first four categories of the wisdom hierarchy (data, information, knowledge, and understanding) relate to the past, dealing only with what has been or what is known. For example, the Bible is full of data and information, many which are contradictory. Such as the image in Figure 3, we can see different numbers of shelves, depending upon how we look at the image. The wisdom comes from understanding these differences and coming up with things to do as a result of these differences. I wouldn't send this drawing of shelves to a carpenter building them for me. Christian knowledge and understanding of the information usually comes from religious studies. The last category, wisdom, has a focus upon the future. We can use wisdom to create the

---

[65] See especially Evans 1985.

future rather than just grasp the past. But let me tell you, achieving wisdom isn't easy since we must effectively and thoroughly process through the other four categories while keeping an open-mind.

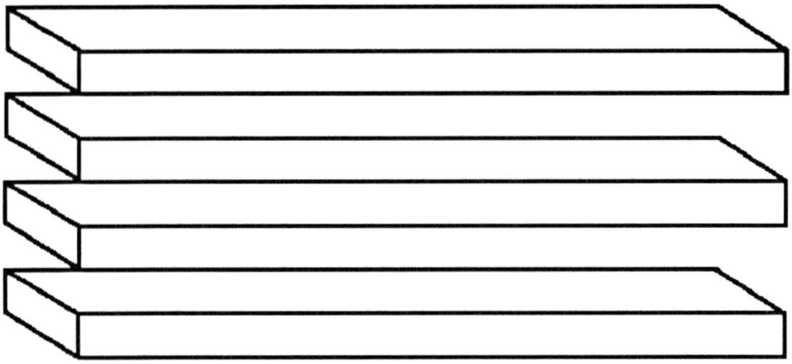

Figure 3. Different Number of Shelves Image.
How many are there, three or four?

Conclusion.

Sadly, most people today prefer to be intellectually lazy and let others assess the data for them and tell them what it means. Furthermore, we tend to interpret information based solely upon our own biases and frame of references. As such, most Christians are biblically illiterate, meaning they don't know what their religion is about[66]. The best advice that can be given was stated almost two hundred years ago by James Madison. "Knowledge will forever govern ignorance and a people who mean to be their own governors must arm themselves with the power which knowledge gives"[67]. We make hundreds of decisions every day, many of them in the name of Christianity. Many of these are defective decisions, which result from misleading experience, misleading prejudgments, inappropriate self-interest, and inappropriate attachments[68].

Until we overcome our intellectual laziness involving our faith, we'll continue to make defective decisions. Yes, this should worry

---

[66] Collier 2012, 54.
[67] 1822.
[68] Finkelstein et al. 2009.

us since many Christians are biblically illiterate and believe their Christian leaders completely[69]. Popular Christianity often degenerates rather than celebrate intellectual and critical inquiry. Our illiteracy supports the fundamental basis of modern Christian religion. Philip Gulley, a pastor of an Indiana Christian church, has a unique perspective about this. "Take an ancient doctrine, insist it originated with God, devise a ritual that reinforces it, wrap it in a prayer, reward those who perpetuate it, and condemn to Hell those who don't, and what you have is a significant portion of today's church"[70]. Christianity should become better than this.

References.

Ackoff, R.L. (1989). "From Data to Wisdom," *Journal of Applies Systems Analysis.* 16: 3-9.

Allen, P.L. (2000). *The Wages of Sin: Sex and Disease, Past and Present.* Chicago: University of Chicago Press.

Baker, B. (2000). *The Gray Matter: The Forgotten Story of the Telephone.* St. Joseph, Mich.: Telepress.

Bohr, N.H.D. (1913). "On the Constitution of Atoms and Molecules." *Philosophical Magazine.* 26: 1-25. Article located on website for the Hamed Maleki Institut für Physik Johannes Gutenberg-Universität. http://www.cond-mat.physik.uni-mainz.de/~oettel/ws10/bohr_PhilMag_26_1_1913.pdf. Accessed 11 September 2011.

Bowler, P.J. (2003). *Evolution: the History of an Idea.* 3rd Edition. Berkeley, Calif.: University of California Press.

Clark, M. (2002). *Paradoxes from A to Z.* New York: Routledge.

Collier, G.D. (2012). *Scripture, Canon, & Inspiration.* Cloverdale, Ind.: CWP Press.

Collins, K.J. (2007). *The Theology of John Wesley: Holy Love and the Shape of Grace.* Nashville, Tn: Abingdon Press.

Crouch, T. (primary contributor). (2011). "Clément Ader." *Encyclopædia Britannica.* http://www.britannica.com/ EBchecked/topic/5780/Clement-Ader. Accessed 15 June 2011.

Custer, G.A. and Custer, E.B. (1950). *The Custer Story: The Life and Intimate Letters of General George A. Custer and His Wife Elizabeth.* Edited by Marguerite Merington. New York: Devin-Adair.

---

[69] Gulley 2010, 38.
[70] 2010, 76.

Daigneault, A. and Sangalli, A. (2001). "Einstein's Static Universe: An Idea Whose Time Has Come Back?" *Notice of the American Mathematical Society*. 48: 9-16. http://www.ams.org/notices/200101/fea-daigneault.pdf. Accessed 9 June 2011.

Dalton, J. (1803). "On the Absorption of Gases by Water and Other Liquids." In *Memoirs of the Literary and Philosophical Society of Manchester*, Second Series, 1, 271-87 (1805). Read October 21, 1803 [from Alembic Club Reprint #2]. http://web.lemoyne.edu/~GIUNTA/dalton52.html. Accessed 8 June 2011.

Dawkins, R. (2006). *The God Delusion*. New York: Bantam Books.

Eastwood, C. (director). (1986). *Heartbreak Ridge*. Internet Movie Database, http://www.imdb.com/title/ tt0091187/ Accessed 14 June 2011.

The Economist (2006). Book review of *The God Delusion* by Richard Dawkins. (September 23). http://www.economist.com/node/8380365. Accessed 14 June 2011.

Einstein, A. (1920). Relativity: The Special and General Theory. German original in 1916. Translated by Robert W. Lawson. New York: Henry Holt and Company. http://www.ibiblio.org/ebooks/Einstein/Einstein_Relativity.pdf. Accessed 25 September 2011.

Einstein, A. (1922). "Ether and the Theory of Relativity" An address delivered on May 5, 1920 in the University of Leyden. German original. Translated by George B. Jeffery and Wilfrid Perrett in *Sidelights on Relativity*, 5-14. London: Methuen. http://www.ibiblio.org/ebooks/Einstein/Sidelights/Einstein_Sidelights.pdf. Accessed 10 September 2011.

Encyclopædia Britannica (2011). "Frederick de Moleyns." *Encyclopædia Britannica*. http://www.britannica.com/EBchecked/topic/388296/Frederick-de-Moleyns. Accessed 15 June 2011.

Encyclopædia Britannica (1911) "Urbain Jean Joseph Leverrier". *Encyclopædia Britannica*. http://www.1911encyclopedia.org/Urbain_Jean_Joseph_Leverrier. Accessed 9 June 2011.

Evans, C.S. (1985). *Philosophy of Religion: Thinking about Faith: Contours of Christian Philosophy*. Downers Grove, Ill.: InterVarsity Press Academic.

Evans, J.E. and Maunder, E. (1903). "Experiments as to the Actuality of the 'Canals' Observed on Mars." *Monthly Notices of the Royal Astronomical Society*. 63: 488-99. http://adsabs.harvard.edu//full/seri/MNRAS/0063//0000488.000.html. Accessed 9 June 2011.

Fara, P. (primary contributor). (2011). "Erasmus Darwin." *Encyclopædia Britannica*. http://www.britannica.com/EBchecked/topic/151960/Erasmus-Darwin. Accessed 15 June 2011.

Finkelstein, S.; Whitehead, J.; and Campbell, A. (2009). "Think Again: Why Good Leaders Make Bad Decisions and How to Keep it from Happening to You." *Harvard Business Review*. 87(2): 60-66.

Fuerbringher, O. (1966). "Is God Dead," Time Magazine. (April 8). http://www.time.com/time/magazine/article/0,9171,835309,00.html. Accessed 11 September 2011.

Gould, S.J. (2002). *The Structure of Evolutionary Theory*. Harvard University: Belknap Harvard.

Gray, C. (2011). "Aleksandr Fyodorovich Mozhaiski." This article was posted on the Flying Machines website. http://www.flyingmachines.org/moz.html. Accessed 15 June 2011.

Gulley, P. (2010). *If the Church Were Christian: Rediscovery the Values of Jesus*. New York: HarperCollins Publishers.

Haraburda, S.S. (2008). *Premonitions of the Palladion Project: A Modern Project Management Fable*. Morristown, N.C.: Lulu Enterprises Publishing.

Haraburda, S.S. (2007). "PROGRAM MANAGEMENT: The 'Seven Sins of Memory' – How They Affect Your Program." *Defense AT&L*. 36(1): 30-32. Ft. Belvoir, Va.: Defense Acquisition University Press.

Haraburda, S.S. (2003). "Performance Measurement: Newport Chemical Agent Disposal Facility Project Management Team – Leveraging Fidelity of Performance-Based Metric Tools for Project Management," Program Manager. 32(1): 32-35. Ft. Belvoir, Va.: Defense Acquisition University Press.

Haraburda, S.S. (2001). "Transport Phenomena of Flow through Helium and Nitrogen Plasmas in Microwave Electrothermal Thrusters," Ph.D. dissertation, Michigan State University.

Holt, J.C. (2006, 22 October). "Beyond Belief." *The New York Times Sunday Book Review* http://www.nytimes.com/2006/10/22/books/review/Holt.t.html. Accessed 14 June 2011.

Hubble, E.P. (1929). "A Relation between Distance and Radial Velocity among Extra-Galactic Nebulae" *Proceedings of the National Academy of Sciences of the United States of America*. 15(3): 168-73. This was communicated January 17, 1929. http://www.pnas.org/content/15/3/168.full.pdf. Accessed 9 June 2011.

Hughes D. (2009). *Power and Poverty: Divine and Human Rule in a World of Need.* Downers Grove, Ill.: InterVarsity Press Academic.

Lamont-Brown, R. (2004). *Humphry Davy: Life Beyond the Lamp.* Stroud, UK: Sutton Publishing.

Lippy, C.H. (2007). "Slave Christianity." Chapter Ten in *Modern Christianity to 1900: A People's History of Christianity*, 6: 291-316, edited by Amanda Porterfield. Minneapolis, Mn.: Fortress Press.

Luther, M. (1958). "Concerning the Ministry." Original German in 1523 Translated by Conrad Bergendoff in *Luther's Works.* Philadelphia, Pa: Fortress Press. 40: 3-44.

Madison, J. (1822). "James Madison to W.T. Barry," (August 4). Writings 9: 103-9. In "Epilogue: Securing the Republic," Volume 1, Chapter 18, Document 35 of *The Founders' Constitution,* 1987. Edited by Philip B. Kurland and Ralph Lerner. Chicago: The University of Chicago Press. http://presspubs.uchicago.edu/founders/documents/v1ch18s35.html. Accessed 11 September 2011.

Maxwell, J.C. (1878). "Ether." *Encyclopædia Britannica*, 9th Ed 8: 568-72. http://en.wikisource.org/wiki/Encyclop%C3%A6dia_Britannica_Ninth_Edition/Ether. Accessed 9 June 2011.

Maxwell, J.C. (1864). "A Dynamical Theory of the Electromagnetic Field." *Philosophical Transactions.* Royal Society of London. 155: 459-512. http://rstl.royalsocietypublishing.org/content/155/459.full.pdf+html. Accessed 11 September 2011.

Mehra, J. (1982). "The Bohr – Sommerfeld Theory of Atomic Structure." Chapter II in *The Quantum Theory of Planck, Einstein, Bohr and Sommerfeld: Its Foundation and the Rise of Its Difficulties 1900-1925 1 (The Historical Development ... and the Rise of Its Difficulties 1900-1925,* 155-258. New York: Springer.

Nagel, T. (2006). "The Fear of Religion." *The New Republic.* (October 23). http://www.tnr.com/article/the-fear-religion. Accessed 14 June 2011.

The New York Times. (2011). "Alcock and Brown Fly Across Atlantic; Make 1,980 Miles in 16 Hours, 12 Minutes; Sometimes Upside Down in Dense Icy Fog." *The New York Times.* Front Page, June 16, 1919. Copy of page located at the Aviation History On-Line Museum. http://www.aviation-history.com/airmen/ alcock.htm. Accessed 15 June 2011.

Pew Research Center. (2010, 28 September). "U.S. Religious Knowledge Survey." *The Pew Forum on Religion & Public Life.*

http://www.pewforum.org/U-S-Religious-Knowledge-Survey.aspx. Accessed 15 September 2012.

Randolf, S. and Phillips, H. (1935). "Did Whitehead Precede Wright in World's First Powered Flight?" *Popular Aviation*. (January). Article contents posted on the Wright Brothers Aeroplane Company museum website. http://www.wright-brothers.org/History_Wing/History_of_the_Airplane/Who_Was_First/Gustav_Whitehead/Whitehead_Articles.htm. Accessed 15 June 2011).

Russell, J.B. (1997). "The Myth of the Flat Earth". *American Scientific Affiliation Annual Meeting.* (Aug). This paper and presentation summarized his book, *Inventing the Flat Earth: Columbus and Modern Historians*, 1997 Westport, Ct.: Praeger. http://www.asa3.org/ASA/topics/history/1997Russell.html. Accessed 9 June 2011.

Rutherford, E. (1911). "The Scattering of α and β Particles by Matter and the Structure of the Atom," *Philosophical Magazine*. 21: 669-88. Article located on website for the Hamed Maleki Institut für Physik Johannes Gutenberg-Universität. http://www.cond-mat.physik.uni-mainz.de/~oettel/ws10/rutherford_PhilMag_21_669_1911.pdf. Accessed 11 September 2011.

Ryden, B.S. (2003). "General Relativity," Ohio State University Astronomy 162 course notes for February 11, 2003. http://www.astronomy.ohio-state.edu/~ryden/ast162_6/notes24.html. Accessed 9 June 2011.

Ryne, L. (2011). "Leif Ericson: Columbus Predecessor by Nearly 500 Years." Excerpted from "Norwegian Explorers" on the ODIN website, produced for the Norwegian Ministry of Foreign Affairs by Nytt fra Norge. http://www.mnc.net/norway/ericson.htm. Accessed 14 June 2011.

Schilpp, P.A. (1938). *The Quest for Religious Realism: Some Paradoxes of Religion*. New York: Harper & Brothers Publishers. The Mendenhall lectures, seventeenth series, delivered at DePauw University.

Schrödinger, E. (1926). "Quantisierung als Eigenwertproblem," Annalen der Physik. 384(4): 361-76. German original. This was the first of four articles involving this equation. http://onlinelibrary.wiley.com/doi/10.1002/andp.19263840404/abstract. Accessed 25 September 2011.

Second Infantry Division, Korean War Veterans Association. (2011). "History of the 2nd Infantry Division during the Korean War: Heartbreak Ridge." This was an article about one of the major battles of this division during the Korean War. http://www.2id.org/heartbreakridge.htm. Accessed 14 June 2011.

Simon, B. (2002). *Undead Science: Science Studies and the Afterlife of Cold Fusion.* Piscataway, N.J.: Rutgers University Press.

Simpson, D.A. (2005). "Phrenology and the neurosciences: contributions of F. J. Gall and J. G. Spurzheim." *ANZ Journal of Surgery.* 75(6); 475-82.

Smith, E.J.; Davis Jr., L.; Coleman Jr., P.J.; and Jones, D.E. (1965). "Magnetic Field Measurements Near Mars". Science, New Series 149 (3689): 1241–42.

Smithsonian National Air and Space Museum. (2011). "Milestones of Flight: Ryan NYP 'Spirit of St. Louis'." *Smithsonian National Air and Space Museum.* http://www.nasm.si.edu/exhibitions/GAL100/stlouis.html. Accessed 15 June 2011.

Stone, I.F. (1988). *The Trial of Socrates.* New York: Little, Brown.

Thomson, J.J. (1904). "On the Structure of the Atom: an Investigation of the Stability and Periods of Oscillation of a number of Corpuscles arranged at equal intervals around the Circumference of a Circle; with Application of the Results to the Theory of Atomic Structure." *Philosophical Magazine*, 39: 237-65. http://www.chemteam.info/ Chem-History/Thomson-Structure-Atom.html. Accessed 8 June 2011.

Thomson, J.J. (1897). "Cathode Rays." *Philosophical Magazine*, 44: 293. In Stephen Wright, *Classical Scientific Papers, Physics*, 1964. London: Mills and Boon. http://web.lemoyne.edu/~GIUNTA/thomson1897.html. Accessed 8 June 2011.

Trinko, T. (2010, 3 October). "Flawed Pew Poll on Religious Knowledge Falsely Flatters Atheists." American Thinker. http://www.americanthinker.com/2010/10/flawed_pew_poll_on_religious_k.html. Accessed 15 September 2012.

Vacandard, E. (1907). *The Inquisition: A Critical and Historical Study of the Coercive Power of the Church.* French original 1902. Translated by Bertrand Conway. New York: Longmans, Green and Co. http://www.gutenberg.org/cache/epub/26329/pg26329.html. Accessed 1 July 2011.

Van Evrie, J.H. (1864). *Subgenation: The Theory of the Normal Relation of the Races; An Answer to "Miscengenation."* New York: John Bradburn.

Westerkamp, M.J. (2007). "Gendering Christianity." Chapter Nine in *Modern Christianity to 1900: A People's History of Christianity*, 6: 261-90, edited by Amanda Porterfield. Minneapolis, Mn.: Fortress Press.

Chapter 3. Christian Rules Violate Jesus' Lessons

Can a true Christian comply with modern Christian rules and still follow the teachings of Jesus? This is the controversy of Christian ethics. Doing the right things based upon the right knowledge for the right reasons should be the goal of every Christian. But what are the right things, right knowledge, and right reasons? This understanding should begin outside the Church since Christian ethics has a strong foundation in the writings of ancient and renaissance philosophers such as Aristotle, Kant, Descartes, Epicurus, Cicero, Epictetus, and Seneca. This includes evolutionary development over two millennia starting with the teachings of Jesus together with analyses by key intellectuals such as Augustine. Preventing another recurrence of Christian-sanctioned cruelty, especially against those who questioned Christian authority, the resulting ancient rules should be modified for a modern world characterized by terrorism, drugs, environmental pollution, corruption, and human trafficking.

Being wise is good. But, being wise about the right knowledge is even better. So, what is the right knowledge, especially about Christianity? Where do I find it? How do we know it is the right knowledge? Can the right knowledge today be the wrong knowledge tomorrow, such as the Christian faith advocating slavery a few centuries ago while opposing it today? Was historical right knowledge, such as support of slavery, really the right knowledge back then? We should be asking ourselves these and many more similar questions. Having the right knowledge is only part of this. Doing the right thing based upon the right knowledge for the right reason is the best a Christian should do. So, what is the essence of Christian ethics? Georgia Harkness, professor of applied theology, stated a good definition of this.

Christian ethics means a "systematic study of the way of life exemplified and taught by Jesus, applied to the manifold problems and decisions of human existence"[71].

Secular Ethics.

Today, many think about ethics as institutional rules of behavior, moral philosophy and consider little about the development of their own personal character and consideration about their environment. However, it's best to consider ethics with a larger emphasis upon philosophy that permits one to become fully a self-conscious moral person committed to maintaining traditions that are essential to fulfilling one's Christian responsibilities with integrity[72]. Many Americans were taught to live a secular life using the Western value system of right and wrong, as described by Major General Buckingham in 1985:

> *"Our Western value system of right and wrong is based primarily on what Jesus taught concerning the origin and value of human life, augmented by the Old Testament lawgivers and prophets. This is what we commonly call the Judeo-Christian tradition. Although these teachings have been eroded and in some cases prostituted radically through the centuries, they still strongly influence the attitudes of Americans and other Westerners and form the core of our ethical concepts. In the Judeo-Christian view, man was created by God in His image; that is, with awareness, with purpose, with personality, and with inherent worth. All forms of human life are equally endowed by God with worth and dignity. There is no distinction between*

---

[71] 1957. In Chapter 1, "What is Christian Ethics?" of this book. Georgia Harkness taught at the Pacific School of Religion in Berkeley, California.

[72] See Shay 1994 and French 2003. These are two useful studies that emphasize issues of moral character in war and that draw from classical literature. The first involves the catastrophic combat experiences of the Vietnam War Soldiers and Soldiers in the Iliad. The second, with a forward from US Senator John McCain, contains a discussion of historical military values, including ancient Greeks, Romans, Vikings, Celts, Chinese monks, and Japanese samurai.

male and female, between black or white, rich or poor, aristocrat or peasant, Americans or Cambodians, Jews or Arabs, old or young, born or unborn, smart or dumb, with regard to inherent worth and dignity. All are created with equal worth, with equal dignity, with equal status, and with equal rights within the human race".

One can further define secular ethics differently depending upon one's desired philosophical outlook on life. The following are six popular ones. The philosophies of Aristotle's *eudaemonism* described a practical life of moderation with each person performing the duties for which equipped to ensure happiness[73]. The hedonistic ethics of Epicurus described the maximum pleasure-seeking life of "eat, drink and be merry, for tomorrow we die"[74]. The formal rational duty ethics of Kant required people to act according to an inherent sense of duty, as portrayed by Mr. Spock, the logical half-human in Gene Roddenberry's *Star Trek*[75]. Ethics of Bentham and Mill's utilitarianism was a pursuit for the

---

[73] 1812. "But the man of Perfected Self-Mastery is in the mean with respect to these objects: that is to say, he neither takes pleasure in the things which delight the vicious man, and in fact rather dislikes them, nor at all in improper objects; nor to any great degree in any object of the class; nor is he pained at their absence; nor does he desire them; or, if he does, only in moderation, and neither more than he ought, nor at improper times, and so forth; but such things as are conducive to health and good condition of body, being also pleasant, these he will grasp at in moderation and as he ought to do, and also such other pleasant things as do not hinder these objects, and are not unseemly or disproportionate to his means; because he that should grasp at such would be liking such pleasures more than is proper; but the man of Perfected Self-Mastery is not of this character, but regulates his desires by the dictates of right reason".

[74] Gordon 2003. "My beginning students know little about philosophy, but they do know what (in their own view) Epicurus taught: eat, drink and be merry, for tomorrow we die. When on one occasion, I pointed out that that is quite wrong". However, this is a common misconception is that the quote is attributed to Epicurus, but that quote is probably from Isaiah 22:13: "And behold joy and gladness, slaying oxen, and killing sheep, eating flesh, and drinking wine: let us eat and drink; for tomorrow we shall die".

[75] Blackman and Utzinger 2009.

greatest amount of happiness for the maximum number of people[76]. The "Social Adjustment" philosophy of John Dewey emphasized the process of improving virtuous conduct by valuing one as a good citizen in an ordered democratic society[77]. Finally, the stoic life was the pursuit of virtue[78].

Figure 4. Plato, Seneca, and Aristotle.
An illustration in the medieval manuscript, *Devotional and Philosophical Writings* (C. 1325-1335).

Although there are both positive and negative aspects with each of these six philosophies, Christianity is more closely related to the Stoic ethic; as such, the remainder of this secular ethics section will

---

[76] Driver 2009. "The Classical Utilitarians, Jeremy Bentham and John Stuart Mill, identified the good with pleasure, so, like Epicurus, were hedonists about value. They also held that we ought to maximize the good, that is, bring about 'the greatest amount of good for the greatest number'".
[77] 1916.
[78] Evans 2011.

involve a stoic frame of reference. Additionally, I learned much of my ethical values while serving as a military officer. During most of my life, I was held to the standard of minimizing the risks to my Soldiers, acting carefully, avoiding waste of lives, not fighting battles that can't be won, and not seeking victories where the costs exceed the value[79]. I fully understood that Soldiers were trained to kill. They may be ordered to, or they may order others to break the Sixth Commandment, the ultimate moral predicament.

To understand the foundation of this, we must understand the stoic school of philosophy, which is embedded in much of Western civilization[80]. This is contained in the writings of René Descartes, David Hume, Immanuel Kant, Michel de Montaigne, Blaise Pascal, and Baruch Spinoza. Although secular in nature, it does include some of the ancient Christian theology, including Augustine, Thomas à Kempis, and Justus Lipsius[81]. In fact, Lipsius developed a Christianized form of Stoicism, referred to as neo-Stoicism, in the sixteenth century. His work influenced the evolution of Catholicism, Calvinism, and Lutheranism[82]. Furthermore, Stoicism was symbolized by the famous Serenity Prayer: "God grant me the serenity to accept the things I cannot change, the courage to change the things I can, and the wisdom to know the difference"[83]. It really was about what we can control, in essence, a cultivation of the "inner citadel" of our soul[84].

Stoicism's four great teachings in the quest for virtue are: willing to endure pain for human good [courage]; pursuing right intentions over that of right results [wisdom]; understanding that fortune doesn't create human happiness [moderation]; and using self-control to prevent harming others and property [justice][85].

---

[79] Walzer 1981
[80] Evans 2011.
[81] Taylor 2007, 116, 119.
[82] See especially Taylor 2007.
[83] Niebuhr 1987, 251.
[84] See especially Hadot 2001. The soul, the guiding principle within us, is in Aurelius' description of an inviolable stronghold of freedom, known as the "inner citadel."
[85] Holowchak 2008, 13, 91, 134, 141, 159.

Furthermore, Stoicism states that life is unfair and that there is no worldly benefit for living a moral life in the world. For example, martyrs and honest men may die poor; while dishonest men may die rich. Stoicism is also evident in both the Old Testament's (OT's) Job about God's good servant, and in Shakespeare's *King Lear* about an exemplary father. This philosophy reminds us that there's an unyielding struggle for right actions in an unfair world. Aeschylus, founder of the Greek tragedy, understood this philosophy and wrote about it in his *Agamemnon*, and which Robert F. Kennedy quoted in his Indianapolis speech on the assassination of Martin Luther King, Jr., "He who learns must suffer. And even in our sleep, pain which cannot forget falls drop by drop on the heart until, in our own despair, against our will, comes wisdom through the awful grace of God"[86].

Character, then, is really formed by free choice, a gift from God, and isn't something forced upon by others. A good character is accomplished by pursuing virtue and avoiding vice, which is shaped through times of both poverty and wealth. According to Epictetus, absolute virtue is comprised of righteousness, honor, and decency, and doesn't include health, wealth, or even life[87]. Regrettably, many Christian groups use shame and guilt to persuade others to act. Yet, the Stoic believes that guilt is an individual free choice. This Stoic philosophy doesn't recognize social guilt in shaping one's character since it considers guilt involves individual choice and even individual misconduct[88]. Everything that we do is based upon our own decisions. These choices are based upon either internal or external values. Epictetus further states, "of things some are in our power and others are not. In our power, are opinion, movement towards a thing [aim], desire, aversion [turning from a thing]; and in a word, whatever are our

---

[86] Kennedy 1968 and Aeschylus 1920. A link to the audio of the Kennedy speech can be found at the Kennedy Presidential Library website too. The Aeschylus quote is: "Man by Suffering shall Learn. So the heart of him, again Aching with remembered pain, Bleeds and sleepeth not, until Wisdom comes against his will."
[87] Brennan 1994, 2. This was based upon a course taught at the Naval War College.
[88] Stockdale 1995, 180, 234-36.

own acts; not in our power are the body, property, reputation, offices [magisterial power] and, in a word, whatever are not our own acts"[89]. He further cautions us that if we focus upon external things, especially those that we can't control, we'll neglect our inner self. These external things are, "weak, slavish, subject to restraint and in the power of others". In most circumstances, external things in life don't necessarily hurt us, but our views of them could.

But, how do we know what is moral and what is immoral? Some believe that all moral purpose should be based upon reason and not the emotions of desire, pleasure, and fear. According to Admiral Stockdale, everything in life should be based upon "decisions of the will"[90]. This is difficult since emotions are just as important as reason for decisions, according to recent scientific studies[91]. If happiness is what we want, then we shouldn't let emotionally based fears about our body, relationships and worldly possessions govern our decisions[92]. Returning to the ancient philosophers, we can learn much about life today. Not much has changed regarding morality during the past several millennia. For example, Africanus, conqueror of Hannibal, stated that virtue can't be found in selfish interests but through service to others. We should, "know that for all who shall have preserved, succored, enlarged their country, there is a certain and determined place in Heaven where they enjoy eternal happiness"[93].

In addition to life, business follows secular ethics. In my experience working in corporate America, I've found that very often businesses aren't bound by any ethics other than abiding by the law. Supporting this position is Milton Friedman, who held that corporations have the obligation to make a profit within the framework of the legal system, nothing more. He explicitly states that the duty of the business leaders is, "to make as much money as

---

[89] 1888.
[90] 1995, 182.
[91] See Bagozzi et al. 2003 and Isen and Shalker 1982. These are just a couple of studies that indicate that emotions affect decisions.
[92] Seneca 1958, 51, 55, 59, 68.
[93] Cicero 1887

possible while conforming to the basic rules of the society, both those embodied in the law and those embodied in ethical custom[94]. Ethics in business for Friedman is nothing more than abiding by customs and laws. The reduction of business ethics to abidance to laws and customs, however, has drawn serious criticisms. Counter to Friedman's logic, the legal procedures are technocratic, bureaucratic, rigid and obligatory whereas an ethical act is a conscientious, voluntary choice[95]. Nevertheless, business ethics reflects the philosophy of business, one of whose aims is to determine the fundamental purposes of a company. If a company's purpose is to maximize shareholder returns, then sacrificing profits to other concerns is a violation of its fiduciary responsibility. Many churches today operate primarily as a business, focused upon fiduciary responsibilities only.

Individuals and businesses make numerous decisions each day. The real ethical concern is whether they can determine if their decisions are moral or immoral? We should also understand the popular paraphrase of Seneca Epistle 77.20, "life's like a play; it's not the length but the excellence of the acting that matters"[96]. Meanwhile, Epictetus reminds us that "to select the part belongs to another"[97]. Our character, the excellence of our life, should mean more to us than our reputation since it's best to have a good character than a false reputation. Marcus Aurelius, the Roman Emperor from 161 until 180 and another ancient Stoic philosopher, believed that we, "must stand erect, not be kept erect by others"[98]. An example of this can be found in the novel, *Fame Is the Spur*, about an idealist British political leader becoming more corrupt in

---

[94] 1970.
[95] Agamben 1993, 43.
[96] Ker 2009, 118. The author lists Seneca's text in Latin along with its English translation. Latin text is "quomodo fabula, sic vita: on quam diu, sed quam bene acta sit, refert. nihil ad rem pertinent quo loco desinas. quocumque voles desine: tantum bonam clausulam inpone. vale." translated into English, "As in a story, so too in life: it is not how long, but how well it was acted, that matters. It is irrelevant in what place you cease. Cease wherever you want: just make sure to put a good end on it. Farewell."
[97] 1888.
[98] 1862.

pursuit of higher office by gradually renouncing his virtues. His soul withered in his unrelenting pursuit of personal ambition[99]. That's the risk that all have when pursuing advancements in life. Rather than seeking fame, fortune, and power, which are popular lifetime goals, we should first conquer our own desires by altering our desires instead of changing our environment[100].

There are some situations in which violating secular or religious laws is the moral course of action. That is because these laws are inflexible by requiring violation as the right thing to do. Modern Americans are losing sight of the values that benefit others along with losing confidence in understanding those values as a whole[101]. As such, we should avoid subscribing to the popular "ethics without morality" in which the moral aspects of ethics are increasingly becoming obsolescent[102].

One of my favorite books, *Once an Eagle*, is about two military officers and their advancements through the military hierarchy[103]. The first officer, Courtney Massengale, was a cynical careerist with social connections and corrupt morality portraying the Epicurean philosophy of materialism[104]. The other officer, Sam Damon, exemplified the stoic philosophy by pursuing real achievement instead of a quest for status. Both officers achieved similar achievements, but Massengale's was service to self, while Damon's was service to others.

---

[99] Spring 1940. A film was made of this book directed by Roy Boulting in 1947.
[100] Descartes 1649, 41. "My third Maxime was, To endevour always rather to conquer my self then Fortune; and to change my desires, rather then the order of the world: and generally to accustome my self to beleeve, That there is nothing wholly in our power but our thoughts; so that after we have done our best, touching things which are without us, all whats wanting of success in respect of us is absolutely impossible."
[101] Moskos et al. 2000, 4.
[102] Coker 2002, 2 and 2008, 97, 137. Ethics without Morality involves the existential and metaphysical ideals that have traditionally underpinned a life dedicated to professionalism seem increasingly obsolescent.
[103] Myrer 1968. A mini-series was made of this book directed by E.W. Swackhamer and Richard Michaels from 1976 – 1977..
[104] See especially Epicurus 1925.

Aside from this fictional story, let me provide you a real example. Air Force Colonel James Burton, a senior military officer, fully understood secular ethics using the stoic philosophy. He was best known for his "to be or to do, that is the question" speech in June 1974 to his colleagues and subordinates at the Pentagon[105]:

> *"You have to make a choice about what kind of person you are going to be. There are two [military] career paths in front of you, and you have to choose which path you will follow. One path leads to promotions, titles and positions of distinctions. To achieve success down that path, you have to conduct yourself a certain way. You must go along with the system. . . . The other path leads to doing things that are truly significant for the Air Force, but you may have to cross swords with the party line on occasion. You can't go down both paths, you have to choose. Do you want to be a man of distinction or do you want to do things that really influence the shape of the Air Force? To be or to do, that is the question".*

In another real, but personal, example from the Spring of 1985, I was a platoon leader in a chemical company stationed at Fort Hood, Texas. My battalion commander was within his first year of command and was a full-bird colonel, which was unusual since command of a battalion is normally for lieutenant colonels, a lower-ranking officer. I believed that he pulled strings at the Pentagon for this command for self-interest reasons since the experience of commanding of a battalion or higher-level unit is required for promotion to brigadier general. Without it, he wouldn't receive any more promotions.

On one of several occasions in which he didn't support his troops happened during weapons qualifications within my company. I had the misfortunate of serving as the Officer in Charge (OIC) of

---

[105] 1993. An HBO film was made of his book directed by Richard Benjamin in 1998.

the range at the time. Being fully prepared to run the range safely, I had previously taken the range safety class and taught our Soldiers marksmanship techniques as required. On the day of the range firing, everything was completed, along with having the requisite safety support in place. After about an hour into weapons firing, my battalion commander visited the range to see how things were going. After giving him an update, I noticed a jeep with a red placard displaying three stars on it enter the range. My battalion commander also noticed the jeep and quickly moved to hide behind the range tower, leaving me alone to greet Lieutenant General Walter F. Ulmer, Jr., commanding general of III Corps and Fort Hood. I was in disbelief that my battalion commander quickly escaped to leave me alone with this powerful person. General Ulmer served as Commandant of Cadets at West Point in 1976, where he was responsible for the first admission of female cadets and the cheating scandal involving several hundred of the junior classmen[106]. After I provided him a quick overview of the range operations, he quickly followed me to talk to several Soldiers. These Soldiers were nervous talking to a three-star general. I know this, because they couldn't remember the marksmanship training that they took earlier in the morning. After talking to a few of the Soldiers, General Ulmer was convinced that none received any training as required and ordered me to halt range operations and immediately conduct the training. "Yes Sir!" I complied and quickly told my range safety officer to order a "cease fire" and stop range firing. Then, General Ulmer returned to his jeep and drove off. Afterwards, out of nowhere, my battalion commander magically appeared. He knew I had conducted the training, but refused to appear and defend me. My battalion commander never did get his star though. I guess the other generals knew about this character and his lack of support for his troops. I, on the other hand, later commanded a battalion successfully enough to command a brigade, a higher level position.

My other personal example involved my relationship with my company commander, a captain and another Epicurean officer, that same year. Early one evening, just before I was to leave for home,

---

[106] Time Magazine 1976.

my company commander called me to tell me that he was at the motor pool and discovered that one of my jeeps there had a fire extinguisher that needed to be secured. He ordered me to recall my entire platoon back into work and secure that extinguisher. I told him that I'd get that extinguisher secured and hung up the phone. What I didn't tell him was that I wasn't going to recall my platoon back to work since I'd personally drive to the motor pool and secure the extinguisher as ordered. It didn't make sense to me to order everyone back to work after they had spent a long twelve-hour day of training and they were already at homes with their families. I'd take care of the person or persons responsible for the unsecured extinguisher the following day. And, I was willing to take responsibility for any consequences of my decision to not recall them back to work for this petty thing. I didn't realize that the consequence involved the commander removing me as a platoon leader for insubordination a few days later. This devastated me and my hopes for a long productive military career. After over a year in the unit, I was just about to become the executive officer, or second in command, of the company. Now, I was no longer in the company and was sent to be a staff officer in another battalion. But, I felt that I did the right thing by not making all of my Soldiers and their families suffer for the mistake of one careless individual. I was the one who was punished, and punished for doing what I believed was the right thing to do. On an interesting note of delayed justice, this company commander was relieved from command a few months later, which is the military way of saying that he was fired too. Unlike my long successful military career, I heard that he never received another promotion and left the Army at his rank of captain. With this and many other examples during my entire military career, I demonstrated the Stoic philosophy of Damon, making me feel good about my soul.

So, from a secular point of view, ethics to me in a very general sense is about doing the right things for the right reasons. Doing the rights things, even though no one knows about it, is much better to me than being known as a person who does the right things, especially if done for the wrong reasons. There are even some situations in which violating inflexible secular or religious laws is the right moral course of action. For example, killing everyone with a different religion even though the Bible commands it is morally wrong today[107]. Unfortunately, this lack of clear guidance causes us today to lose sight of the values that benefit others, in addition to lose confidence in understanding those values as a whole[108]. The resultant subscription to the popular "ethics without morality" is making the moral aspects of ethics increasingly obsolescent[109]. It's probably best that we realize that we today don't live in a Hobbesian world, one in a pure state of nature[110]. Ethics in the real world involves real people in real situations.

Ethics of Jesus.

Next, the ethics of Christianity includes the ethics of Jesus, as understood through His actions and teachings. To assess this part of the Christian ethics, we should ask "What Would Jesus Do" (WWJD) ethically. However, most people today don't ask themselves this ethical question. And, if they did, the answer wouldn't be based upon a logical analysis of the available facts. Instead, they assume His ethics was the same as their idea of Christian ethics, two thousand years later. This modern view is based upon the combination of democracy, nationalism, and capitalism, all blended together with scientific and technological achievements. This is then mixed with the Western world's way of life, patriotism, along with humanitarian concern for the weak, the helpless, and the suffering. In addition, this includes complete respect for law, especially involving kindness, generosity, and citizenship. The combination of all of that is what many regard as "acting like a Christian"[111]. But, the ethics of Jesus isn't this complex. Let me begin this with a brief story about my personal experience as a teenager involving the legend of Santa, you know,

---

[107] Deuteronomy 17:2-7.
[108] Moskos et al. 2002, 4.
[109] Coker 2002, 2 and 2008, 97, 137. Ethics without Morality involves the existential and metaphysical ideals that have traditionally underpinned a life dedicated to professionalism seem increasingly obsolescent.
[110] Hobbes 1651. In this book, Hobbes argues for a social contract and rule by an absolute sovereign, which will avert chaos and civil war.
[111] Harkness 1957. In Chapter 1, "What is Christian Ethics?" of this book.

the one about the jolly ole man who brings everyone gifts in celebration of Jesus' birthday. As a young child, I once viewed Santa as the sure-fire magical self-interest way to receive toys, lots of them. Maybe, this is how many people view Jesus, a magical way to get into Heaven. Just believe in him, and He will welcome us with open arms, no matter what. No matter how evil we are and no matter how hateful we are of others, popular Christian belief is faith is enough. For me, this belief isn't enough.

There was a time when I was a non-believer in Santa. Maybe, I was even a non-believer in Jesus at that time too, even though I attended Catholic mass religiously every week. But, my belief in Santa changed in the basement of the Herpolsheimer's Department store, commonly known as Herp's, during the late 1970's. This store was located in the heart of downtown Grand Rapids, Michigan. Most Americans may remember that this was mentioned several times in the recent *Polar Express* movie[112]. Portrayed in the movie, many Grand Rapids' children visited the Herp's Santa each Christmas Season, some like me having their picture taken with him.

I spent my pre-school days growing up in Grand Rapids, living near both of my grandparents. My childhood memories were magical in which anything was possible. My parents and grandparents helped me live in this magical period by supporting the Santa legend every year. Why would I doubt this? Santa was a popular topic of discussion at my elementary schools by not only the students, but by the teachers as well. There were Christmas songs too, both on the radio and sung at school. Also during the Christmas season, Christmas shows populated the television airwaves. These included Charlie Brown's concern about the commercialism of the season. *Rudolph* had a message on diversity. And, the *Drummer Boy* was part of the real Christmas Story. Finally on Christmas morning, I would awaken to see the stockings filled with goodies and additional presents under the tree. As a Christian child, I believed that Santa was the gift from God to

---

[112] Van Allsburg 1985. A film was made of his children's book directed by Robert Zemeckis in 2004.

Christian Rules Violate Jesus' Lessons

celebrate the birth of His son, Jesus. I even thought that God used Santa, the real one from Herp's, to give every good child gifts on Jesus' birthday.

As I was growing up, I soon became a disbeliever. I couldn't understand how one person, with flying reindeer, could deliver presents to every child in every town on our planet Earth. It seemed impossible. So, too, the story of Jesus seemed impossible. I later had a shocking discovery that my parents had bought the Santa gifts several days prior to Christmas, and that this Santa myth was probably a parental trick to convince children to behave, at least once every year. Maybe, Jesus, too, was a religious trick to convince everyone to behave. While attending Creston High School in Grand Rapids, my grandmother asked me to do something. She was a sales representative for Herp's; and, she asked me if I wanted to be one of the Herp's Santa's that year. I couldn't believe this, since I was just a teenager, both tall and thin. I also needed the money, so of course I said, "yes".

My first day playing Santa was very memorable. I learned some of the key phrases that I needed to say, such as "Ho Ho Ho," and "What would you want Santa to bring you?" I also learned some key facts, such as the nine reindeer names. However, the most humiliating event of this day was putting on make-up, such as grey chalk for my eyebrows and red blush for my cheeks. Teenage boys didn't wear make-up, at least none that I knew. Then, it was time for me to walk out of the dressing room and begin my official duties as Santa. To say that I was nervous would be an understatement. There were several kids waiting to see me and were shouting that "Santa is coming". So, I began to populate a myth that I didn't believe in. How hypocritical of me? But, then again, there are many hypocritical religious leaders who populate the myth of Jesus that they don't believe.

Figure 5. Saint Nicholas of Myra Saves Three Innocents from Death.
Николай Мирликийский избавляет от смерти трёх невинно осуждённых by Ilya Repin (1888)[113].

During my two years of playing Santa, I experienced the power of commercials. Most kids wanted the items that they saw on TV, such as the *Hungry Hungry Hippos* game. Also, some very young children were scared of me and didn't want to get anywhere near me - I guess that they were told never to trust strange old men. Jesus can be scary to many people too. Several times, I saw the sparkle in a child's face when he was talking to me. I, as Santa, made him happy. During the evenings when I wasn't Santa, I

---

[113] From The Yorck Project: 10.000 Meisterwerke der Malerei 2002. The compilation copyright is held by Zenodot Verlagsgesellschaft mbH and licensed under the GNU Free Documentation License.

would operate the monorail in the basement, otherwise known as the *Santa Train*. I wonder if this train was the inspiration for the train in the *Polar Express* movie. Finally, I conducted research into the Santa legend for an English term paper, learning more about the Turkish Bishop, known as Saint Nick, and about the "*Yes, Virginia, there is a Santa*", newspaper article[114]. I began to see Santa not as the jolly old elf from the North Pole, but as the symbol of the Christmas season.

Being the Herp's Santa for two years, from 1978 through 1979, was a very memorable experience for me. Herp's no longer exists today, giving way to the malls on the outskirts of the city. But, Santa still exists to millions of children throughout the world today. For them, Christmas without Santa is like peanut butter without jelly. Today, I can truly relate to the Santa from the *Polar Express*, especially from his statement that the true spirit of Christmas lies in the heart. This is like believing that wind exists even though we can't see the wind. But, we can see what the wind does to others. This is the same with Jesus. We know that the spirit of Santa exists, just look at the face of young children during the Christmas season. Since the time I was Santa and became a member of the "Long Red Line", I passed on the Santa experience to my daughters and look forward to doing the same to my grandchildren. I wonder if I can hear the *Polar Express* bell that only rings for those who truly believe in Santa. They should also have a bell that only rings for true followers of Jesus. I doubt many people would hear the Jesus bell.

Believing in Jesus is similar to the belief in Santa. Even though stories about both are impossible by today's mortal understandings, the legends and stories of both exists to millions throughout the world. And, the true spirit of both lies in the heart. But, belief in Jesus is just not enough. Even Lucifer, the mythical chief of the fallen angels, believes in Jesus; but, Lucifer isn't going to spend eternity in Heaven with Jesus, despite his belief in Him[115]. So, what does it really mean being a Christian?

---

[114] Church 1897.
[115] Kent 1907.

Being a Christian isn't about the rules but about the relationship we have with Jesus. This relationship provides an objective reference for determining the difference between right and wrong, regardless of the situation. Without this reference, we can become captive in our own subjectivity, defining ethics based upon what we think we can keep. Unfortunately, modern Christians only find a patchwork today of homilies and sermon dictates, some of which are unclear and others of which are contradictory. Furthermore, the modern culture focuses upon individuality, competition, and consumerism, all which provide obstacles to following Jesus[116].

The foundation of information about Jesus and His actual words originated from the Bible. During my readings of this Book and analyzing its information, I can tell you that Jesus didn't provide His followers with any such manual of Christian membership or church rules, at least not in the Bible. Furthermore, it would be presumptuous for any mortal human to attempt what Jesus was too wise to do. Yet, one continues to hear many preachers and read many theological books about the dictates of Jesus and His rules for Christian behavior. People should realize that there exists no perfect record of the life and teachings of Jesus, not even in the Bible. As such, I fully understand that no fallible human mind, including mine, can fully understand the divine consciousness of Jesus and assess without error what His opinion would be involving all modern decisions. Yet, many Christian leaders claim this understanding. Based upon our lives, would Jesus confirm us as friends on Facebook?

Direct information about Jesus can be found in the Bible's four gospels, each containing information about His actual life and teachings. In the Gospel of John, Jesus taught people, but mostly about Himself, such as Him being the "light of the world"[117]. In this gospel, Jesus directed His disciples to love one another[118]. In the Gospel of Mark, Jesus was described as a teacher of mysterious

---

[116] Giannet 2002.
[117] John 8:12.
[118] John 15:12.

teachings about God that were so obscure that none of His disciples were able to understand them. Yet, this gospel lacked much information about daily ethical living[119]. The Gospel of Matthew is really a reproduction of Mark, such as love being the master virtue of Jesus, with stoic ethical philosophies added[120]. These stoic philosophies were probably added since the author of Matthew didn't possess information about Jesus' character and wanted to write something about it. So, it's likely that he used the most prominent and respected philosophy at the time, which was Stoicism[121]. Besides adding ethical information to the Jesus story, Matthew also contained several contradictions involving His teachings. For example, in the Sermon on the Mount, Jesus instructed that anger was wrong, but He later attacked the money changers while He was angry[122]. In Matthew 5:22, He taught that calling another person a fool was punishable with eternity in Hell, yet He called the scribes and Pharisees fools in Matthew 23:17. Unfortunately, the problem with Matthew is that the stoic ethics combined with a vengeful god didn't logically fit with the love of enemies[123]. In the Gospel of Luke, Jesus had good news for his people, including non-Jews such as a Roman officer[124]. This gospel included famous parables not included in the other gospels, such as the parables of the *Good Samaritan*, the *Rich Fool*, and the *Rich Fool and Lazarus*[125].

From these gospel words, I can't tell you His opinions about modern issues. But, I can tell you what I do know about Him. First, the life and teaching of Jesus with regard to man's moral duty and ethical living can be found in "obedient love". This meant to love God and our neighbors as ourselves. Jesus combined Old Testament thought with the general guidance of God-centered moral living, and didn't use any other sources for His ethical directives. Almost everything that Jesus taught can be found in the

---

[119] See Stowers 2010.
[120] Matthew 19:16-22 and Mark 10:17-31.
[121] See Stowers 2010.
[122] Matthew 21:12-13.
[123] See Stowers 2010
[124] Luke 7:1-9.
[125] Luke 10:25-37, 12:13-21, 16:19-31.

Old Testament. The Old Testament, we must remember, was His Bible. He didn't dispute its contents. Instead, Jesus fully embraced it. How do I know this? He frequently quoted from it to support His teachings. Yet, He didn't comply with everything in it for all situations, sometimes even changing the rules. For example in the Sermon on the Mount, he told His followers that, "You have heard that it was said .... But I say to you ...."[126]. This indicated how he used Old Testament rules, which was a foundation that He elaborated upon. As a result, His teachings violated the traditional political and religious patriarchal order, not to mention the gender roles of the time. He aggressively challenged the legalistic and unreasonable requirements imposed by the religious leaders, such as the Pharisees[127]. He opposed their hypocrisy and self-righteousness, which He told his people were morally hollow and alienated them from God[128].

Despite all the uncertainties involving His teaching, it is clear to me that they involved God's reign over people's hearts. Jesus always made human need the source of obedient love of God. For example, human service was more important than the law of the Sabbath[129]. He socialized with both publicans and sinners to save them even at the cost of becoming ceremonial unclean. His words were meant for everyone in every country and within every race, gender, class, culture, and economic station. Whether they were women, children, slaves, Jew, Roman, Samaritan, or social outcasts, all persons were of equal value to Jesus.

Sacrificial offerings to God were also very important to Jews[130]. Before one offered gifts to God, Jesus instructed that person should first reconcile their problems against their neighbor[131]. Jesus wasn't concerned about these gifts. Instead, He wanted one to have a loving relationship with others. Thus, our ethical behavior

---

[126] Matthew 5:20-48.
[127] Mark 12:38-40.
[128] Giannet 2002.
[129] Exodus 20:8-11, 31:12-17; Deuteronomy 5:12-15; Nehemiah 13:15-22; and Jeremiah 17:19-27.
[130] See Leviticus 1-7.
[131] Matthew 5:23-24.

must be in order before our religious behavior was considered acceptable. Contrary to what one may have heard from religious leaders today, Jesus' words were clear on this subject. He placed a higher value for your loving ethical character above either material things or institutions.

Figure 6. Curses Against the Pharisees.
Imprécations contre les pharisiens (c. 1886-1894) by James Tissot.

Besides love, Jesus discussed salvation. Yet, there was significant confusion about the criteria for salvation, such as whether one can be saved by faith alone. Knowledge about His ethics wasn't enough. Discussed in Matthew 5:43-48, loving our enemies and praying for those who are persecuting us were difficult, unless we're willing to transcend our selfish ego and genuinely accept the awe-inspiring mystery of God[132]. However, if we insisted upon solely complying with man-made ethical codes instead of following the words and examples of Jesus, we risk living a life of the pious religious leaders whom Jesus disliked[133].

---

[132] See especially Hick 1995.
[133] Giannet 2002.

The legend of Santa provides a good analogy for this. Jesus and Santa are both magical men who bring joy and happiness to millions throughout the world. And, the true spirit of both legends lies in the heart. But, belief, or faith, in Jesus just isn't enough. The ethics of Jesus is designed for this world, where persecution, lust and hatred are continuing realities. In the words of John Yoder, a Mennonite theologian[134]:

> *"The kingdom of God is a social order and not a hidden one. It is not a universal catastrophe independent of the will of men; it is that concrete jubilary obedience, in pardon and repentance, the possibility of which is proclaimed beginning right now, opening up the real accessibility of a new order in which grace and justice are linked, which men have only to accept. It does not assume time will end tomorrow; it reveals why it is meaningful that history should go on at all"*

Jesus taught an ethic completely integrated with His Jewish religion. Yes, Jesus was a faithful Jew. However, He focused primarily upon the ethical and spiritual character of a person, not the rules. His most harsh words were toward those who preached, but didn't practice what they preached[135]. Jesus didn't come to make us religious, righteous, or moral. Basically, His ethics involved His proclamation of a God-centered, love-filled life lived in obedience to God. Both love of God and love of others were very important to Jesus[136].

Early Christian Church Ethics.

The ethics of Jesus was simple. It was based upon his Greatest Commandments[137]. Yet, mortal humans over time made this more complex. This evolved into the Christian ethics we know today. Initially, Christianity transformed an older religion, so that the link

---

[134] 1972, 108.
[135] Matthew 23:3-24.
[136] Schnackenburg 1965.
[137] Matthew 22:36-40.

between it and Judaism was close. In fact, it was much closer than that between Buddhism and Hinduism or between Islam and Christianity[138]. The combination of the New with the Old Testaments further strengthened this linkage by providing the Gentile converts with fundamental Christian interpretation of existing sacred Jewish literature.

For Christians, many questions arose about the Bible and its role upon the Christian culture. What part of the Bible was more important than the others? Which stories in the Old Testament supported the Christian faith and which stories didn't? In the New Testament (NT), was one part more authoritative than another? Who determined which part was more important than another? Were there Scriptures that were more important than others? If one Scripture contradicted another, which one should we believe and follow? How could we know? Who could we trust? These and many others plagued the early Christians. In fact, modern Christians ask similar questions today. The answers to these questions throughout history evolved into our modern Christian culture.

So, what do we really know about the early Christians? What were their biggest contributions to Christianity? These can be found in the written words of the New Testament, which incidentally were written long after Jesus' departure from this world. For example, the gospels were nothing more than a product of the Church's experience in the first century and not an accurate newspaper-type firsthand account of Jesus' words and actions. There was even general agreement among current New Testament scholars that none of the gospels was completely historical[139]. In addition to the gospels, much of the modern Christian faith developed from letters Paul wrote. Let me say that Paul was a devout Christian, a great theologian, and an effective missionary. Nevertheless, it was his words, not Jesus' words, that formed much of the basic structure of the Christian faith. Some of Paul's words, though, contradict

---

[138] See especially Olcott 1919, Dasgupta 1922, and Becker 1909.
[139] Harkness 1957. In Chapter 4: "Ethical Perspectives of the Early Church" of this book.

modern ethics. For example, many today have a personal problem with Paul's words requiring women to keep silent in the Church[140]. All the same, we shouldn't advocate discarding his words completely because it contained several contradictions or mistakes. Instead, we should interpret the words of the New Testament to that which is most faithful to the total picture of Jesus.

There's no dispute that the Bible and its development had a significant role upon the Christian culture. Yet, confusion existed about which part of the Bible was more important than the others. For example, some of the stories in the Old Testament supported the Christian faith while others didn't. In the New Testament, too, some parts became more authoritative than others. However, it was a mortal person who determined which part and which Scriptures were more important. Confusion became more pronounced when several Scriptures contradicted others, making it impossible for Christians to determine which one should be believed and followed. In many cases, people allowed others whom they trusted to make this determination for them. These were the growing pains that plagued the early Christians. What's more, modern Christians have the same concerns today. The analyses, discussions, and decisions involving these concerns evolved into the current Christian culture.

Aside from the development of the Bible, the early religious cultural evolution can be viewed in three distinct phases[141]. The first phase involved the transformation of Jewish Christians into the Church of the Gentiles. This Church still followed their Jewish culture, which was both very strong and individualistic. The next phase involved the growth of the Church through an underground movement characterized by persecution and struggle for survival. There was no established Christian culture, yet these followers were united in faith while separated from the pagan culture that surrounded them. Besides, the State and the Church were enemies in this phase, requiring the Church to depend upon its internal resources for survival. The last phase involved the emergence of a

---

[140] 1 Corinthians 14:34.
[141] Dawson 1954.

Christian culture that further changed the ancient secular world and its political order with Christian values and ideas. Christianity then became the official Roman religion with the Church acquiring immense wealth and power. In addition to being the head of the Christian community, bishops assumed powerful civic duties. Likewise, the Roman emperors influenced Christian doctrine and even presided at the ecumenical councils described later. The resulting religious canon laws then became embedded into the secular laws[142].

On the surface, the people viewed the Church through its ceremonial Christian rites, which usually involved liturgies as an expression of its faith and culture. The ceremonies were first performed in the Constantinian basilicas that incorporated the secular Roman-Hellenistic culture[143]. The liturgies themselves were artistic and expressed in poetry, music, and art. Furthermore, the early Christian liturgies included Jewish poetry of Psalms, which the Jews already used in their synagogues. This poetry expressed spiritual things better than classical secular poetry and could reflect individual expressions of both thoughts and feelings. In many of the newly converted countries, it was the monasteries that propagated this liturgical culture. Furthermore, the early Christians developed several rites and ceremonies that continue to be celebrated today, especially those involving baptism, Lent, Easter, and Pentecost.

Symbology within the early Church, especially during its ceremonies, became very important. These were often developed at the expense of an accurate representation of important events. For example, the Lord's Supper during which His Apostles ate was different than its liturgical replication as celebrated in a typical Roman Catholic Mass. Additionally, Jesus, His followers, and early Christians knew nothing about stone altars with shining candelabra, incense, and hymns associated with worship in a modern immense building called a church[144]. Furthermore, since

---

[142] Dawson 1954.
[143] See especially Austin 1981.
[144] See especially Vacandard 1907.

most of the lay members of the Church were illiterate, the liturgy was the only way for Christians to learn about their faith. Thus, the knowledge of Christianity for the general public was acquired orally. Because the written Bible wasn't produced until the 1450s by Johannes Gutenberg in Mainz, Germany, the early Christians relied upon their local religious leaders for interpretations of their religious beliefs[145].

Accordingly, from where did these interpretations come? I recommend reviewing many of the interpretations that are found in records of the first seven ecumenical councils, as listed in Table 7. They provide a written theological record of the evolution from the ancient world to Christianity, including the early development of its doctrine and its conflict with paganism[146]. This record represents the primary foundation of the Christian ethical culture with input from key intellectuals such as Titus Flavius Clemens, Origen Adamantius, John Chrysostom, Theodoret of Cyrus, Tertullianus, and Augustine[147]. The one who was more aware of the psychological problems of his time and his profound thoughts was Augustine. He was also more responsible than the others for the later development of Christian theology[148].

The early Christians augmented their culture with the personalities of the saints as their mortal role models. These saints personified the expected Christian way of life. The legends and fantasies surrounding these saints provided insight into the expectations of Christians throughout this cultural evolution[149]. For instance, martyrdom replaced the hero of the pagan culture containing

---

[145] Estes 2005.
[146] See especially Schaff and Wace 1899.
[147] Schaff 1910. Especially the following numerous pages: 8, 55-59, 65-67, 106, 112-13, 118-25, 135-37, 144-49, 174, 218-19, 258-59 298, 305, 312, 330-31, 348-49, 358-61, 366, 371-72, 382, 391, 405, 416, 422, 460, 474, 478, 487, 496, 511, 522, 525, 538-48, 561, 573-74, 599-606, 652-69, 675, 679, 692-705, 727-41, 746-50, 755-74, 791-92 810, 833-836, 842 870, 893-95, 937, 946, 948, 956, 979, 1017, 1048-62, 1075, 1117, 1175, 1191, 1209, 1243-44, 1254, 1284, 1297, 1315, 1325, 1376, 1383, 1406, 1440
[148] Dawson 1954.
[149] Dawson 1954.

popular heroic myths and legends. Moreover, they treated virginity with sacred respect. Saint Agnes, a virgin, became an example of a highly respected Christian[150]. In essence, Christians viewed virginity as a living martyrdom, with faith to transcend the human weakness of sexual desires. Also, monks living a celibate monastic life distinguished themselves from the rest of the faithful. These self-sufficient monks' support of their communities caused a rise of monasticism throughout the world, which in turn resulted in an expansion of followers based on Christian principles. Furthermore with the decline of the economic secular culture in the West during the fifth century, these monasteries became the spiritual source of the Christian faith[151].

Table 7. Ecumenical Councils.

Council	Location	Year	Emperor	Pope
First	Nice	325	Constantine	Silvester
Second	Constantinople	381	Theodosius	Damasus
Third	Ephesus	431	Theodusius II, Valentinian III	Celestine Leo I
Fourth	Chalcedon	451	Valentinian III Marcian Pulcheria	Leo I
Fifth	Constantinople	553	Justinian I	Vigilius
Sixth	Constantinople	680-81	Constantine Pogonatus	Agatho I
Seventh	Nice	787	Constanine VI Irene	Hadrian

Source: See especially Schaff and Wace 1899

From the beginning, acquiring new Christian members and keeping them weren't done by force. During the first three centuries, the early Christians never thought of using any physical or emotional force to convert or punish anyone. Although the Old Testament decreed the death penalty for apostasy or heresy, Origen and other

---

[150] Kirsch 1907.
[151] Dawson 1954.

ecclesiastical writers favored toleration instead of force[152]. These early Christians preferred following the advice of Jesus as exemplified in Him forbidding Peter from using his sword[153]. They viewed Jesus' purpose as coming to suffer, not to defend Himself or to protect us from God.

Figure 7. The Kiss of Judas and Peter Cutting off the Ear of Malchus.
O beijo de Judas e Pedro cortando a orelha de Malchus (1786) by José Joaquim da Rocha.

Then beginning with the reign of Roman Emperors Valentinian I and Theodosius I in the latter part of the fourth century, the Christian faith began to change. Specifically, the laws against

---

[152] Vacandard 1907. See Chapter I: "First Period I-IV century – The Epoch of the Persecutions."
[153] John 18:11 and Matthew 26:52.

Christian Rules Violate Jesus' Lessons

heretics continued to increase with surprising regularity[154]. By the middle of the fifth century, Theodosius II enforced the policy that his first duty was to protect the true religion of the empire[155]. By then, the Christian religion was also the State religion, with secular philosophies embedded. Emperors began using religion as a method to rule over and control their people. Although minor physical force such as flogging was acceptable, other forms of force like the rack and iron pincers were sconsidered cruel. For example, flogging and whipping others were frequently used by schoolmasters and parents to instill discipline. Within the Church, excommunication, a non-physical punishment, was the only penalty for heresy. However, some religious leaders, such as bishops Priscillian and Optatus, believed that the Church should execute heretics while citing the Old Testament as the authority[156]. In ironic justice, Priscillian was the first person executed for heresy[157].

Although persecution of heretics was rare through the eleventh century, Christians began increasing cruelty against heretics then[158]. For example, French King Robert II was very concerned about the effects of heresy upon his kingdom that he initiated the punishment

---

[154] Vacandard 1907. See Chapter II: "Second Period from Valentian I to Theodosius II – The Church and the Criminal Code of the Christian Emperors Against Heresy."
[155] Vacandard 1907.
[156] Vacandard 1907.
[157] McKenna 1938, 56. "Priscillian was not condemned to death for heresy, but for the civil crime of magic, and his condemnation cannot be regarded as the prototype of the mediaeval inquisition. ... St. Martin of Tours, who was in Treves when the trial of Priscillian was going on, pleaded with Maximus not to allow the condemned bishop to be put to death. After the execution of Priscillian, St. Ambrose visited Treves and refused to associate with the bishops who were actually seeking to have the followers of Priscillian put to death. In a letter to Bishop Thuribius of Astorga on Priscillianism Pope Leo I (440-61), however, approved of the salutary effects that had resulted from this trial by the civil ruler. Maximus was therefore justified in saying to St. Martin that the heretics (Priscillian, etc.) were condemned by the secular courts rather than by the persecution of the bishops."
[158] Vacandard 1907. See Chapter III: "Third Period From 1100 to 1250 – The Revival of the Manichean Heresies in the Middle Ages."

of burning heretics at the stakes[159]. Burning at the stake continued to be common throughout France during the twelfth and thirteenth centuries, mostly as a result of the people's passion. With popular support to prevent heresy and save Christian souls, Roman Emperor Henry III hanged heretics in Goslar, located in present-day central Germany[160]. The Church's role in these executions was either remaining aloof or just expressing disapproval. Strengthening the union between the Church and the State, the coronation oath in France required the King to swear that he would exterminate all heretics from his kingdom[161].

Figure 8. Inquisition Scene.
Tribunal de la Inquisición o Auto de fe de la Inquisición (1819) by Francisco Goya.

This gradually grew into the horrible practices of the medieval Inquisition. Its primary mission was simple – to save souls, even if it killed them. The Church attempted to distance itself from this, but it wasn't without guilt since it used everything within its power to convince the State to torture others. The Church accomplished

---

[159] Vacandard 1907.
[160] Vacandard 1907.
[161] Vacandard 1907. See Chapter VI: "Fifth Period – Gregory IX and Frederic II – The Establishment of the Monastic Inquisition."

this without physical force because it had something much better. It had the power of excommunication, which was consider more horrible than the torture itself. The head of the State, risking excommunication and eternal damnation of his soul, eagerly sided with the demands of the Church and readily tortured the people[162]. By now, the Church had forgotten Jesus' teachings of tolerance and adopted the Roman civil laws involving ancient paganism cruelty[163].

After several more centuries, the Church developed more efficient tools to deal with its enemies: torture and execution devices. These enemies were usually accused of practicing sorcery, magic and witchcraft[164]. The medieval Church considered witchcraft a challenge to the order of society and to the majesty of God himself. As such, the Church sanctioned witch hunts to search for witches or evidence of witchcraft. These usually resulted in wide-spread panic, mass hysteria, lynchings, and burnings. In many cases, legally sanctioned witchcraft trials were conducted with judges of Christian bishops acting as God's defenders[165]. From the fifteenth through eighteenth centuries, there were about eighty thousand witchcraft-related trials resulting in about thirty-five thousand executions[166]. It wasn't until the eighteenth century, when prosecution of witchcraft ended. The objective existence of sorcery and witchcraft were then understood to be errors of either superstition or fraud[167]. For instance, a famous heretic burned at the stake was Joan of Arc. Actually though, she was executed for political reasons, yet done legally under the authorities of the Inquisition[168]. Had the Bishop of Beauvais, Pierre Cauchon, not

---

[162] Vacandard 1907. See Chapter VII: "Sixth Period – Development of the Inquisition (Innocent IV and the Use of Torture)."
[163] Vacandard 1907.
[164] Vacandard 1907. See Chapter VIII: "Theologians, Canonists, and Casuists of the Inquisition."
[165] Russell 1972, 2-3.
[166] Monter 2002, 12. Approximate amount of trials/executions from 1450-1750 (in thousands) for British Isles & North America (5/2); Germany, Netherlands, Switzerland, Lorraine, Austria & Czech (50/25); France (3/1); Scandinavia (5/2); Poland, Lituania, Hungary, & Russia (7/2); and Spain, Portugal, & Italy (10/1).
[167] Russell 1972, 28.
[168] Vacandard 1907. See Chapter IX: "The Inquisition in Operation."

been an English partisan, I believe that the tribunal over which he presided likely wouldn't have brought in a guilty verdict.

Figure 9. Joan at the Stake
by Jules Eugène Lenepveu (1890).

So, why did I spend so much time discussing the Inquisition? I wanted you to know that human passions were primarily responsible for the many abuses of the Inquisition. Much of this happened because the rulers in both the Church and the State felt it their combined duty to defend both society and God in the world. They convinced the people of their divine authority, possessing God's permission to punish all crimes against His law. Heresy was a religious crime, yet it was punishable by the State[169]. Throughout this medieval time, Rome used Christianity as a significant source of its political authority. Likewise, the Papacy's attention and activity became more directed towards acquiring power in the new lands, like Britain and later Germany. Thus the medieval Pope was characterized as the highly political position of the head of Christendom and a key leader of society[170]. This was best exemplified in the words of Edward Gibbon, an eighteenth century English historian and Member of Parliament. "The various modes of worship, which prevailed in the Roman world, were all considered by the people as equally true; by the philosopher as equally false; and by the magistrate as equally useful"[171].

During the Spanish Inquisitions alone, Christianity caused about five million deaths. Yet, this was small when compared to the more than fifty million killed for all religious reasons[172]. Particularly, Christian wars involved warriors killing to achieve God's purpose. These included the Pope-sanctioned Crusades against the Muslims in the Holy Lands during the eleventh through thirteenth centuries; the sixteenth century French Wars of Religion between the Catholics and Protestants; the seventeenth century Taiping Rebellion in China involving a protestant rebellion civil war against the imperial State; and the seventeenth century Thirty Years War between the Catholics and Protestants in the German states, Sweden, and Poland[173]. So, why did Christians follow these aggressive dictates? The best answer I can provide comes from the slogan of the Crusades, *Deus vult*, meaning "God wills it"[174]. Also during the Middle Ages, Christian Soldiers were required to perform penance after war for any sin that they may have done,

---

[169] Vacandard 1907. See Chapter X: "A Criticism of the Theory and Practice of the Inquisition."

[170] Dawson 1954.

[171] 1782. This is popularly quoted as" Religion is regarded by the common people as true, by the wise as false, and by the rulers as useful" and most likely misattributed to Seneca. I could not locate this quote in any of Seneca's works.

[172] Plaisted 2006.

[173] See Bréhier 1908, Encyclopædia Britannica 2011a and 2011b, and Spahn 1912.

[174] Phillips 2010, 3-28.

such as killing out of anger instead of duty in the service of justice[175]. Much of the influence behind early Christianity came from the principle of the Peace of Augsburg of 1555, *cuius regio, eius religio*, meaning "Whose realm, his religion"[176]: In a nutshell, the religion of the ruler dictated the religion of the ruled[177].

Figure 10. Inquisition Torture Chamber.
by Bernard Picard (1716). Obtained from Louis-Ellies Dupries' *Mémoires historiques pour servir à l'histoire des Inquisitions*.

---

[175] Verkamp 1993, 11. First millennium "warriors returning from battle would or should be feeling guilty and ashamed for all the wartime killing they had done. Far from having such feelings dismissed as insignificant or irrelevant, returning warriors were encouraged to seek resolution of them through rituals of purification, expiation, and reconciliation. To accommodate these latter needs, religious authorities of the period not infrequently imposed various and sundry penances on returning warriors, depending on the kind of war they had been engaged in, the number of their killings, and the intention with which they had been carried out."
[176] Krasner 1999, 79.
[177] See especially Miller et. Al. 2010.

This leads me to believe that no matter whom we are and no matter what we do, someone can attempt to use their Christian faith to find fault in us. Jesus didn't do this. For instance, while Jesus was teaching in the Temple in Jerusalem, some of the religious leaders interrupted Him and brought in an adulterous woman for His judgment[178]. He refused to condemn her. If Jesus refused to condemn an adulterer, a person who willingly violated God's seventh commandment, why should a Christian? Throughout its history, there was no lack of Christians eager to tell others what to do. Instead of trying to please everyone, Christians today, should understand Abraham Lincoln's words to nineteenth century Christians about emancipation. "These are not, however, the days of miracles, and I suppose it will be granted that I am not to expect a direct revelation. I must study the plain physical facts of the case, ascertain what is possible and learn what appears to be wise and right. The subject is difficult, and good men do not agree"[179]. No matter how hard he tried, Lincoln could never please puritanical moralists and idealists. So, why should anyone else?

Excluding the violence committed against others, the Christian ethics during this evolutionary period can be summarized with a list of seven things a Christian should do and shouldn't do. This involves living the *Seven Virtues* while avoiding the *Seven Deadly Sins*. In the late thirteenth century, Aquinas developed the *Seven Virtues* of justice, courage, temperance, prudence, faith, hope and charity[180]. Prior to that in the late sixth century, Pope Gregory the Great directed that all Christians were to abstain from *Seven Deadly Sins* of pride, greed, envy, wrath, lust, gluttony, and sloth[181]. These requirements of what to do and not to do found their way into early literature such as Dante's epic poem, the *Divine Comedy*. This poem listed these same seven virtues and sins respectively

---

[178] John 7:53-8:11.
[179] Lincoln 1967.
[180] Pegis 1945, 466-80. From Summa Theologica, First Part. Habits, Virtues and Vices. Faith, Hope, and Charity are theological virtues, while Justice, Courage, Temperance and Prudence are cardinal virtues. Summa Theologica was written from 1265-74.
[181] Gregory the Great 1844.

representing paradise of virtues and the sin's effects upon a person's soul after death[182].

Figure 11. Jesus and the woman taken in adultery by Gustave Doré (1865).

Modern Age Christian Ethics.

Now, this brings us to the modern age of Christianity. There has never been any progress without some mixture of human error and sin. Yet, Christianity today is further along the road toward a true Christian ethics than was Paul in his attitudes toward women, or Martin Luther in regard to the economic status of peasants, or John

---

[182] 1867.

Calvin in regard to infant damnation[183]. And, it's more than just pursuing *Seven Virtues* while avoiding the *Seven Deadly Sins*. The Bible remains the primary source of the Christian ethics even though there exist numerous translations and radical interpretation differences. Yet, it isn't the sole source. Even Roman Catholic Bishops, the senior Christian leaders, state that an examination of the Bible "do not provide us with detailed answers to the specifics of the questions we face today"[184].

Thus, with the increased literacy rate and availability of written works, there are numerous theological books that contribute to the overall Christian ethic, normally written by various Christian leaders. Except in such authoritarian churches of the Roman Catholic and Eastern Orthodox, the voice of the Church is rarely equated with the voice of Jesus. On the contrary, Protestant religious ethics don't believe that any single Christian or group of Christians fully understand Christian moral truth with a complete monopoly upon the gospels and its ethical interpretations[185]. Additionally, many of the churches today don't always practice what they preach.

In my opinion, the Church only possesses the moral authority to speak to others about its ethics only when it holds itself accountable at the same time. Then again, the Church is inconsistent in its message if it preaches adoption over abortion but then creates a climate of ostracizing women who become pregnant. Also, I hear about many churches holding people accountable for their behavior, and it's almost always about sex. For example, somebody having an affair typically results in the church attempting to save the marriage before considering anything else[186]. Essentially, the Inquisition is alive and well today as many Christians still feel the obligation to persecute others in the name of Jesus.

---

[183] 1 Timothy 2:11-14, Luther 1525, Schaff 1910.
[184] National Conference of Catholic Bishops 1983, 26.
[185] Harkness 1957. In Chapter 1, "What is Christian Ethics?" of this book.
[186] Mason 2011. This as a lecture the author provided at the Currie Strickland Lectures at Howard Payne University on March 15, 2011.

Many Christians believe it better to be "right" than to have a relationship with another. However, Jesus didn't teach us to be right. I shared an analogy with my daughters involving righteousness and driving in which I commented that graveyards are filled with many drivers who had the right of way. No matter what anyone tells them, many people would rather be "right" and have no qualms about telling others that they are right, even if it killed them and even if it caused them to violate Jesus' lessons.

So, what is a modern Christian? Believing in Christian doctrine and calling ourselves Christians without a change in personality or behavior towards that of Jesus isn't enough. Otherwise, we'll be nothing more than a hypocrite without compassion to human suffering. Not only that, bad Christians become barriers to God's words when compared to good non-Christians[187]. So, how do we define a good modern Christian? Do we have to possess the *Seven Virtues* and avoid the *Seven Deadly Sins*? If we do, is it enough? Do we have to profess the right Christian beliefs, belong to the right Church, and faithfully observe the sacraments? Do we have to live a completely God-centered life while following the teachings of Jesus?

For me, a true Christian fully believes and follows the teachings of Jesus. The love of God and our neighbor is the supreme virtue. Self-love and self-centeredness are the supreme sins. This means that the real Christian ethics should include thinking about the effects of decisions beyond self. These ethics shouldn't be a version of looking out for "number one". This is difficult since the fabric of modern secular society is full of dishonesty and other characteristics that are contrary to the Christian character. What's more, many churches are plagued with dishonesty and sinful actions. For an appalling number of people, they tend to make decisions using two criteria: doing what other people do or doing what they can get away without detection or penalty. Furthermore,

---

[187] Harkness 1957. In Chapter 5: "God, Sin, and Christian Character" of this book.

Christian ethics becomes questionable if it either accommodates secular standards completely or refuses to learn from the past[188].

Now, what is the modern Christian Church? What does it do? Is it just a group of modern real Christians? Does it have a mission? According to Jesus, He only mentioned the word "Church" twice in the Bible, one identifying Peter as the rock upon which to build the Church and the other stating that Heathens neglect to hear the Church[189]. But, I prefer to think of the Church as a group of people whom Jesus says gather in His name[190]. It should be faithful to its mission as the carrier of the gospels and should be a fellowship of persons sincerely trying to follow the teachings of Jesus[191].

Unfortunately, many Christian religions tend to make people feel worthless and broken. Instead, they should be spiritually uplifting and enriching. Regrettably, they make people feel guilty for virtually everything: being born a sinner, experiencing human pleasures, not believing with enough zeal, not witnessing effectively, marrying someone outside the church, skipping church, attending the wrong church, and questioning religious beliefs[192].

So, how does one become a member of a Christian church? Christian initiation of full membership into the Church involves formal religious education. For example, Catholics initiate members using Catechism, derived from the discourses of Saint Cyril of Jerusalem and the homilies of Saint Augustine[193]. Aside from watching other Christians as role models, religious education is generally the process that people learn about Christian ethics. For many ancient and modern Christians, this religious education is both brutal and effective. I should know, at least from a modern perspective.

---

[188] Harkness 1957. In Chapter 1, "What is Christian Ethics?" of this book.
[189] Matthew 16:18, 18:17.
[190] Matthew 18:20.
[191] Harkness 1957. In Chapter 1, "What is Christian Ethics?" of this book.
[192] Gulley 2010, 31-32.
[193] Vaticana 2003, Cyril of Jerusalem 1969, and Augustine 2007.

From 1969 through 1972, I attended the Immaculate Conception School, which was part of the Catholic Church located in Franklin, New Jersey. This elementary school had three nuns, who were Sisters of Charity of Saint Elizabeth. One of them taught my first grade class. You would never have thought that light-weight frail nuns could strike terror into anyone's life. And, I'm not talking about the loving nun played by Sally Field in *The Flying Nun* sitcom in the late 1960s, nor about the humorous incompetent one in the *Sister Mary Elephant* comedy skit by Cheech and Chong in 1973[194]. From my experience in this Catholic school, I know about the real terror of nuns. I think that even the local parish priests feared them too. On one memorable agonizing occasion, one of my classmates did something he wasn't supposed to do. He talked in class to another student without permission. And, he was caught by this "eagle eye" nun. The punishment for his crime was for him to meet "Charlie Brown". Now, who wouldn't want to meet Charles Shultz's famous gentle cartoon character? He was the lovable star of several popular films in the 1960s, such as *A Charlie Brown Christmas* and *It's the Great Pumpkin, Charlie Brown*[195]. Yet, this nun's "Charlie Brown" was nothing like this person. Instead, it was her devious name for a large, thick, wooden paddle. Its purpose was painfully simple – corporal punishment to discipline children who violate rules.

As a six-year old who didn't know any better, I thought it was funny to see someone caught and sentenced to face the wrath of this Machiavellian nun. Why not? The Saturday morning cartoons I usually watched each week such as Looney Tunes' *Bugs Bunny* and *The Road Runner* conditioned me to find humor in anyone caught and punished for violating a rule[196]. Watching super genius Wile E. Coyote suffer in his attempt to catch the Road Runner was funny. Unable to control myself as I watched my fellow classmate meet "Charlie Brown", I giggled. Sadly, it was loud enough for that "rabbit ears" nun to hear. When she was done disciplining the talkative student, she informed everyone that it was my turn. My

---

[194] Ackerman and Wylie 1967, and Marin and Chong 1973.
[195] Melendez 1965 and 1966.
[196] Beck and Friedwald 1989.

guilt? She told me that it was laughing without permission. From my perspective as an adult now, I really shouldn't have taken pleasure in the pain and suffering of others. But, I didn't know any better back then. To this day, I'll never forget the pain and embarrassment I suffered for my insensitive attitude towards others. Although I learned it wasn't good to laugh at someone being punished, this nun used violence and humiliation to teach me this lesson. Like many others throughout history, my religious training began with an unwavering definite fear of God, especially if He used an army of intolerable supernatural nuns to enforce His rules. For this young six-year old boy, Christian ethics meant doing whatever a nun or priest told you. As an adult, I know it means much more than that. Bishop Spong expressed this well. "Religious teachings must turn from its fear-driven moralism and concentrate on deepening relationships, articulating a new, responsible human maturity and recovering the essential goodness of life"[197].

Conclusion.

Today, one needs to be strongly rooted with Christian ethics, especially in a VUCA (volatile, uncertain, complex, and ambiguous) world. Modern Christians live in a world different than one Jesus personally knew. This is a world of sexual exploitation, forced labor, and child slavery affecting millions. Moreover, desperate economic conditions around the world, ignorance, or just plain greed could lead to families selling their children to human traffickers. Many people support both the pimps and human traffickers by paying for sex. The modern world also includes terrorism, drugs, corruption, genocide, population explosion, environmental pollution, animal extinctions, waste of natural resources, etc. These modern problems create ethical issues, such as the ones Chaplain (Colonel) Johnson describes as being relevant to Christian decisions[198]. First issue is that ethical relativism has replaced right and wrong decisions with a "no fault" mentality. Second, loyalty or allegiance to a person or a group, such as a church, subordinates right decisions. Third, concern for

---

[197] Spong 2005, 47.
[198] Johnson 1974.

image trumps right decisions if it embarrasses the individual or group. Finally, success with fame, fortune, or power replaces right decisions.

No matter how hard anyone tries, including Jesus, we should understand that it's impossible to entirely expel evil from the world[199]. Christians shouldn't look upon this as a bad thing, since I firmly believe that evil causes much of the misfortune that we experience and that some of this misfortune forces our soul to grow in a positive and good way. What's more, our true character can't be discovered unless we have a struggle with adversity, as Seneca quotes in *On Providence*. "Fire tests gold, misfortune [tests] brave men"[200]. Searching for absolute ethical and moral purity, the unobtainable purpose of many pious Christian fanatics, isn't the answer either. Furthermore, Christianity demands belief, but belief doesn't prevent unethical conduct[201].

Many times, Christians walk on a tight-rope moving between the extremes of an ethical crusader or ethical chameleon. A crusader is a pious self-righteous individual, while the chameleon dutifully agrees with others, even though this person frequently changes one's mind to remain faithfully loyal[202]. Which one are you, a crusader or chameleon? Is being one more important than another? In my opinion, it depends upon not only the situation, but why. There are three generic internal reasons for doing the right thing. First, it is the right thing to do. Second, it makes us feel good. Third, we personally benefit from doing the right thing. In all three, we do the right thing, but only the first one is purely selfless. Not only doing the right things for the right reasons, Christian ethical decisions should be based upon personal honor, interpersonal relationships with others including non-Christians, and moral implications of the decisions. Anything less than this violates the teachings of Jesus.

---

[199] Solzhenitsyn 2002, 299-314.
[200] 64. In Latin: "Ignis aurum probat, miseria fortes uiros".
[201] Saranam 2005, 57.
[202] Johnson 1974.

References.

Ackerman, H. and Wylie, M. (creators). (1967). *The Flying Nun*. The Internet Movie Database. http://www.imdb.com/title/ tt0061252/ Accessed 10 July 2011.

Aeschylus. (1920). *The Agamemnon.* Greek original 458 BCE. Translated by Gilbert Murray, London: Oxford University Press. Project Gutenberg. http://www.gutenberg.org/cache/epub/14417/pg14417.html. Accessed 26 June 2011.

Agamben, G. (1993). *The Coming Community*. Italian original 1990. Translated by Michael Hardt. Minneapolis, Minn.: University of Minnesota Press.

Aristotle. (1812). *Ethics*. Greek original 340 BCE. Translated by J.A. Smith. Book III, Section XI. http://www.gutenberg.org/cache/epub/8438/pg8438.html. Accessed 26 June 2011.

Augustine. (2007). *Essential Sermons: The Works of Saint Augustine*. Latin original ca. 354-430. Translated by Edmund Hill and edited by Boniface Ramsey. Hyde Park, N.Y.: New City Press.

Aurelius, M. (1862). *The Meditations*. Greek original 167. Translated by George Long. Book Three. The Internet Classics Archive, Massachusetts Institute of Technology. http://classics.mit.edu/Antoninus/meditations.3.three.html. Accessed 25 June 2011.

Austin, M.M. (1981). *The Hellenistic world from Alexander to the Roman conquest: a selection of ancient sources in translation*. Cambridge, Mass.: Cambridge University Press.

Bagozzi, R.P.; Dholakia, U.M.; and Basuroy, S. (2003). "How Effortful Decisions Get Enacted: The Motivating Role of Decision Processes, Desires, and Anticipated Emotions." *Journal of Behavioral Decision Making*, 16: 273–295.

Beck, J. and Friedwald, W. (1989). *Looney Tunes and Merrie Melodies: A Complete Illustrated Guide to the Warner Bros. Cartoons*. New York: Henry Holt and Company.

Becker, C.H. (1909). *Christianity and Islam*. German original 1907. Translated by Henry J. Chaytor, London: Harper & Brothers. http://www.gutenberg.org/cache/epub/11198/pg11198.html. Accessed 10 July 2011.

Blackman, R.H. and Utzinger, J.M. (2009). "A Post-Roddenbery Star Trek," *The Cresset, Michaelmas*, 73 (1): 36-39.

Bréhier, L. (1908). "Crusades." *The Catholic Encyclopedia*. 4. New York: Robert Appleton Co. http://www.newadvent.org/ cathen/04543c.htm. Accessed 26 August 2011.

Brennan, J.G. (1994). *Foundations of Moral Obligation: the Stockdale Course*. Novato, Calif.: Presidio Press.

Buckingham, C.T. (1985). "Ethics and the Senior Officer: Institutional Tensions." *Parameters. Journal of the US Army War College*. 15 (Autumn): 23-32. http://www.carlisle.army.mil/usawc/Parameters/Articles/1985/buck.htm. Accessed 27 November 2011.

Burton, J.G. (1993). *The Pentagon Wars: Reformers Challenge the Old Guard*. Annapolis, Md.: Naval Institute Press.

Church, F.P. (1897, 21 September). "Is There a Santa Claus?" *The Sun of New York*.

Cicero, M.T. (1887). "Scipio's Dream." In *On the Republic*. Greek original 51 BCE. Translated by Andrew P. Peabody in *Cicero De Officiis (On Moral Duties)*. Boston, Mass.: Little, Brown, and Co. Project Gutenberg. http://www.gutenberg.org/cache/epub/7491/pg7491.html. Accessed 26 June 2011.

Coker, C. (2002). *Waging War without Warriors? The Changing Culture of Military Conflict*. International Institute for Strategic Studies (IISS) Studies in International Security. London: Lynne Rienner Publishers.

Coker, C. (2008). *Ethics and War in the 21st century*. New York: Routledge.

Cyril of Jerusalem. (1969). *The Works of Saint Cyril of Jerusalem*. Greek original ca. 313-86. Translated by Leo P. McCauley and Anthony A. Stephenson. Washington, D.C.: The Catholic University of America Press.

Dante (Durante degli Alighieri). (1867). *The Divine Comedy: The Vision of Paradise, Purgatory, and Hell*. Italian original ca. 1308-1321. Translated by Henry W. Longfellow. Leipzig, Ger.: Bernhard Tauchnitz.

Dasgupta, S. (1922). *A History of Indian Philosophy*. Cambridge, Mass.: Cambridge University Press. Vol. 1. http://www.gutenberg.org/cache/epub/12956/pg12956.html. Accessed 10 July 2011.

Dawson, C. (1954). "Christian Culture in the Ancient World." *Folia Magazine*, 8(2). Article available at Catholic Education. http://www.catholiceducation.org/articles/history/world/wh0130.htm. Accessed 10 July 2011.

Descartes, R. (1649). *Discourse de la Méthode*. French original 1637. Translation printed by Thomas Newcombe in *A Discourse of a Method for the Well Guiding of Reason and the Discovery of Truth in the Sciences*. London. http://www.gutenberg.org/files/25830/25830-h/25830-h.htm. Accessed 2 September 2011.

Dewey, J. (1916). *Democracy and Education: An Introduction to the Philosophy of Education.* New York: Macmillan.

Driver, J. (2009). "The History of Utilitarianism," *Stanford Encyclopedia of Philosophy.* http://plato.stanford.edu/ entries/utilitarianism-history/. Accessed 26 June 2011.

Encyclopædia Britannica. (2011a). "Wars of Religion." *Encyclopædia Britannica Online.* http://www.britannica.com/EBchecked/topic/497152/Wars-of-Religion. Accessed 26 August 2011.

Encyclopædia Britannica. (2011b). "Taiping Rebellion." *Encyclopædia Britannica Online.* http://www.britannica.com/EBchecked/topic/580815/Taiping-Rebellion. Accessed 26 August 2011.

Epictetus. (1888). *The Enchiridion.* Greek original 125. Translated by George Long in *The Discourses of Epictetus.* London: George Bell and Sons. http://www.gutenberg.org/files/10661/10661-h/10661-h.htm. Accessed 26 June 2011.

Epicurus. (1925). *Principle Doctrines.* Greek original ca. 341-270 BCE. Translated by Robert D. Hicks. The Internet Classics Archive, Massachusetts Institute of Technology. http://classics.mit.edu/Epicurus/princdoc.html. Accessed 26 June 2011.

Estes, R. (2005). *The 550th Anniversary Pictorial Census of the Gutenberg Bible.* Mainz, Ger.: Gutenberg Research Center.

Evans, M. (2011). "Captains of the Soul: Stoic Philosophy and the Western Profession of Arms in the Twenty-first century." *Naval War College Review.* 64 (Winter): 35, 42-46.

French, S.E. (2003). *The Code of the Warrior: Exploring Warrior Values Past and Present.* Lanham, Md.: Rowman & Littlefield.

Friedman, M. (1970, 13 September). "The Social Responsibility of Business is to Increase Profit", *The New York Times Magazine.* 33: 122-26. http://www.colorado.edu/studentgroups/libertarians/issues/friedman-soc-resp-business.html. Accessed 25 June 2011.

Gibbon, E. (1845). "The Internal Prosperity in the Age of the Antonines." Chapter II in *The History of the Decline and Fall of the Roman Empire.* London: Strahan and Cadell, 1782. Vol. I. Revised ed with notes by Rev. Henry H. Milman. http://www.gutenberg.org/files/890/890-h/890-h.htm. Accessed 2 September 2011.

Giannet, S.M. (2002). "The Radical Ethics of Jesus. A Commentary on Feasibility." *The American Journal of Biblical Theology.* 3 (39). http://www.biblicaltheology.com/Research/ GiannetS02.html. Accessed 8 July 2011.

Gordon, D.R. (2003). "The Philosophy of Epicurus: Is It an Option for Today?" In *Epicurus: His Continuing Influence and Contemporary Relevance*, edited by Dane R. Gordon and David

B. Suits, 5. New York: Rochester Institute of Technology Cary Graphic Arts Press.

Gregory the Great. (1844). *Morals on the Book of Job*. Latin original ca. 540-604. Translated by John H. Parker and J. Rivington. Oxford: J.H. Parker. Vol. III, Book XXXI. Section 87. http://www.lectionarycentral.com/ GregoryMoraliaIndex.html. Accessed 29 July 2011.

Gulley, P. (2010). *If the Church Were Christian: Rediscovery the Values of Jesus*. New York: HarperCollins Publishers.

Hadot, P. (2001). *Inner Citadel: The Meditations of Marcus Aurelius*. French original 1992. Translated by Michael Chase. Cambridge, Mass.: Harvard University Press.

Harkness, G.E. (1957). *Christian Ethics*. Nashville, Tenn.: Abingdon Press, 1957. http://www.religion-online.org/showbook.asp?title=802. Accessed 2 September 2011.

Hick, J. (1995). *A Christian Theology of Religions: A Rainbow of Faiths*. Louisville, Ky: Westminster John Knox Press.

Hobbes, T. (1651). *Leviathan*. Printed for Andrew Crooke at the Green Dragon in St. Paul's Churchyard. http://www.gutenberg.org/files/3207/3207-h/3207-h.htm. Accessed 22 June 2011.

Holowchak, M.A. (2008). *Stoics: A Guide for the Perplexed*. New York: International Publishing Group.

Immaculate Conception Regional School. (2011). *Immaculate Conception Regional School website*. http://www.icrsschool.com. Accessed 10 July 2011.

Isen, A.M. and Shalker, T.E. (1982). "The effect of feeling state on evaluation of positive, neutral, and negative stimuli: When you 'accentuate the positive,' do you 'eliminate the negative'?" *Social Psychology Quarterly*, 45 (1): 58–63.

Johnson, K.D. (1974). "Ethical Issues of Military Leadership." *Parameters. Journal of the US Army War College*. 4 (2): 35-39. http://www.carlisle.army.mil/usawc/Parameters/Articles/1974/johnson.pdf. Accessed 27 November 2011.

Kennedy, R.F. (1968). "Statement on the Assassination of Martin Luther King," Indianapolis, Ind.: Speech (April 4). John F. Kennedy Presidential Library and Museum. http://www.jfklibrary.org/Research/Ready-Reference/RFK-Speeches/Statement-on-the-Assassination-of-Martin-Luther-King.aspx. Accessed 25 June 2011.

Kent, W. (1908). "Devil." *The Catholic Encyclopedia*. 4. New York: Robert Appleton. http://www.newadvent.org/cathen/04764a.htm. Accessed 10 September 2011.

Ker, J. (2009). *The Deaths of Seneca*. Oxford: Oxford University Press.

Kirsch, J.P. (1907). "St. Agnes of Rome." *The Catholic Encyclopedia*. 1. New York: Robert Appleton http://www.newadvent.org/cathen/01214a.htm. Accessed 26 August 2011.

Krasner, S.D. (1999). *Sovereignty: Organized Hypocrisy*. Princeton, N.J.: Princeton University Press.

Lincoln, A. (1967). "Reply to Christians of Chicago, 1862." In *The Political Thought of Abraham Lincoln*, edited by Richard N. Nurrent, 216-17. Indianapolis, Ind.: Bobbs-Merrill.

Luther, M. (1525, May). "Against the Robbing and Murdering Hordes of Peasants." Article found at University of South Carolina website from Professor Kathryn Edwards History 310 course, *Age of Reformation*. http://www.cas.sc.edu/hist/faculty/edwardsk/hist310/reader/lutheragainst.pdf. Accessed 31 July 2011.

Marin, R. (Cheech) and Chong, T. (1973). *Sister Mary Elephant*. Lyrics available at MetroLyrics http://www.metrolyrics.com/sister-mary-elephant-lyrics-cheech-and-chong.html. Accessed 10 July 2011.

Mason, G.A. (2011). "Preaching on Ethics in the Local Church." *Christian Ethics Today*. 19 (2): 6-8.

McKenna, S. (1938). "Chapter 3: xx." In *Paganism and Pagan Survivals in Spain up to the Fall of the Visigothic Kingdom*. Esopus, N.Y.: Mount Saint Alphonsus. http://libro.uca.edu/mckenna/paganism.htm. Accessed 17 July 2011.

Melendez, B. (director). (1965). *A Charlie Brown Christmas*. The Internet Movie Database. http://www.imdb.com/title/tt0059026/ Accessed 10 July 2011.

Melendez, B. (director). (1966). *It's the Great Pumpkin, Charlie Brown*. The Internet Movie Database. http://www.imdb.com/title/tt0060550/ Accessed 10 July 2011.

Miller, F.P.; Vandome, A.F.; and McBrewster, J. (2010). *Cuius Regio, Eius Religio*. Saarbrücken, Germany: VDM Publishing House.

Monter, E.W. (2002). "Witch trials in Continental Europe, 1560-1660." In *Witchcraft and Magic in Europe*, edited by Bengt Ankarloo and Stuart Clark, Part 1:1-52. Philadelphia, Penn.: University of Pennsylvania Press.

Moskos, C.C.; Williams, J.A.; and Segal, D.R. (2000). "Armed Forces after the Cold War." In *The Postmodern Military: Armed Forces after the Cold War*, edited by Charles C. Moskos, John A. Williams, and David R. Segal, 1-13. New York: Oxford University Press.

Myrer, A. (1968). *Once an Eagle*. New York: Harper Collins Publishers.
National Conference of Catholic Bishops (American). (1983, 3 May). "The Challenge of Peace: God's Promise and Our Response." Washington, D.C. : Office of Pub. and Promotion Services, United States Catholic Conference. http://www.osjspm.org/the_challenge_of_peace_1.aspx. Accessed 2 September 2011.
Niebuhr, R. (1987). *The Essential Reinhold Niebuhr: Selected Essays and Addresses*. Edited by Robert McAfee Brown. New Haven, Conn.: Yale University Press.
Olcott, H.S. (1919). *The Life of Buddha and Its Lessons*. Adyar, Madras, India: Theosophical Publishing House. 2nd ed. http://www.gutenberg.org/files/18194/18194-h/18194-h.htm. Accessed 10 July 2011.
Pegis, A.C. (ed). (1945). *Basic Writings of Saint Thomas Aquinas: Man and the Conduct of Life*. New York: Random House.
Phillips, J.P. (2010). *Holy Warriors: A Modern History of the Crusades*. New York: Random House.
Plaisted, D.A. (2006). *Estimates of the Number Killed by the Papacy in the Middle Ages and Later*. University of North Carolina archive. www.cs.unc.edu/~plaisted/estimates.doc. Accessed 2 September 2011.
Russell, J.B. (1972). *History of Medieval Christianity*. Ithaca, N.Y.: Cornell University Press.
Saranam, S. (2005). *God Without Religion: Questioning Centuries of Accepted Truths*. East Ellijay, Ga.: The Pranayama Institute.
Schaff, P. (1910). "Calvin's Theology." In *History of the Christian Church, Volume VIII: Modern Christianity*. New York: Charles Scribner's Sons. http://www.ccel.org/s/schaff/history/8_ch14.htm. Accessed 30 July 2011.
Schaff, P. and Henry W. (eds). (1899). "The Seven Ecumenical Councils." In *A Select Library of the Nicene and Post-Nicene Fathers of the Christian Church*. 2nd Series. Vol. 14. Grand Rapids, Mich.: Eerdmans Publishing Company. http://www.ccel.org/ccel/schaff/npnf214.toc.html. Accessed 2 September 2011.
Schnackenburg, R. (1965). "Jewish Moral Teaching and Jesus' Moral Demands," Chapter 2 in *Jesus and the New Testament*, 54-89. London: Burns & Oates. http://theology1.tripod.com/readings/Schnackenburg.htm. Accessed 6 August 2011.
Seneca, L.A. (64). *De Providentia (On Providence)*. Latin original. http://www.thelatinlibrary.com/sen/sen.prov.shtml. Accessed 26 June 2011.

Seneca, L.A. (1958). Selected works. Latin original ca. 40-64. Translated by Moses Hadas. In *The Stoic Philosophy of Seneca: Essays and Letters*. New York: W.W. Norton & Company.

Shay, J.S. (1994). *Achilles in Vietnam: Combat Trauma and the Undoing of Character*. New York: Simon & Schuster.

Sisters of Charity of Saint Elizabeth. (2011). *Sisters of Charity of Saint Elizabeth website*. http://www.scnj.org. Accessed 10 July 2011.

Solzhenitsyn, A.I. (2002). *The Gulag Archipelago, 1918–1956*. Abridged. New York: Harper Perennial Modern Classics.

Spahn, M. (1912). "The Thirty Years War." *The Catholic Encyclopedia*. 14. New York: Robert Appleton Company. http://www.newadvent.org/cathen/14648b.htm. Accessed 26 August 2011.

Spong, J.S. (2005). *The Sins of Scripture: Exposing the Bible's Texts of Hate to Reveal the God of Love*. New York: Harper Collins Publishing.

Spring, H. (1940). *Fame is the Spur*. New York Literary Guild of America.

Stockdale, J.B. (1995). *Thoughts of a Philosophical Fighter Pilot*. Stanford, Calif.: Hoover Institution Press.

Stowers, S.K. (2010). "Jesus the Teacher and Stoic Ethics in the Gospel of Matthew." In *Stoicism in Early Christianity*, edited by Tuomas Rasimus, Troels Engberg-Pedersen, and Ismo Dundenberg, 59-76. Peabody, Mass.: Grand Rapids, Mich.: Baker Publishing Group. http://www.brown.edu/Departments/Early_Cultures/events/documents/ Stowers.pdf. Accessed 9 July 2011.

Taylor, C. (2007). *A Secular Age*. Harvard University: The Belknap Press.

Time Magazine. (1976, 27 December). "ARMED FORCES: A Barrage Hits West Point's Code," http://www.time.com/time/magazine/article/0,9171,947758,00.html. Accessed 1 July 2011.

Vacandard, E. (1907). *The Inquisition: A Critical and Historical Study of the Coercive Power of the Church*. French original 1902. Translated by Bertrand Conway. New York: Longmans, Green and Co. http://www.gutenberg.org/cache/epub/26329/pg26329.html. Accessed 1 July 2011.

Van Allsburg, C. (1985). *The Polar Express*. New York: Houghton Mifflin.

Vaticana, Libreria Editrice. (2003, 4 November). *Catechism of the Catholic Church*. Citta del Vaticano. http://www.vatican.va/archive/ENG0015/_INDEX.HTM. Accessed 10 July 2011.

Verkamp, B.J. (1993). *Moral Treatment of Returning Warriors in Early Medieval and Modern Times*. Scranton, Penn.: University of Scranton Press.

Walzer, M. (1981, March). "Two Kinds of Responsibility." *Parameters. Journal of the US Army War College*. 11: 42-46. http://www.carlisle.army.mil/usawc/Parameters/Articles/1981/1981%20walzer.pdf. Accessed 27 November 2011.

Yoder, J.H. (1972). *The Politics of Jesus*. Grand Rapids, Mich.: Eerdmans.

Chapter 4. Bible Can Justify Opposite Claims

The Bible is the primary written source of Christianity. Yet, this book contains numerous contradictory statements, which amounts to controversies in the Bible. How can we logically use this book to support our assertion if others can use the same book to disprove it? Through two millennia of transcriptions, including changes in definitions, culture, technology, and world beliefs, there exists no correct transcription of the original texts. More to the point, it isn't even completely historically factual. There were no audio or visual recording of the events, not to mention the lack of timely news reports. Regardless, the Bible should be taken as a whole, contradictions and all. The primary message is that God loves us and everyone else.

The basis of Christianity comes from the Bible. It's really a collection of dozens of separate books written by authors from all walks of life ranging from kings to laborers, and from military leaders to professional workers. Yet, these authors, who mostly never met one another, wrote them over a time span of more than a thousand years and were originally written in Hebrew, Greek and Aramaic – not English[203]. Regrettably, biblical words have been used to justify killing, including justifying violence to racial minorities, women, Jews, and homosexuals[204].

Instead, I've heard it many times that the Bible is God's love story to His people, but most Christians don't really know what this means. In addition to being a military history book, it's a law book full of rules that must be obeyed. It also contains fascinating stories, many of which contain R-rated adult themes. For instance, it contains stories about abortion, adultery, exhibitionism,

---

[203] See especially Ackroyd and Evans 1970.
[204] See especially Spong 2005.

homosexuality, incest, murder, polygamy, rape, robbery, slavery, suicide, torture, and war.

What do these stories really tell us? What should we learn from them? Are the messages today different than the messages intended thousands of years ago? And what do they say about our Christian faith? Are these stories accurate? Why are there so many interpretations and so many different denominations? What are we to believe; and who are we to believe? There are so many questions. Still, there are differing answers to each, depending on who we ask. Assisting us, there are tons of books available that provides us in-depth knowledge into the Bible, so I won't do that for you in this book. However, I'll briefly discuss its contents, the impact of language translations upon various versions, the context at the time it was written, the different interpretations, some of its controversial contradictions, and the resultant numerous denominations. For me, the message isn't that complicated. Simply stated, the Bible is nothing more than God's message through both literal and non-literal stories that He loves me and everyone else.

Content

In addition to more than seven million Christian book titles and fifty-six thousand Christian periodicals, there are over seventy million Bibles distributed annually[205]. The Bible contains many books, written by many authors from different times. Now, how were these books determined worthy of inclusion? What were the criteria? And, who made the decision? Why were some books not selected? To understand the Bible, we must understand why the contents were included[206]. These were decisions made by men, not God, though. True, we can say that the contents were inspired by God. But, God didn't make these decisions, and He definitely didn't personally write the books. After spending countless hours looking through Scriptures, I couldn't locate anything indicating that God wanted a complete, closed, never-changing, single collection of books for a Bible. Nor, could I find anything written

---
[205] Gordon Conwell Theological Seminary 2011.
[206] For a good simple source, see McDonald 2011.

that He inspired the Bible, let alone telling us that our current Bible is both infallible and accurate[207]. Scriptures are inspired; the Bible isn't[208]. Furthermore, God does inspire different people to do different things, even contrary to one another, while others may erroneously think their poor decisions were God-inspired.

Let me describe my recent divine inspiration. I had a dream one night early in 2011. This was a very vivid dream about writing my book, which was very clear to me the following morning. However, it still took me almost two years to put these ideas into written words. Much of this time was spent researching the source documents of my ideas to ensure that the facts in this book were verifiable facts. Then, I wrote my interpretation of these facts and laid out my understanding of everything I knew. Even now, can I truly say that I was divinely inspired? I really don't know for sure, and I most definitely can't prove it to you. What I do know is that I felt compelled to write this book, and that this book reinforced my understanding of the teachings of Jesus. Maybe, this is indeed divinely inspired. Having this personal experience, I fully understand how Christians can believe that their own decisions could be divinely inspired.

Now, back to the contents of the Bible. Only a few of the books specifically identify its author, leaving the others to guesses. Tables 8 and 9, obtained from the Christian Apologetics & Research Ministry (CARM), contain lists of the books of the Bible, its traditional author, and the approximate date written[209]. Instead of spending countless hours researching for this data, I chose to use the information from CARM, which is a non-profit Christian ministry that analyzes all religions such as Islam, Jehovah's Witnesses, Mormonism, Roman Catholicism, Universalism, and Wicca[210]. For me, this was close enough to the truth. I also listed the original language.

---

[207] Collier 2012, 103 and 122-23.
[208] 2 Timothy 3:16 states that God inspired all Scriptures. However, 2 Corinthians 11:17 implies that some Scriptures weren't inspired.
[209] Bradlaugh 1881.
[210] Slick 2011b.

Table 8. Books of the Bible – Old Testament.

Book	Author	Date Written	Original Language
Pentateuch:			
Genesis	Moses	≈ 1445 BCE	Hebrew
Exodus	Moses	1445-1405 BCE	Hebrew
Leviticus	Moses	1405 BCE	Hebrew
Numbers	Moses	1444-1405 BCE	Hebrew
Deuteronomy	Moses	1405 BCE	Hebrew
Historical:			
Joshua	Joshua	1404-1390 BCE	Hebrew
Judges	Samuel	1374-1129 BCE	Hebrew
Ruth	Samuel	1150 BCE	Hebrew
1 Samuel	Samuel	1043-1011 BCE	Hebrew
2 Samuel	Ezra (possible)	1011-1004 BCE	Hebrew
1 Kings	Jeremiah (possible)	971-852 BCE	Hebrew
2 Kings	Jeremiah (possible)	852-587 BCE	Hebrew
1 Chronicles	Ezra (possible)	450-425 BCE	Hebrew
2 Chronicles	Ezra (possible)	450-425 BCE	Hebrew
1 Esdras	Ezra	330 BCE	Hebrew
Ezra	Ezra	538-520 BCE	Hebrew, Aramaic
Nehemiah	Nehemiah	445-425 BCE	Hebrew
Tobias	Tobias	7th Century BCE	Hebrew, Aramaic
Judith	unknown	2nd Century BCE	Hebrew
Esther	Modecai (possible)	465 BCE	Hebrew
1,2,3,4 Maccabees	unknown	135 – 63 BCE	Greek
Wisdom:			
Job	Job (possible)	Unknown	Hebrew
Psalms	David and others	≈ 1000 BCE	Hebrew
Odes	unkown	unknown	Hebrew, Greek
Proverbs	Solomon and others	950-700 BCE	Hebrew
Ecclesiastes	Solomon	935 BCE	Hebrew
Song of Solomon	Solomon	965 BCE	Hebrew
Sirach	Jesus, son of Sirach	180 – 175 BCE	Hebrew

Table 8. Books of the Bible – Old Testament. (continued).

Book	Author	Date Written	Original Language
Major Prophets:			
Isaiah	Isaiah	740-680 BCE	Hebrew
Jeremiah	Jeremiah	627-585 BCE	Hebrew, Aramaic
Lamentations	Jeremiah	586 BCE	Hebrew
Baruch	Baruch	599 BCE	Hebrew
Ezekiel	Ezekiel	593-560 BCE	Hebrew
Daniel	Daniel	605 – 536 BCE	Hebrew, Aramaic
Minor Prophets:			
Hosea	Hosea	710 BCE	Hebrew
Joel	Joel	835 BCE	Hebrew
Amos	Amos	755 BCE	Hebrew
Obadiah	Obadiah	840-586 BCE	Hebrew
Jonah	Jonah	760 BCE	Hebrew
Micah	Micah	700 BCE	Hebrew
Nahum	Nahum	663-612 BCE	Hebrew
Habakkuk	Habakkuk	607 BCE	Hebrew
Zephaniah	Zephaniah	625 BCE	Hebrew
Haggai	Haggai	520 BCE	Hebrew
Zechariah	Zechariah	520-518 BCE	Hebrew
Malachi	Malachi	600-450 BCE	Hebrew

Sources: Bechtel,1910; Bradlaugh 1881; Drum 1912; Gigot 1907, 1909, 1912; Pope 1910; and Souvay 1909

According to Dr. James Denison, President of the Center for Informed Faith, the early Christians used four criteria for accepting a book into its Christian Scripture, which later became the New Testament. First, an apostle or eyewitness must have written the book. Second, the book must be both credible and believable. Third, the entire Church, not just a single congregation, must accept it. And, finally, the entire Church must approve it[211].

---

[211] 2006, 5-6.

Table 9. Books of the Bible – New Testament.

Book	Author	Date Written	Original Language
Gospels:			
Matthew	Matthew	60s CE	Greek
Mark	Mark	Late 50s CE	Greek
Luke	Luke	60 CE	Greek
John	John	80s – 90s CE	Greek
Apostolic History:			
Acts	Luke	61 CE	Greek
Pauline Epistles:			
Romans	Paul	55 CE	Greek
1 Corinthians	Paul	54 CE	Greek
2 Corinthians	Paul	55 CE	Greek
Galatians	Paul	49 CE	Greek
Ephesians	Paul	60 CE	Greek
Philippians	Paul	61 CE	Greek
Colossians	Paul	60 CE	Greek
1 Thessalonians	Paul	50-51 CE	Greek
2 Thessalonians	Paul	50-51 CE	Greek
1 Timothy	Paul	62 CE	Greek
2 Timothy	Paul	63 CE	Greek
Titus	Paul	62 CE	Greek
Philemon	Paul	60 CE	Greek
General Epistles:			
Hebrews	Unknown	60s CE	Greek
James	Jesus' Half Brother	40s – 50s CE	Greek
1 Peter	Peter	63 CE	Greek
2 Peter	Peter	63-64 CE	Greek
1 John	John	Late 80s CE	Greek
2 John	John	Late 80s CE	Greek
3 John	John	Late 80s CE	Greek
Jude	Jesus' Half Brother	60s-70s CE	Greek
Apocalypse:			
Revelation	John	80s – 90s CE	Greek

Source: Bradlaugh 1881

From 50 through 100 CE, the New Testament books were written. However, other books were written during this period that could have been included, such as *Didache* in 70 CE and the *Epistle of*

Barnabas in 100 CE[212]. Around 200, the *Muratonian Canon* with the oldest known list of books was developed[213]. By 367, Bishop Athanasius of Alexandria wrote the number and order of the books in his *39th Festal, Easter*, letter of 367[214]. Almost a thousand years later, during the Council of Florence in 1442, the entire Church recognized twenty-seven books, though didn't declare them unalterable[215]. Finally, the Council of Trent in 1546 made decisions on the Christian biblical canons for the Catholic Church, the *Thirty-Nine Articles* in 1563 for the Church of England, the Westminster Confession of Faith in 1647 for Calvinism, and the Synod of Jerusalem in 1672 for the Orthodox Church[216].

Moreover, the Catholic and Orthodox Bibles contain the *Apocrypha*, ancient books not recognized by Protestants in theirs[217]. Apocryphal writings "denoted a composition which claimed a sacred origin, and was supposed to have been hidden for generations, either absolutely, awaiting the due time of its revelation, or relatively, inasmuch as knowledge of it was confined to a limited esoteric circle"[218]. Table 10 lists the books generally considered part of this *Apocrypha*, classified by either Jewish or Christian origin.

I caution you when reading these books of the *Apocrypha* since there is no standard English translation[219]. Furthermore, there are different titles used for the same texts, along with the same titles used for different texts. As well, these texts vary in depth and breadth of coverage since not every text is fully translated[220]. Correspondingly, there remains a wide disagreement on authors,

---

[212] Draper 2006 and Wake 1863.
[213] Kirsch 1911.
[214] Athanasius 1892
[215] Hahn 2011.
[216] Bruce 1988.
[217] Koester 1990, 43-48.
[218] Reid 1907.
[219] Metzger 1987, 165-90.
[220] Metzger 1987, 251-286.

Table 10. Books of the Bible – Apocrypha.

Jewish Origin:

Henoch	Jannes and Mambres
Assumption of Moses	3,4 Machabees
Secrets of Henoch	Psalms of Solomon
3,4 Esdras	Prayer of Manasses
Apocalypse of Baruch	Sibylline Oracles
Apocalypse of Abraham	Testaments of the Twelve
Apocalypse of Daniel	Patriarchs
Jubilees	Ascension of Isaias

Christian Origin:

Infancy Gospel of James	Acts of Bartholomew
Gospel of the Infancy	Acts of Peter and Paul
Gospel of Gamaliel	Acts of Paul
Transitus Mariæ	Acts of Paul and Thecla
Gospel according to the Hebrews	Acts of Philip
	Acts of Matthew
Gospel According to the Egyptians	Teaching of Addai
	Acts of Simon and Jude
Gospel of Peter	Acts of Barnabas
Gospel of Philip	Gesta Matthiæ
Gospel of Thomas	Testamentum Domini
Gospel of Bartholomew	Nostri Jesu
Gospel of the Twelve Apostles	Preaching of Peter
Report of Pilate to the Emperor	Judicium Petri
Gospel of Nicodemus	Preaching of Paul
Minor Pilate Apocrypha	Epistles of the Blessed Virgin
Narrative of Joseph of Arimathea	Epistle of Peter to James the Less
Legend of Abgar	
Letter of Lentulus	Epistles of Paul to the Corinthians
Acts of Peter	
Acts of John	Correspondence of Paul and Seneca
Acts of Andrew	
Acts and Martyrdom of Matthew	Apocalypse of Mary
	Apocalypses of Peter
Acts of Thomas	Apocalypse of Paul

Source: see Reid 1907

Bible Can Justify Opposite Claims 95

dates, geographical origins, and theological orientations[221]. If you are interested in reading these, though, I recommend James Elliott's 1993 *The Apocryphal New Testament*, which is a based on the 1924 work of M. R. James while retaining the same value. I believe that the introductions and bibliographies in Elliot's book make this a better choice. There's no doubt that the books of the *Apocrypha* were and continue to remain controversial; but, it can't be denied, though, that fourteen of them were included in the original King James Bible.

As for the official selection of New Testament books, there were many who challenge the list chosen and recommend the inclusion of other books. For example, Archbishop William Wake formally disputed "the authority of those uncharitable, bickering, and ignorant Ecclesiastics who first suppressed" the New Testament Scriptures in his *Forbidden Books of the Bible*. A Church of England priest, Wake was the Archbishop of Canterbury from 1715 until 1737[222]. Wake, in his book, claimed that the dissension, personal jealousy, intolerance, and bigotry contributed to the evolution of the Bible. Moreover, according to Edward Hancock, a later contributor to Wake's book, "bishops who extracted these books from the original New Testament, under the pretense of being Apocryphal, and forbade them to be read by the people, is proved by authentic impartial history too odious to entitle them to any deference"[223]. They both implied that the Nicene Council was a pious fraud in suppressing these books. Moreover, Wake's book includes text from those missing books[224].

---

[221] Shepherd 2010, 40.
[222] Encyclopædia Britannica 2011
[223] Wake 1863. Archbishop Wake refers to this as, "The Suppressed Gospels and Epistles of the Original New Testament of Jesus the Christ and Other Portions of the Ancient Holy Scriptures. Now Extant, Attributed to His Apostles, and other Disciples, and Venerated by the Primitive Christian Churches During the First Four Centuries, But Since, After Violent Disputations Forbidden by the Bishops of the Nicene Council, in the Reign of the Emperor Constantine and Omitted from the Catholics and Protestant Editions of the New Testament, by Its Compilers." Accessed 7 August 2011 http://www.gutenberg.org/files/6516/6516-h/6516-h.htm.
[224] Mary, Protevangelion, 1 Infancy, 2 Infancy (Young Childhood), Nicodemus, Christ and Abgarus, Laodiceans, Paul and Seneca, Acts of Paul and Thecla, 1

Also missing from the Bible are the *Gnostic Gospels*, which is a collection of books based upon the teachings of Jesus and several prophets[225]. Andrew Bernhard comments in his 2006 text-critical edition of non-canonical gospels that the definition of "gospel" should be used for any text describing the teachings or activities of Jesus. These gospels were written from the second to the fourth century. Recently, these gospels received widespread attention as a result of Dan Brown's 2003 best-selling novel *The Da Vinci Code*, which used them in its story. Brown's book was a very intriguing and disturbing fictional book involving treachery, religious fanaticism, secret societies and an ancient conspiracy, making it widely popular globally. It also raised several thought-provoking questions about the reliability and accuracy of the Bible[226]. Even though it was cleverly written, Brown's book contained numerous factual errors; yet, many people continue to believe these factual errors to be correct[227].

Can we learn from reading these non-canonical books[228]? At least, reading them provides us more insight into the environment of the times and into additional literature that could supplement our further understanding of the canonical books. Table 11 contains a list of some of those missing books along with a brief description of each. For me, the four canonical Gospels are interpretive portraits of Jesus, not direct eyewitness accounts[229]. Regrettably, most people believe them to be accurate biographies of Him and an accurate history of the time. What most people fail to understand is that the early Christians believed that the remembered oral words of Jesus were more important than the written documents[230]. Initially, these stories were communicated orally, and it wasn't

---

Clement, 2 Clement, Barnabas, Ephesians, Magnesians, Trallians, Romans, Philadelphians, Smyrnaeans, Polycarp, Philippians, 1 Hermas—Visions, 2 Hermas—Commands, and 3 Hermas—Similitudes
[225] Arendzen 1909.
[226] Abanes 2004, 5.
[227] I'm not going to list these errors. If interested, you could easily find them.
[228] See especially Pagels and King 2007.
[229] Spong 2005, 279.
[230] Metzger 1987, 3.

until decades later when they were written down. Sadly, it's these written words that we assume today to be an accurate account of Jesus.

Conversely, we can find others who would disagree with Wake while others advocate for the inclusion of these missing books. For one, Timothy Keller, an Adjunct Professor of Practical Theology at Westminster Theological Seminary and pastor of Redeemer Presbyterian Church (PCA) in New York City, wrote that many scholars don't accept these missing books from the Bible and aren't accepted by scholars. Actually, he believes that they aren't better than the ones contained in the Bible and that any claim of them being "better sources than the recognized gospels on the teachings and deeds of Jesus is simply unsupportable"[231]. So, what should we believe? Should we try to get these missing books included in the Bible? Instead, should we protest any attempts to get them included? If you want to read them, you can easily obtain free copies of these books on the Web for your review. I obtained many of my copies from the *Project Gutenberg* site of free electronic books founded by Michael Hart in 1971.

What about the writers of the books in the Bible? How likely is it that the traditional authors listed in Table 8 and Table 9 above were the actual writers? Does it matter? Some people determine the credibility of a book based upon the credentials of the author. This means that for many people, the author is important. For me, I prefer to weigh the contents of the writings as being more important than the writer. As such, I consider the source of the documents in my assessment of the writing's credibility. With that said, let me provide you my personal opinion of who wrote some of the books of the Bible. And, I refer to the mortal authors, not the divine inspiration of God, in my opinion.

The first five books of the Old Testament (Genesis, Exodus, Leviticus, Numbers and Deuteronomy), are referred to as the

---

[231] 2004.

Table 11. Some Books Missing From the Bible.

Book	Description
Books of Adam and Eve	Considered written by unknown Egyptians. Parts of these can be found in the *Talmud*, the *Koran* and elsewhere. It was important in the original literature of early humans. The original manuscript was written in Arabic.
Prayer of Azarias	This prayer had been cut from the Bible. But in the Vulgate, the Greek translation of Daniel, it's inserted in the third chapter between the twenty-third and twenty-fourth verses. It was Azarias' prayer while he was standing in the fiery furnace with his two friends, Ananias and Misael.
General Epistle of Barnabas	Many ancient church authorities deem this to be canonical and genuine. It was read widely in the churches at Alexandria. It's supposed to have been written by Barnabas, an apostle and companion of Paul.
Prophecy of Baruch	Baruch, a disciple of Jeremiah., wrote it After Nebuchadnezzar plundered the temple of Jerusalem, Baruch described Jeremiah predicting the return of the Babylonians.
Gospel of the Birth of Mary	Written by Matthew, it's considered genuine and authentic by the early church. It was later rejected by various edicts and councils of the early Church. It described Mary's origin and her life leading to the birth of Jesus.
First Epistle of Clement to the Corinthians	Clement was a disciple of Peter. This was publicly read in the early church. This was rejected by early church fathers because they claimed it didn't honor the Trinity doctrine. This letter chastised the congregation for sedition and blasphemy.
Book of Enoch (Ethiopian Enoch)	The early church widely read and used this book during the first three centuries. The Council of Laodicia discredited and banned it. It was discovered in the Dead Sea Scrolls.
Book of the Secrets of Enoch	Widely used by early Christians, it was found in Russia and Servia. It explained and verified some of the darker and more mysterious passages of the New Testament.
Shepherd of Hermas	Hermas, the brother of Bishop Pius of Rome, wrote it. Early church leaders read it for direction and confirmation of the faith. It contained visions on how to live a godly, faithful Christian life.
Letter of Herod to Pilate the Governor	These connected the death of Jesus to Roman History. It gave us an overview of what happened to Herod after Jesus' crucifixion.
Letter of Pilate to Herod	This was the response to Herod's letter. Pilate also described several events regarding Jesus' death and resurrection.

Table 11. Some Books Missing From the Bible (continued).

Book	Description
Epistles of Ignatius	Ignatius was the Bishop of Antioch in Syria from 67-107. He wrote letters dealing with morality, faith, martyrdom and Jesus to various congregations while a prisoner and on his journey to Rome to martyrdom
First Gospel of The Infancy Of Jesus Christ	Written by Thomas. Used by early Christians along with the other four gospels. The Synod at Angamala condemned these gospel in 1559. Mohammed may have used it to compile the *Koran*.
Epistles of Jesus Christ and Abgarus, King of Edessa	Discussed in the public registers and records of the city of Edessa in Mesopotamia. It was written in the Syriac language. They are considered Apocryphal. The Epistles contain two letters: King Abgarus' request for help from Jesus, and His reply.
Book of Jasher	It's an ancient Hebrew manuscript that is mentioned twice in the Bible (Joshua 10: 12 and 2 Samuel 1:17). This book provided insight into the historical period from creation through the time of Joshua. Although a man named Jasher wrote the book, the Hebrew word Jasher meant straight or upright. Therefore, the translated name of this book could be The Book of the Straight or Upright
Epistle of Jeremiah	Unknown author's letter written in Greek to the Jewish captives of Nebuchadnezzer. It's a warning to the people to beware of idolatry. The early church declared it canonical.
Wisdom of Jesus, Son of Sirach	The early church used it. Written in Hebrew by Jesus, son of Sirach, between 190 and 170 BCE. It's about morality and wisdom.
Book of Judith	Written by Joachim during the reign of Manasses. The Protestants excluded it from the Bible because it didn't exist in the Hebrew Bible. It described a virtuous woman who, by her actions, saved Israel from destruction by Holofernes and his vast army.
First and Second Books of Maccabees	Written by an unknown Palestinian from 135 – 63 BCE, these contained a history of the Jews. Both books can be found in the Catholic Bible
Third and Fourth Books of Maccabees	Written by a Jew, they were used by the Greek Church. The Third book was intended to comfort to the persecuted Jews in Alexandria during the reign of Ptolemy Philopator. And, the Fourth one described the destruction of Jerusalem.

Table 11. Some Books Missing From the Bible (continued).

Book	Description
Prayer of Manasseh	Manasseh was an immoral king of Judah because he worshipped false gods. While in prison, he repented of his gross sins against God with this prayer. After his imprisonment, he removed all false gods and their altars. As part of his repentance, he then restored the worship of God to Judah.
Gospel of Nicodemus	Written by Nicodemus, a disciple of Jesus Christ. It was used by early Christians and churches until the end of the third century. It was considered canonical until its later removal by various edicts and councils of the early church.
Acts of Paul and Thecla	It's believed to have been a forgery, even though they were considered genuine by the early Christians. Emperor Zeno had a vision of Thecla, who promised him the restoration of his empire. Emperor Zeno's empire was restored and he built a beautiful temple in honor of Thecla in Seleucia, Isauria. Assumed to have been written during the Apostolic Age[232].
Report of Pilate to Augustus Caesar	Pilate sent this letter to Caesar with his private report of the occurrences surrounding Jesus' crucifixion.
Report of Pontius Pilate to Tiberius	Written by Pilate to Tiberius Caesar, describing the details about Jesus' crucifixion and events immediately following.
Letter of the Smyrnaeans	Written from the church at Smyrna to the church of Philomelium to describe Polycarp's martyrdom which took place in either 155 or 166.
Odes of Solomon	The origin and date of writing are unknown. It contained beautiful songs of joy and peace. Some believed them to be songs written by newly baptized Christians.
Psalms of Solomon	An ancient Semitic writer wrote this collection of eighteen war songs during the middle of the first century BCE. These war songs were widely circulated and held a prominent position in the early church. It's an eyewitness account of ancient history, telling the story of a great nation in the greatest crisis of its existence.
Wisdom of Solomon	Written in Greek, probably not by Solomon. It contained information on wisdom, how to obtain it and its benefits.

---

[232] The Apostolic Age represents the time from Jesus' crucifixion in 30 CE until the death of John in 115 CE.

Table 11. Some Books Missing From the Bible (continued).

Book	Description
Book of Susanna	It's about a good woman wrongly accused by two lustful men of committing immoral acts with them. It included how Daniel defended and saved her life. Excluded from the Bible because it wasn't written in Hebrew originally.
Thomas' Gospel of the Infancy of Jesus Christ	Thomas wrote this and connected it with the Gospel of Mary. It's an account of the miracles and supernatural actions that occurred during the infancy of Jesus.
Book of Tobit	Tobit and his son Tobias wrote this during the early seventh century. Fragments of the book were found in the Dead Sea Scrolls. The Protestants rejected The Book of Tobit as non-canonical and had it removed from the Bible.
Testaments of the Twelve Patriarchs	A Pharisee, wrote these as biographies between 107 and 137 BCE. Considered an actual source to the books of the Bible. For example, the Sermon on The Mount contained phrases from these testaments. Paul, too, used them.

Source: Brinkley 2005.

Pentateuch. Moses was supposed to have been the writer of these[233]. However, most secular scholars suggest that these were not written by a single author and were likely written over several centuries[234]. I don't believe that Moses wrote the first five books of the Old Testament, either, which included a description of his death. Yet, it's written in the Gospels that Jesus claimed that he had[235]. I also don't believe that King David wrote Psalms either. Still, it's written in the Gospels that Jesus claimed that he had[236].

Matthew, the tax collector and apostle, is the traditional author of the Gospel of Matthew. On the contrary, many scholars suggest that the author wasn't an eyewitness, but instead probably written by an ethnic Jewish scribe and written between 70 and 100[237]. Luke, the companion of Paul, is the traditional author of the Gospel of Luke and Acts. But, the author was probably an unknown

---

[233] Jacobs 1995, 375.
[234] McDermott 2002, 21.
[235] Mark 1:44, Matthew 8:4, 19:7-8, 22:24, Luke 5:14, 20:28, and 24:27.
[236] Mark 12:36-37, Matthew 22:43-45, and Luke 20:42-44.
[237] Duling 2010, 302-3.

amateur Hellenistic historian[238]. John, an apostle, is the traditional author of the Gospel of John, three Epistles, and Revelation. However, many scholars believe that he wasn't the author of these five books[239]. But, does it really matter who the mortal authors of the books are?

Many Christians believed that God wrote the Bible through divine inspiration of men as stated in 2 Timothy 3:16. Yet, there were some Christians who believe the complete opposite, such as Bart Ehrman, the James A. Gray Distinguished Professor of Religious Studies at the University of North Carolina at Chapel Hill[240]. He was also the New York Times bestselling author of *Misquoting Jesus* and *Jesus, Interrupted*. Professor Ehrman specifically wrote that, "many of the books of the New Testament were written by people who lied about their identity, claiming to be a famous apostle -- Peter, Paul or James"[241]. Once again, there exist many learned scholars today who will be willing to provide contradictory assessments. Ultimately, only you can decide for yourself what you will use as the basis of your Christian faith.

As for its contents and analyses thereof, I prefer the tradition-rhetorical criticism process explained by Assistant Professor April DeConick of the Illinois Wesleyan University. This process is an approach to understanding literature by considering the author's attempt to modify religious traditions while allowing for the traditions of the time[242]. This process involves assessing the conflicts present that motivated the author to create the text, the religious traditions of the time, the actual modifications of the tradition resulting from the new text, and the author's most likely meaning of the text. Moreover, the books of the New Testament should best be understood from the environment of the authors, such as the Judaism and Hellenistic religious environment.

---

[238] Aune, 1987, 77.
[239] Harris 1985, 355.
[240] 2003.
[241] 2001.
[242] DeConick 2001, 15-16 and 21.

Otherwise, the reader would be unable to comprehend the writing and quickly succumb to illogical arguments given by experts.

Translations and Interpretations

Let me begin this section with a personal example. This is a story about my youth and my love of treasure hunting. It's been more than forty years since any of this happened; but, this is my remembrance of it, putting these into written words for the first time. And, it's my first-hand account of the events. Although some of this information may not be entirely accurate, the story and its overall meaning are indeed accurate. And, this is how I judge the translations, transcriptions, and interpretations of the Bible. Now, here's my brief biographical story about treasures.

My grandfather, Bert Fortuna, Sr., had three things that he loved to do: fishing, hunting, and lovemaking. Yes, I said lovemaking. And, this is what my grandmother said. So, it must be true. Who could contradict her on this subject? As a child, I enjoyed two of these loves with him. We'd spend time together fishing near Spike Horn Acres, which was my grandfather's cabin near White Cloud, Michigan, north of the city of Newaygo and near Croton Dam. I remember fondly of those seemingly long trips north from Grand Rapids. Sometimes, we'd stop for fresh plain cake donuts if we departed early in the morning. On the return trip, we'd usually stop for ice cream sundaes, especially those scrumptious hot fudge ones for me. All wonderful memories for a child who enjoyed sweets.

My grandfather taught me how to fish and spent time with me while fishing near this cabin. Sometimes, we'd fish in one of the small creeks running nearby; other times, we'd go via car to a hidden lake further into the woods. These were definitely fun times, even when we came back with no fish. But, there was always a story of how the big one got away.

In addition to fishing, I learned some hunting techniques, specifically how to use a bow and arrow. Behind the cabin was the family shooting range, which we used for practicing both bow and gun. Accordingly, I acquired skill in using different types of bows, from the simple ones to the compound bows. On one occasion while I hunted deer alone with my bow, I wandered into a nearby clearing, where I sat beneath a tree. Being overcome with the boredom of waiting for one to appear, I fell asleep. About an hour later, I heard a noise, which was a doe in the field about fifty yards in front of me. It spent several minutes just staring at him. And, before I managed to get the bow ready to shoot, the doe darted off. No one believed this story except for my grandfather.

The most memorable hunting experiences involved hunting for treasure, such as boxes of hidden loot from pirates and crooks. The two of us would-be treasure hunters would talk about different plans necessary to find these throughout Michigan. We even talked about obtaining a metal detector to search for a variety of expensive metallic objects, such as golden doubloons, below the surface. My grandfather provided me locations of these treasures, such as in the basement of abandoned buildings and old barns. However, spooks, probably dead burglars, guarded these boxes of loot. Once, we attempted to enter the cellar of an old farmhouse near Cedar Rapids. My grandfather had a map of the basement, which contained an "*X*" marking the site of the hidden treasure. Unfortunately, it was nowhere near the stairs. In the vicinity of the buried treasure was a decaying bed on a floor of broken glass with a large boot nearby, which was supposed to be a boot worn by one of the spooks sleeping on the bed. As we both began to descend slowly into this dark basement, my grandfather quickly ran upstairs and darted out of the house screaming that he saw the spook waking up. This convinced me to leave too, daring not to enter the basement and look for the treasure, leaving it to the scary spook for another day.

Through these experiences, I became very fascinated with haunted houses, believing that they contained the spirits of deceased beings who may have been former residents or were familiar with the property. As my grandfather explained, these ghosts were the spirits of dead people who haven't passed over, becoming trapped inside the property where their memories and energy were strong. I further understood that these haunted buildings often contained spooks that made noises, appeared as apparitions, and moved physical objects. As a child, I had no desire to meet a spook face-to-face. Not even as an adult, either. They were just too scary.

In addition to searching for treasures in old abandoned houses, we would even search for treasure within old barns near the side of the roads. These barns were often found in a state of disrepair, maybe because they were no longer the centers of family and community life they once were. No matter if we grew up on the farm or in the city, I felt that barns spoke to the feeling of country life and America's rural past, being a symbol of rural architecture, rural life, and the rural community. Therefore, these barns, despite their shortcomings, continued to appeal to my senses, my memories and my imagination, such as searching for hidden treasures. On our way north to the cabin, we sometimes took a side trip to look for old barns. Even though we wandered through a half dozen of these barns throughout several trips, the one I remembered best was the barn with new windows in the hayloft area. According to my grandfather, the spooks installed them so that they could clearly see anyone approaching the barn, meaning there must be a treasure somewhere near. Because of that observation window, there was no way we were going to search that barn.

Sometimes, someone comes along in your life who knew how to get your attention while putting important things into perspective. That person would tell us how life works, providing their insights that life is really not complicated or political or negative. They would even listen to our opinions and value them, even if we were very young and inexperienced, especially for an eight-year old boy. My grandfather was one of those few people in my life. As one can imagine, I have wonderful memories of my grandfather from him showing his love through the time he spent sharing his loves, especially fishing and hunting.

So, why did I spend some time writing about my grandfather and treasure hunting in this chapter about the Bible? First, my hunt for treasures has changed since I was a child. As a child, I sought the treasure of fortune, the one with lots of gold, diamonds, and monetary currency. As an adult, I no longer seek fortune. Instead,

I hunt for the meaning of life today. I fully appreciate the fact that I can't take my money with me when I die. As you should be able to tell by now, this book contains knowledge I found in my quest for this meaning. The other reason why I wrote about my grandfather is that this is a story that several people have questioned. For one, my mother told me several times that my grandfather wasn't a good father to her and that he didn't treat women as equals to men. This may be true, but my story doesn't involve those topics. The primary topic of my story was that my grandfather loved his grandson and showed his love with his time and efforts. And, that was my interpretation of this story.

Now, back to the interpretations of the Bible. Previously, I discussed the mortal writers of the biblical books and not the assumed divine influence. I find it very difficult to believe that God wrote every word in every language of those books throughout thousands of years. Believing in complete divine authorship requires us to assume that God is a super manipulator by helping each writer write and transcribe the Bible. This would require us to believe that He was a super manipulator by watching each scribe copy the texts and each translator from one language to another, to ensure that there would be no mistakes, errors, or omissions of His words[243].

We must remember that every translation of the oldest document from Greek, Hebrew, or Aramaic, reflected the biases of the numerous translators throughout time. There were no existing accurate or correct translations of the manuscripts, not even an original one. However, some copies were clearly more accurate than others. But, which ones were better? I caution you to never take a translation as an authority over a document written in its original language of Greek, Hebrew, or Aramaic. Such as, we must consider word choice, punctuation, word order, terms and terminology, past usage of words, present usage of words, and correct understanding of basic scriptural words and terms. Furthermore, we must understand that most documents written in

---

[243] Spong 2005, 24.

the original host language didn't have punctuation or word structure like the English language does.

Another fact is that many Jews couldn't even read Hebrew, and this disturbed the Jewish leaders. Actually, most of the Old Testament was written in Hebrew spanning more than a thousand years[244]. Around 300 BCE, a translation of the Old Testament from Hebrew into Greek was undertaken which was completed about a hundred years later. Gradually this Greek translation of the Old Testament, called the *Septuagint*, was widely accepted and was even used in many synagogues during Jesus' time[245]. Moreover, the New Testament was first written in Greek. We might think this was unusual and would have assumed that it was written in either Hebrew or Aramaic. But, the Greek language was the scholastic language during the latter part of the first century CE[246].

To fully understand the translated texts, we should have a fundamental understanding of paleography. This is the scientific study of ancient writing, which was written on papyrus, parchment, paper, potsherds, wood, or waxed tablets[247]. Prior to the seventeenth century, this science didn't exist, requiring early scholars to make guesses regarding the ages of documents. This science today requires an understanding in the production of the books, specifically the materials, textual formatting, and writing devices such as ink.

As mentioned previously, none of the original archetypal texts of any book in the New Testament exists today[248]. Further compounding the concerns is that the early Greek New Testament documents were written with no spacing between the words, requiring some training to individualize the words[249]. The following is an example of this paragraph with no spacing or punctuation.

---

[244] Brotzman 1994: 37-62.
[245] Vander Heeren 1912.
[246] Davidson 1995, 117-23.
[247] Metzger 1981, 3.
[248] Comfort 2005, 6.
[249] Black 2009, 7; and Comfort 2005, 53.

ASMENTIONEDPREVIOUSLYNONEOFTHEOR
IGINALARCHETYPALTEXTSOFANYBOOKIN
THENEWTESTAMENTEXISTSTODAYFURTHE
RCOMPOUNDINGTHECONCERNSISTHATTHE
EARLYGREEKNEWTESTAMENTDOCUMENT
SWEREWRITTENWITHNOSPACINGBETWEEN
THEWORDSREQUIRINGSOMETRAININGTOIN
DIVIDUALIZETHEWORDSTHEFOLLOWINGIS
ANEXAMPLEOFTHISPARAGRAPHWITHNOSP
ACINGORPUNCTUATION

Can you imagine reading an entire book written like that of this preceding paragraph example without spacing and punctuation? And, can you imagine doing so without errors or misinterpretations from the original writer? I couldn't do it, even after reading several books about it[250].

The *Latin Vulgate*, a collection of texts that Saint Jerome compiled and translated during the latter part of the fourth century, was dominant in Western Christianity through the Middle Ages[251]. The first mass produced printed Christian book was the Bible, a version based on the Latin edition from about 380. John Wycliffe was the first to translate it into English[252]. Johannes Gutenberg printed this in mass quantities in Mainz, Germany from 1452 -1455. Of interest, translated in the thirteenth century, the Old French Bible is the oldest complete biblical translation to survive in Western Europe[253]. Since then, the Bible was translated into numerous languages.

Now back to my discussion about translations. There have been numerous linguistic and ideological approaches to translating these documents. For instance, one translation could be a literal word for word approach, while another could be a translation of the

---

[250] See especially Smith 1893.
[251] See especially Edgar 2011.
[252] 1320-1384.
[253] Sneddon 1993.

Bible Can Justify Opposite Claims

meaning of a phrase or thought. Unfortunately, all languages have several idioms and concepts that aren't easily translated. The result is a debate about whether it's better to translate word for word literally or to translate a parallel idiom in the target language. English language examples of literal translations include the New American Bible, King James Version, New Revised Standard Version, and New American Standard Bible. More relevant translations with similar idioms include the New International Version and New Living Translation. Even though the text becomes easier to read, the further away one deviates from word for word literal translations, the more the translators must rely upon the theological, linguistic or cultural understanding of the original text. Maybe that is why Matthew 1:23 uses the text of Isaiah 7:14 to state that Jesus be born of a virgin. According to several scholars, this was an incorrect assessment of that passage since Isaiah used that Hebrew word *almah* (עלמה), a young woman, and not *bethulah* (בתולה), a virgin, will be with child[254]. This singular word choice was another example involving linguistic, historical, literary, and cultural factors involved in assessing the meanings of the biblical stories.

Additional causes of biblical translation errors came from misquotes. Many people believed that certain quotes or sayings appeared biblical in nature. I've assessed eight popular misquotes, providing comments about each in Table 12. I personally heard people tell me that these were definitely in the Bible. Some of them, I used to believe were true. Upon further investigation, I know better now. I wonder if you, the reader, too have heard many of them attributed to the Bible.

For my analyses of the Bible, I used some of the information involving the ancient texts. For your information, the name of an ancient book in leaf form, not in a roll, is called a codex. An

---

[254] Heine 2007, 119. The Hebrew word of "almah" in Isaiah 7:14 is translated as a "young woman", while, the Hebrew word "bethulah" means "virgin." Throughout Isaiah, "bethulah" appeared four times (23:12, 37:22, 47:1, 62:5), so its author was most likely aware of the word's meaning. However, the reference to a "young woman" doesn't mean that she wasn't a "virgin" too.

example of this is the *Codex Vaticanus*, written in Greek in uncial letters during the fourth century. Unfortunately, this document was mutilated such that the first twenty folios were missing along with parts of others[255]. Uncial, by the way, referred to separate-letter form of writing. Whereas, minuscule referred to cursive-letter form of writing. Dating these documents involved archaeological evidence, codicology, comparative paleography and "Nomina Sacra"[256]. "Nomina sacra" were specific words that were abbreviated to set them apart as sacred[257]. For example, the word "God" was fully written as *Θεός* in Greek with the nominative as *ΘΣ*. Also in Greek, the word "Lord" was written as *Κύριος* with its nominative as *ΚΣ*; and, the word "Jesus" was written as *Ἰησοῦς* with its nominative as *ΙΣ*. Let me mention that a portion of the New Testament was made on papyrus[258]. These papyri codices were identified by a symbol similar to the character of 𝔓 followed by a superscript. Today, we have 127 known papyri; with $\mathfrak{P}^7$ representing part of Luke 4[259].

Besides translation errors, we have those involving interpretations. The word "Heaven", as an example, has different meanings and its intended meaning should depend upon what the author intended, not the reader. Also, "Heaven" could mean God, human communion, or even divine love. Even our knowledge of the character of Jesus involves interpretations. Written within the Gospels, Jesus said that he wasn't equal with God[260]. Even Jesus denied divine personal attributes in Mark 10:17-18 when He denied being good since only God alone is good. So, why should we believe that Jesus is a divine god? My understanding of this belief is traced back to the First Council of Nicea in 325 where

---

[255] Benigni 1908.
[256] Comfort 2005, 104.
[257] Köstenberger and Kruger 2010, 191.
[258] Aland and Aland 1989, 83-102.
[259] See especially Elliott 2000.
[260] John 14:28; Matthew 24:36.

Table 12. Eight Popular Misquotes of the Bible.

Misquotes	Comments
Better to reign in Hell than serve in Heaven.	It's from John Milton's *Paradise Lost*, a poem about the fall of man involving Satan's temptation[261].
Cleanliness is indeed next to godliness.	This exact phrase comes from John Wesley's 1778 sermon based upon 1 Peter 3:3-4. However, the theme may an ancient one since Francis Bacon provided a similar saying in his 1605 *The Advancement of Learning*.
Do unto others as you would have them do unto you.	This was similar to Matthew 7:12.
A fool and his money are soon parted.	The quote was actually a proverb found in Thomas Tusser's poem *Five Hundred Points of Good Husbandry*[262].
God helps those who help themselves.	Sidney Algernon, an English politician and army colonel executed for his part of a plot against King Charles II of England, wrote this. It was later published in 1698 after his death[263]. Also, Benjamin Franklin quoted this in his 1757 *Poor Richard's Almanac*. Although credited to Algnernon, its original origin is really based upon Aesop's Fables from the sixth century BCE[264]. Nevertheless, the Bible specifically stated the opposite[265].
The lion shall lie down with the lamb.	There were a couple of Bible verses similar to this quote. The closest is probably from Isaiah 11:6.
Money is the root of all evil	This one isn't technically a misquote, but one of omission. It's missing part of the sentence that radically changes the meaning. It is missing the first three words, "The love of," from 1 Timothy 6:10. Money isn't inherently evil, and can be used for good things. However, the love of money causes a person to be selfish.
Spare the rod, spoil the child	There were a couple of Bible verses similar to this quote. The closest was probably from Proverbs 13:24.

---

[261] 1667. In Book I, line 263.
[262] 1557, 19. "A foole and his monie be soone at debate, which after with sorrow repents him too late."
[263] Contained in chapter 2 section 23 is, "Help thyself, and God will help thee."
[264] In the fable, "Hercules and the Waggoner" is quoted as, "heaven helps those who help themselves."
[265] Isaiah 25:4.

Figure 12. Papyrus 20.
Contains James 2:19-3:9 (c. third century).

bishops met to determine the nature of Jesus. Using a voting process, they essentially elected Jesus to the exalted position of a god. Risking excommunication or execution if they voted otherwise, those voters reluctant to believe the same were coerced by other mortal men in their voting and succumbed to the majority opinion[266]. So, what is the truth behind the divinity of Jesus? Is there any direct evidence for this belief, or should we take this as faith based upon the opinions of other mortals?

Accordingly, which is more important, the interpretation by others or by us when understanding the Bible? My response to this question is that the truth is more important. Yet, finding the truth isn't that easy. Several Christian leaders, such as Augustine, had a tremendous influence upon Christianity[267]. His historical interpretations has added to the foundation of our Christian faith and getting us closer to the biblical truths. Accordingly, a personal understanding of these contributions adds to our own biblical understanding. As we can tell by now, truth is not found in any single scriptural passage, but in all of them. One Scripture should never trump that of another. Furthermore, let me tell you that God deplores selecting and using Scriptures in a smorgasbord manner[268]. Many times, there won't be a single passage that provides us comfort or answers a question. Much of the Bible isn't even factually true, since much of the texts involve figurative words, such as referring to Herod as a fox in Luke 13:31-32 and hypocritical religious leaders as whitewashed tombs in Matthew 23:27. Popular examples of modern figurative phrases include "light as a feather", "racking our brains", "moving like the wind", and "falling in love". The literal phrases for these, respectively, could be written as "incredibly light", "intensely thinking", "swiftly moving", and "beginning to love". Although reading the Bible literally distorts the message, most Christians throughout history read the Bible literally anyways[269]. It's no wonder that most biblical scholars and other historians today prefer seeking non-canonical Christian texts for answers with some of them placing more value on them instead of upon canonical texts[270].

---

[266] Gulley 2010, 19.
[267] See especially Beduhn 2010.
[268] Isaiah 28:12-13.
[269] Lose 2011.
[270] Van Voorst 2000, 3.

As we can see, determining the true meaning of someone else's words is a significant concern for us. Assisting me in this, I researched several books and articles focused upon the study of interpretations of the Bible, otherwise known as "biblical hermeneutics". This assessment of the various, and sometimes contradicting, interpretations involves analyses in the culture of the writers. It also requires an understanding of the context of the stories, along with the historical semantic changes in the words used. Furthermore, some of the stories in the Bible aren't historical records but that of metaphors, parables, and proverbs[271]. I'll dive deeper into this in the following section for context.

Even an extensive search for the truth may lead to no answer at all. Let's not forget that the Gospels were certainly not written until some thirty years after the Ascension. Not knowing is entirely acceptable. We should be fully aware that all translations and interpretations of the biblical books have errors. Some of these errors are deliberate, many of them with good intent. Furthermore, some of these errors involve definitions of words that changed with time. For me, the best translation accurately communicates the author's true meaning of the original text into the translated language.

Context

When I was a young teenager, I read the Bible from cover-to-cover. Why did I do this? Recently, I've seen several plans for daily Scripture readings that would allow us to read the Bible in just 365 days. Thus, many today think this is important. Back when I was a teenager, I began studying the Christian faith in preparation for confirmation as a Roman Catholic. I definitely didn't want any terrorizing nun to discipline me for not doing my best in these studies. Also, several of my relatives back then told me that my grandfather was a wise Christian and understood his faith better than most. They also told me that he was wise because he had read the entire Bible and knew what it contained. So, to lay claim upon this pursuit of Christian wisdom too, I read the Bible –

---

[271] See especially Virkler and Ayayo 2007.

all of it from cover to cover. Afterwards, I was proud of myself for having read it entirely. And, several of my relatives were proud of me too. Well, not until after I told them I did it. In spite of this, I wasn't any smarter or wiser for this effort. It was hard to read, and it definitely wasn't organized in any logical manner. When it came to reading the Gospels, I felt like I was reading the same story four different times. In the end, all that I gained for my effort was lots of confusing information. And, it was very sketchy at that. I didn't analyze the stories that I read to develop any reasonable knowledge or understanding. In the end, I definitely wasn't any wiser as a result.

So, what was missing? How could anyone who read the entire Bible not be wise? I didn't understand any of it at the time. But, I understand more now. I didn't understand the controversies of Christian wisdom, which I described in a previous chapter of this book. So, what can we do to improve our knowledge and understanding through reading of the Bible? One thing we should consider is assessing the context of the stories in relation to both the culture and situation at the time. For most people, including myself, we tend to assess the stories we read through the lens of our personal situation and modern biases. But, this prevents us from really understanding the intended message.

Today, if you live in the United States, you probably have frequent access to modern conveniences and technologies that fill your daily lives that were unknown to ancient people during the biblical times. These include communication devices, computers, microwaves, toilets, medicines, vehicles, electrical appliances, televisions, audio / video players, cameras, power tools, electronic gadgets, light bulbs, and the list continues. It's definitely overwhelming. In fact, we probably can't imagine life without them. Even the food we eat, such as instant food year-round, and the clothes we wear, such as ones made from light-weight durable form-fitting material, are modern.

Now compare this to life during the biblical times. Father Professor Frédéric Manns, a Franciscan friar from the Order of Friars Minor, wrote about several cultural aspects of life during the time of Jesus[272]. Why should we believe someone like him about life in ancient Palestine? He was also the director of the Franciscan Biblicum Stadium in Jerusalem[273]. And, these friars have been the custodians of the Holy Land since 1219[274]. What did he use for his assessment? His information came from a variety of local Middle-East resources, including archeological excavations, such as the one Charles Warren did in 1867 along the south and southwest walls of the Temple Hill in Jerusalem. Warren's work revealed information necessary in helping us understand the culture of the people who wrote the Bible, including those in the biblical stories[275]. Even Augustine assumed that our moral views are influenced by the literary context in which we assess our ethical situations, constrained by the limitations of language[276].

To begin, Jesus was a Jew, fully living within the Jewish culture of the time. As with other Jewish males, Jesus was circumcised eight days after his birth. The circumcision ceremony included drinking and dancing. He later learned to read and write, probably using the Torah, along with the other Jewish boys[277].

From an economic perspective back then, beggars were common in Jerusalem. The town had bakers, butchers, shoemakers, money changers, farmers, perfumers and artisans[278]. It also had contemptuous professions of donkey drivers, sailors, dog dung collectors, tanners, dice players, tax collectors, publicans, coachmen, shepherds, shopkeepers, butchers, and physicians[279]. People considered butchers despicable because they were suspected of selling meat from animals with physical defects.

---

[272] 1998. Father Manns is a professor at the Franciscan Biblicum Studium in Jerusalem.
[273] Information obtained from the Faculty of Biblical Sciences and Arcaeology. "MANNS Frédéric, ofm." Studium Biblicum Fanciscanum in Jerusalem. Retrieved on August 14, 2011 http://198.62.75.4/www1/ofm/sbf/segr/profs/Manns.html.
[274] Bihl 1909.
[275] See especially Wilson et al. 1871.
[276] Stock 2001, 4 and 57.
[277] See especially Manns 1998.
[278] Artisans sold souvenirs to pilgrims.
[279] See especially Manns 1998.

Likewise, physicians were scorned because they were known for giving preferential treatment to the rich while neglecting the poor. Much of what little that the Jews had back then was given to the Roman government. Hence, taxation to pay for the Roman occupation of Palestine was a harsh burden to its people. Refusal to lessen the burden was the motive behind the Jewish War and the Siege of Jerusalem in 70 CE. There were numerous complaints of corruption. The Quirinus census, conducted around 6 CE, was to determine the number of subjects and the estimate of their possessions for tax assessments. This census involved the Roman Provinces of Syria and Judea when Publius Sulpicius Quirinius was governor of Syria[280]. This census was even mentioned in Luke 2:1-7.

Family life was very different than that within the modern Western world. Ancient Jewish fathers had the right to sell their daughters into slavery. Likewise, these young girls didn't have the authority to reject a marriage proposal arranged for them. However, future husbands had to pay a dowry to compensate for the economic loss of a daughter from the family. Also, marriage to a relative was common. Adultery was punishable by death. And, women had to wear veils and were prohibited from speaking to men[281]. Marriages back then were celebrated for three days. However, if during the wedding night, the bride didn't display any signs of virginity, she was denounced immediately. Yes, the right of divorce was exclusively that of the men. Furthermore, displeasure was even grounds enough for a divorce[282].

Food was different then too. Wheat and barley were cooked or parched on a hot plate, or ground into flour by crushing the grain between two pieces of stone. The common vegetables were lentils,

---

[280] Ben-Sasson 1976. Page 246: "When Archelaus was deposed from the ethnarchy in 6 CE, Judea proper, Samaria and Idumea were converted into a Roman province under the name Iudaea."; page 274: "Josephus connects the beginnings of the extremist movement with the census held under the supervision of Quirinius, the legate of Syria, soon after Judea had been converted into a Roman province."
[281] See especially Manns 1998.
[282] See especially Manns 1998.

coarse beans, and cucumbers. They didn't have squash, pumpkins, tomatoes or potatoes. Onions, leeks, and garlic were used for flavoring. Fruit available were figs, dates, grapes, and pomegranates. They used olives for oil. They ate fish along both the Mediterranean and the Sea of Galilee. Although they didn't have sugar, they used honey for sweetening. Dates, honey and nuts were used for candy. Even though grapes were eaten fresh or dried into cakes, most of them were used for wine[283].

Wool or linen was used for most of the clothing worn then. Men and women wore similar clothes, which included a loincloth; a tunic reaching to the ankles and close-fitting at the neck; and an outer garment useful as a storm garment or a covering at night during journeys. Shoes were usually pieces of hide drawn together with thongs or cords. To increase its life, people often carried their shoes when they entered cities. The headdress was usually a folded square cloth worn as a veil for protection against the sun, or wrapped as a turban. Men wore their hair and beards long. Women also used artificial curling[284].

As for life expectancy, the common ancient Palestinian had to survive under harsher conditions than those enjoyed by kings. Their life expectancy was less than forty, and was still lower for women who had to survive multiple pregnancies[285]. If I lived back then, I wouldn't be alive today since I'm much older than forty years. The life expectancy in the world today is between sixty-five and seventy years[286]. Much of this huge increase is based upon the modern conveniences and improved sanitary conditions. However, this depends upon where we live today. This ranges from a life expectancy of about forty-five years in Afghanistan to about eighty-five years in Japan[287]. Fortunately for me, I live in the United States with an expectancy of about eighty years[288].

---

[283] See especially Manns 1998.
[284] Lussier 2011.
[285] King and Stager 2001, 37.
[286] Central Intelligence Agency 2011a.
[287] Central Intelligence Agency 2011b and 2011c.
[288] Central Intelligence Agency 2011d.

Scriptures were written a long time ago by people who lived in a very different world than we do. Furthermore, the biblical writers expected their readers to understand not only the language, but the historical, geographical and cultural references as well. These authors would view modern people today as gods since we're doing thing unimaginable to them – from instantly telecommunicating anywhere in the world (telephone), people walking on the moon, moving pictures with sound (television), killing others with sticks (rifles), resuscitating the dead (cardiopulmonary resuscitation), magically writing with sticks (pens), to instantly traveling by ground and air (automobiles and airplanes).

So, what does this mean when it comes to understanding the Scriptures? I strongly suggest that we don't accept anything without assessing its context. How do we do that, you might ask? We must consider the surrounding verses, the cultural setting, the author, and its relationship with the rest of the Bible[289]. And, we must understand that the author determines the meaning of the written stories. It's only discovered by the readers. As I previously mentioned, the gospels were written several decades after Jesus' death; and, they didn't necessarily include His actual words

These biblical stories aren't historically accurate. How can they be? There were no audio or video recordings of actual words spoken, nor were there any scribes taking copious notes of those words. We just have some eye witnesses of the events describing their experiences several decades after they happen. Yet, many of these were stories using hearsay information, not direct witness observations. Can you remember what you ate for lunch yesterday? How about a week ago? Or even, a year, ten years, or even thirty years ago? Even for a significant emotional event, such as what I was doing when terrorists attacked the World Trade Center and the Pentagon over ten years ago, I had a difficult time remembering and describing what I did. Using information from my stored email to help me remember, and researching news

---

[289] Dillon 1976, 5.

articles over the Internet, I was able to compose the following remembrance of that fateful day, ten years after it occurred.

I remember exactly what I was doing the morning of Tuesday, September 11, 2001, as though it were yesterday. I went to work as normal without a worry. As the deputy site project manager for the Newport Chemical Agent Disposal Facility, I supported the destruction of about 300 thousand gallons of VX nerve agent, a Weapon of Mass Destruction. This was an important and dangerous job; yet, I didn't worry for my safety or that of my colleagues. I ensured that everything we did was done with available safety protocols to effectively protect both the people and the environment. This facility was located about thirty miles north of Terre Haute, Indiana near the border of Illinois; and, it was in the middle of nowhere.

My duties as a Government civilian employee involved providing technical advice for the facility with overall responsibility for design, systemization, pilot testing, operations, and closure during the entire life cycle of the multi-year project with a total project cost of over $1 billion. I also managed the project risk management program, which included: project control, safety, treaty compliance, and environmental compliance. In my risk management duties, I became fully aware of the project's risks to this chemical weapon stockpile. The Maximum Credible Accident was a plane crash into the stockpile, causing an uncontrolled airborne release of the chemical agent into the population. Until that morning, an accident like this had a very low probability. By noon, it was highly probable.

Around 9:00 am, a couple of hours after we started our day, our administrative assistant interrupted a meeting I had with my boss. He informed both of us that a plane accidentally hit one of the World Trade Center's towers. We didn't take this message too seriously until about a half hour later when additional information arrived. Knowing that the two towers and the Pentagon were deliberately attacked, we realized that our country was under attack. This was another Pearl Harbor event on US soil, and it was happening during my lifetime. We had several hundred employees working at the facility that day, mostly construction workers under the control of our systems contractor, Parsons. Because our employees began getting nervous and our continual failure to contact higher headquarters for direction, Parsons sent their people home at 9:30 am. Government employees were then given the opportunity to take liberal leave, a chargeable vacation, if desired. Otherwise, we were to remain at work.

As a major in the Army Reserves with duties assigned to the Korean Theater, I received military email notification at 11:33 am that THREATCON DELTA was declared throughout the US, requiring the implementation of our Anti-Terrorism Force Protection plan because a terrorist attack was happening. Unfortunately, the Newport Chemical Depot plan was to provide security and force protection for us, which was limited and not designed to defend against a full-scale terrorist attack, especially from the sky. They only had a civilian contracted security force with no air defense capabilities. The depot was now fully closed down with all access points under armed guard. At 11:52 am, my boss finally directed all non-essential personnel to leave. However, I was one of the six essential managers directed to remain at my post. About an hour later, we too were directed to evacuate. Since I lived the closest to the facility, I agreed to remain until everyone left, meaning that I was officially the last person to leave the facility. Before I departed, I ensured that no one was left behind and that all items were powered off. By 1 pm, I had secured the buildings and was on my way home to await further instructions.

I was home by 1:30 pm, where I became glued to the television, watching in complete disbelief the horrors shown. While in the safety of my home, which was only about fifteen miles directly south from the stockpile, I observed several waves of army helicopters fly past my house on their way to the depot. I later learned that the Soldiers of Delta Company of the 1st Battalion, 502nd Infantry in the 101st Airborne Division from Fort Campbell, Kentucky arrived that afternoon to secure our stockpile and protect it from potential follow-on terrorist attacks. We weren't allowed to return back to work until Thursday, the 13th of September, where I observed numerous armed Soldiers throughout the depot securing the stockpile.

Following these events, the complete stockpile was destroyed on August 8, 2008, leaving me without a job at the Newport Chemical Depot. Fortunately, I accepted a position with Crane Army Ammunition Activity and relocated near Crane, Indiana in February 2009. Since the attacks of 2001, I had visited the site of all three crashes. In 2005, I worked at the Pentagon overseeing the Army Science Board. While at the Pentagon, I provided several personal tours of the crash site and the memorial chapel there. In December 2005, I briefly visited Ground Zero in New York City during an Army colonel's holiday outing. And, from 2006 through 2007, I commanded the 464th Chemical Brigade with its headquarters in Johnstown, Pennsylvania, which is about thirty miles directly north of Stonycreek Township, the site of the Flight 93 crash. As the brigade commander, I worked with several Soldiers who were involved in security and recovery actions following the crash in of Flight 93. Because of this attack, I decided to postpone my retirement from the army by nine years and served a combat tour in the Middle East. Shortly before the date of the attack, I had just received the documentation notifying me that I had successfully served twenty years and was eligible to retire. These attacks had a tremendous impact upon my life.

I wouldn't have been able to provide the details of time, nor number of people, and definitely not the military unit identification without using my notes. And, from a contextual point of view, the readers of my 9-11 story above need to consider what I was doing, why I was doing it, and the culture involved. If people from ancient Palestine read this story, they wouldn't realize that several of the key essential people remaining behind were women. This wouldn't be feasible since women were considered objects and not people who can occupy positions of authority. They also wouldn't understand that we had technology of planes and Weapons of Mass Destruction. Nor would they understand that we were living in a peaceful society without threats of attacks from anyone. What's more, the last attack of a foreign country upon the US occurred about sixty years prior. Context means a lot when it comes to understanding the author's intended meanings of his written works.

I recommend that we consider the historical context of the Bible. Let me provide some examples of literary works and compare them each to its historical context. *Beowulf* was a story developed during the eighth century and put into paper about 300 years later[290]. This was a story about monsters and magic, which were considered real during the perilous times when much of the European country was covered by dense forest and inhabited by wild animals. It wouldn't be uncommon for monks during this period to tell biblical stories involving monsters and magic, especially in an effort to win converts, such as the *Ecclesiastical History of the English Nation*[291]. There were many poems written then describing heroic exploits of saints. Later in history, medieval religious literature became quite prominent, such as Passion plays performed on movable stages from town to town to teach illiterate people about biblical stories.

Milton's *Paradise Lost* and *Paradise Regained* in the seventeenth century involved Puritan rebellion against the tyranny of absolutism[292]. These were books of rebellion, defeat, and hope of ultimate victory with Satan as a main character. The context then included the establishment of parliamentary democracy, such as civil rights, and the beginning of modern science.

This was followed by the age of enlightenment of the eighteenth century Europe with books such as Jonathan Swift's *Gulliver's Travels* and Daniel Defoe's *Robinson Crusoe*[293]. Respectively, these stories dealt with the vanity and corruptibility of scholars in a satirical effort along with overcoming fear, and the acceptance of God's will in an autobiographical format. These stories represented the belief held by "many humane thinkers and artists of

---

[290] Unknown Author 1892.
[291] Bede 1910. This book is an account of Britain between the landings of Julius Caesar in 55 BCE and Augustine in 597 CE. It's a key source on the history of Christianity in Britain.
[292] 1667 and 1671.
[293] 1726 and 1719.

the time that human reason could bring light into the darkness of the world [and] that it could prevail over tyranny, ignorance and superstition"[294]. Around this same time, Christian leaders began encouraging their followers to read the Bible.

By the nineteenth century, the Industrial Revolution took over, providing people with a variety of products from efficient large-quantity manufacturing production. Independence and other human rights were the thoughts of the common public. Thomas Paine wrote his *Rights of Man,* arguing that "human beings have basic rights by virtue of their existence as humans, that these natural rights have been usurped by tyrannical rulers supported by the aristocracy, whose position in society derives from wars of plunder, and by the churches, who keep the people in ignorance and through fear of Hell terrorize them into submission"[295]. And in 1792, Mary Wollstonecraft wrote her *A Vindication of the Rights of Women,* demanding both equality and education for women. Other popular literature during this period, affected by the historical conditions of the time, were Mary Shelley's Frankenstein and Jane Austen's series of romantic stories[296]. Shelley's monster book represented the problems inherent in Man playing God, especially using technology to create life. Austen's books involved educated young women and their efforts in finding suitable husbands, while advocating mutual respect and affection between wife and husband[297]. Additionally, many other popular literary classics were written during this period by well-known authors of Charles Dickens; the Brontë sisters of Charlotte, Emily and Anne; and Mary Ann Evans[298].

---

[294] Fleischmann 1999, 27.
[295] Fleischmann 1999, 34.
[296] Shelley 1818 and Koppel 1988. Mary Shelley was Mary Wollstonecraft's second child. Wollstonecraft died ten days after the birth.
[297] See especially Poovey 1984.
[298] See especially Slater 2009, Kenyon 2003, and Graver 1984. Charlotte is known for her *Jane Eyre*, Emily for her *Wuthering Heights*, and Anne for her *The Tenant of Wildfell Hall*. Mary Ann Evans was better known by her pseudonym of George Eliot.

The twentieth century was marked with massive global wars and the development of Weapons of Mass Destruction. Technology had advanced tremendously to provide individual and global powers previously unimagined. Science fiction writing became popular, especially as a way to express humanity versus technology conflicts. George Orwell's *Animal Farm* and *Nineteen Eighty-Four* described socialists who became tyrants[299]. The first of these books was a political fable describing life on a farm after the humans departed, with the animals being dominated by the most intelligent – the pigs. Orwell's other book involved a negative form of Utopia in which people were completely controlled by an over-powering monolithic Government party.

These are just a few of many examples to illustrate the different types of stories written throughout the past millennia and how the historical context of the time had a profound impact upon the texts. All of these stories are popular today; yet, most people view them through the lenses of their modern lives and their experiences. Doing so without understanding the historical context when the stories were originally written puts us at risk of misunderstanding the authors. The same is true when reading the Bible. The stories contained within it don't represent a historical description of the events, as we would find in a newspaper article. Instead, they were allegories, or stories, told to convey a message, many done over a campfire or in a liturgy on a church pulpit. The complete message itself is wrapped in the context of the environment during which they were originally told.

This reminds me of a popular quotation from Ludwig Wittgenstein which reads "the world of the happy is quite another than that of the unhappy"[300]. Unless we understand the world of the author, we can't fully understand the full meaning of its story. I saw a good example of this misunderstanding in the 2011 Christmas Eve edition of Bil Keane's *The Family Circle*. In this comic, the

---

[299] 1945 and 1949.
[300] 1922, 88. In German, T 6.43 reads: "Die Welt des Glücklichen ist eine andere als die des Unglücklichen."

mother is observed reading the Christmas Story[301]. After she read "... and there was no room for them at the Inn", her daughter, Dolly, made a classic observation about this story from her childlike modern cultural perspective. She said, "Joseph should have just gone online and booked a room before they left". Now, how often do we make similar statements about the Bible using our modern culture world as our contextual point of view?

As for experts in the field, it's quite common to find some who are willing to contradict other reputable ones with their interpretation of the same information. For example, two modern scholars, Robert Funk and James Robinson, believe the gospels are reliable, but only admire Jesus as a spiritual leader and not Lord. Two others, Robert Price and Bart Ehrman, believe there's nothing reliable to know who Jesus was, what he said, and what he did[302]. So, even expert interpretations of the Scriptures vary.

The context of the immutable Christian doctrine today was first formulated in the first century when Jesus' followers were baffled and overwhelmed by losing their Lord. This was especially troubling when they thought He was going to be a military style leader, such as King David. Furthermore, in the words of Philip Gulley, "the Bible was theologically inconsistent, written by many different authors with many different world-views, and that having to conform our insights and beliefs to every verse would be impossible"[303]. For example, how can we believe in a virgin birth that isn't supported by the Bible[304]. This belief was developed in an unenlightened era when both women and sexual relationships were believed to be sinful, and wasn't scientifically understood[305]. Where in the bible do we find Scriptures that state that Jesus was born of a virgin? I couldn't find any. If we were to ask these questions of most Christians, I bet their response would be that this is part of one's faith. In other words, we are led to believe in

---

[301] This specific one was probably done by Jeff Keane, his son, since Bil Keane died about a month earlier.
[302] Evans 2008, 19-26.
[303] 2010, 74.
[304] See especially Orr 1907.
[305] Gulley 2010, 86-7.

something that one doesn't really believe based upon logic alone. Instead, we should understand the context of the Scriptures they quote.

Now, what about Judas and the changing environment involving the various Scriptures involving him? Was there really a Judas, a betrayer among the disciples? "Betrayed" is mentioned in 1 Corinthians 11:23-24; but the original context of using this word meant "handed over" and not "betrayed by a betrayer"[306]. Other inconsistencies in the story include 1 Corinthians 15:1-6, written in the 50's CE, which states that Jesus appeared to the twelve, which implied that Judas was present. However, written about thirty years later, Matthew 28:16-20 stated that Jesus appeared to the eleven, which meant that Judas wasn't present. So, why the difference in stories?

In reality, the written story of Judas as a traitor evolved with time. Written in the 70's CE, Mark 14:10-11, 14:20, and 14:44-45, contained little details. About ten years later, Matthew 26:15, 26:25, 26:51-54, and 27:3-10 contained slightly more details. Now five more years later, the stories about Judas in Luke 20:19-20, 22:3, 22:6, and 22:53 contained even more details. Finally, in the last gospel to be written, John 12:6, 13:18, 13:26-30, and 18:2-11 contained the most details. The evidence of an evolving story puts this traitorous story into question. Ironically, let me remind you that *Ἰούδας*, Judas, is also the Greek spelling of Judah, the nation of Jews[307].

Some have logically argued that the story of Judas the traitor was a fabricated story and not one of objective remembrance of historical fact[308]. Indeed, Bishop Spong suggested that the details of this Judas story had a stunning resemblance to several Old Testament stories: shepherd king of Israel betrayed over thirty pieces of silver[309], Ahithophel's betrayal of King David after eating at his

---

[306] Spong 2005, 200.
[307] Robinson 1836, 393; and Robinson 2007, 149.
[308] Spong 2005, 205.
[309] Zechariah 11:12-13.

table and hanging himself[310], and King David's military chief Joab kissing his replacement Amasa on the cheek while disemboweling him with a dagger[311]. From 66 to 73 CE, there was a full-scale war between the Jews and the Romans, resulting in over one million Jewish casualties and the fall of Jerusalem. This included the destruction of its Second Temple[312]. There is a theory that the early Christians wanted to secure favor with Rome by blaming the Jews for their problems too[313]. This context should be considered when assessing both the credibility and the message in the story of Judas.

Failure to understand this contributed to Christian anti-Semitism throughout history, which played a huge role in the Holocaust of WWII and the murder of millions of Jews. With few exceptions, such as Dietrich Bonhoeffer and Martin Niemöller, Christian leaders supported the Nazi agenda[314]. Judgments of Jews as God's hated people provided Christians the scriptural justification to beat, rob, and murder them in the name of God. Why not, it was supported by the Bible. But, let me remind you that Jesus and his followers were Jewish. Furthermore, the early Christians in the decades after His death practiced their religion in synagogues. In essence, the early Christians were synagogue-worshipping Jews[315]. What we should fully understand is that context is just as important in understanding the Bible.

Contradictions and Mistakes

We have heard that nearly everyone admits that the Bible contains errors, such as a faulty creation story here and a historical mistake there. Many people even agree that it contains a contradiction or two. But, do we really know how many there are? It really shouldn't matter how many contradictions and mistakes it contains. It matters more if we can recognize them and have some understanding of the truth behind them. Our understanding does

---

[310] 2 Samuel 15:7 to 17:23.
[311] 2 Samuel 20:8-10.
[312] Dimont 1962, 97-102.
[313] Spong 2005, 209.
[314] Brauch 2009, 54.
[315] Martin 2006.

help us, especially when other Christians search the Bible to locate a verse to support their position, even though other verses in the Bible contradict it.

Let's start my discussion "in the beginning". You may not know it, but there are two different Adam and Eve stories in the Bible with the first one beginning at the 26th verse of the first chapter and the other beginning in the third chapter. The first story is about original blessing, whereas the other is about original sin. Which one do you think is used by Christian leaders today? And when it comes to these leaders supporting their position, they frequently speak the words "This is the word of the Lord", especially in liturgical ceremonies following reading of the Bible. This is usually responded with "Thanks be to God" by the congregation to enhance two-way communication. This commonplace occurrence continues to reinforce to Christians that the Bible and everything in it is directly from God[316]. How can anything He wrote have errors?

Figure 13. Adam and Eve in Worthy Paradise by Peter Paul Rubens (1615).

---

[316] Spong 2005, 16.

Now, let's look at conceptual differences. My first question is whether God is a loving God. Written in 1 Samuel 15:3, God ordered King Saul to kill his enemies and every living thing associated with them. Now, should we believe that this execution order is based upon love? This same Bible gave fathers permission to sell their daughters into slavery[317]. Permission was also given to own slaves from other countries[318]. And now for the common conditions requiring the ultimate punishment – the Death penalty. The Bible required death for violating the Sabbath[319], and blaspheming[320]. And, if we can believe it, this loving God requires the execution of children disobeying parents, for over eating, or for drinking too much[321]. Even though these were all Old Testament passages, many modern Christians continued using select Old Testament Scriptures to support their positions.

As for the New Testament, I'll add technology and advancements in understanding the Scriptures. One example involves Jesus claiming that epilepsy and mental illness are caused by demon possession and that being "deaf and dumb" is caused by the devil tying the tongue of the person[322]. Based upon my knowledge of the medical sciences, I don't believe these statements are correct. So, what does this mean? Did Jesus make an inaccurate statement about the causes of these mental illnesses? Or, were the authors of this story incorrect in their writings? Or, were the interpretations and transcriptions through two millennia responsible for this inaccuracy? More, importantly, does it really matter if this statement is completely factual or even partially factual? During my research into the Bible, I've developed a list of key contradictions, contained in Table 13.

---

[317] Exodus 21:7.
[318] Leviticus 25:44.
[319] Exodus 31:15.
[320] Leviticus 24:13-16.
[321] Deuteronomy 21:18-21.
[322] Mark 1:23-26, 9:14-18, and Luke 9:38-42.

Table 13. List of Biblical Contradictions.

Statement	Contradictory Statement
Man was created after other animals (Genesis 1:25-27)	Man was created before other animals (Genesis 2:18-19)
Adam and Eve was about original blessing (Genesis 1:26-30)	Adam and Eve was about original sin (Genesis 3:1-19)
God was satisfied with His work (Genesis 1:31)	God was dissatisfied with His work (Genesis 6:6)
Salah's father was Arphaxad (Genesis 11:12)	Salah's father was Cainan (Luke 3:35-36)
Marriage to a sister allowed (Genesis 17:15-16 and 20:12)	Marriage to a sister forbidden (Deuteronomy 27:22; Leviticus 20:17)
Abraham's wife was Keturah (Genesis 25:1)	Abraham's concubine was Keturah (1 Chronicles 1:32)
Children punished for parent's sins (Exodus 20:5)	Children not punished for parent's sins (Ezekiel 18:20)
Polygamy allowed (Exodus 21:10; 1 Kings 11:3)	Polygamy forbidden (1 Corinthians 7:2; Deuteronomy 17:17)
God is seen and heard (Exodus 24:10, 33:11-23)	God is invisible and unheard (John 1:18, 5:37)
Killing is allowed (Exodus 32:27)	Killing is forbidden (Exodus 20:13)
David took 700 horsemen (2 Samuel 8:4)	David took 7,000 horsemen (1 Chronicles 18:4)
Elijah ascended to Heaven (2 Kings 2:11)	Only Jesus ascended to Heaven (John 3:13)

Table 13. List of Biblical Contradictions (continued).

Statement	Contradictory Statement
Wisdom is a source of enjoyment (Proverbs 3:13-17)	Wisdom is a source of grief and sorrow (Ecclesiastes 1:17-18)
Godly (people) receive property and worldly goods (Psalms 37:28-37; Job 42:12)	Godly (people) receive misery and destitution (Hebrews 11:35-40; Luke 21:17).
David's throne to last forever (Psalms 89:35-37)	David's throne was cast down (Psalms 89:44)
Man can find God if they seek Him (Proverbs 8:17)	Man can't find God if they seek Him (Proverbs 1:28)
Evil won't happen to the godly (Proverbs 12:21; 1 Peter 3:13)	Evil will happen to the godly (Hebrews 12:6; Job 2:3-7)
Laughter is commended (Ecclesiastes 3:1-4 and 8:15)	Laughter is condemned (Ecclesiastes 7:3-4; Luke 6:25)
God creates evil (Isaiah 45:7)	God does not create evil (1 Corinthians 14:33)
Mary's father-in-law was Jacob (Matthew 1:16)	Mary's father-in-law was Heli (Luke 3:23)
God's spirit is love and gentleness (Galatians 5:22)	God's spirit is vengeance and fury (Judges 15:14; 1 Samuel 18:10-11)
All Scripture is inspired (2 Timothy 3:16)	Some Scripture isn't inspired (2 Corinthians 11:17)
God gives freely to those who ask (James 1:5-6)	God withholds his blessings (John 12:40; Joshua 11:20)

Table 13. List of Biblical Contradictions (continued).

Statement	Contradictory Statement
Jesus 3 days and 3 nights in the grave (Matthew 12:40)	Jesus 2 days and 2 nights in the grave (Mark 15:42-46 and 16:9)
Satan entered Judas during supper (John 13:27)	Satan entered Judas before supper (Luke 22:3-7)
There were 14 generations from Abraham to David and 14 generations from Babylonian captivity to Jesus (Matthew 1:17)	There were 13 generations from Abraham to David and 13 generations from Babylonian Captivity to Jesus (Matthew 1:2-6 and 12-16)
God tempts man (Matthew 6:13)	God doesn't tempt man (James 1:13)
Marriage is encouraged (Matthew 19:5)	Marriage is discouraged (1 Corinthians 7:1-8)
Judas died by suicidal hanging (Matthew 27:5)	Judas didn't die by suicidal hanging (Acts 1:18)
Two thieves rebuked Jesus (Matthew 27:44; Mark 15:32)	Only one thief rebuked Jesus (Luke 23:39-40)
Jesus was all-powerful (Matthew 28:18; John 3:35)	Jesus wasn't all-powerful (Mark 6:5)
Jesus was crucified at the 3rd hour (Mark 15:25)	Jesus was crucified at the 6th hour (John 19:14-15)
Jesus' mission was peace (Luke 2:13-14)	Jesus' mission wasn't peace (Matthew 10:34)
Poverty is a blessing (Luke 6:20-24; James 2:5)	Riches are a blessing (Proverbs 10:15; Job 22:21-25 & 42:12)

Table 13. List of Biblical Contradictions (continued).

Statement	Contradictory Statement
Two angels seen standing at the sepulcher (Luke 24:4)	One angel seen sitting at the sepulcher (Matthew 28:2-5)
Jesus was equal with God (John 10:30; Philippians 2:5-6)	Jesus wasn't equal with God (John 14:28; Matthew 24:36)
Impossible to fall from grace (John 10:28; Romans 8:38-39)	Possible to fall from grace (Ezekiel 18:24; Hebrews 6:4-6; 2 Peter 2:20-21)
God is war (Isaiah 51:15)	God is peace (Romans 15:33)
Abraham had two sons (Galatians 4:22)	Abraham had only one son (Hebrews 11:17)
Two angels seen inside sepulcher (John 20:11-12)	One angel seen inside sepulcher (Mark 16:5)
Holy Spirit bestowed at Pentecost (Acts 1:5-8)	Holy Spirit bestowed before Pentecost (John 20:22)
God knows the hearts of men (Acts 1:24)	God tests men to find out what's in their heart (Genesis 22:12)
Women have rights (Acts 2:18 and 21:9)	Women don't have rights (1 Timothy 2:12; 1 Corinthians 14:34)
Man justified by faith alone (Romans 3:20-4:2; Galatians 2:16-3:11)	Man not justified by faith alone (James 2:21-24; Romans 2:13)
Judging others allowed (1 Corinthians 5:12)	Judging others forbidden (Matthew 7:1-2)

Table 13. List of Biblical Contradictions (continued).

Statement	Contradictory Statement
Dead will be resurrected (1 Corinthians 15:16 and 52; Revelation 20:12-13; Luke 20:37)	Dead will not be resurrected (Job 7:9-10; Ecclesiastes 9:5; Isaiah 26:14)
Jesus ascended from Mount Olive (Acts 1:9-12)	Jesus ascended from Bethany (Luke 24:50-51)
Judas purchased potter's field (Acts 1:18)	Chief Priests purchased potter's field (Matthew 27:6-7)
Lying is allowed (James 2:25)	Lying is forbidden (Revelation 21:8)
Earth will be destroyed (2 Peter 3:10; Hebrews 1:11; Revelation 20:11)	Earth won't be destroyed (Psalms 104:5; Ecclesiastes 1:4)

Transcription Errors

Let me try to explain my fundamental understanding of these contradictions. The current editions of the Bible contain transcription mistakes, many of them. These mistakes can either be unintentional or intentional errors that include: cultural influences, assimilations, and substitutions[323]. An example of an accidental error involves Mark 8:1. In all but eight uncials and all but fifteen cursives, the passage is written παμπολλου οχλου, which means "the multitude being very great"[324]. The other ancient documents contain the familiar expression passage παλιν πολλου, instead of the unusual one of παμπολλου. The resulting change in the passage is "when there was again a great multitude", a slightly different meaning.

---

[323] Burgon 1896, 9.
[324] Burgon 1896, 34.

Other errors involved copying the words from the original documents, such as transposition, addition, omission, and corruption are described in Table 14[325]:

Table 14. Transcription Errors.

Error Type	Description
Dittography	This means writing more than once what should have only been written once. The word God, written as Θεός in Greek, appears twice in Mark 12:27 in several works[326]. Another biblical example involves Matthew 27:17. There use to exist copies of this Gospel that contained a reference to Jesus Barabbas following Pilate's question asking whom he should release. There is speculation that an inattentive second century scribe mistook the final syllable of υμιν, "unto you," for the abbreviated word ιν, meaning "Jesus," and carelessly duplicated the last two letters as υμιν ιν before the word βαραββαν, "Barabbas"[327]. Clearly, Jesus wasn't called Barabbas, a sinner; and, fortunately, this error has been corrected since then. An English example of dittography includes writing the word "latter" instead of "later". "Latter" means nearest the end. "Later" means after something else. This also partially explains why computerized spellchecking of documents doesn't always identify misspelled words.
Fission	This means improperly dividing one word into two words. An English example of this is writing the word "nowhere" into "now here". What's more, writing the phrase "Jesus is nowhere" as "Jesus is now here" by eliminating a space and fusing two words together results in a completely different phrase and meaning.
Fusion	As the opposite of fission, this means combining the last letter of one word with the first letter of the next word. An English example of this writing "Look it is there in the cabinet" instead of "Look it is therein the cabinet," which has a slightly different meaning.

---

[325] See especially Slick 2011a.
[326] Patzia 2011, 232.
[327] Burgon 1896, 53-54.

Table 14. Transcription Errors (continued).

Error Type	Description
Haplography	This is the opposite of dittography, which means the omission of letters, words, or sentences. An example of this is the phrase "money is the root of all evil", as seen in Table 12, that lacks the words "the love of". Other biblical examples can be found in Sir Fredrick Kenyon's 1901 *Handbook to the Textual Criticism of the New Testament*[328]. Omissions in transcription includes scribes who left out words; whether misled by proximity of a similar word, or by recurrence of similar letters[329]
Homophony	This means writing a word with a different meaning for another word when both words have the exact same pronunciation. This is a difficult one to discover since most of the information about Jesus was oral for the first few decades after His death. Illustrating this problem is the English example of "meat" being written for the word "meet" since they both have the exact same sound but different meanings. Also, the words "there," "their" and "they're" is another example, one that is frequently committed.
Metathesis	This means an improper exchange in the order of letters. Some ancient documents containing Mark 14:65 has the phrase ἔλαβον meaning "they took," while others have the phase ἔβαλον with the exchange of only two letters that means "they threw"[330]. An English example of this involves the writing of the word "mast" with either "mats," "cast or "cats," all of which have different meanings.

An example of additions to texts involving dittography is the *Pericope Adulterae*[331]. This text was missing from the earliest and most reliable works, and first appeared in a Greek text during the

---

[328] A good example is at the end of this book from pages 298-312.
[329] Burgon 1896, 66-67.
[330] Patzia 2011, 233.
[331] John 7:53 through 8:1-11.

fourth century[332]. Scholars, such as a Bethel University professor, report that although the story isn't inspired Scripture, it should remain in the Bible because of its long history and resemblance to the oral stories of Jesus[333]. Some claim lectionary influence from scribes in style of words, its locations, and addition was part of this debate[334]. Nevertheless, its inclusion in the Bible in its current location is appropriate[335]. Yet, some religious leaders, such as John Calvin, removed this from their edition of the Bible because of their assumption it may have been spurious[336].

Even the liturgies used by the early Christians influenced the contents of the Scriptures with additional words. An example of this is the Lord's Prayer doxology, "For Yours is the Kingdom and the power and the glory forever. Amen"[337]. This addition to the text is missing from the early Latin texts. Yet, it remains in our modern text because it's found in almost all the early Greek copies.

Occasionally, scribes substituted one common word for another, such as είπε, meaning "quoth", for ελεγε, meaning "said"[338]. Another example is substituting κράβαττον, meaning "bed or poor man's mat", for words with similar meaning, such as κραββατον, κραβάττοις, and κραβάττων[339]. An analogy includes different types of chairs, such as stool, bench, couch, seat, caquetoire, fauteuil, glider, hassock, ottoman, pouffe, bean-bag, recliner, sgabello, throne, and zaisu for furniture. Or, a chair could mean: chairman, leader, chairwoman, chairperson, president for head of an organization. What if it was a verb instead of a noun? This chair

---

[332] Keith 2009, 120. This is missing from third century papyrus P[66] and P[75], along with the Codex Sinaiticus and Vaticanus. It is found in the Vulgate and Codex D from 384 CE.
[333] Zylstra 2008.
[334] Keith 2009, 135-39.
[335] Keith 2009, 139.
[336] Trumble 2010, 62.
[337] Matthew 6:13. οτι σου εστιν 'η βασιλεια και 'η δυναμις και 'η δοξα εις τους αιωνας. αμην.
[338] Burgon 1896, 19.
[339] Burgon 1896, 19. I used the online Greek Concordance for some of the other words used for κράβαττον in the Bible:. http://concordances.org/greek/krabatton_2895.htm. See John 5:8-12 for this example.

could mean the act of presiding over something and could be written as lead, run, guide, moderate, or conduct. Which one is correct? Does it really matter? It does if we're concerned with the literalistic translations and meaning of each word. For me, it doesn't since I'm more concerned with reading the stories of the Bible metaphorically by looking into its meaning[340].

Translation Errors.

In addition to transcription errors, we should consider translation and other meaning-related errors[341]. To understand these errors, I suggest we understand Etymology, which is the study of the origins of words[342]. Because the Bible wasn't written in a culture-independent non-arbitrary language, understanding its meanings requires understanding the potential semantic changes of words[343]. As languages evolve over time, the meaning of words frequently change. This causes confusion and misunderstanding when communicating with other people. My favorite example of this is the meaning of the word "doctor," which is near and dear to my own professional non-medical salutation. Although frequently used for physicians today, the original meaning didn't include them. Instead, the doctorate (Latin: *doceō*, I teach) appeared in medieval Europe as a license to teach at a university[344]. For example, the early church used the term "doctor" for Apostles, church fathers and other Christian authorities who taught and interpreted the Bible[345].

Examples of other words that have changed over time include: awful, brave, cavalier, and girl. "Awful" originally was a positive word meaning deserving of awe[346]. "Brave" was a negative word meaning cowardice[347]. "Cavalier" used to mean brave and gallant,

---

[340] See also Fokkelman 1999, 203.
[341] See especially Stern 1931.
[342] See especially Liberman 2009.
[343] Wierzbicka 1992, 200.
[344] Latin of doceō for I teach.
[345] Super 1905, 610.
[346] Steinmetz 2008, 101.
[347] Sedgwick 2009, 26.

and now means careless, free and easy[348]. Finally, the word "girl" changed from meaning a young person of either gender to now just a young female[349]. So, what caused this? Table 15 describes five probable causes of this change[350]:

Table 15. Translation Errors.

Error Type	Description
Specialization	This is a narrowing of meaning. Similar to what happened to the word "girl", the word "deer" used to mean any kind of beast and now means a specific one.
Generalization	This is a widening of meaning. The word "clerk" used to mean a member of the clergy, and now means an office worker.
Amelioration	This is an elevation of meaning. Similar to what happened to the word "brave", the word "pretty" used to mean a negative sense of cunning or crafty and now describes beauty.
Pejoration	This is the degradation of meaning. Using the example of the word "awful", King James in 1688 described the new St. Paul's Cathedral as "amusing, awful and artificial". respectively referring it to mean "wonderful, impressive as full of awe, and skillfully displaying art".
Transfer	This is a complete change in meaning. The word "bureau" used to mean course woolen cloth in the twelfth century, a counting table in the fourteenth century, and to the room containing the counting table in the seventeenth century.

My intent here wasn't to make you an expert in semantic changes, but to inform you that changes in definitions have occurred and will definitely continue to change in the future. More to the point, we should be aware that linguistic expressions are very likely to change their meaning unpredictably over time through both lexical and grammatical semantic changes[351]. Many have even argued

---

[348] Steinmetz 2008, 39.
[349] Steinmetz 2008, 82.
[350] Culpeper 1997, 38.
[351] Hollmann 2009, 525 and 536.

philosophically that our human languages are limited, meaning they can't be used to completely describe ethical and religious concepts[352]. This brings up another concept regarding language, involving yet another controversy.

The controversy (or paradox) of the heap, aka *Sorites Paradox*, considers a heap of sand, from which grains are individually removed. This classical controversy of definitions begins with the question of whether it still a heap when only one grain remains. If not, when did it change from a heap to a non-heap? The definition of this word or concept is really ambiguous, leaving room for doubt and multiple interpretations[353]. Unfortunately, I believe that a perfectly precise language is an unobtainable entity. Understanding the limitations of language should include classical logic, which leads to the principle of bivalence in which every statement is either true or false[354]. The first recorded attempt to understand this vagueness of languages began with the logistician Eubulides in the fourth century BCE with this paradox[355].

The heart of this controversy involved the phenomenon of vagueness. I prefer to think of this as the controversy of vagueness. Names, verbs, adjectives, adverbs and other types of words in any language were all susceptible to this controversy[356]. Ludwig Wittgenstein, an influential twentieth century philosopher, considered vagueness to be pervasive in all natural languages. Whenever we have seen a need for a better definition, a new word or definition was developed. But, this required developing the specific conditions for its use, which can't be done for every known and potential possibility[357]. When it comes to describing ethical and religious items, Wittgenstein stated that we don't need

---

[352] Grayling 1988: 56.
[353] Burns 1991, 3.
[354] Williamson 1994, 1.
[355] Łukowski 2011, 132.
[356] Hyde 2011.
[357] Wolach 2007.

a language to describe them since they're "indeed the inexpressible. This shows itself; it is the mystical"[358].

My last discussion about the biblical contents comes John Hayes and Carl Holladay's 2007 book on biblical exegesis describing their critical interpretation of the Bible. According to them in better understanding the truths emanating from the Bible, we should consider five elements. First, we should search for original words, especially those involving biblical interpretations since there are different forms in which these ancient words were written and preserved[359]. Second, we should assess the environment, including time and location, of the historical development of the textual interpretations[360]. Next, we should evaluate the textual language, together with its syntax and grammar[361]. Fourth, we should analyze the composition and rhetorical style of the words with the aim of assessing its literary structure, style, purpose, mood, and imagination[362]. Finally, we should consider the impact that the historical development of the words has upon this understanding. All cultures have traditions that assist in providing self-understanding and their sense of history that are passed from one generation to the next[363]. If we consider all of these elements in our own interpretation of the Bible, we would be much closer to its truths – God's truths.

Denominations

Aside from our own understanding of the Bible, the Christian churches each have their own interpretations. Unfortunately, many of them have become consumed with their quests for power and authority using the Bible as its source, making it difficult for God's true words to be heard[364]. To increase this power, they tend to scare its followers into believing that their denomination is the one and

---

[358] 1922, 90. In German, T 6.522 reads: "Es gibt allerdings Unaussprechliches. Dies zeigt sich, es ist das Mystische."
[359] 34.
[360] 53.
[361] 81.
[362] 92.
[363] 115.
[364] Spong 2005, 25.

Bible Can Justify Opposite Claims   143

only true path to God, implying that all of the others are false[365]. Most Christians are incapable of challenging this power since they're almost completely ignorant of God's work after the biblical narrative ends[366]. For the two millennium of Christian theology, there have been unnecessary debates, conflicts, and deaths over minor issues of the faith[367].

Christianity, nonetheless, is the largest religion in the world with about two billion followers. The next two religions are Islam with 1.2 billion and Hinduism with just under one billion. What I find interesting is that nonbelievers in God, as a group with about 750 million, is the fourth largest group in the world[368]. Christianity is also a huge economic power with over $30 trillion personal income of church members, over $500 billion contributed to Christian causes, and over $200 billion in Church income annually[369]. Additionally, the annual earnings for Christians is more than $8 thousand per capita versus non-Christian of less than $3 thousand. The literacy of Christians is between 80 and 90% versus non-Christians of between 60 and 80%. So, what do these numbers really mean? Christians are richer and more educated than anyone else on average in the world. Furthermore in the past century, the typical character of Christians is becoming more diversified as demonstrated by about 80% of Christians being Caucasian in 1900; and, by 2005, Caucasian Christians becoming minorities about 40%[370].

By country, over 250 million Christians reside in the US, over 165 million in Brazil, 110 million in China, 100 million in Mexico, 85 million in Russia, 74 million in Philippines, 68 million in India, 62 million in Germany, and 61 million in Nigeria. Regrettably, this single religion has over 40 thousand denominations, with over five

---

[365] Gulley 2010, 22.
[366] See especially Olson 1999.
[367] Olson 1999, 17.
[368] Zuckerman 2007, 55.
[369] See especially Johnson 2011.
[370] See especially Rhodes 2005

million congregations or worship centers. These denominations range from less than 100 to more than millions of followers[371].

Religion is most assuredly one of the most powerful human forces. It lifts the heart, challenges the mind and inspires great achievements[372]. Molded by religion, our beliefs affect how we live. Accordingly, understanding the truths within the Bible is an excellent way to improve our life, and afterlife. An understanding in the variety of beliefs in the different denominations helps us towards our search for the real Jesus. Choosing one as our Christian religion has a tremendous influence upon our path towards the truth. I don't claim to possess this truth, and I don't believe anyone else has the complete truth. Nevertheless, my intent in this section wasn't to dive deeply into each of these denominations and compare them to one another. I leave that up to you, the reader, to the extent that you deem necessary.

Why are there so many churches in one street, many across the street from one another? Why aren't they full and why don't their leaders work together? When I attended a United Methodist Church in New Martinsville, West Virginia, I was shocked to realize that this small town of about five thousand had three churches with this same denomination. This is definitely a problem since we should be united so that the world may believe[373]. Instead, we're divided, making it hard for the rest of the world to believe the Christian message[374]. For your reference, I have listed six of the major denominational groups in Table 16.

Conclusion.

In my overall opinion, the stories in the Bible really should be understood allegorically and not literally. We don't need to be a literalist in order to be a Christian. Christian allegories aren't literal accounts of the actual events, making them obstacles to faith, barriers to membership and embarrassing remnants of a naïve

---

[371] See especially Rhodes 2005
[372] See especially Mead 2001.
[373] John 17.
[374] See especially Maseko 2008.

understanding of the world. No one should disagree that God is perfect and everything He does is perfect. So how can those Churches and organizations who advocate that the imperfect Bible with all of its contradictions and mistakes is the literal word of God? Logically, it doesn't make sense to me that a perfect God can make an imperfect book.

Table 16. Major Christian Denominations.

Denomination	Description
Roman Catholic	It was founded in Rome in 1054 as a result of the Great Schism[375]. They have over one billion followers[376]. Its original language was Latin. They use the *Roman Missal* as their worship literature[377].
Orthodox	It was founded in Constantinople in 1054 as a result of the Great Schism too. They have over 200 million followers. Its original language was Greek[378].
Lutheran	Martin Luther founded it in Germany in 1517 with his publication of *Ninety-five Theses* against indulgences[379]. They have about eighty-five million followers. The original languages were German and Latin. They use the *Book of Concord* as their worship literature[380].
Presbyterian	John Calvin founded it in Scotland in 1560[381]. They have about fifty million followers. The original languages were French and Latin. They use the *Directory for Worship* as their worship literature[382].

---

[375] See especially Salembier 1907.
[376] I obtained these numbers of followers on January 21, 2012, from the www.adherets.com website, which is a growing collection of over 40 thousand adherent statistics and religious geography citations with references to published membership/adherent statistics and congregation statistics for over 4,200 religions, churches, denominations, religious bodies, faith groups, tribes, cultures, and movements.
[377] Websites: www.catholic.org and www.vatican.ve.
[378] Website www.ec-patr.org/athp/index.php?lang=en.
[379] Gassmann et al. 2001, xvi.
[380] Website www.ilc-online.org.
[381] Walker 1906, 392.
[382] Websites www.ipc-ealing.co.uk and www.pcusa.org.

Table 16. Major Christian Denominations (continued).

Denomination	Description
Methodist	John Wesley founded it in England in 1739[383]. They have about fifty million followers. The original languages were English and Latin. They use the *Book of Discipline* as their worship literature[384].
Anglican / Episcopalian	King Henry the VIII founded it in England in 1532 with his issuance of an *Act of Restraint of Appeals*[385]. They have about eighty million followers. The original languages were English and Latin. They use the *Book of Common Prayer* as their worship literature[386].

Unfortunately, even today, many scholars who suggest that the Bible is inaccurate face punishments and sanctions from Christian leaders. Such is the recent case of Professor John Schneider, who was removed from his Calvin College position because of his controversial study considering whether the Adam and Eve story should be considered allegorical instead of historical fact. Regrettably, this Christian college, founded by the Christian Reformed Church, considers the biblical text literally[387].

Sadly, most Christians treat the Bible as a holy relic, something to worship[388]. Definitely not something to read or understand. Why? We live in a world where people prefer simple sayings, such as quick sound-bites of single scriptural verses such as John 3:16, instead of hard work to understand the context and meanings of biblical sources to discover the truth. The New Testament as an example isn't really about Jesus being a god and defining our life's purpose as found in His death. Instead, our life should be found in His example of "accepting the excluded, healing the sick, strengthening the weak, loving the despised, and challenging the

---

[383] Overton 1891 and Tomkins 2003, 75.
[384] Website new.gbgm-umc.org for United Methodist churches.
[385] Kirkpatrick 2008, 25-26.
[386] Website www.anglicancommunion.org.
[387] Murray 2011.
[388] Collier 2012, 51-57.

powerful"[389]. Consequently, the acid test of Christianity is whether its followers are people who do justice, love kindness, and walk humbly on the Earth.

What's more, the Bible shouldn't be used as a law book with someone quoting scriptural sound-bites to justify their position. If they do, they are likely conducting spiritual malpractice. Instead, the Bible should be taken as a whole, contradictions and all. The primary message is that God loves everyone. Likewise, we, too, should love God and everyone else. Any other message is probably a contradiction to the overall meaning of the Bible.

References.

Abanes, R. (2004). *The Truth Behind the Da Vinci Code*. Eugene, Or.: Harvest House Publishers.

Ackroyd, P.R. and Evans, C.F. (eds). (1970). *The Cambridge History of the Bible*. (1). New York: Cambridge University Press.

Adrian Room. (1986). *Dictionary of True Etymologies*. New York: Routledge & Kegan Paul.

Aesop. (2011). "Hercules and the Waggoner." In *Aesop Fables*. Ca. 600 BCE. http://www.gutenberg.org/files/11339/11339-h/11339-h.htm. Accessed 5 August 2011.

Aland, K. and Aland, B. (1989). *The Text of the New Testament*. Original German in 1981. 2nd Edition. Translated by Erroll F. Rhodes. Grand Rapids, Mich.: Eerdmans Publishing Company.

Algernon, S. (1698). *Discourses Concerning Government*. London.

Arendzen, J. (1909). "Gnosticism." *The Catholic Encyclopedia*. 6. New York: Robert Appleton Company. http://www.newadvent.org/cathen/06592a.htm. Accessed 10 December 2011.

Athanasius. (1892). *Festal Letter XXXIX*. Greek original in 367. Translated by R. Payne-Smith in *Nicene and Post-Nicene Fathers*, 2nd Series. 4. Edited by Philip Schaff and Henry Wace. Buffalo, N.Y.: Christian Literature Publishing Co. Revised and edited for New Advent by Kevin Knight. http://www.newadvent.org/fathers/2806039.htm. Accessed 23 September 2011.

Aune, D.E. (1987). *The New Testament in Its Literary Environment*. Philadelphia, Penn.: The Westminster Press.

---

[389] Gulley 2010, 26.

Bacon, F. (1893). *The Advancement of Learning*. Latin original in 1605. Transcribed by David Price from 1893 edition. London: Cassell & Company. http://www.gutenberg.org/dirs/etext04/adlr10h.htm. Accessed 5 August 2011.

Barrett, D.B. and Johnson, T.M. (2001). "Martyrology: The Demographics of Christian Martyrdom, AD 33 – AD 2001." Part 4 in *World Christian Trends AD 30 – AD 2200: Interpreting the Annual Christian Megacensus*. Pasadena, Calif.: William Carey Library. http://www.gordonconwell.edu/resources/documents/WCT_Martyrs_Extract.pdf. Accessed 13 August 2011.

Bechtel, F. (1910). "The Books of Machabees." *The Catholic Encyclopedia*. Vol. 9. New York: Robert Appleton Company. http://www.newadvent.org/cathen/09495a.htm. Accessed 7 August 2011.

Bede. (1910). *The Ecclesiastical History of the English Nation*. Latin original in 731. Translator not clearly indicated (appears to be L.C. Jane's 1903 Temple Classics translation), introduction by Vida D. Scudder. London: J.M. Dent. http://www.fordham.edu/halsall/basis/bede-book1.asp. Accessed 30 September 2011.

Beduhn, J.D. (2010). *Augustine's Manichaean Dilemma, I: Conversion and Apostasy 373-388 C.E.* Philadelphia, Penn.: University of Pennsylvania Press.

Ben-Sasson, H.H. (1976). *A History of the Jewish People*. Cambridge, Mass.: Harvard University Press.

Benigni, U. (1908). "Codex Vaticanus." *The Catholic Encyclopedia*. 4. New York: Robert Appleton Company. http://www.newadvent.org/cathen/04086a.htm. Accessed 27 December 2011.

Bernhard, A.E. (2006). *Other Early Christian Gospels: A Critical Edition of the Surviving Greek Manuscripts*. Library of New Testament Studies. 315. New York: T & T Clark.

Bihl, M. (1909). "Order of Friars Minor." *The Catholic Encyclopedia*. Vol. 6. New York: Robert Appleton Company. http://www.newadvent.org/cathen/06281a.htm. Accessed 14 August 2011.

Black, D.A. (2009). *Learn to Read New Testament Greek*. Nashville, Tenn.: B&H Publishing Group.

Bradlaugh, C. (1881). *When Were Our Gospels Written?* London: Freethought Publishing. http://www.gutenberg.org/files/36267/36267-h/36267-h.htm. Accessed 6 August 2011.

Brauch, M.T. (2009). *Abusing Scripture: The Consequences of Misreading the Bible*. Downers Grove, Ill.: InterVarsity Press.

Brinkley, B. (2005). *The Lost Books of the Bible: The Supernatural.* Berkeley, Calif.: Oracle Research Publishing.

Brotzman, E.R. (1994). *Old Testament Textual Criticism: A Practical Introduction.* Grand Rapids, Mich.: Baker Book House Company.

Brown, D. (2003). *The Da Vinci Code.* New York: Doubleday Publishing.

Bruce, F.F. (1988). *The Canon of Scripture.* Downers Gove, Ill.: InterVarsity Press.

Burgon, J.W. (1896). *The Causes of the Corruption of the Traditional Text of the Holy Gospels: Being the Sequel to the Traditional Text of the Holy Gospels.* Edited by Miller, Edward. Lonodon: George Bell and Sons. http://www.gutenberg.org/files/21112/21112-h/21112-h.htm. Accessed 7 August, 2011.

Burns, L.C. (1991). *Vagueness: An Investigation Into Natural Languages and the Sorites Paradox.* Dordrecht, The Netherlands: Kluwer Academic Publishers.

Central Intelligence Agency. (2011a). "World." *The World Factbook.* https://www.cia.gov/library/publications/the-world-factbook/geos/xx.html. Accessed 14 August 2011.

Central Intelligence Agency. (2011b). "Afghanistan." *The World Factbook.* https://www.cia.gov/library/publications/ the-world-factbook/geos/af.html. Accessed 14 August 2011.

Central Intelligence Agency. (2011c). "Japan." *The World Factbook.* https://www.cia.gov/library/publications/the-world-factbook/geos/ja.html. Accessed 14 August 2011.

Central Intelligence Agency. (2011d). "United States." *The World Factbook.* https://www.cia.gov/library/publications/ the-world-factbook/geos/us.html. Accessed 14 August 2011.

Collier, G.D. (2012). *Scripture, Canon, & Inspiration.* Cloverdale, Ind.: CWP Press.

Comfort, P. (2005). *Encountering the Manuscripts: An Introduction to New Testament Paleography & Textual Criticism.* Nashville, Tenn.: Broadman & Holman Publishers.

Culpeper, J. (1997). *History of English.* London: Routledge.

Davidson, J. (1995). *The Gospel of Jesus: In Search of His Original Teachings.* Shaftesbury, U.K.: Element Books Limited.

DeConick, A.D. (2001). *Voices of the Mystics: Early Christian Discourse in the Gospel of John and Thomas and Other Ancient Christian Literature.* London: Sheffield Academic Press.

Defoe, D. (1719). *The Life and Adventures of Robinson Crusoe*. London: W. Taylor. http://www.gutenberg.org/files/521/521-h/521-h.htm. Accessed 30 September 2011.

Denison, J.C. (2006). "The Real Painter of the Gospel: The Da Vinci Code in the Light of History." (Feb) 5-6. Article available on the Mimosa Lane Baptist, Mesquite, Texas website. http://www.mimosalane.org/images/davincicode.pdf. Accessed 7 August 2011.

Dillon, W.S. (1976). *Commentary on the Book of Matthew*. River Grove, Ill.: Voice of Melody.

Dimont, M.I. (1962). *Jews, God and History*. 2nd Ed. New York: New American Library.

Draper, J.A. (2006). "The Apostolic Fathers: The Didache." *The Expository Times*. (February) 117(5): 177-81.

Drum, W. (1912). "Tobias." *The Catholic Encyclopedia*. Vol. 14. New York: Robert Appleton Company. http://www.newadvent.org/cathen/14749c.htm. Accessed 7 August 2011.

Duling, D.C. (2010). "Gospel of Matthew." Chapter 18 in *The Blackwell companion to the New Testament*, edited by David E. Aune, 296-318. West Sussex, U.K.: Blackwell Publishing.

Edgar, S. (ed). (2011). *The Vulgate Bible: Douay-Rheims Translation*. 5 vol. Cambridge, Mass: Harvard University Press.

Ehrman, B.D. (2001, 25 March). "Who Wrote the Bible and Why It Matters." *Huffington Post*. http://www.huffingtonpost.com/bart-d-ehrman/the-bible-telling-lies-to_b_840301.html. Accessed 6 August 2011.

Ehrman, B.D. (2003). *Lost Scriptures: Books that Did Not Make it into the New Testament*. New York: Oxford University Press.

Elliot, J.K. (1993). *The Apocryphal New Testament: A Collection of Apocryphal Christian Literature in an English Translation Based on M.R. James*. New York: Oxford University Press.

Elliot, J.K. (2000). *A Bibliography of Greek New Testament Manuscripts*. Society for New Testament Studies Monograph Series 109. Cambridge: Cambridge University Press.

Encyclopædia Britannica. (2011). "Archbishop of Canterbury.". *Encyclopædia Britannica Online*. http://www.britannica.com/EBchecked/topic/93055/archbishop-of-Canterbury. Accessed 9 August 2011.

Evans, C.A. (2008). *Fabricating Jesus: How Modern Scholars Distort the Gospels*. Downers Grove, Ill.: InterVarsity Press.

Fleischmann, R. (1999). *A Survey of English Literature in its Historical Context*. Student study guide of English Literature for Die

Universtät Koblenz-Landau. http://www.uni-bielefeld.de/lili/personen/fleischmann/surveyelit.pdf. Accessed 17 August 2011.

Fokkelman, J.P. (1999). *Reading Biblical Narrative: An Introductory Guide*. Original in Dutch. Leiderdorp, The Netherlands: Deo Publishing.

Franklin, B. (1757). *Poor Richard's Almanack*. Philadelphia, Penn.

Gassmann, G.; Howard, D.H.; and Oldenburg, M.W. (2001). *Historical Dictionary of Lutheranism*. Lanham, Md.: Scarecrow Press.

Gigot, F. (1907). "Baruch.'" *The Catholic Encyclopedia*. Vol. 2. New York: Robert Appleton Company. http://www.newadvent.org/cathen/02319c.htm. Accessed 7 August 2011.

Gigot, F. (1909). "Ecclesiasticus." *The Catholic Encyclopedia*. Vol. 5. New York: Robert Appleton Company. http://www.newadvent.org/cathen/05263a.htm. Accessed 7 August 2011.

Gigot, F. (1912). "Book of Wisdom." *The Catholic Encyclopedia*. Vol. 15. New York: Robert Appleton Company. http://www.newadvent.org/cathen/15666a.htm. Accessed 7 August 2011.

Gordon Conwell Theological Seminary. (2011). "Status of Global Mission, 2011, in Context of 20th and 21st Centuries." (January) http://www.gordonconwell.edu/resources/documents/StatusOfGlobalMission.pdf. Accessed 1 October 2011.

Graver, S. (1984). George *Eliot and Community: A Study in Social Theory and Fictional Form*. Berkeley, Calif. University of California Press.

Grayling, A.C. (1988). *Wittgenstein: A Very Short Introduction*. New York: Oxford University Press.

Gulley, P. (2010). *If the Church Were Christian: Rediscovery the Values of Jesus*. New York: HarperCollins Publishers.

Hahn, P. (2011). "Development of the Biblical Canon." Adapted from materials used for Professor Hahn's University of St. Thomas courses. http://www.columbia.edu/cu/augustine /a/canon.html. Accessed 7 August 2011.

Harris, S.L. (1985). *Understanding the Bible*. Palo Alto, Calif.: Mayfield.

Hayes, J.H. and Holladay, C.R. (2007). *Biblical Exegesis: A Beginner's Handbook*. 3rd Edition. Louisville, Ky.: Westminster John Knox Press.

Heine, R.E. (2007). *Reading the Old Testament with the Ancient Church: Exploring the Formation of Early Christian Thought*. Grand Rapids, Mich.: Baker Academic.

Hollmann, W.B. (2009). "Semantic Change." Chapter 35 in *English Language: Description, Variation and Context,* edited by

Jonathan Culpeper, Francis Katamba, Paul Kerswill,and Tony McEnery. Basingstoke, U.K.: Palgrave Macmillan. 525-537. http://www.lancaster.ac.uk/staff/hollmann/WBH_SemChange_fi naldraft.pdf. Accessed 1 January 2012.

Hyde, D. (2011). "Sorites Paradox," *The Stanford Encyclopedia of Philosophy* (Winter), Edward N. Zalta (ed.), http://plato.stanford.edu/archives/win2011/entries/sorites-paradox. Accessed 18 December 2011.

Jacobs, L. (1995). *The Jewish Religion: a Companion.* Oxford: Oxford University Press.

James, M.R. (ed). (1924). *The New Testament Apocrypha.* Oxford: Clarendon Press.

Johnson, T.M. (2004, September). "World Christian Trends 2005." IFMA/EFMA, St. Louis. http://www.gordonconwell.edu/ resources/documents/IFMA_World_Trends.pdf. Accessed 1 January 2012[390].

Keane, B. (2011, 24 December). "The Christmas Story." Comic. *The Family Circus.*

Keith, C. (2009). *The Periscope Adulterae, the Gospel of John, and the Literacy of Jesus.* Leiden, The Netherlands: Brill.

Keller, T. (2004). "Lost books of the Bible." This article was excerpted from his article "The Gnostics and Jesus" Redeemer Report for the Redeemer Presbyterian Church, New York. The Truth About Da Vinci Code website. http://www.thetruthaboutdavinci.com /lost-books-of-the-bible-article.html. Accessed 7 August 2011.

Kenyon, F.G. (1901). *Handbook to the Textual Criticism of the New Testament.* London: MacMillan and Company.

Kenyon, K.S. (2003). *The Brontë Family: Passionate Literary Geniuses.* Minneapolis, Minn.: Lerner Publications.

King, P.J. and Stager, L.E. (2001). *Life in Biblical Israel.* Louisville, Ky: Westminster John Knox Press.

Kirkpatrick, F.G. (2008). *The Episcopal Church in Crisis: How Sex, The Bible and Authority are Dividing the Faithful.* Westport, Conn.: Praeger Publishers.

Kirsch, J.P. (1911). "Muratorian Canon." *The Catholic Encyclopedia.* Vol. 10. New York: Robert Appleton Company. http://www. newadvent.org/cathen/10642a.htm. Accessed 7 August 2011.

Koester, H. (1990). *Ancient Christian Gospels: Their History and Development.* Harrisburg, Penn.: Trinity Press.

---

[390] Johnson is from the Center for the Study of Global Christianity at the Gordon Conwell Theological Seminary.

Koppel, G. (1988). *The Religious Dimension in Jane Austen's Novels.* Ann Arbor, Mich.: UMI Research Press.

Köstenberger, A.J. and Kruger, M.J. (2010). *The Heresy of Orthodoxy: How Contemporary Culture's Fascination with Diversity Has Reshaped our Understanding of Early Christianity.* Wheaton, Ill.: Crossway.

Liberman, A. (2009). *Word Origins And How We Know Them: Etymology for Everyone.* New York: Oxford University Press.

Lose, D. (2011, 6 August). "4 Good Reasons Not to Read the Bible Literally." *Huffington Post.* Retrieved August 6, 2011 http://www.huffingtonpost.com/david-lose/4-good-reasons-not-to-read-bible-literally_b_919345.html. Accessed 6 August 2011.

Lussier, E. (2011). "Daily Life in Ancient Israel." *The American Ecclesiastical Review.* Washington, D.C.: The Catholic University of America Press. http://www.catholicculture.org/culture/library/view.cfm?recnum=1356. Accessed 14 August 2011.

Łukowski, P. (2011). *Paradoxes.* Series: Trends in Logic. (31). Original Polish. Translated by Marek Gensler. Dordrect, The Netherlands: Springer.

Manns, F. (1998, Autumn). "Everyday Life in the Time of Jesus." *Holy Land.* Translations by Fathers A. Parent and James Heinsch. Washington: Holy Land Franciscans. http://198.62.75.1/www1/ofm/mag/TSmgenB3.html. Accessed 14 August 2011.

Martin, R.P. (2006). "How the First Christians Worshiped" in *Introduction to the History of Christianity*, edited by Tim Dowley. 123-29. Minneapolis, Minn.: First Fortress Press.

Maseko, A.N. (2008). *Church Schism & Corruption.* Durban, South Africa: Lulu Publishing.

McDermott, J.J. (2002). *Reading the Pentateuch: a Historical Introduction.* New York: Paulist Press.

McDonald, L.M. (2011). *The Origin of the Bible: A Guide For the Perplexed.* New York: Continuum Books.

Mead, F.S. (2001). *Handbook of Denominations in the United States.* Nashville: Abingdon Press.

Metzger, B.M. (1981). *Manuscripts of the Greek Bible: An Introduction to Greek Paleography.* New York: Oxford University Press.

Metzger, B.M. (1987). *The Canon of the New Testament: Its Origin, Development and Significance.* New York: Oxford University Press.

Milton, J. (1667). *Paradise Lost.* England. http://www.gutenberg.org/cache/ epub/20/pg20.html. Accessed 5 August 2011.

Milton, J. (1671). *Paradise Regained*. England. http://www.gutenberg.org/cache/epub/58/pg58.html. Accessed 30 September 2011.
Murray, D. (2011, 19 August). "Not So Fast, Calvin." *Grand Rapids Press*.
Olson, R.E. (1999). *The Story of Christian Theology: Twenty Centuries of Tradition & Reform*. Downers Grove, Illinois: InterVarsity Press.
Orr, J. (1907). *The Virgin Birth of Christ: Being Lectures Delivered Under the Auspices of the Bible Teachers' Training School*. (April). New York: Charles Scribner's Sons.
Orwell, G. (1945). *Animal Farm: A Fairy Story*. London: Secker and Warburg.
Orwell, G. (1949). *Nineteen Eighty-Four*. London: Secker and Warburg.
Overton, J.H. (1891). *John Wesley*. London: Methuen & Co.
Pagels, E. and King, K.L. (2007). *Reading Judas: The Gospel of Judas and the Shaping of Christianity*. New York: Penguin Group.
Paine, T. (1791). *The Rights of Man*. London: J.S. Jordan
Patzia, A.G. (2011). *The Making of the New Testament: Origin, Collection, Text & Canon*. Downers Grove, Ill.: InterVarsity Press.
Poovey, M. (1984). *The Proper Lady and the Woman Writer: Ideology as Style in the Works of Mary Wollstonecraft, Mary Shelley, and Jane Austen*. Chicago: University of Chicago Press.
Pope, H. (1910). "Book of Judith." *The Catholic Encyclopedia*. Vol. 8. New York: Robert Appleton Company. http://www.newadvent.org/cathen/08554a.htm. Accessed 7 August 2011.
Reid, G. (1907). "Apocrypha." *The Catholic Encyclopedia*. 1. New York: Robert Appleton Company. http://www.newadvent.org/cathen/01601a.htm. Accessed 2 October 2011.
Rhodes, R. (2005). *The Complete Guide to Christian Denominations: Understanding the History, Beliefs, and Differences*. Eugene, Or.: Harvest House Publishers.
Robinson, E. (1836). *A Greek and English Lexicon of the New Testament*. Boston, Mass.: Crocker and Brewster.
Robinson, J.M. (2007). *The Secrets of Judas: The Story of the Misunderstood Disciple and His Lost Gospel*. New York: HarperCollins.
Salembier, L. (1907). *The Great Schism of the West*. London: Kegan Paul, Trench, Trübner & Co.
Sedgwick, F. (2009). *Where Words Come From: A Dictionary of Word Origins*. New York: Continuum International Publishing Group.

Shelley, M. (1818). *Frankenstein, or the Modern Prometheus*. London: Lackington, Hughes, Harding, Mavor & Jones. http://www.gutenberg.org/files/84/84-h/84-h.htm. Accessed 1 October 2011.

Shepherd, W.H. (2010). "Early Christian Apocrypha: A Bibliographic Essay." *Theological Librarianship*, an Online Journal of the American Theological Library Association. 3(1): 40-47. https://journal.atla.com/ojs/index.php/theolib/article/viewFile/125/430. Accessed 10 December 2011.

Slater, M. (2009). *Charles Dickens: A Life Defined by Writing*. New Haven, Conn.: Yale University Press.

Slick, M. (2011a). "Introduction to Bible Difficulties and Bible Contradictions." *Christian Apologetics & Research Ministry*. http://carm.org/introduction-bible-difficulties-and-bible-contradictions. Accessed 5 August 2011.

Slick, M. (2011b). "When Was the Bible Written and Who Wrote It?" *Christian Apologetics & Research Ministry*. http://carm.org/when-was-bible-written-and-who-wrote-it. Accessed 7 August 2011.

Smith, R.M. (1893). *Studies in the Greek New Testament*. Nashville, Tenn.: Publishing House Methodist Episcopal Church.

Sneddon, C.R. (1993). "A neglected mediaeval Bible translation." *Romance Languages Annual*. 5(1): 11-16. West Lafayette, Ind.: Purdue Research Foundation. http://tell.fll.purdue.edu/RLA-Archive/1993/French-html/Sneddon,Clive.htm. Accessed 10 December 2011.

Souvay, C. (1909). "Esdras." *The Catholic Encyclopedia*. Vol. 5. New York: Robert Appleton Company. http://www.newadvent.org/cathen/05535a.htm. Accessed 7 August 2011.

Spong, J.S. (2005). *The Sins of Scripture: Exposing the Bible's Texts of Hate to Reveal the God of Love*. New York: Harper Collins Publishing.

Steinmetz, S. (2008). *Semantic Antics: How and Why Words Change Meaning*. New York: Random House.

Stern, G. (1931). *Meaning and Change of Meaning with Special Reference to the English Language*. Göteborg, Sweden: Elanders Boktryckeri Aktiebolag.

Stock, B. (2001). *After Augustine: The Meditative Reader and the Text*. Philadelphia, Penn.: University of Pennsylvania Press.

Super, C.W. (1905). "Physicians and Philosophers." *Popular Science Monthly*. Science Press. 67(7): 608-21. http://www.archive.org/stream/popularsciencemo67newy#page/608/mode/1up. Accessed 12 August 2011.

Swift, J. (1726). *Gulliver's Travels Into Several Remote Nations of the World.* London: Benjamin Motte. http://www.gutenberg.org/files/829/829-h/829-h.htm. Accessed 30 September 2011.

Tomkins, S. (2003). *John Wesley: A Biography.* Oxford: Lion Publishing.

Trumble, A. (2010). *The Finger: A Handbook.* Victoria, Australia: Melbourne University Press.

Tusser, T. (1812). *Five Hundred Points of Good Husbandry.* Original in 1557. In William Mavor edition. London: Lackington, Allen, and Company.

Unknown Author. (1892). *Beowulf.* Old English original ca. eleventh century. Translated by Lesslie Hall. Boston, Mass.: D.C. Heath & Co. http://www.gutenberg.org/files/16328/16328-h/16328-h.htm. Accessed 30 September 2011.

Van Voorst, R.E. (2000). *Jesus Outside the New Testament.* Grand Rapids, Mich.: Eerdmans Publishing.

Vander Heeren, A. (1912). "Septuagint Version." *The Catholic Encyclopedia.* 13. New York: Robert Appleton Company. http://www.newadvent.org/cathen/13722a.htm. Accessed 27 December 2011.

Virkler, H.A. and Ayayo, K.G. (2007). *Hermeneutics: Principles and Processes of Biblical Interpretation.* 2nd Edition. Grand Rapids, Mich.: Baker Academic.

Wake, W. (1863). *The Forbidden Books of the New Testament.* Ca. 1657 – 1737. Contributed by William Hone and Edward Hancock. London: E. Hancock & Co. http//www.gutenberg.org/files/6516/6516-h/6516-h.htm. Accessed 7 August 2011.

Walker, W. (1906). *John Calvin: The Organiser of Reformed Protestantism, 1509 – 1564.* New York: The Knickerbocker Press.

Wesley, J. (2011). "On Dress." *Sermon 88.* Original 1778. Sermon available at the United Methodist website. http://new.gbgm-umc.org/ umhistory/wesley/sermons/88/ Accessed 5 August 2011.

Wierzbicka, A. (1992). *Semantics, Culture, and Cognition: Universal Human Concepts in Culture-Specific Configurations.* New York: Oxford University Press.

Williamson, T. (1994). *Vagueness.* London: Routledge.

Wilson, C.W.; Warren, C.; Morrison, W.; and Stanley, A.P. (1871). *The Recovery of Jerusalem: A Narrative of Exploration and Discovery in the City and the Holy Land.* New York: Appleton.

Wittgenstein, L. (1922). *Tractatus Logico-Philosophicus.* Original German in 1921. Translated by C.K. Oggen. London: Kegan Paul, Trench, Trubner and Company. http://www.gutenberg.org/ files/5740/5740-pdf.pdf. Accessed 18 December 2011.

Wolach, D.M. (2007, December). "Wittgenstein and the Sorites Paradox." *Sorites.* 19: 58-60. http://www.sorites.org/Issue_19/wolach.htm. Accessed 18 December 2011.

Wollstonecraft, M. (1792). *A Vindication of the Rights of Women.* Boston, Mass.: Peter Edes

Zuckerman, P. (2007). "Atheism: Contemporary Rates and Patterns." In *Cambridge Companion to Atheism,* edited by Michael Martin. New York: Cambridge University Press. Dr. Zuckerman is a professor of sociology at Pitzer College, Claremont, California.

Zylstra, S.E. (2008, 23 April). "Is 'Let Him Who is Without Sin Cast the First Stone' Biblical?" *Christianity Today.* http://www.christianitytoday.com/ct/2008/aprilweb-only/117-31.0.html. Accessed 1 January 2012.

Chapter 5. Christian Leaders Defy Jesus' Lessons

> *Christian leaders have the most influence over Christians. But, many of these leaders don't follow the words of Jesus. If you don't believe me, read historical books or just read the news today. They are both full of infamous examples of poor Christian leaders. Still, there are many good ones out there too. Unless you knew what to look for, finding one would be difficult. An excellent way to identify them is to study biblical leaders and understand both their good and bad leadership skills. We don't have to follow every Christian leader and their dictates. Choosing which one to follow is one of our most critical decisions.*

All organizations – businesses, governments, militaries, religious institutions, sports, you name it – indulge in deep-rooted questionable practices. Think about it. If you don't believe this, just read the news. Examples include Halliburton overcharging government contracts, Los Angeles police brutally beating Rodney King in 1991, US military aviation officers sexually assaulting women during the 35th Annual Tailhook Association Symposium, Catholic priests sexually abusing their parishioners throughout the world, and the Black Sox Scandal of 1919[391]. Why, you might ask, does this happen? It's a simple answer – they have bad leaders. The ethical practices of their followers reflect their leaders.

The most important task of any leader involves human emotion. In essence, the leader has the maximum influence over their follower's emotions[392]. Thus, these followers are more likely to emulate those of the leader. As such, it's the Christian leaders who have the most impact upon the beliefs of their followers. We can

---

[391] See especially Chatterjee 2009, Cannon 1999, Office of the Inspector General 1993, US House Committee on Armed Services 1992, Doyle et.al. 2005, and Asinof 1963.
[392] Goleman et.al. 2002, 5.

easily assess the beliefs of the leaders through our observations of the behavior and actions of their followers. So, what does this mean to you, the reader? Most people are followers, which is true for most Christians. This means they learn their faith from their leaders. My own knowledge too, both good and bad, came from my present and previous leaders. Understanding this concept places you in more control over your future. Choosing your leader, or choosing to follow your leader, is a very important personal decision. To help you make this decision a wise one is the purpose of this chapter.

So, how do we recognize these leaders? Religious churches have different titles for their leaders. The Jews have Rabbis and Muslims have Imams. In Christianity there are a variety of titles for its leaders. These include in alphabetical order: Abbot, Apostle, Bishop, Brother, Cardinal, Chaplain, Elder, Father, Minister, Missionary, Mother, Pastor, Pope, Prelate, Presbyter, Prior, Reverend, Sister, and Teacher. Regardless of their titles, even if they want to be called "Lord High Muckity Muck", these are the people who lead others within the Christian religion. They don't even have to be in a position of authority or have a leadership related title. Christian leaders could even be the regular member of the Church with no duties and with no responsibilities, but are leaders because they influence others, such as a family member, friend, or colleague. Since leaders are human, one can expect both good and bad leaders. I'll discuss several key examples of each, along with my personal thoughts on the qualities and attributes of good Christian leaders.

Infamous Examples

Beginning my discussion are examples of Christian leaders who I believe don't live and profess the teachings of Jesus for their followers. These examples, in alphabetical order, provide us traits that we shouldn't want from our leaders.

Tony Alamo

He was the founder of the *Alamo Christian Ministries*. In addition to a conviction for tax evasion in 1994, he abused his followers. In

2009, he was convicted of ten federal counts of taking minors across state lines for sex, and was sentenced to 150 years in federal prison[393].

Marshall Applewhite

Leading the *Heaven's Gate* group, he self-proclaimed himself both prophet and messiah[394]. Particularly, he claimed to be an extraterrestrial from the Kingdom of Heaven. To improve his credibility among Christians, he further claimed that his soul once resided in the body of Jesus after traveling here in a spaceship thousands of years ago[395]. Applewhite and several others even castrated themselves to demonstrate control over their physical values of carnal need since sex was completely forbidden. Although he considered sex to be primitive animalistic acts, Appleweight believed heterosexuals were "less evolved than homosexuals, who had at least overcome the attraction to the other gender"[396]. On March 26, 1997, thirty-nine followers in a hilltop Rancho Santa Fe, California mansion committed suicide by using plastic bags for suffocation while under the influence of sedatives and alcohol[397]. They killed themselves because Applewhite convinced them that their suicides were necessary for their souls to exit their "human vessels" and travel aboard a spaceship following comet Hale-Bopp. Professors Hexham and Poewe from the University of Calgary stated that these leaders used twisted logic to lead thirty-nine "well-educated people to commit suicide because they believed that a space craft was tailing the Hale-Bopp Comet. .... Behind all of these movements and belief lies a mythology of creation which rejects evolution as a scientific concept but, except in the fundamentalist case, cannot return to a Biblical view of creation"[398].

---

[393] Gambrell 2009.
[394] Galanter 1999, 176-78.
[395] Bowne and Harrison 2008, 174.
[396] Bearak 1997.
[397] CNN 1997.
[398] 1997.

Jim Bakker

He created the Praise The Lord (PTL) organization. He was convicted of fraud and conspiracy charges after illegally soliciting millions of dollars from his followers. Bakker bilked over one hundred thousand of his PTL followers out of about $150 million, from which he bought a 2,300 acre Christian theme park, expensive homes, cars, and jewelry. He even had a scandalous affair with his secretary, Jessica Hahn, paying her almost $300 thousand of PTL money to buy her silence[399]. He only served a little more than four years in a white-collar prison for this theft. Hahn later was paid $1 million to pose nude in *Playboy* and received additional money in a video, *Jessica Hahn Bares It All*[400].

Wayne Bent

He was the founder of the *Lord Our Righteousness Church*, which was sometimes called "Strong City"[401]. He was sentenced to eighteen years after being convicted of criminal sexual contact of a minor in 2008[402].

Harold Camping

He is known for leading numerous Christians in the Judgment Day Rapture parties on May 21, 2011. In 1970, he published an article about the biblical calendar in a Christian journal for scientists, in which he hinted at the "possibility of the end of the age occurring in our time". Camping later taught others that "God wants people to worship privately in their homes instead – with no leaders, no baptism and no communion"[403]. He specifically described the ultimate terror of Judgment Day in his 2005 book. As a false teacher of doom and gloom, Camping was a self-taught Bible instructor, a civil engineer, owner of Camping Construction Company, and co-founder of the non-profit ministry of Family Stations. I find it very interesting that none of his six living children, twenty-eight grandchildren and thirty-eight great

---

[399] Mizell 1997, 158.
[400] Mizell 1997.
[401] aka: Michael Travesser.
[402] Associated Press 2011.
[403] Associated Press 2003.

grandchildren believed in his theories[404]. Matthew Turner, a Washington Post writer, expressed the events on the 21st of May for this Judgment Day party and its effects upon Christianity and its believers:

> *"And on May 22, while those of us who think that the May 21 Christians are crazy will probably be laughing or poking fun or explaining what we believe to be biblical reasons why they shouldn't have put a date on God's Judgment, the May 21st kids will be facing their "day of reckoning, waking up to realize that their parents, pastors, and theologies were wrong. Many of those kids will lose something that day. The questions that many of them will ask will get answered with lies and excuses and bad biblical reasoning. Some of them will be angry with God for not bringing about Judgment Day. Some of them will lose their faith and yet be unable to escape it. And some of them will go on like nothing happened and probably end up setting and believing in another date".*

Following the Judgment Day events without rapture, Camping went on to claim that "we can be sure that the whole world, with the exception of those who are presently saved (the elect), are under the judgment of God, and will be annihilated together with the whole physical world on October 21, 2011, on the last day of the present five months period. On that day the true believers (the elect) will be raptured"[405]. Now, another date was prophesized by this Christian leader. Of concern is that this single individual has Family Radio at his fingertips, along with millions of dollars available to post warnings while advocating his ideas on billboards throughout the United States. Without this, his predictions wouldn't be heard by millions. What's even more troubling is that millions of Christians took this prophet seriously, resulting in several suicides. Despite these deaths, Camping had the nerve to

---
[404] Rey 2011.
[405] Reimink 2011.

suggest that this was just a botched mathematical error and suggested a new date in October[406]. It's no wonder that Camping's daughter Susan Espinoza told reporters that she's sorry to disappoint them, but Family Radio has been "directed to not talk to the media or the press"[407].

This apocalyptic prediction, though, was honored as a recipient of a 2011 Ig Nobel Prizes, which honors achievements that "first make people laugh, and then make them think". It's intended to celebrate the unusual, honor the imaginative, spurring people's interest in science, medicine, and technology. For 2011, several doomsday predictors were awarded the Ig Nobel Prize for Mathematics jointly, reminding the "world to be careful when making mathematical assumptions and calculations"[408]. Those predictors being honored, in addition to Camping were: Dorothy Martin for predicting the world would end in 1954, Pat Robertson for predicting the world would end in 1982, Elizabeth Clare Prophet for predicting the world would end in 1990, Lee Jang Rim for predicting the world would end in 1992, and Credonia Mwerinde for predicting the world would end in 1999[409]. In my personal opinion, these Christian "end of days" prophets should have read Mark 13:32 and be content that only God knows the exact date. Even the Mayans, known for their accurate astronomical predictions, were wrong with their December 21, 2012 end of the world date[410].

Graham Capill

He was the former leader of Christian Heritage in New Zealand. He was sentenced to nine years in 2005 for child sexual abuse against girls younger than twelve[411].

---

[406] Oltean 2011.
[407] Stevens 2011.
[408] Improbable Research 2011.
[409] Improbable Research 2011.
[410] Stevenson 2012. Many believed these prophesies, including school officials in Michigan resulting in dozens of schools cancelling classes during the week prior to the date amid rumors of violence. Even Christian groups were spreading rumors involving the world's end in 2012.
[411] New Zealand Herald 2005 and 2011.

Joseph Di Mambro

He was the leader of the *Order of the Solar Temple*[412]. Luc Jouret, a physician and New Age lecturer, along with Di Mambro founded this group in Geneva in 1984 to advocate that the Earth would face a worldwide catastrophe in the mid-1990s. To further enhance its credibility, they linked their group to the revival of the Knights Templar, a military-religious order founded in the twelfth century and later suppressed by Papal command two centuries later. This linkage helped them convince several of the members to donate to them over $1 million[413]. In anticipation of this apocalyptic event, Di Mambro further convinced its members into believing it was necessary to enter a higher spiritual plane without the constraints of a mortal human body. The result from 1994 to 1997 was more than seventy members killing themselves in Switzerland and in Quebec. Their farewell letters mentioned that their deaths would be an escape from the "hypocrisies and oppression of this world". These deaths occurred around the dates of the equinoxes and solstices, which were likely part of the group's mixed Christian and New-Age beliefs. What's more, just prior to these deaths, Di Mambro declared a three-month old infant to be the antichrist, which motivated its members to murder the infant with a wooden stake driven through its heart along with killing the baby's parents[414].

Matthew F. Hale

He was the former leader of Creativity Movement, also known as the Church of the Creator. He was sentenced to forty years for soliciting an undercover FBI informant to kill a federal judge[415].

Warren Jeffs

He was the President of Fundamentalist Church of Jesus Christ of Latter Day Saints , a polygamist Mormon sect. He was convicted of sexual assault in 2011, mainly resulting from his seventy-eight

---

[412] This organization went by the French title of " l'Ordre du Temple Solaire"
[413] Encyclopædia Britannica 2011.
[414] Lewis 2006, 1.
[415] Wilgoren 2005.

marriages, many of them to underage girls. Even though he won't be released from prison until 2038 at the age of ninety-three, he still controls his followers[416]. Jeffs also awaits trial in other states and in the federal court system[417].

Figure 14. Jim Jones as the Loving Father of the "Rainbow Family"
Brochure of Peoples Temple portraying the cult leader (1978)[418].

Jim Jones

He was the charismatic Christian leader of the *Peoples Temple*. Jones was personally responsible for the deaths of about a thousand people on November 18, 1978, in Jonestown, located in northwestern Guyana[419]. Except for him, these people died of an apparent cyanide poisoning. Instead, Jones committed suicide with a self-inflicted gunshot wound. As a leader, Jones successfully

---

[416] Hylton 2012.
[417] Wagner 2011.
[418] Retrieved from the website of the Jonestown Institute which states: "Tape transcripts, summaries, some primary source documents, and all photographs on this site are free and available to the public for use by crediting: The Jonestown Institute, http://jonestown.sdsu.edu".
[419] Galanter 1999, 113-17.

convinced his followers that he represented "divine principle, total equality, a society where people own all things in common, where there's no rich or poor, where there are no races. Wherever there are people struggling for justice and righteousness, there I am. .... Some people see a great deal of God in my body. They see Christ in me, a hope of glory"[420]. One of his followers and former Peoples Temple member, Hue Fortson, said that he allowed "Jones to think for me because I figured that he had the better plan. .... I gave my rights up to him. As many others did"[421]. Many of these deaths included children, who were given no choice[422]. And, it included the deliberate murders of Congressman Leo Ryan and NBC reporter Don Harris at a nearby airstrip. Alan Riding, a New York Times journalist, accurately summarized Jones effectively in his 2011 article.

> *"In Jonestown, Jim Jones was the demonic almighty. Yet it's easily forgotten that initially he was considered a force for good. Born in 1931, he was just 23 when he opened one of the first integrated churches in Indianapolis. Seven years later, as head of the city's Human Rights Commission, he attempted to integrate other churches and local restaurants. To boost his appeal, though, he was already faking miracles. .... Tragically, these idealists embraced death as a final refuge, still unaware that Jones, not society, had betrayed them".*

William Kamm

He was an Australian religious sect leader of the *Order of St. Charbel*. He was also known as the "Little Pebble" and as the antipope Peter II. He was sentenced to prison in 2005 for sexual attacks on a fifteen-year-old girl. Also in 2007, his sentence was

---

[420] Nelson et al 2006.
[421] Nelson et al 2006.
[422] Many of the adults were pressured to take the poison.

increased after being found guilty for sexual abuses against another teenage girl[423].

Henry Lyons

He was the former President of the National Baptist Convention, USA, Inc. In 1999, he was convicted for racketeering and grand theft[424].

Marcial Maciel (Degollado)

He founded the *Legionaries of Christ* in Mexico in 1941. The Vatican labeled him a person "devoid of scruples and of genuine religious sentiment". They did this because Maciel had a long history of sexual abuse, including fathering several children, despite him creating a vast network of Mexican schools and supporting philanthropic efforts for its children[425].

Sam Mullet

He was a bishop in an Amish community. He claimed that he "should be able to punish people who violate the laws of the church"[426]. However, other Amish bishops in eastern Ohio rebuked him after determining that he wasn't justified in attempting to excommunicate eight families in 2005. Even though the Amish live a modest lifestyle traveling by horse and buggy and forgoing most modern conveniences, they all have deep religious beliefs. This includes distancing themselves from the outside world and yielding to a collective order. They also believe the Bible requires women to grow their hair long, and men to grow beards and stop shaving once they marry. Mullet led other Amish members in publicly humiliating others who disobeyed him. This included beating those who "disobeyed him, made some members sleep in a chicken coop and had sexual relations with married women to 'cleanse them'"[427]. As a result, Amish in several states were frightened after several of Mullet's followers during the fall of

---

[423] Courier Mail 2011, Herald Sun 2007, and Webber 2008.
[424] New York Times 1999.
[425] Lacey and Malkin 2010.
[426] Eckholm 2011.
[427] Sheeran and Seewer 2011.

2011 forcibly cut Amish men's beards and Amish women's hair, along with taking photos of them. These frightened Amish people made tearful calls to authorities, along with arming themselves with pepper spray and shotguns.

Credonia Mwerinde

She was the leader of the *Movement for the Restoration of the Ten Commandments of God*[428]. Mwerinde, an ex-prostitute, along with Joseph Kibweteere, a lay worker within the Catholic Church, founded this group in 1987[429]. Claiming to have personally seen the Virgin Mary, she convinced her followers of an apocalyptic event, including the end of the world, if the Ten Commandments were disregarded. Her apocalyptic messages specifically predicted the destruction of the world on December 31, 2000. She even demanded the following rules from her followers: "refraining from sex, the separation of family members, separate dormitories for men and women, wearing uniform green, black, and white clothing, keeping the members from forming friendships by moving them around frequently and unexpectedly, hard labor, communicating only through gestures except for prayer and singing, reduced contact with non-members, and the giving up of all earthly goods for the promise of Heaven"[430]. Dominic Kataribabo, a Catholic priest with a doctorate degree, improved the credibility of the cult[431]. On March 14, 2000, the group held a large farewell party[432]. Three days later, over nine hundred members died in Uganda[433]. Unfortunately, most of the deaths were clearly not suicides, based upon the evidence of the large number of women and children, including strangulations[434]. Contributing to this was the prevalent culture of extreme religious fanaticism. Missionaries known for defying political institutions first introduced Christianity into Urganda in the late nineteenth century.

---

[428] Nelson 2000.
[429] Santucci 2000.
[430] Santucci 2000.
[431] BBC 2000b.
[432] Borzello 2000.
[433] Nelson 2000.
[434] Murphy 2000.

Initially, the State hunted and persecuted Christians. Causing more confusion were the two big churches, the Roman Catholic and Episcopal, often attacking each other[435]. Furthermore, Ugandans were already suffering from mass killings under Idi Amin, and being exposed to a devastating epidemic we now know as AIDS. These made it easy for a charismatic self-proclaimed prophet to blame the State and Christian churches for bringing the wrath of God upon them[436].

Sister Anna Nobili

She was a former lap-dancer who performed in Italian nightclubs for many years. Later she used her skills to minister in prisons and hospitals with a modern dance, called "The Holy Dance". She joined the *Working Lady Nuns of Nazareth House*[437]. Pope Benedict XVI shut down the monastery's lap-dancer-turned-nun concerts and removed the monks, ending their 500-year presence. This monastery contained many of the historical relics from Jesus' life, such as nails and splinters from His cross, thorns from his crown, and the bone of the finger from Thomas that penetrated His wounds[438].

Fred Phelps

He was the leader of anti-gay *Westboro Baptist Church*. Also, Phelps was convicted for disorderly conduct and battery in 1995[439]. His non-Christian behavior has been felt by others outside of the United States, such as in the United Kingdom, who believed he was "engaging in unacceptable behaviour by fostering hatred which might lead to intercommunity violence"[440]. On a personal note, my first encounter with his followers was during the 2005

---

[435] See especially Bwire 2007.
[436] BBC 2000a.
[437] Trujillo 2009.
[438] Kington 2011. I placed this example here, not because I found any fault in her ministry. Instead, it was her lack of judgment in upsetting her superiors through defiance and other insubordinate actions. This failure to lead up to her supervisors caused her ministry to shut down, preventing her future impact upon Christian followers.
[439] Barnes 2011 and Cutbirth 2010.
[440] Guardian 2009.

anniversary walk in Washington DC of the September 11th attack of the United States. I felt outrage towards his followers who carried signs that read "Thank God for Terrorists", "Thank God for Dead Soldiers", "Thank God for 9/11". These were definitely not signs about a loving god[441].

Figure 15. Members of the Westboro Baptist Church.
They demonstrate at the Virginia Holocaust Museum. With permission from J.C. Wilmore, a writer and photographer (2 March 2010).

Howard Douglas Porter

He was the pastor at Hickman Community Church. Porter was convicted of first-degree murder, embezzlement, elder abuse, and attempted murder in 2008[442].

Jung Myung Seok

He was a South Korean religious sect leader and founder of Providence, which was a non-Catholic, non-Orthodox, and non-

---

[441] To counter the Phelps protests at funerals of soldiers, a group of motorcycle riders formed the Patriot Guard Riders to provide a nonviolent, volunteer buffer between the protesters and mourners.
[442] See especially Kurst-Swanger 2008, 197; Fladager 2008; and Munoz 2006.

Protestant Christian group. Seok was convicted for raping several of his followers[443].

Catholic Priests

They have led their parishioners with their Christian faith for centuries. Yet, recently, many of them have invoked the name of God to justify violation of the children entrusted to them. This included their superiors doing the same to justify covering up these violations. These superiors, mostly bishops, claimed that the unity of the church was more important than the truth[444].

Additional Examples

I will also tell you that *Peoples Temple, Order of the Solar Temple, Heaven's Gate,* and *Movement for the Restoration of the Ten Commandments of God* are cults; and, in cults, intellectual curiosity and empathy are discouraged[445]. Though, not all secret societies are entirely secret, with well-known members, objectives, and teachings[446]. I recommend anyone considering membership in any Christian church to understand cults, including reading personal accounts of former cult members, such as Professor Janja Lalich at California State University. She was a member of the *Democratic Workers Party* (DWP) for eleven years, a group she considered a political cult led by Professor Marlene Dixon of the University of Chicago[447]. In her book, she compared her personal experiences with the DWP and that of *Heaven's Gate*. I also recommend learning about human behavior, such as reading books or articles by Marc Galanter, a professor of psychiatry at New York University. He described three key forces in a charismatic group: group cohesiveness, shared belief, and altered consciousness[448]. Historically, cults referred to a minor religious sect that practiced its own rituals; however, today it refers to a

---

[443] Associated Press 2007, Callick 2007, and Ji-sook 2008.
[444] Spong 2005, 13.
[445] Scheeres 2011, xi.
[446] Daraul 1989, 9.
[447] 2004, xvii.
[448] 1999, 13-76.

secretive and dangerous group led by a charlatan[449]. Individuals becoming part of a religious cult may do baffling things such as shaving their heads, giving away their most prized possessions, or committing suicide[450]. Examples of claiming to raise the dead, taking multiple spouses, and committing murder demonstrate that cult members are making irrational and harmful decisions[451]. It should be no surprise to anyone that an estimated two million people in the United States have joined cults in the past several decades, many of which are beneficial legitimate organizations though, such as self-help groups and book clubs[452]. In the words of Lalich, "without the leader, there would be no draw, no call, no promise of an ideal. And without devotees responding to that call, there would be no group"[453]. You should always be concerned that a cult leader may be just a manipulative person who believes the purpose of having power is abusing it[454].

In addition to the several examples provided, I would be remiss if I failed to mention several quasi-religious groups such as the *Freemasonry*, *Hibernians*, *Illuminati*, *Knights of Malta*, *Knights Templar*, and *Christian Identity*. The first one is a popular one throughout the world with many good deeds. Nevertheless, several Christian churches have felt threatened by its practices. For example, Catholics since 1738 have been under penalty of excommunication, *incurred ipso facto*, if they enter or promote in any way Masonic societies[455]. The religious law now in force pronounces excommunication upon "those who enter Masonic or Carbonarian or other sects of the same kind, which, openly or secretly, plot against the Church or lawful authority and those who in any way favour these sects or do not denounce their leaders and principal members"[456]. Next, the *Hibernians* grew up gradually among the Catholics of Ireland owing to the dreadful hardships and

---

[449] Galanter 1999, ix.
[450] Galanter 1999, 1
[451] Lalich 2004, 2.
[452] Lalich 2004, 8.
[453] 226.
[454] Browne and Harrison 2008, 175.
[455] Ratzinger 1983.
[456] Gruber 1910a.

persecutions to which they were subjected with the primary intent and purpose to promote friendship, unity and Christian charity[457]. The *Illuminati* was a secret group advocating a society regulated by reason as man's only code of law applying the practices of Freemasonry and practical liberalism. In 1783, the anarchistic tendencies of the order provoked public denunciations which later caused Pope Pius VI to condemn the group[458]. Membership into the *Knights of Malta* was based upon nobility, Christian faith, integrity and social position. As for doing good deeds during war, since 1870, this group provided ambulance service on the battlefield[459]. The *Knights Templar* was disbanded in the early fourteenth century through treacherous interaction between the State and the Church. This resulted in Pope Clement V supporting the persecution of the Templars as heretic, which later ended in fifty-four Templars being publicly burned in 1310[460]. The *Christian Identity* claimed to be the descendants of the lost tribes of "white" Israel through a long history of violence[461]. This group was also known as being part of the Christian far-right and Armageddon survivalists using the "gun and gospel" approach[462].

Summary Thoughts

So, what did these leaders offer their followers? I couldn't answer this any better than Cherise Fantus, the Editor-in-Chief of *The Scribe* at the University of Colorado. These religious leaders, with their unrivaled egotism and insatiable ambition, offered their followers a "Christian Get Out of Jail Free Card" for their unquestioned unwavering complete loyalty and obedience. In the words of Fantus, "someone who already goes to church every Sunday now has permission to commit all the crimes they want with no repercussions. Yes, no repercussions – because completing a year of attending church does not result in a time-

---

[457] McFaul 1910.
[458] Gruber 1910b.
[459] Moeller 1910. Also known as the Hospitallers of St. John of Jerusalem.
[460] Moeller 1912.
[461] Quarles 2004, 7-9.
[462] Quarles 1999, 164.

served stamp, it results in a complete dismissal of charges"[463]. Furthermore, numerous religious leaders throughout time have invoked the name of God to justify violation of the children entrusted to them, including their superiors doing the same to justify covering up these violations. Unity of the church was deemed more important than the truth to them[464]. Their questionable, evasive, dishonest decisions destroyed the essential trust necessary for effective leadership. These aren't the leaders Jesus wanted. I know this to be true since He rebuked the religious leaders of His day for not practicing what they preached[465].

Figure 16. Burning of Templars.
Verbrennung von Templern. (British Library, Royal 14 E V f. 492v) by Verbrennung von Templern (1479-1480).

---

[463] 2011.
[464] Spong 2005, 13.
[465] Mark 11:27-12:44 and Luke 10:30-37.

Infamous Popes

My next set of examples of bad Christian leaders have been the supreme leader of the Catholic Church, the world's largest Christian group – the Pope. Don't get me wrong; we have had many great and wonderful Popes who have lived the examples of Jesus. However, we must realize that every group of people, such as politicians and corporations, is a reflection of the population it uses for its membership. The Church isn't immune from the sins of the people. The papacy throughout its two millennium history, too, is no exception. As can be expected, we can easily find documented examples of Popes who have not lived the teachings of Jesus. During my research into this area, I've found many examples of Popes whom haven't lived up to the standards one expects of the Holy See. Nevertheless, the following set of examples shouldn't suggest that we attack the papacy[466]. Instead, it just indicates that even the process for selection of the leader of the Catholic Church throughout its history, which was, and still is, a man-made process, isn't infallible. I found many examples of popes who were accused of adultery, bribery, murder, and other despicable crimes. These are listed in chronological order below. However though, in my professional opinion, many of these were nothing more than unproven accusations, usually given by a single person or a group of people who despised their pope. In spite of that, several of these appear to be more than just accusation.

Hormisdas

Beginning my list is Hormisdas, 514-23. He was a married man whose son later became Pope Silverius, being on the list for violating the rule of celibacy[467].

Adrian II

Next in the list was a married priest, Adrian II, 867-72[468]. Don't get me wrong. I have nothing against a married Pope, and not even a priest. Ethically, though, they violated their own religious oaths.

---

[466] See especially Foote and Wheeler 1887.
[467] Kirsch 1910a.
[468] Loughlin 1907a.

Stephen VI

This very colorful pope from 896-7, exhumed Formosus' rotting corpse and put him on trial in the so-called *Cadaver Synod* in January 897[469]. And, no, I'm not making this up. With the corpse propped up on a throne, an appointed deacon answered for the deceased pontiff. The charges against Formosus included performing the functions of a bishop when he had been deposed and for receiving the pontificate while he was the bishop of Porto. The corpse was quickly found guilty, stripped of its sacred vestments, and then deprived of three blessing fingers of its right hand. He was then clad in the garb of a layman, and quickly buried. To further add insult to this corpse, it was then re-exhumed and thrown in the Tiber River. Finally, all of his ordinations were later annulled[470].

Figure 17. The Cadaver Synod of 897.
Le Pape Formose et Etienne VII - Concile cadavérique de 897 (1870) by Jean-Paul Laurens. Pope Formosus and Stephen VII.

---

[469] Donald Wilkes 2001, 8. In some sources, he is listed as Stephen VII.
[470] Mann 1912a.

Sergius III

Immediately following Stephen VI was Sergius III from 904 to 911. According to several records, he was accused of ordering the murder of another pope, along with fathering an illegitimate son who later became Pope John XI from 931–35. I should caution you that this was based upon the words of a chronicler who was also biased against Sergius III. These accusations were highly doubtful since they're only made by bitter or ill-informed adversaries, and are inconsistent with what is said of him by respectable contemporaries[471]. I'll let you, the reader, determine if you believe the accusations against Sergious III.

John XII

Next on my list is John XII from 956-64. He was known for turning the Lateran Palace into a brothel[472]. In addition to this, he was accused of adultery, incest, murder, perjury, sacrilege, and simony[473]. Finally, as his life story concludes, the husband of a woman with whom he was having an affair beat him. He died three days later, supposedly without receiving confession or the Last Rites sacraments[474].

Boniface VII

This pope from 974 was accused of murdering his predecessor, plundering the Basilica, and then murdering Pope John XIV. After he died, Bonifice's body was dragged through Rome's streets and then thrown under the statue of Marcus Aurelius in the Lateran Palace naked, covered only with wounds[475].

---

[471] Mann 1912b.

[472] Logan 2002, 100-102. The Lateran Palace was an ancient Roman palace which later became the main Papal residence. It is adjacent to the Basilica di San Giovanni in Laterano, otherwise known as the cathedral church of Rome.

[473] Simony means paying for sacraments, including for holy offices or hierarchy positions in the church. This word was named after Simon Magus, mentioned in Acts 8:9-24.

[474] Kirsch 1910b.

[475] Oestereich 1907.

Clement V

This pope from 1305-14 was on my list because of his cruel suppression of the Knights Templar. He stole their property and shared them with the king of France. He had several members burned alive. He also started a new crusade against the Turks. Dante, by the way, placed him in Hell[476]. Admired for the blending in his *Divina Comedia* of Roman literature and Christian teachings, Dante's work represented the spirit of Christianity through the lens of the Middle Ages[477].

Figure 18. The Army of the Second Crusade.
They find the remains of the soldiers of the First Crusade by Gustave Doré (1877).

---

[476] Shahan 1908.
[477] MacCaffrey 1914.   Discussed in Chapter I.   CAUSES OF THE REFORMATION.

Urban VI

Accused of ordering the brutal torture of several cardinals is Urban VI, from 1378-89. He was also the first Pope of the Western Schism, which ultimately lead to three people claiming the Papal throne at the same time[478]. He was also the last pope elected outside the College of Cardinals. The cardinals who elected him decided that they'd made the wrong decision by electing a new Pope in his place, who took the name of Clement VII and started a second Papal court in Avignon, France. Later he launched a program of violence against those he thought conspired against him, imprisoning people at will and mistreating them brutally. This second election threw the Catholic Church into turmoil, quickly escalating from a religious problem to a diplomatic one that divided Europe. This schism ended about forty years later when all three of the reigning Popes abdicated together and a successor, Pope Martin V, was elected[479].

Innocent VIII

About a century later, Innocent VIII, 1484-92, joins this list with several illegitimate children[480].

Alexander VI

Following him is Alexander VI, from 1492-1503, known for maintaining a harem in the Vatican[481]. Available historical records indicate that he held a feast with fifty naked dancing courtesans[482]. This feast was known as the *Banquet (or Ballet) of Chestnuts*[483]. He was also reported to have had four children from a mistress[484]. These records indicated that he died via poison that he intended for Cardinal Adriano da Corneto[485].

---

[478] Salembier 1912.
[479] Mulder 1912.
[480] Weber 1910.
[481] Hills 1922, 51.
[482] Burchardus 1921, 154-55.
[483] Mancheter 1992, 79.
[484] Manchester 1992, 79. Vannozza dei Cattanei: Giovanni, Cesare, Lucrezia, and Gioffre.
[485] Loughlin 1907b.

Julius II

Last in my list is Julius II, from 1503-13. He was accused of acquiring the papacy by fraud and bribery, holding it with violent force. This earned him the epithet of *pontefice terribile*. However, he was also a patron of arts, supporting the works of Bramante, Raphael, and Michelangelo[486]. Additionally, he laid the cornerstone of Basilica of St. Peter[487].

Summary Thoughts

These early abuses, which were more colorful than the soap opera stories on television, were undoubtedly symptoms of a period of unrest for the Church. Many of the problems were attributed to the interference of secular authorities. You should already understand that the State had influence over ecclesiastical appointments, causing Christians to become disgusted in the capabilities of their Christian leaders[488]. This led to several religious revolts, including those led by Martin Luther. He upset Pope Leo X with the turmoil created in Germany by his theses and sermons. The Pope appointed a commission to examine the issues and summoned Luther to appear[489]. Inflexible theology had lost its hold upon many educated men who refused to yield a ready obedience to the Papal decrees. By the eighteenth century, many of the world's educated and powerful people began questioning the rigid foundation of Christianity[490]. Prior to these protests, the Christian world was really one large religious family that acknowledged the Pope as the global Father of Christendom. This provided the Pope the role of supreme arbitrator of disputes between states. After the religious unity of Europe collapsed, the Papal influence over state matters diminished. This provided them influence more on

---

[486] The work he supported includes the famous frescoes of Michelangelo in the Sistine Chapel and of Raphael in the Stanze, the Court of St. Damasus with its loggias, the Via Giulia and Via della Lungara, the colossal statue of Moses for the mausoleum of Julius II in the church of San Pietro in Vincoli.
[487] Ott 1910.
[488] MacCaffrey 1914.
[489] MacCaffrey 1914. Discussed in Chapter II. THE RELIGIOUS REVOLUTION: LUTHERIANISM AND ZWINGLIANISM.
[490] Discussed in Chapter VIII RATIONALISM AND ITS EFFECTS.

spiritual matters[491]. Maybe this is why we haven't seen examples of Papal abuses of power since.

Throughout history, including current times, the senior Catholic leadership tended to squash anyone trying to modernize or even liberalize interpretation of its doctrine. In essence, if it didn't support the beliefs of the Constantine era, it wasn't Catholic. These were especially true of current concerns, such as ordination of women, marriage of priests, ministry to homosexuals, and human sexuality. But then, why should we expect anything different from older men who live by strict ancient rules laid down thousands of years ago? Why should they understand the rest of the world's desire to modernize?

Good Leadership

Listing examples of leadership failures is easy to do since they're readily available and easy to identify. But, what is good leadership really about? Many people claim they know about leadership and often use their current or previous leadership position as proof of that knowledge. Being in a position of authority provides one leadership experience; but, it doesn't make one a good leader. Neither does just telling someone to do something. In fact, giving "lip service" is a poor leadership technique. Successfully influencing others involves more than just the right combination of words[492]. I'll begin this section with some key skills I learned the hard way, which I obtained through experience in increasing levels of leadership in the Army.

But why should you listen to me and believe what I have to say? I received several years of leadership training from the US Army, starting with my pre-commissioning training from the Reserve Officers' Training Corps (ROTC) while I was an undergraduate college student. Following commissioning as a lieutenant, I completed basic officer training. This provided me with leadership training focused upon leading a platoon of approximately thirty Soldiers. And, I received technical information associated with my

---

[491] Discussed in Chapter IX THE PAPACY.
[492] Patterson et. Al. 2008, 5.

military field of Weapons of Mass Destruction (WMD). A few years later, I attended an advanced officer course. In this course, I learned additional leadership training, focused upon commanding a company of approximately two hundred Soldiers. Several more years later, as a captain, I completed the command and staff colleges of each of the military services. I learned about staff leadership skills necessary for support of larger multi-discipline organizations. The culmination of my leadership training was the completion of the US Army War College as a colonel. This final training focused upon strategic leadership of large organizations operating in a complex international environment.

From this leadership training, I can easily tell you that leadership is simply "influencing people by providing purpose, direction, and motivation"[493]. It, also, involves organizational values of loyalty, duty, respect, selfless service, honor, integrity, and personal courage[494]. And, leadership core competencies include: leading others, influencing others outside their control, leading by example, communicating effectively, creating a positive environment, improving self and followers, and obtaining results[495]. But, leadership isn't about knowledge of good leadership. It involves actions, skills, and capabilities, much of which isn't learned in a classroom or from reading a book. Much of the Army's leadership philosophy may be ineffective outside the military today. For instance, its hierarchical structure and promotion system imply that age and experience automatically produce greater knowledge and ability. This implies that the senior-ranking person is inherently superior to a subordinate[496]. In spite of this, the leader doesn't have to be in a position of authority. Even students and non-supervisors can lead others.

I also learned about the three distinct levels of leadership: direct, senior and executive levels[497]. I won't describe the differences

---

[493] 2007, 1.
[494] 2007, 2.
[495] 2007, 3.
[496] Pape 2009.
[497] Lewis et al 1987, 34.

between these three. But although the leadership actions at each level is different, the character of the good leaders remain the same. Based upon several Harvard University studies, we can use three generic types to categorize leaders. The first is focused primarily upon internal goals and agendas. The second is a team player focused upon relationships with others. And, the third type is focused upon internal values[498]. Essentially, much of my formal training of leadership in the Army was usually a study of biographies and actions of important military leaders though.

From this training, I can describe some of the skills that good leaders possess. First, many effective leaders were *charismatic*, such as Winston Churchill and Mother Teresa[499]. Although not normally charismatic, Churchill demonstrated this skill during World War II by convincing his nation that they could survive and overcome Hitler's terrible overwhelming danger. Mother Teresa also exhibited charisma by using it to inspire the members of the Missionaries of Charity to transcend their own self-interests to give "wholehearted and free service to the poorest of the poor"[500]. Second, they were also *adaptable* by being dynamic in response to the different situations they are faced with. This was Dwight Eisenhower's style[501]. Being one of my favorite leaders, Ike commanded the largest coalition army in history and guided his country through a turbulent decade in American politics, leaving the office more popular than any of his successors[502]. If leaders were to be successful while being adaptable, their core objectives shouldn't change. Instead, there were a variety of ways to achieve those goals[503]. Third, good leaders *inspire* actions by appealing to

---

[498] Lewis et al 1987, 35-39.
[499] For Churchill, see especially Hayward 1998. For Mother Teresa, see Klenke 1996, 78.
[500] Website: http://www.mcpriests.com.
[501] See especially Wukovits and Clark, 2006.
[502] See especially Smith 2012 and Weigley 1981. Ike commanded the Supreme Headquarters of the Allied Expeditionary Force from 1943 through 1945. This force contained several million soldiers, sailors and airmen in combined armies, navies, and air forces of 26 nations, including Canada, China, France, the Netherlands, Poland, United Kingdom, and the United States.
[503] Starry 1987, 13.

their followers' ideals and morals, such as empowering them to use their own beliefs and personal strengths. These inspirational leaders included Martin Luther King Jr. and Walt Disney[504]. Fourth, they possessed a *good character*, which may be defined as the commitment to an admirable set of values, and the courage to display those values in one's life, no matter the cost. For us to understand this, we should understand the ethics that have guided the great civilizations and great societies of the past. We should also understand that almost everything we do has a value component. We both reveal our values and teach them to others through everything we do and say[505]. Fifth, effective leaders possessed both *confidence and trust*. Leadership can be used for either good or bad. George Washington used it for the benefit of his people[506]. Sixth, good leadership required *openness to change* individually. Effective leaders knew how to identify the operational environment in addition to how to change their behavior and their decisions to match that environment[507]. Seventh, the *lead by example* leaders don't necessarily tell people what to do. Furthermore, they don't force people to do things that they're not willing to do themselves, such as Rosa Parks and Abraham Lincoln. Parks, the African-American woman who in 1955 refused to relinquish her bus seat to a white man helped inspired the civil rights movement[508]. Lincoln understood the equality of men and saw slavery as being wrong. He did what he thought was right at the risk of public scorn from others[509]. Finally, as *servant leaders*, they definitely take care of the needs of others before taking care of their own. They don't act like a dictatorial king to their followers, serving them rather than forcing them to act. One of my favorite servant leaders was Gandhi. He practiced what he preached and inspired non-violent protest throughout India in 1919[510].

---

[504] For MLK, see especially Phillips 1998. For Disney, see especially Williams 2004.
[505] Sorley 1989, 11-12.
[506] See especially Rees 2007.
[507] Snowden and Boone 2007.
[508] Bredfeldt 2006, 21-22.
[509] See especially Williams et. al. 1994.
[510] Polelle 2008, 22-24.

What do good leaders avoid? First, they don't rely solely upon ***rewards and punishments*** to motivate their followers. An example of this was Senator Joseph McCarthy and his anti-Communist investigation[511]. In response to this investigation and the excessive punishments given, Senator Ralph Flanders from Vermont introduced a resolution in June 1954 accusing McCarthy of misconduct for his anti-Communist accusations and punishments of American citizens[512]. By the end of the year, the Senate formally condemned him for conduct unbecoming a senator. Second, ***cruel treatment*** of defenseless people is also a poor leadership trait. Such is the case of Second Lieutenant William Calley's leading the massacre of defenseless civilian Vietnamese. Doing the right thing by not being cruel may be much harder, but is required of good leaders as demonstrated by Second Lieutenant Cleo Buxton with his humane treatment of prisoners during WW II. Buxton accomplished this by knowingly risking charges of a capital offense of desertion and insubordination for saving these prisoners and disobeying orders from his superior officers to execute them[513]. Based upon the West Point Cadets Prayer, a leader must be able to "choose the harder right instead of the easier wrong"[514]. Third, many poor leaders ***conceal*** information from their followers. They believe that flawed data or withholding data supports their leadership. It does, but in a bad way. They tend to support this with their Machiavelli philosophy that people usually make decisions more from appearance than from reality[515]. In my opinion, I'd rather my people know the real information and negotiate a compromise in my decisions, using something similar to the *Marquis of Queensburg Rules* for ensuring a fair and

---

[511] See especially Giblin 2009.
[512] Giblin 2009, 244.
[513] Lewis et al 1987, 34-35. Cleo Buxton founded the Association for Christian Conferences, Teaching and Service (ACCTS) in 1972. He was also the first General Secretary of the Officers' Christian Fellowship, an organization I have been a member of since 1983.
[514] Wheat 1942, 9. Colonel Wheat was both a chaplain and English Professor at the US Military Academy from 1918 – 1926. The prayer, written before 1920, was approved by then West Point's Commandant Douglas MacArthur.
[515] Benner 2009, 400.

equitable decision is made[516]. Fourth, another poor leadership trait demonstrated by many in leadership positions is *micromanagement*. Moreover, extreme detailed planning is a waste of time. In complex and ever-changing situations, it's best to provide a rough outline for the plan and allow the followers the freedom to make decisions independently[517]. That's even good advice for the leader too, especially following the advice of Napoleon, "you engage and then you see"[518]. Finally, this includes *toxic* leadership. Lieutenant General Ulmer, the one who chewed me out when I was a platoon leader, had significant concerns about leaders who are toxic. Although they're usually bright, energetic and technically competent, toxic leaders alienate and abuse their followers. They create a hostile climate, rule by fear and reject bad news. They're self-serving and arrogant. They usually become leaders because of their skill in upward relationships[519].

More important than training was the experience I had in applying my leadership skills at various organizational levels starting with platoon leader of about thirty Soldiers, culminating with brigade command of more than two thousand Soldiers and civilians located throughout several states. Through my nearly thirty year career, I made both good and bad decisions. Fortunately, I learned through the failures of my bad decisions. When I commanded my brigade, I definitely couldn't succeed by micromanaging. And, I definitely didn't possess all of the technical knowledge and skills of each of my people. Many of the tasks I knew little about included fire-fighting, civil engineering, construction, and mess operations. Still, I was successful in leading them to successfully complete their tasks. I admit that I didn't know everything, and I didn't trust any leaders who claim that they did.

Chiefly, what did I do to succeed as a leader? There was nothing magical or difficult about it. Since leading others was my single greatest privilege, I ensured that completing my missions always

---

[516] Moore 1994, 193.
[517] Dörner, 1996 161.
[518] Betts 2001. In French: "On s'engage et puis on voit".
[519] Ulmer 2012.

involved taking care of my people. I ensured that every person felt as though he or she was an active contributor and member of a close-knit team, sharing a common goal and objective. As professionals, we're each expected to accomplish the mission, know the standard, strive to exceed it in every area, be technically proficient, be a team player, be safe in all areas, improve ourselves, and keep a positive attitude. A good attitude was a large part of being successful in any organization. This included having a healthy sense of humor. I believed that a positive leadership climate built organizational cohesion, maintained discipline and adherence to standards, while promoting mission accomplishment. I also led by example, with integrity, honesty, and loyalty. I definitely didn't sit on my butt and worry about it. But, did all of this work? Most of the time it did. I even had to fire a young captain who informed me that he didn't want to be a leader. I also disciplined other military officers who worked for me, especially those who committed criminal actions, such as international weapons smuggling and sexual harassment.

My biggest leadership challenge happened when I commanded the 472nd Chemical Battalion, which was broken when I assumed command. The previous battalion commander abdicated, the executive officer was absent without leave (AWOL), and many key leadership positions were vacant. The battalion also had a group of individuals in key positions on the headquarters staff who continually abused the system, such as working fewer hours than mandated and misusing Government property. This created a serious leadership and morale problem throughout, resulting in many tasks not being accomplished. Adding more complexity to an already bad situation, the unit was identified as a potential deployment asset for the 2003 offensive operations in Iraq. Further adding more chaos to the situation, construction improvements of the unit headquarters' facility forced my headquarters and four of my companies to relocate to three separate locations throughout the Chicagoland area. To effectively lead this unit, I found several replacements for key staff, including an executive officer. I also made crucial decisions to remove non-performing leaders from the unit, especially those who didn't want to be leaders. I also spent much of my personal time reducing the informal power of the group of people who'd been abusing the system, which proved effective after nearly a year of diligence. Under my direction, the unit began to thrive successfully. When it was time to turn leadership over to my successor two years later, I was confident that the leadership and morale issues had been resolved. Even though these issues took much time and created additional challenges, I was able to accomplish the key missions of the unit, which included mobilizing several hundred Soldiers for the wartime efforts.

This was just one of the numerous leadership challenges I overcame throughout my professional career. Leaders do things and they accomplish things. They take a limited amount of resources, organize them, and use them to accomplish a finite goal[520]. This sounds easy and simple. But the details are both complex and hard. This includes the leadership skills. Fortunately early in my career, I learned about the technical skills involved in leadership, which involved what a leader does. This included establishing an organizational vision for what the organization should be in the future. A leader must accomplish work of the organization through others, which can be done through team building. Next, the leader must be willing and able to negotiate major change to accomplish the vision. Then, the leader must plan and execute the actions necessary to accomplish the required tasks involved. To ensure required information is transmitted, the leader must communicate.

But I found out the hard way that leadership involves more than just the technical skills of establishing vision, team building, managing change, planning, executing, and communicating. It involves soft skills, which is who the leader is. A good leader doesn't stop growing and developing as a person, but pursues life-long learning. This person has a good understanding of his uniqueness and capabilities. An effective leader has a high emotional intelligence, being fully aware of and knowing how to properly respond the emotions of others. Doing the right things for the right reasons is important too. The leader must possess strong

---

[520] Starry 1987, 13.

people skills and know how to relate to others. You could say that leadership is really about influencing through a relationship with others. These soft skills are necessary for persuading, motivating, developing, and managing relationships with others[521].

Leaders lacking in soft-skills face hard realities though. Their poor relational skills are usually near or at the top of every list that explains why leaders fail. There is a wide variety of reasons for this. For example, leadership arrogance overshadows soft skills, in that they tend to view their strengths, talents, and gifts as more valuable than the soft skills. Narrowness is another reason that soft-skills are difficult for leaders since they are so excited about creating plans that they can't see the people side of execution. Another reason is the blindness of leaders who don't see any lack of soft skills, especially if they don't think they need any improvements in this area. Even though there are many more, the last reason I'll mention is self-interest in that they tend to personalize their actions and words, such as honoring others as a way to honor themselves.

I also learned that some changes in the way leaders act could mitigate some of these reasons. First, the leaders should understand that people enjoy them when they enjoy the people. Followers are also drawn to sincere humility and to those who demonstrate that they understand them. Leaders shouldn't maximize their capabilities while minimizing those of others. Instead, they should be humbled by gifts and strengths of others rather than becoming irritated by them. And they should ask for information about their people's challenges. When they discuss their challenges, they should avoid offering solutions and instead inform them it was helpful to learn about those challenges.

As a caution, leaders possessing all of these good skills while avoiding the poor ones don't always make good decisions. Please believe me when I say that intelligent, responsible people with the best information and intentions sometimes make decisions that are hopelessly flawed. These bad decisions are usually affected by

---

[521] Army Civilian Study Panel 2003.

three factors that distort information: inappropriate self-interest, distorting attachments, and misleading memories. Overcoming this requires challenging the data and recognizing errors in the data[522]. We shouldn't forget that professionals built the Titanic, while an amateur built the Ark.

At the end of the day, what should we remember about a good leader? This person lives the values of the organization, has empathy towards others, has sound judgment, and has operational knowledge. They lead by example, communicate, develop others, and get results. Good leadership is essential to the success of any organization. It's nothing more than influencing others. They motivate and inspire others to work toward a common purpose to achieve an objective[523]. This person also shouldn't have to impose authority, especially by being bossy[524]. The real test of any leader are the actions of the followers.

Christian Leadership

What about leadership within the Church? Using the Bible for role models and examples of leadership, we can find some who were charismatic while others were uninspiring. Likewise, some were successful and others weren't. The following are several important biblical leaders and my brief discussion about what we could learn from each.

Jesus

I'll begin this section with the best Christian leader ever, which almost everyone should agree. Jesus served as the supreme example of good Christian leadership through servant-hood, humility, taking risks, sharing responsibilities with others, and building a team[525]. He placed the needs of others ahead of His own. He wasn't judgmental and definitely wasn't hypocritical. Like all great leaders, His leadership was challenged frequently. An

---

[522] Campbell et.al. 2009.
[523] US Army 2006, A-2 to A-3.
[524] Bradley 1981, 2. These were spoken to the staff and faculty of the US Army War College at Carlisle Barracks, Pennsylvania on October 8, 1971.
[525] See especially C. Gene Wilkes 1998.

example of this involved a mob demanding that a woman accused of adultery be stoned as required by law[526]. In my opinion, He made the right decision with the right answer and with compassion towards others[527]. Now, you're probably reading this and thinking that the adulterous woman should be punished or suffer a consequence for her lack of morality – or perhaps a social stigma. But, if we review the definition of "adulterer", we find that it's a person who has sexual relations with anyone outside a marriage union. This could define two monogamous unmarried people living together or anyone who is single and sexually active. So, now, how many adulterers do you know?

Figure 19. Flagellation of Our Lord Jesus Christ.
Flagellation de Notre Seigneur Jesus Christ (1880) by William-Adolphe Bouguereau.

---

[526] John 7:53 through 8:1-11.
[527] Greenleaf and Spears 2002, 42.

As His main message, Jesus preached about love. The greatest of these was the willingness to lay down one's life for another[528]. Jesus loved us so much that He laid down His life for us[529]. The Romans punished Him because they viewed Jesus was a subversive. The Pharisees punished Him for blasphemy and contempt of the law. His followers later understood that Jesus died for their salvation. For these reasons, Jesus was and is regarded as the greatest leader, one to be emulated by all Christian leaders[530].

Abraham

He was a transformational leader who motivated others to ignore self-interests and worked for the larger benefits of an organization[531]. He established and spread the radical belief in only one God[532]. Simply stated, he was a monotheist living in a pagan society. More importantly, Abraham demonstrated both courage and confidence by waging war on several kingdoms with only a few hundred people to rescue his nephew Lot[533]. He even loved others, including strangers, as demonstrated through his hospitality towards them. He negotiated with God to save Sodom and Gomorra from destruction if he could find a few innocent people living there[534]. While risking death for his different beliefs, Abraham succeeded in transforming the religious direction[535].

Jacob

This grandson of Abraham was a hardheaded leader[536]. He stole his father's birthright from his physically stronger brother, Esau[537]. An angel renamed him "Israel" before the birth of his youngest son,

---

[528] John 15:13.
[529] 1 John 3:16.
[530] Barrett and Johnson 2001, 230.
[531] Borek et.al. 2005, 23-33
[532] Woolfe 2002, 24.
[533] Genesis 14.
[534] Genesis 18: 20-33.
[535] Friedman 2000.
[536] Borek et. al. 2005, 34-44.
[537] Genesis 25-27.

Benjamin[538]. However, he made a mistake in naming his son, Joseph, as his successor while this son was still young and irresponsible[539]. This favoritism infuriated his brothers who publically responded that they wouldn't accept him as ruler.

Joseph

One of my favorite leaders was Joseph, so much that I took this name for my Catholic confirmation[540]. He was clearly a great decision-maker and strategic planner[541]. After his brothers sold him into slavery as a teenager, Joseph suffered as a slave for more than ten years[542]. When he had the justified chance to avenge his unfair imprisonment, he chose a better path[543]. Unlike the story of

Figure 20. Joseph Interprets Pharoah's Dream. by James Tissot (1896).

---

[538] Genesis 32: 28-29.
[539] Friedman 2001.
[540] Confirmation is one of the seven Sacraments. The other six are baptism, communion, confession, marriage, anointing the sick, and taking of holy orders. Roman Catholics going through confirmation choose a saint they feel an affinity for as their confirmation name. Although Saint Joseph refers to the husband of the Virgin Mary, I considered the eleventh son of Jacob as the source of my selection.
[541] Borek et. al. 2005, 44-45.
[542] Genesis 38-45.
[543] Friedman 2001.

The Count of Monte Cristo, Joseph wasn't interested in vengeance[544]. People who spend their time trying to get even aren't suitable as leaders, who should instead be more interested in what is best for the entire organization.

Moses

Another great leader in the Bible was Moses[545]. Born a Levite and raised an Egyptian, he didn't conform to either culture. While defending a fellow Hebrew from lethal brutal oppressive beatings, Moses killed an Egyptian[546]. Understanding the capital penalty for this act, he fled to the desert. While hiding in the desert, God called out to him through a "burning bush" to lead His people. Instead of taking the safe action of hiding, Moses accepted the call and faced almost-certain death[547]. Accordingly, he later sent ten plagues on the Pharaoh, fled a hostile country with limited food, and led thousands of people through a parted sea[548].

Joshua

He was a skilled military leader, who motivated others with effective plans. This ultimately helped his people knock down an impregnable fortress[549]. Prior to this, Moses sent a dozen people to recon the Promised Land. Most of them returned and reported that the land was occupied by strong fierce warriors living in large fortified cities. Despite these pessimistic reports, Joshua urged his people to take the land anyways, based solely upon his faith in the promises of God[550]. Through the famous battle causing the fall of Jericho, he succeeded in completing his mission of leading Abraham's descendants to dwell in the Promised Land.

---

[544] *The Count of Monte Cristo* was originally published in the *Journal des Débats* in eighteen parts from August 28, 1844 to January 15, 1846.
[545] See especially Coates 1988.
[546] Coats 1988, 49.
[547] Exodus 3:4.
[548] Exodus 6-14. The ten plagues were: blood, frogs, gnats, flies, pestilence, boils, hail, locusts, darkness, and death of the firstborn.
[549] Joshua 6:1-27.
[550] Numbers 13-14.

Saul

Although he initially possessed humility and courage, Saul failed as a leader ultimately[551]. The problem was that he was jealous and tried to kill others who were better than him, specifically his son-in-law David[552]. Leaders with an obsession of jealousy are dangerous. For example, Saul's obsession resulted in the destruction of an innocent town of priests[553]. Jealousy can easily distract the leader from his mission. Seeking revenge isn't a way to inspire followers. Instead, it sends the message that one is small-minded[554].

Figure 21. Saul Attempts to Kill David by Gustave Doré (1866).

David

I've no doubt that David was one of the greatest kings of Israel. I'm sure you know the story of his fight with Goliath, the Palestinian invincible champion. He began his leadership career as an outcast, and when he took over formal power from Saul, he chose advisors with expertise and wisdom to perform their jobs. Yet, he could have been much greater even though he was a

---

[551] Borek et. al. 2005, 133-142.
[552] Woolfe 2002, 36.
[553] 1 Samuel 22.
[554] Friedman 2001.

faithful and determined servant of God doing His will despite the cost[555]. Many have heard about the story of his affair with Bath-Sheba and the punishment he received from his transgression[556]. But, some may not have heard the story about his eldest son, Amnon, raping his half-sister Tamar[557]. Unfortunately, David failed to punish Amnon for the assault. This failure resulted in an armed rebellion against the king, ending in unnecessary loss of human lives. Leaders shouldn't ignore or cover up injustices, even if they involve someone they are close to[558].

Solomon

David's son, Solomon, became the wisest ruler of Israel, preferring wisdom over fame, fortune, and power – or so we are told[559]. Under his rule, his fame increased, his kingdom grew in prosperity, and he became powerful. He built a great Temple and an even larger palace[560]. Solomon was competent, had good character, and was a good communicator with people[561]. He even had numerous wives and concubines. Yet, Solomon's failure as a leader was that as he became older, the accumulation of fortune became more important than improving his country and his followers[562]. All of this placed an enormous tax burden upon his people. After his death, his kingdom split into two and began its downward descent. Fame, fortune and power might be byproducts of good leadership; but, it should never be the goal.

Daniel

He was a wise, faithful, and brave leader. As a young man, he was taken from his Israelite home and forced into Babylonian captivity, becoming an obedient subordinate leader[563]. While in captivity, he refused to follow the same customs and laws of his captives.

---

[555] See especially Jost 2003
[556] 2 Samuel 11-12.
[557] 2 Samuel 13.
[558] Friedman 2001.
[559] 1 Kings 3:9.
[560] 1 Kings 5-6.
[561] See especially Williams 2010.
[562] Friedman 2001.
[563] Borek et. al. 2005, 191-98.

Nevertheless, God gave Daniel insight through dreams and visions such that his answers to the King's questions were much better than all the kingdom's magicians and enchanters[564]. Although required by a royal written decree to follow the Babylonian ways, Daniel refused[565]. Because of his mortal disobedience of the king, Daniel accepted the consequence of being thrown into a den of lions to bravely face the consequence of his decision.

Figure 22. Crucifixion of St. Pete. by Masaccio (1426).

Peter

In the New Testament, we can read about Peter, the self-correcting leader. In his youth, Peter was both fearful and inconsistent. Towards the end of his life, he became more confident, displaying both conviction and compassion[566]. He was known to inspire thousands and to bring new believers into the faith. While

---

[564] Daniel 1:20.
[565] Daniel 6:4-10.
[566] Acts 2:14-4:31.

preaching to others and healing the sick, Peter became a servant leader who focused upon his followers instead of himself. While addressing the organizational challenges of the early Church, he placed the needs of others first. Although he denied Jesus several times, he eventually corrected his ways and became the rock of His church.

Martyrs

Now, let's talk about martyrs, which many claim provide other examples of good Christian leadership[567]. I don't completely support this claim. But, martyrdom does imply that following Jesus may be hazardous to one's mortal life. Let's use a generic definition of a martyr being a believer in Jesus, who later lost his life prematurely in a situation of witness as a result of human hostility[568]. Using this definition, Jesus was clearly a martyr. Yet, this generic definition doesn't require heroic sanctity because "many Christians have been killed shortly after their conversion and before they had any chance to develop Christian character, holiness, or courage"[569]. Using this generic definition, Judas was a martyr. He believed in Jesus, died prematurely involving the witness of Jesus through his own human hostility. Yet, I don't believe he was a good Christian leader. With this generic definition, Table 17 contains names of early Christian martyrs.

So, how likely is it that a Christian will be martyred? Based upon my preconceived ideas, I originally thought the probability of this was an unlikely event. That is until I did the final calculation recently. Using historical records, the estimated total number of people born since 33 CE was slightly more than 36 billion. During this same time, about 12 billion were evangelized. This is roughly about a third of every living person since Jesus died. Of that number of evangelized people, only slightly more than 8 billion became Christian, which is about a fourth of every living person. Since then, there were over 69 million martyrs. Today, we have about 160 thousand martyrs each year. Based upon these statistics,

---

[567] See especially Hassett 1910.
[568] Barrett and Johnson 2001, 234.
[569] Barrett and Johnson 2001, 229.

"one out of every 120 Christians in the past has been martyred, or in the future is likely to so be"[570]. Are you willing to be that one out of every 120 Christians? If so, you may want to view Table 18 listing the numerous methods of martyrdom and the magnitude of each. Dying in prison, being shot, and starving to death are the top three methods. Fortunately, being eaten by piranhas, run over by a tank, or thrown to crocodiles are a couple of the least likely.

Table 17. Early Christians Martyrs.

Martyr	Date (CE)	How	Where
Judas Iscarat	33	Suicide	Jerusalem
James, son of Zebedee	44	Beheaded	Jerusalem
James, son of Alphaeus	54	Stoned	Jerusalem
Philip	60	Hanged	Hierapolis, Turkey
Simon Zelotes	61	Crucified	Suanir, Iran
Barnabas	61	Stoned	Salamis, Cyprus
James, Jesus' brother	62	Stoned	Jerusalem
Matthias	64	Burned	Axum, Ethiopia
Paul, Saul of Tarsus	64	Beheaded	Rome, Italy
Simon Peter	64	Crucified	Rome, Italy
Judas Thaddeus	66	Clubbed	Ardaze, Turkey
Bartholomew	68	Crucified	Albana, Armenia
John Mark	68	Trampled	Alexandria
Andrew	69	Crucified	Patras, Greece
Matthew	70	Stabbed	Nubia, Ethiopia
Thomas	82	Speared	Mylapore, India
Timothy	90	Beheaded	Ephesus, Turkey
Luke	91	Hanged	Rome, Italy
John Boanerges	96	Boiled in Oil	Ephesus, Turkey

Source: see Barrett and Johnson 2001, 229.

---

[570] Barrett and Johnson 2001, 229.

Table 18. Methods of Christian Martyrdom.

Method	Magnitude	Method	Magnitude	Method	Magnitude
Assassinated	3	eaten alive	3	put to death	5
Annihilated	7	eaten by piranhas	2	quartered	3
attacked during sleep	4	electrocuted	4	racked to death	4
bayoneted	5	electronically killed	2	roasted alive	4
beaten to death	7	executed	4	run over by tank	2
beheaded	4	exposed to elements	6	run over by vehicle	4
bled to death	6	frightened to death	3	savaged by dogs	3
boiled in oil	2	frozen to death	6	savaged by animals	5
blown up	5	garroted	4	sawed in two	3
brainwashed to death	5	gassed	6	shedding blood	6
broken on wheel	2	gibbeted	4	shot	10
buried alive	4	guillotined	4	shot by sniper	6
burned at stake	4	hacked to death	5	slashed to death	7
buried in sand	4	hanged	5	slaughtered	7
butchered	9	hanged upside down	3	speared to death	4
cannibalized	3	hunted to death	4	stabbed to death	5
chemically killed	7	immolated	4	starved to death	10
clubbed to death	5	immured	2	stoned	3
crucified	4	impaled	4	strangled	4
crushed to death	3	injected	5	suffocated	4
cut to pieces	5	killed by contract	3	targeted in war	5
decapitated	4	killed by mob	7	terrorized to death	6
deprive of medication	6	killed extra-judicially	5	throat slit	7
died after beating	8	killed during genocide	9	thrown from aircraft	2
died prison release	6	killed with sword	9	thrown off building	3
died in custody	5	knifed	7	thrown over cliff	4
died in interrogation	4	lashed to death	4	thrown overboard	4
died in prison	10	left to die	6	thrown to crocodiles	2
died in slavery	6	liquidated	7	thrown to lions	3
died of injuries	9	lowered into sewage	4	thrown to sharks	2
died on release	7	lynched	4	tied behind vehicle	3
died under torture	6	machine-gunned	6	torched	5
disemboweled	3	massacred	8	torn apart by horses	3
dismembered	5	murdered	5	tortured to death	5
driven mad	5	mutilated to death	4	trampled to death	4
driven to suicide	3	poisoned	4	wiped out	6
drowned	6	pushed under traffic	3		
drugged to death	4	pushed under train	3		

10 – Over 10 million
9 – From 4-10 million
8 – From 2-4 million
7 – From 1-2 million
6 – From 500,000 to 1 million
5 – From 100,000 to 500,000
4 – From 10,000 to 100,000
3 – From 1,000 to 10,000
2 – From 100 to 1,000
1 – Under 100

Source: Barrett and Johnson 2001, 230.

Summary Thoughts

So, what does the Bible reveal about good Christian leadership? My favorite example is that of the parable of the *Good Samaritan*[571]. Jesus didn't yield to the religious elite, especially those involved in abusing their power. Back then, the road from Jerusalem to Jericho was both dangerous and difficult. And, the Jews and Samaritans hated each other[572]. Moreover, tensions were particularly high in the early decades of the first century because Samaritans had desecrated the Jewish Temple at Passover with human bones. In Jesus' culture, contacting a dead body resulted in becoming defiled, or unclean[573]. Priests aggressively avoided uncleanness. The priest and Levite may therefore have assumed that the fallen traveler was dead and avoided him to remain ritually clean. In this parable, Jesus showed us that man was created instead for the sake of man, inferring a mutual obligation between everybody, regardless of religious membership[574].

In the words of Calvin, "we must not live of ourselves, but for our neighbors"[575]. Is there anything else from this that we should understand? Martin Luther King, Jr. provides us these words. "We are called to play the Good Samaritan on life's roadside, but that will be only an initial act. One day we must come to see that the whole Jericho Road must be transformed so that men and women will not be constantly beaten and robbed as they make their journey on life's highway. True compassion is more than flinging a coin to a beggar"[576].

What about religious leaders today? Do they follow these biblical or historical examples? Regrettably, many don't. Besides, many religious leaders who hold power tend to advocate institutional maintenance instead of human needs. They claim that their religion wasn't the means for spiritual growth of people, but the

---

[571] Luke 10:25-37.
[572] Forbes 2000, 55-71.
[573] Vermès 2004, 153-54.
[574] Calvin 1956.
[575] 1949.
[576] 1967.

end state of that growth. On the contrary, meeting the spiritual growth of the people was the goal of Jesus. Whenever he spoke of the institutional religions, He didn't have kind words[577].

Figure 23. Parable of the Good Samaritan.
by Jan Wijnants (1670).

Let me now describe three military chaplains I worked with, each having different leadership skills. The first one, from the 34th Support Battalion at Fort Hood, Texas, was a Vietnam veteran who wore a Combat Infantryman's Badge. He eagerly provided spiritual support to Soldiers wherever they were. Although trained to fire weapons, he was forbidden to use them as a chaplain; but, that didn't prevent him from hauling and loading ammo for the Soldiers. During several trips to the field for training exercises,

---

[577] Matthew 23:25.

ones that I planned and organized as the unit's assistant operations officer, I had the pleasure of several one-on-one discussions with him. One of those discussions involved the Christian concept of forgiveness. He once told me that he too was human and found it extremely difficult to forgive one person, that person being Jane Fonda. This chaplain served as an infantryman in Vietnam and saw first-hand the spiritual damage she did to Soldiers there as a result of her seemingly innocent visit to North Vietnam. Although she may not have known any better at the time, she has since expressed remorse for her actions in July 1972. In spite of that, many people still refuse to forgive her[578]. Maybe because Ms. Fonda was still responsible for her pro-North Vietnamese, anti-American conduct, especially her pose with an anti-aircraft gun demonstrating the shooting down of American planes along with her propaganda broadcasts directed toward American troops[579]. Even good Christian leaders find it hard to continually follow Jesus in everything they do.

The second chaplain, from the 472nd Chemical Battalion, in Chicago, was a young lady with little military experience. She knew very little about how the military operated, but was willing to learn in order to help the Soldiers and their families as much as possible. When I first met her as I took over command of my battalion, she was disillusioned with the military and eagerly wanted to leave. Her previous commanders abused her emotionally and blamed her for the poor climate throughout their command, even though she had nothing to do with it. I knew better and didn't do that to her, or anyone else for that matter. I treated her with respect and took her recommendations seriously. She quickly discovered that I genuinely cared about all of my Soldiers, giving her hope that at least some military officers were good. Towards the end of my battalion command tenure, she told me something that I never forgot. When I was having difficulties motivating several of my stubborn subordinate officers, she saw my frustrations and later told me that I could use her in my motivational discussions. She suggested that during future

---

[578] Associated Press 2000 and Curran 2005.
[579] See especially Andersen 1990, and Holzer and Holzer 2002.

discussions to give her a signal. She would then pick up and throw a chair across the room. Afterwards, I would tell everyone that "you're upsetting everyone on my staff by not accomplishing your tasks that even the chaplain is upset and throwing chairs". Although I didn't get the opportunity to do it, I thought it was a good idea and grateful that she was willing to do this. Although she was a young and inexperienced leader, she was a good Christian leader.

The third chaplain, from the 464th Chemical Brigade, was a senior officer with about thirty years of military experience. This person was very knowledgeable about both the military and his Christian denomination. When I say his denomination, I mean that he was very focused upon witnessing his own narrow view of Christianity while downplaying the faith of the others. As the brigade commander, I expected my command chaplain to provide effective religious support to everyone. When I say religious support, I mean all religions, including Judaism, Muslim, and others. I had Wiccans and Atheists in my command, and had to support their needs too. I fully understood that the Bible is full of Scriptures requiring Christian evangelism; yet as a commander, I had to maintain the Government's neutrality towards religion by avoiding alienation of my Soldiers by officially supporting one religion over that of another[580]. This chaplain, though, didn't see any value in supporting the religious needs of others. In my opinion, Jesus would have supported them, based upon His parable of the *Good Samaritan*. This chaplain, a high ranking Christian leader in the military, acted like the non-neighborly leader in this parable, decreasing his effectiveness as a leader.

Conclusion.

Luckily, Jesus didn't provide us with complex insight into His message. So, why do scholars and other Christian leaders attempt to make it complicated? His message wasn't intended solely for these leaders or anyone else who attended seminary or theological training. Any leader who tells you that only they know His

---

[580] For example, see Mark 16:15-16, Matthew 28:18-20, Romans 10:10-17, and Acts 1:8.

message because of their extensive theological training is missing the point. It should be clear that Christian leaders take care of their people, expect the unexpected, live and eat with their people, plan, self-evaluate, remain flexible, and prepare successors[581]. More to the point, Christian leadership should include integrity, honesty, compassion, diplomacy, perception, common sense, and forgiveness. Serving as a Christian leader involves servant leadership, which is a radical commitment to their follower's life that requires acting in love no matter what it costs that leader[582]. The true Christian leader doesn't act like the religious leaders in the *Good Samaritan* parable. They must be compassionate and live the words of Jesus, teaching and showing others the real meaning of Christian behavior. In the wise words of Tiberius, "A good shepherd shears his sheep, he doesn't flay them"[583].

Unlike the uneducated Christian followers from centuries ago, the typical Christian today has a particularly high level of suspicion of organized religion, including an acute sensitivity to hypocrisy. Leaders who think otherwise today won't lead many. Ultimately, a member of any Christian organization should be cautious of its leaders and assess whether they truly support the teachings of Jesus. Choosing to follow a leader is one of our biggest decisions. Being wise about this selection is very important. Otherwise, we risk following a leader who would impose God upon the world through bigotry, injustice, and intolerance.

References.

Andersen, C.P. (1990). *Citizen Jane: The Turbulent Life of Jane Fonda*. New York: Henry Holt.

Army Civilian Study Panel. (2003). *The Army Training and Leader Development Panel Report – Phase IV (Civilian Study)*. Fort Leavenworth, Kansas: US Army Combined Arms Center.

Asinof, E. (1963). *Eight Men Out: The Black Sox and the 1919 World Series*. New York: Henry Holt and Company.

Associated Press. (2011, 28 September). "High Court to Review Wayne Bent Ruling."

---

[581] See especially Briner and Pritchard 1997.
[582] Matthew 20:26-27; John 13:16; Philippians 2:5-11; and 2 Corinthians 4:5.
[583] Balk 2008, 137. "Boni pastoris est tondere pecus, non deglubere".

Associated Press. (2007, 16 May). "Alleged South Korean Rape Cult Leader Arrested in China."

Associated Press. (2003, 23 January). "Christian radio host tells listeners to abandon church."

Associated Press. (2000, 20 June). "Jane Fonda Regrets N. Vietnam Photo."

Balk, A.P. (2008). *Saints & Sinners: An Account of Western Civilization.* Helsinki: Thelema Publications.

Barnes, R. (2011, 3 March). "Supreme Court rules First Amendment protects church's right to picket funerals." *Washington Post.* http://www.washingtonpost.com/wp-dyn/content/article/2011/ 03/02/ AR2011030202548.html. Accessed 30 October 2011.

Barrett, D.B. and Johnson, T.M. (2001). *World Christian Trends AD 30 – AD 2200: Interpreting the Annual Christian Megacensus.* Pasadena, Calif.: William Carey Library.

BBC. (2000a, 20 March). "Cults: Why East Africa?" *BBC News.* http://news.bbc.co.uk/2/hi/africa/683388.stm. Accessed 23 October 2011.

BBC. (2000b, 29 March). "The preacher and the prostitute." *BBC News.* http://news.bbc.co.uk / 2/hi/africa/694729.stm. Accessed 23 October 2011).

Bearak, B. (1997, 28 April). "Eyes on Glory: Pied Pipers of Heaven's Gate." *The New York Times.* http://www.nytimes.com/1997/ 04/28/us/eyes-on-glory-pied-pipers-of-heaven-s-gate.html? pagewanted=all&src=pm. Accessed 16 October 2011.

Benner, E. (2009). *Machiavelli's Ethics.* Princeton, N.J.: Princeton University Press.

Betts, R.K. (2001). "Compromised Command." A review essay of *Waging Modern War* by Wesley Clark. *Foreign Affairs.* 80(4) http://www.foreignaffairs.com/articles/57062/richard-k-betts/ compromised-command. Accessed 22 January 2012.

Borek, D.; Lovett, D.; and Towns, E. (2005). *The Good Book on Leadership: Case Studies from the Bible.* Nashville, Tenn.: Broadman & Holman Publishers.

Borzello, A. (2000, 20 March). "A Party, Prayers, Then Mass Suicide." *The Guardian.* http://www.guardian.co.uk/world/2000/mar/ 20/3. Accessed 23 October 2011.

Bradley, O.N. (1981). "On Leadership." *Parameters. Journal of the US Army War College.* 11 (September): 2-7. http://www.carlisle. army.mil/usawc/parameters/Articles/1981/ 1981%20bradley.pdf. Accessed 27 November 2011.

Bredfeldt, G. (2006). *Great Leader, Great Teacher: Recovering the Biblical Vision for Leadership.* Chicago: Moody Publishers.

Briner, B. and Pritchard, R. (1997). *The Leadership Lessons of Jesus: A Timeless Model for Today's Leaders.* Nashville, Tenn.: Broadman & Holman Publishers.

Browne, S. and Harrison, L. (2008). *End of Days: Predictions and Prophecies about the End of the World.* New York: Penguin Group.

Burchardus, J. (1921). *Pope Alexander VI and His Court: Extracts From the Latin Diary of Johannes Burchardus.* Edited by F. L. Glaser. New York: Nicholas L. Brown.

Bwire, R. (2007). *Ashes of Faith: A Doomsday Cult's Orchestration of Mass Murder in Africa.* Amsterdam: Fontier Publishing.

Callick, R. (2007, 15 May). "Asian cult leader arrested." *The Australian.* http://www.theaustralian. com.au/news/world/ asian-cult-leader-arrested/story-e6frg6so-1111113538594. Accessed 30 October 2011.

Calvin, J. (1956). *Commentary on a Harmony of Evangelists: Matthew, Mark, Luke.* Volume 3. Latin original ca 1509-64. Translated by William Pringle. Grand Rapids: William B. Eerdman Publishing Company. http://www.ccel.org/ccel/calvin/ calcom33. Accessed 26 November 2011.

Calvin, J. (1949). *Commentary Upon the Acts of the Apostles.* Volume 1. Translated by Henry Beveridge. Grand Rapids: William B. Eerdman Publishing Company. http://www.ccel.org/ccel/calvin/calcom36. Accessed 26 November 2011.

Campbell, A.; Whitehead, J.; and Finkelstein, S. (2009). "Why Good Leaders Make Bad Decisions." (February) *Harvard Business Review.*

Camping, H. (2005). *Time Has an End: A Biblical History of the World 11,013 BC – 2011 AD.* New York: Vantage Press.

Camping, H. (1970). "The Biblical Calendar of History." *Journal of the American Scientific Affiliation.* 22: 98–105. http://www.asa3.org/ASA/PSCF/1970/JASA9-70Camping.html. Accessed 23 October 2011.

Cannon, L. (1999). *Official Negligence: How Rodney King and the Riots Changed Los Angeles and the LAPD.* Bolder, Co.: Westview Press.

Chatterjee, P. (2009). *Halliburton's Army: How a Well-Connected Texas Oil Company Revolutionized the Way America Makes War.* New York: Nation Books

CNN. (1997, 27 March). "Mass Suicide Involved Sedatives, Vodka and Careful Planning." http://www.cnn.com/US/9703/27/suicide/index.html. Accessed 16 October 2011.

Coates, G.W. (1988). *Moses: Heroic Man, Man of God*. Sheffield, England: Sheffield Academic Press.

Courier Mail. (2011, 2 January). "Religious sex fiend asks psychic's aid." http://www.couriermail. com.au/news/religious-sex-fiend-asks-psychics-aid/story-e6freomx-1225980159274. Accessed 29 October 2011.

Curran, T. (2005, 23 April). "Man Spits Tobacco Juice on Jane Fonda During Book Tour." *Bangor Daily News*.

Cutbirth, J. (2010, 11 April). "Phelps' Son Says "God Hates Fags" Church Could Turn Violent." *Huffington Post*. http://www.huffingtonpost.com/joe-cutbirth/phelps-son-says-god-hates_b_533132.html. Accessed 30 October 2011.

Daraul, A. (1989). *A History of Secret Societies*. New York: Citadel Press.

Dörner, D. (1996). *The Logic of Failure: Recognizing and Avoiding Error in Complex Situations*. New York: Metropolitan Books.

Doyle, T.P.; Sipe, A.W.R.; and Wall, P.J. (2005). *Sex, Priests, and Secret Codes: The Catholic Church's 2000-Year Paper Trail of Sexual Abuse*. Santa Monica, Calif.: Volt Press.

Dumas, A. (1846). *The Count of Monte Cristo*. London: Chapman and Hall. http://www. gutenberg.org/files/1184/1184-h/1184-h.htm. Accessed 29 April 2012.

Eckholm, E. (2011, 23 November). "7 in Renegade Amish Group Charged With Assaults." *The New York Times*. http://www.nytimes.com/2011/11/24/us/7-arrested-in-hair-cutting-attacks-on-amish-in-ohio.html. Accessed 26 November 2011.

Encyclopædia Britannica. (2011). "Order of the Solar Temple." *Encyclopædia Britannica*. Encyclopædia Britannica Online.. http://www.britannica.com/ EBchecked/topic/1418448/Order-of-the-Solar-Temple. Accessed 16 October 2011.

Fantus, C. (2011, 2 October). "Christianity as a Get out of Jail Free Card." *The Scribe*. http://www.uccsscribe.com/opinion/christianity-as-a-get-out-of-jail-free-card-1.2643324. Accessed 30 October 2011.

Fladager, B. (2008, 4 August). "Press Release: Porter Convicted of Murder." Office of the District Attorney, Stanislaus County, California. http://www.stanislaus-da.org/ News/pdf2008/press-release-porter-08-04-08.pdf. Accessed 30 October 2011.

Foote, G.W. and Wheeler, J.M. (1887). "Crimes of the Popes." Chapter VII in *Crimes of Christianity*. London: Progressive Publishing Company.

Forbes, G.W. (2000). *The God of Old: The role of the Lukan parables in the purpose of Luke's Gospel*. Sheffield, England: Sheffield Academic Press.

Friedman, H.H. (2001). "Moral Leadership: Ancient Lessons for Modern Times." *Journal of College and Character*. 2 (11).

Friedman, H.H. (2000). "Abraham as a Transformational Leader." *Journal of Leadership Studies*. 7 (2): 88-95.

Galanter, M. (1999). *Cults: Faith, Healing, and Coercion*. New York: Oxford University Press.

Gambrell, J. (2009, 13 November). "Tony Alamo, Evangelist, Sentenced To 175 Years For Sex Crimes." *The Huffington Post*. http://www.huffingtonpost.com/2009/11/13/tony-alamo-evangelist-sen_n_357709.html. Accessed 29 October 2011.

Giblin, J.C. (2009). *The Rise and Fall of Senator Joe McCarthy*. New York: Clarion Books.

Gigot, F. (1910). "Joseph." *The Catholic Encyclopedia*. 8. New York: Robert Appleton Company. http://www.newadvent.org/cathen/08506a.htm. Accessed 17 June 2012.

Goldberg, B. (2003). *Arrogance: Rescuing America From The Media Elite*. New York: Warner Books.

Goleman, D.; Boyatzis, R.; and McKee, A. (2002). *Primal Leadership: Learning to Lead With Emotional Intelligence*. Boston, Mass.: Harvard Business School Press.

Greenleaf, R.K. and Spears, L.C. (2002). *Servant Leadership: A Journey Into the Nature of Legitimate Power and Greatness*. Mahwah, N.J.: Paulist Press.

Gruber, H. (1910a). "Masonry (Freemasonry)." *The Catholic Encyclopedia*. 9. New York: Robert Appleton Company. http://www.newadvent.org/cathen/ 09771a.htm. Accessed 26 October 2011.

Gruber, H. (1910b). "Illuminati." *The Catholic Encyclopedia*. 7. New York: Robert Appleton Company. http://www.newadvent.org/cathen/07661b.htm. Accessed 26 October 2011.

Guardian. (2009, 5 May). "The Home Office list of people banned from the UK: Full list of the 16 barred individuals and the government's reasons for preventing them from coming to the UK." http://www.guardian.co.uk/uk/2009/may/05/list-of-people-banned-from-uk. Accessed 30 October 2011.

Haraburda, S.S. (2007). "CBRNE Leadership Rules." *Army Chemical Review*. Winter (PB 3-07-3): 4-7. http://www.wood.army.mil/chmdsd/pdfs/2007%20Winter/Haraburda.pdf. Accessed 30 October 2011.

Hassett, M. (1910). "Martyr." *The Catholic Encyclopedia*. 9. New York: Robert Appleton Company. http://www.newadvent.org/cathen/09736b.htm. Accessed 27 November 2011.

Hayward, S.F. (1998). *Churchill on Leadership: Executive Success in the Face of Adversity*. New York: Three Rivers Press.

Herald Sun. (2007, 14 February). "Little Pebble Seduced 14-y-o, Court Told." http://www.heraldsun.com.au/news/national/little-pebble-seduced-14-y-o-court-told/story-e6frf7l6-1111112994588. Accessed 29 October 2011.

Hexham, I.; Poewe, K. (1997). "UFO Religion - Making Sense of the Heaven's Gate Suicides". *Christian Century*. 114: 439-44. http://people.ucalgary.ca/~nurelweb/papers/ irving/HGCC.html. Accessed 16 October 2011.

Hills, N.D. (1922). *Great Mean as Prophets of a New Era*. New York: Fleming H. Revell.

Holzer, H.M. and Holzer, E. (2002). *Aid and Comfort: Jane Fonda in North Vietnam*. Jefferson, N.C.: McFarland and Company.

Hylton, H. (2012, 10 February). "Jailed Polygamist Warren Jeffs Prepares His Flock for Doomsday." *Time*. http://www.time.com/time/nation/article/0,8599,2106545,00.html. Accessed 5 May 2012.

Improbable Research. (2011). "The 2011 Ig Nobel Prize." http://www.improbable.com/ig/winners/#ig2011. Accessed 23 October 2011.

Ji-sook, B. (2008, 21 February). "Cult Leader Extradicted to Korea." *Korea Times*. http://www.koreatimes.co.kr/www/news/include/print.asp ?newsIdx=19368. Accessed 30 October 2011.

Jost, L. (2003). *Leadership on the Line*. Winnipeg: Christian Press.

King, M.L. Jr. (1967). "Beyond Vietnam -- A Time to Break Silence." Speech delivered April 4 in Riverside Church, New York City. Copy available at American Rhetoric. http://www.americanrhetoric.com/speeches/mlkatimetobreaksilence.htm. Accessed 26 November 2011.

Kington, T. (2011, 25 May). "Pope Ousts 'Loose Living' Monks of Rome's Santa Croce Monastery." *The Guardian*. http://www.guardian.co.uk/world/2011/may/25/pope-ousts-loose-monks-rome. Accessed 20 August 2011.

Kirsch, J.P. (1910a). "Pope St. Hormisdas." *The Catholic Encyclopedia.* 7. New York: Robert Appleton Company. http://www.newadvent.org/ cathen/07470a.htm. Accessed 22 November 2011.

Kirsch, J.P. (1910b). "Pope John XII." *The Catholic Encyclopedia.* 8. New York: Robert Appleton Company. http://www.newadvent.org/cathen/ 08426b.htm. Accessed 22 November 2011.

Klenke, K. (1996). *Women and Leadership: A Contextual Perspective.* New York: Springer Publishing.

Kurst-Swanger, K. (2008). *Worship and Sin: An Exploration of Religion-Related Crime in the United States.* New York: Peter Lang Publishing.

Lacey, M. and Malkin, E. (2010), 12 May). "A Priest's Legacy Survives, and Divides, in Mexico." *New York Times.* http://www.nytimes.com/2010/05/13/world/americas/13maciel.html. Accessed 20 August 2011.

Lalich, J. (2004). *Bounded Choice: True Believers and Charismatic Cults.* Berkeley, Calif.: University of California Press.

Lewis, J.R. (2006). *The Order of the Solar Temple: The Temple of Death.* Burlington, Vt.: Ashgate Publishing Company.

Lewis, P.; Kuhnert, K.; and Maginnis, R. (1987, summer). "Defining Military Character." *Parameters. Journal of the US Army War College.* 17: 33-41. http://www.carlisle.army.mil/usawc/parameters/Articles/1987/1987%20lewis%20kuhnert%20maginnis.pdf. Accessed 27 November 2011.

Logan, F.D. (2002). *A History of the Church in the Middle Ages.* New York: Routledge.

Loughlin, J. (1907a). "Pope Adrian II." *The Catholic Encyclopedia.* 1. New York: Robert Appleton Company. http://www.newadvent.org/cathen/ 01156a.htm. Accessed 22 November 2011.

Loughlin, J. (1907b). "Pope Alexander VI." *The Catholic Encyclopedia.* 1. New York: Robert Appleton Company. http://www.newadvent.org/cathen/ 01289a.htm. Accessed 26 November 2011.

MacCaffrey, J. (1914). *History of the Catholic Church from the Renaissance to the French Revolution.* Dublin. http://www.gutenberg.org/cache/epub/2396/pg2396.html. Accessed 22 November 2011.

Manchester, W. (1992). *A World Lit Only by Fire: The Medieval Mind and the Renaissance: Portrait of an Age.* Boston, Mass.: Little, Brown and Company.

Mann, H. (1907). "Pope Benedict IX." *The Catholic Encyclopedia*. 2. New York: Robert Appleton Company. http://www.newadvent.org/cathen/02429a.htm. Accessed 22 November 2011.

Mann, H. (1912a). "Pope Stephen (VI) VII." *The Catholic Encyclopedia*. 14. New York: Robert Appleton Company. http://www.newadvent.org/cathen/14289d.htm. Accessed 22 November 2011.

Mann, H. (1912b). "Pope Sergius III." The Catholic Encyclopedia. Vol. 13. New York: Robert Appleton Company. http://www.newadvent.org/cathen/13729a.htm. Accessed 22 November 2011.

McFaul, J. (1910). "Ancient Order of Hibernians (in America)." *The Catholic Encyclopedia*. 7. New York: Robert Appleton Company, http://www.newadvent.org/cathen/07320a.htm. Accessed 26 October 2011.

Mizell, L.R. Jr. (1997). *Masters of Deception: The Worldwide White-Collar Crime Crisis and Ways to Protect Yourself*. New York: John Wiley & Sons.

Moeller, C. (1910). "Hospitallers of St. John of Jerusalem." *The Catholic Encyclopedia*. 7. New York: Robert Appleton Company. http://www.newadvent.org/cathen/07477a.htm. Accessed 26 October 2011.

Moeller, C. (1912). "The Knights Templars." *The Catholic Encyclopedia*. 14. New York: Robert Appleton Company, http://www.newadvent.org/ cathen/14493a.htm. Accessed 26 October 2011.

Moore, R.L. (1994). *Selling God: American Religion in the Marketplace of Culture*. New York: Oxford University Press.

Mulder, W. (1912). "Pope Urban VI." *The Catholic Encyclopedia*. 15. New York: Robert Appleton Company. http://www.newadvent.org/cathen/ 15216a.htm. Accessed 22 November 2011.

Munoz, O. (2006, 30 November). "Preacher Arrested in Alleged Murder Plot." *Washington Post*. http://www.washingtonpost.com/wp-dyn/content/ article/2006/11/30/ AR2006113001176.html. Accessed 30 October 2011.

Murphy, D.E. (2000, 24 March). "Urganda Cultists Believed Slain by Their Leaders." *L.A. Times*. http://articles.latimes.com/2000/mar/24/news/mn-12255. Accessed 23 October 2011.

Muverengwi, P. (2011). *The Faces of Hypocrisy in the Christian Church*. Bloomington, Ind.: AuthorHouse.

Nelson, C. (2000, 31 March). "Urganda Sect Death Toll at 924." *Associated Press*.

Nelson, S.; Smith, M.; and Walker, N. (2007). *Jonestown: The Life and Death of Peoples Temple*. PBS Episode. http://www.pbs.org/wgbh/ americanexperience/films/jonestown. Accessed 16 October 2011.

New York Times (1999, 1 April). "Tearful Baptist Leader Is Given 5 1/2-Year Term in Graft Case." http://www.nytimes.com/1999/04/01/us/tearful-baptist-leader-is-given-5-1-2-year-term-in-graft-case.html?ref=henryjlyons. Accessed 30 October 2011.

New Zealand Herald. (2011 9 September). "Paedophile politician released." http://www.nzherald.co.nz/nz/news/article.cfm?c_id=1&objectid=10750558. Accessed 29 October 2011.

New Zealand Herald. (2005, 14 July). "Capill sentenced to nine years for child sex crimes." http://www.nzherald.co.nz/nz/news/article.cfm?c_id=1&objectid=10335782. Accessed 29 October 2011.

Office of the Inspector General. (1993). *The Tailhook Report: The Official Inquiry into the Events of Tailhook '91*. New York: St. Martin's Press.

Oestereich, T. (1907). "Boniface VII (Antipope)." *The Catholic Encyclopedia*. 2. New York: Robert Appleton Company. http://www.newadvent.org/ cathen/02661c.htm. Accessed 22 November 2011.

Oltean, D. (2011, 24 October). "Harold Camping is World's Worst Prophet." *Central Michigan Life*. http://www.cm-life.com/2011/10/24/column-harold-camping-the-worlds-worst-prophet. Accessed 29 October 2011.

Ott, M. (1910). "Pope Julius II." *The Catholic Encyclopedia*. 8. New York: Robert Appleton Company. http://www.newadvent.org/cathen/ 08562a.htm. Accessed 22 November 2011.

Quarles, C.L. (2004). *Christian Identity: The Aryan American Bloodline Religion*. Jefferson, N.C.: McFarland.

Quarles, C.L. (1999). *The Ku Klux Klan and Related American Racialist and Antisemitic Organizations: A History and Analysis*. Jefferson, N.C.: McFarland.

Pape, J.M. (2009). "Reassessing Army Leadership in the 21st Century." *Military Review*. 95-102 (January-February).

Patterson, K.; Grenny, J.; Maxfield, D.; McMillan, R.; and Switzler, A. (2008). *Influencer: The Power to Change Anything*. New York: McGraw-Hill.

Phillips, D.T. (1998). *Martin Luther King, Jr., on Leadership: Inspiration & Wisdom for Challenging Times.* New York: Warner Books.

Polelle, M.R. (2008). *Leadership: Fifty Great Leaders and the Worlds They Made.* Westport, Ct.: Greenwood Press.

Ratzinger, J. (Pope Benedict XVI). (1983). "Declaration on Masonic Associations." Vatican XXX. Congregation for the Doctrine of the Faith. http://www.vatican.va/roman_curia/congregations/cfaith/documents/rc_con_cfaith_doc_19831126_declaration-masonic_en.html. Accessed 29 October 2011.

Record, J. (2005, winter). "Why the Strong Lose." *Parameters. Journal of the US Army War College.* 35: 16-31. http://www.carlisle.army.mil/usawc/parameters/Articles/05winter/record.pdf. Accessed 27 November 2011.

Rees, J.C. (2011). *George Washington's Leadership Lessons: What the Father of Our Country Can Teach Us about Effective Leadership and Character.* Hoboken, N.J.: John Wiley & Sons.

Reimink, T. (2011, 4 October). "Harold Camping says Judgment Day will occur Oct. 21 (for real this time)." *The Grand Rapids Press.* http://www.mlive.com/news/index.ssf/2011/10/harold_camping_says_judgment_d.html. Accessed 23 October 2011.

Rey, A.R. (2011, 21 May). "Critical Harold Camping Facts." *The Christian Post.* http://www. christianpost.com/news/who-is-harold-camping-anyway-50368/ Accessed 23 October 2011.

Riding, A. (2011, 7 October). "The Jonestown Massacre Revisited." *The New York Times.*

Salembier, L. (1912). "Western Schism." *The Catholic Encyclopedia.* 13. New York: Robert Appleton Company. http://www.newadvent.org/cathen/ 13539a.htm. Accessed 22 November 2011.

Santucci, J. (2000). *The Movement for the Restoration of the Ten Commandments of God.* Department of Comparative Religion, California State University, Fullerton. http://faculty.fullerton.edu/jsantucci/M.R.T.C._Overview.pdf. Accessed 16 October 2011.

Scheeres, J. (2011). *A Thousand Lives: The Untold Story of Hope, Deception, and Survival at Jonestown.* New York: Free Press.

Shahan, T. (1908). "Pope Clement V." *The Catholic Encyclopedia.* 4. New York: Robert Appleton Company. http://www.newadvent.org/cathen/ 04020a.htm. Accessed 22 November 2011.

Sheeran, T.J. and Seewer, J. (2011, 24 November). "Amish Beard Cutting Arrests: FBI Detains Sam Mullet And Six Others Following Attacks." *Associated Press.* http://hosted.ap.org/

dynamic/stories/U/US_AMISH_ATTACKS?SITE=AZSUN&SECTION=HOME&TEMPLATE=DEFAULT. Accessed 26 November 2011.

Smith, J.E. (2012). *Eisenhower in War and Peace*. New York: Random House.

Snowden, D.J. and Boone, M.E. (2007). "A Leader's Framework for Decision Making." *Harvard Business Review*.

Sorley, L. (1989, March). "Doing What's Right: Shaping the Army's Professional Environment." *Parameters. Journal of the US Army War College.* 19: 11-15. http://www.carlisle.army.mil/usawc/parameters/Articles/1989/1989%20sorley.pdf. Accessed 27 November 2011.

Spong, J.S. (2005). *The Sins of Scripture: Exposing the Bible's Texts of Hate to Reveal the God of Love*. New York: Harper Collins Publishing.

Starry, D.A. (1987, September). "Running Things." *Parameters. Journal of the US Army War College.* 16: 13-20. http://www.carlisle.army.mil/usawc/parameters/Articles/1987/1987%20starry.pdf. Accessed 27 November 2011.

Stevens, J. (2011, 22 October). "Doomsday Prophet Remains in Hiding." *The Daily Mail*. http://www.dailymail.co.uk/news/article-2052114/You-come-Harold-Doomsday-prophet-remains-hiding-world-survives-Rapture--AGAIN.html. Accessed 23 October 2011.

Stevenson, M. (2012, December 12). "End of the World 2012? Not Just Yet." *Huffington Post*. http://www.huffingtonpost.com/2012/12/21/end-of-the-world-2012_n_2344389.html?ir=World. Accessed 22 December 2012.

Trujillo, A. (2009, 7 April). "'Lap-Dancing Nun' Performs for Church." *BBC World Service*. http://news.bbc.co.uk/2/hi/europe/7988322.stm. Accessed 20 August 2011.

Turner, M.P. (2011, 21 May). "The Harm that 'Judgment Day' Will Do." *Washington Post*. http://www.washingtonpost.com/blogs/guest-voices/post/may-21-2011-the-harm-that-judgment-day-will-do/2011/05/16/AFdYwp4G_blog.html. Accessed 23 October 2011.

Ulmer, W.F. Jr. (2012). "Toxic Leadership: What Are We Talking About?" *Army*. 62 (6): 47-52. http://www.ausa.org/publications/armymagazine/archive/2012/06/Documents/Ulmer_0612.pdf. Accessed 15 June 2012.

US Army. (2007). *Army Leadership*. Army Regulation 600-100. Washington, D.C.: Government Printing Office.

US Army. (2006). *Army Leadership: Competent, Confident, and Agile.* Field Manual 6-22. Washington, D.C.: Government Printing Office.

US House Committee on Armed Services. (1992). *Women in the Military: The Tailhook Affair and the Problem of Sexual Harassment.* Washington, D.C.: US Government Printing Office.

Vermès, G. (2004). *The Authentic Gospel of Jesus.* London: Penguin Books.

Vermès, G. (1981). *Jesus the Jew: a Historian's Reading of the Gospels.* Philadelphia, Penn.: Fortress Press.

Wagner, D. (2011, 9 August). "Polygamist sect leader Warren Jeffs gets life in prison." *USA Today.* http://www.usatoday.com/news/religion/2011-08-09-polygamist-sect-leader-warren-jeffs-life-sentence_n.htm. Accessed 29 October 2011.

Webber, G. (2008). *A Wolf among the Sheep.* Montreal: KeyStone Press.

Weber, N. (1910). "Pope Innocent VIII." *The Catholic Encyclopedia.* 8. New York: Robert Appleton Company. http://www.newadvent.org/cathen/ 08019b.htm. Accessed 22 November 2011.

Weigley, R.F. (1981). *Eisenhower's Lieutenants: The Campaign of France and Germany, 1944–1945.* Bloomington: Indiana University Press.

Wheat, C.E. (1942). "Cadet Prayer History." *Assembly.* Newburgh, N.Y.: Published for the Association of Graduates, United States Military Academy by the West Point Alumni Foundation, Inc., 1(3): 8-9. http://digital-library.usma.edu/libmedia/ archives/assembly/vol1no3.pdf. Accessed 27 November 2011.

Wilgoren, J. (2005, 7 April). "40-Year Term for Supremacist in Plot on Judge." *The New York Times.* http://www.nytimes.com/2005/04/07/national/07hale.html?ref=matthewfhale. Accessed 29 October 2011.

Wilkes, C.G. (1998). *Jesus on Leadership.* Carol Stream, Ill.: Tyndale House Publishers.

Wilkes, D.E. Jr. (2001, 31 October). "The Cadaver Synod: Strangest Trial in History." *Flagpole Magazine.* http://www.law.uga.edu/dwilkes_more/his31_cadaver.html. Accessed 22 November 2011.

Williams, F. J.; Pederson, W.D.; and Marsala, V.J. (1994). *Abraham Lincoln – Sources and Style of Leadership.* Westport, Ct.: Greenwood Press.

Williams, P. (2010). *The Leadership Wisdom of Solomon: 28 Essential Strategies for Leading With Integrity*. Cincinnati, Oh.: Standard Publishing.

Williams, P. (2004). *How to Be Like Walt: Capturing the Disney Magic Every Day of Your Life.* Deerfield Beach, Fl.: Health Communications.

Woolfe, L. (2002). *The Bible on Leadership: From Moses to Matthew: Management Lessons for Contemporary Leaders*. New York: American Management Association.

Wukovits, J. and Clark, W.K. (2006). *Eisenhower: Lessons in Leadership*. New York: Palgrave MacMillan.

Chapter 6. Many Christians Also Defy Jesus

Many believe they are members of God's only church and that all others are Heathens, even though these Heathens worship Jesus and are obedient to God. Basically, these Christians serve God but fail to love His people. Other problems with Christians include hypocrisy, bigotry, materialism, and persecution of others. They prefer to judge others, instead of accepting, loving, and supporting them. They like to tell other people how to behave and act as if they never do anything wrong. Instead, their focus should be on their relationship with Jesus, not on just following a bunch of "rules".

From early on we're conditioned to belong to groups. We're bombarded by information to join groups, organizations, alliances, committees, clubs, unions. You name it. Today it's all about Social-media, and belonging. It makes us feel better to "belong" to various groups. Just like most people, I'm a member of numerous groups too, as shown in Table 19. But, why do we join? The primary reason is for self-fulfillment or individual satisfaction. This includes companionship with others, survival and security as a large group, affiliation and of status being a member, power through leadership roles, and achievement gained from being in a group that accomplishes things.

Once in a group, we hold a position, or multiple positions, with roles and responsibilities. For example, in my family I perform the duties of different positions, including being a husband, father, son, brother, and uncle. As in most families, I sometimes don't do a good job in one or more of these roles. But, I honestly try to do the best I can in each of them. In one of my professional organizations, I served in a variety of different positions, serving at the local, state, and national levels[584]. In my business groups, these were my job positions, with both formal and informal duties. As you can see from Table 19, I've not listed any of my memberships in several Christian congregations and parishes. Yet, I held positions of member, Sunday school teacher, and even superintendent of religious education. Today, I prefer to say I'm a Christian, being a member of God's universal church as a whole, while attending worship "where and when" I desire. If someone wants to know my religious opinion, they have to ask for it; otherwise, I'll keep it to myself. I'll definitely not force my opinions down someone's throat, like some Bible-thumping Holier-than-thou religious zealots I know. I prefer to witness through my actions and deeds instead.

Joining gives us the sense of belonging to something. There's nothing wrong with that, except that group-think saturates us. We lose our ability of individual thinking and decision making relative to areas of our lives, and it can hamper our ability of reason and rationale relative to independent thinking. As the old saying goes, "we can't see the forest for the trees". Described in George Orwell's *Nineteen Eighty Four,* group-think, which includes double-speak and double-talk, influences group membership. Before I begin my discussion into this interesting area, which will include examples, I'll start with the behaviors and dynamics involved with groups. Then, I'll finish by addressing Christian members.

Group Behavior

People have behaviors, and so do groups. It's this behavior that defines how the group operates and thinks. Being a member of a group, people exhibit the behaviors of that group. Individually, the members develop common attitudes, values, and beliefs, all of

---

[584] As a member in the National Society of Professional Engineers, I was the vice president of the local chapter for several years. At the state level, I was the chair of the awards committee. At the national level, I was one of a few vice-chairs of the Professional Engineers in Government special interest group, along with being a member of the Licensure and Qualifications for Practice Committee.

which contribute to group cohesion[585]. Usually, it's these similarities that attract individuals to the group in the first place[586]. However, if a member of the group has incompatible attitudes, values, and beliefs, the group will aggressively attempt to alter this incompatibility, even if with only partial success[587].

Table 19. List of My Group Memberships

Group Type	Membership
Family	Haraburda households.
Alumni	Creston High School. Grand Rapids Junior College. Central Michigan University. Michigan State University. Defense Acquisition University. Several military War Colleges.
Military	Association of the United States Army. Reserve Officers Association. United States Army.
Veteran	American Legion. Veterans of Foreign Wars.
Professional	American Institute of Chemical Engineers. American Institute of Aeronautics and Astronautics. American Society for Quality. National Society of Professional Engineers.
Business	Business companies. Military organizations. Owen County Chamber of Commerce.
Athletic	United States Judo Association.
Volunteer	Terre Haute Children's Museum Board of Directors. Malcolm Baldrige National Quality Award Examiner. Friends of McCormick Creek's State Park.

The behavior of the group is defined by its culture, with established expectations. Each group has a way of maintaining and regulating its environment, resulting in predictable and expected actions. These groups provide its members expectations of likes and

---

[585] Hollander and Hunt 1963, 295-311.
[586] Johns. et al 1984, 33.
[587] Henderson 1985, 75.

dislikes, along with skills and weaknesses[588]. In good news about becoming more mature in their faith, Americans are moving from individual spirituality to collective spiritual activism. However in a recent study, the percentage of adult Americans identifying themselves as Christians has decreased more than ten percent over the last couple of decades[589]. Furthermore, the group influences members' judgment, behaviors, and decisions to accept only their information as the truth. And, the members are influenced to conform to the group's expectations[590]. All of which inhibits the faith maturity levels of its members.

There are several different ways to look at the maturity level of an individual, which can be used to assess the maturity of a religious group too. Considering historical theories, we can start with the simple three developmental stages proposed by psychologist Gordon Allport in 1950, ranging from raw credibility through satisfying rationalism to religious maturity. He believed that a person could become more mature, emotionally, socially, intellectually, and spiritually throughout life. But, I prefer the more recent model that developmental psychologist James Fowler proposed in 1981. His involved seven distinct progressive stages: primal, intuitive-projective, mythic-literal, synthetic-conventional, individuative-reflective, conjuctive, and universalizing faith. This ranged from early learning about life, through different understandings of faith, to the ultimate stage of enlightenment with a comprehensive understanding of everything in the universe[591]. Most Christian groups do not allow an individual to progress past the synthetic-conventional faith to a more mature level. Thus, I don't believe many, if any, Christian groups have matured past this group level either. In other words, these groups refuse to become mature in their faith.

What's more, ethics is usually an important element of being a member. As such, lying about your activities in a group isn't

---

[588] Brown 2011, 22.
[589] van Wormer and Besthorn 2011, 319-20.
[590] Witte 1996, 254.
[591] Parker 2006.

acceptable. A recent example of a former Soldier comes to mind, which outraged most current and former Soldiers. On the television series *America's Got Talent*, Timothy Michael Poe informed the public that a rocket-propelled grenade hit him in the head while serving as an infantryman in Afghanistan. It was a very emotional story; yet, it was a complete fabrication. He intentionally lied to the public to improve his financial earnings by attempting to explain his audible stutter. Although he served in Afghanistan, he was a truck driver and not an infantryman. As for his injuries, he fell from a truck and wasn't hit in the head with a grenade. Also, the photos he used to support his story on television were of a different Soldier[592].

Group Dynamics

Cohesion is the interaction of group members in such a way as to sustain their commitment to each other, their group, and their goals. This cohesion doesn't always contribute to effectiveness; therefore, the group's commitment is important. Furthermore, the individuals must subordinate their personal welfare, including life if necessary, to that of their group[593]. Adding to this cohesion is the worldwide spread of modern communications networks, cell phones, television, and the internet, which provides a global means to communicate information quickly[594]. Also, teamwork is a dynamic process with people sharing common goals and working together towards a common goal. This should be accomplished through interactive collaboration, open communication and shared decision-making[595].

In Golding's *Lord of the Flies,* we have a fictional story about a group of British boys stranded on an uninhabited island who try to govern themselves, sometimes with disastrous results[596]. Although fictional, this story reflected real dynamics in a group. This story describes the tension between groupthink and individuality,

---

[592] See especially Daly and Kaplan, 2012, and Wong 2012.
[593] Johns. et al 1984, 4 and Henderson 1985, 3-4.
[594] Brown 2011, 22.
[595] See especially Xyrichis and Ream 2008.
[596] 1954.

between rational and emotional reactions, and between morality and immorality. From a Christian perspective, we can easily see that one of the characters, Simon, represented the teachings of Jesus. This person exhibited peace, tranquility and positive teamwork. However, some of the other boys saw this as a threat to their power. As a result, they had him brutally murdered. Although many of the other boys didn't support this murder, they went along because of the group. Why do people do this?

In the 1950s, Solomon Asch, Swarthmore College professor of psychology, conducted several experiments involving conformity within a group of people[597]. He measured whether people would modify their decisions based on the majority opinion. Many of the test subjects changed their individual assessment to the erroneous majority. The reasons for their changes were belief that either the majority was correct, the individual doubting their assessment, or they were willing to be wrong in order to conform to the group. In fact, we might call this last reason as being civilized, with people living by the rules peacefully and in harmony.

The last concept I want to touch upon regarding this topic is group narcissism. This is similar to individual narcissism involving an unrealistic belief in one's greatness[598]. The group version is a collective belief for the group. Table 20 provides several examples comparing individual to collective narcissistic thinking. Many groups, unfortunately, behave narcissistically and are unwilling to listen to anyone with contradictory messages.

Group Membership Process – Boot Camp Story.

Becoming a member of a group isn't always an easy process. In college, students join fraternities and sororities through a formal process by Rushing to become familiar with the group, receiving a Bid or invitation from the group to join them, and participating in

---

[597] This great scientist was born in Poland and lived there as a child in the early twentieth century. He studied the effects of propaganda at the beginning of the Second World War and fully understood the effects of the propaganda being used by the Third Reich during the war on its public.

[598] See especially de Zavala et. al. 2009.

recruitment activities. A similar process is used for joining any type of group, such as military, athletic, religious and professional organizations. However, problems normally encountered involve abusive, degrading, and often deadly hazing of potential new members. Fortunately, I've never encountered this. Yet, entry into a group is often rigorous to ensure that the right people with the right skills and attitude are allowed in. I'm a member of one of the largest groups in the world, the US Army, which is considered the best and most powerful army in history.

Table 20. Individual vs Collective Narcissistic Thinking

Individual	Collective
I'm extraordinary.	My group is extraordinary.
I'm more attractive than others.	My group is more attractive.
I rarely fail.	My group rarely fails.
I influence others.	My group influences others.
People don't listen to me.	People don't listen to my group.

Source: de Zavala et.al. 2009.

To me, the US Army is the best army (group) based upon my understanding of history. This includes the Egyptian army of the thirteen century BCE, which fought and won battles with other countries in the region[599]. The Persian army in the fifth century BCE conquered southern Asia[600]. The Macedonia army conquered them in the fourth century BCE under the leadership of Alexander the Great[601]. The Roman army controlled Europe, northern Africa, and parts of southwest Asia in the early centuries of BCE and CE[602]. The Huns under the leadership of Attila forced the Roman Empire to fall in the fifth century CE[603]. The Arab army controlled much of Europe, Africa, and southern Asia in the eighth century[604]. The Mongolian army under the leadership of Genghis Khan and his grandson Kublai controlled the largest empire in world history at

---

[599] See especially Hasel 1998.
[600] See especially Sekunda 1992.
[601] See especially Cawthorne 2004.
[602] See especially Keppie 1998.
[603] See especially Kelly 2009.
[604] See especially Wickham 2005.

the time in the thirteen century[605]. The British army (and navy) controlled all of the world's oceans in the eighteenth century[606]. In the 1930s and 1940s, the Third Reich German army challenged all of the world's armies at the time. Next, the Soviet armies had a large military power that eventually lost the Cold War to the United States[607]. Finally today, the US Army has troops scattered throughout the world and provides humanitarian assistance in additional to regional security. My army in 1991, identified as the second largest in the world at the time, entered Iraq, which was protected by the world's fourth largest army. After about four days, the Iraqi army lost. With this now said, the following is my brief story of being admitted as a member of this US Army group over thirty years ago.

In June 1981, just a couple of weeks following my graduation from high school, I boarded a Greyhound bus in Grand Rapids, Michigan, taking me to the military welcome center in Detroit. I was now on my way to become a Soldier, being both scared and excited about the upcoming adventure. If my father and grandfather could survive Army basic training, so could I. My final destination that summer was Fort Jackson, South Carolina.

I arrived at the post a few minutes before midnight. After another couple of hours of in-processing at the reception station, I went to bed a few minutes. Unfortunately, my platoon was awaken at four, providing this sleepy Soldier less than an hour of sleep. I quickly realized that I wasn't going to have time to rest anytime soon. During my first few days, I spent several days receiving several painful shots and filling out numerous bureaucratic paperwork. I was measured for uniforms and obtained the first taste of what it was like to accept orders. I also became very acquainted with fireguard duty and Charge of Quarters (CQ) duties, both of which interrupted Soldiers' sleep each night for at least an hour, making our six hours of sleep really about five hours. Quickly, my connection to the civilian world was severed, which was made very

---

[605] See especially Turnbull 2003.
[606] See especially James 1994.
[607] See especially Bartov 1992.

clear when my civilian clothes were locked in a closet, not to be seen until graduation two months later. Also, the drill sergeants often shouted, "Hurry up! We don't have all day, boys and girls! Fall in!" making the magnitude of being a Soldier finally registering for the first time. Nevertheless, during these first few days, I was bored. I wasn't learning anything hard yet. Like many of the other basic training recruits who were also away from home for the first time, my homesickness hit me like a lightning bolt. However, that didn't stop the sergeants from calling us recruits "Rocks" for appearing incapable of following simple instructions.

Unexpectedly, I noticed something different that my father didn't experience – female Soldiers. They ate in the same mess hall, wore the same uniforms and received the same training; and, it wasn't difficult for me and the other male Soldiers from realizing that they were women. Based upon reading historical books and watching "war" movies, I grew up learning that women in uniform was a concept that was difficult for American society to accept, especially during the 1940s. Back then, women's jobs were those of hostess, librarians, clerks, cooks, waitresses, chauffeurs, and messengers"[608]. In 1978, the Army dissolved the Women's Army Corps (WAC) to allow them to serve in the Army without restrictions on their service, without special privileges, and without obstacles to advancement[609]. Because the Army changed, I learned

---

[608] Bellafaire 2005. *"Traditional restrictions on female employment in American society were broken during World War II by the critical labor shortage faced by all sectors of the economy. As "Rosie the Riveter" demonstrated her capabilities in previously male-dominated civilian industries, women in the Army broke the stereotypes which restricted them, moving into positions well outside of traditional roles. Overcoming slander and conservative reaction by many Americans, a phenomenon shared by their British and Canadian sisters in uniform, American women persisted in their service and significantly contributed to the war effort. The 1943 transition from auxiliary status to the Women's Army Corps was de facto recognition of their valuable service. The Women's Army Corps was successful because its mission, to aid the United States in time of war, was part of a larger national effort that required selfless sacrifice from all Americans. The war effort initiated vast economic and social changes, and indelibly altered the role of women in American society."*
[609] Morden 1990. The author, Colonel Morden enlisted in the Women's Army Auxiliary Corps from Michigan on 15 October 1942 and served throughout

to be a Soldier with women in the same barracks, taking the same classes, which was a huge distraction at the time.

I completed my in-processing, including getting my first military "buzz cut" haircut, which lasted about one minute in the barber chair. It was a shocking experience to watch the guys with long hair making the adjustment to military life. One of them even walked in and spoke to the Army barber as if he was talking to a hairdresser. "I like it long in the front with bangs touching the eyebrows and short on the sides covering the ears". No matter what we said, the barber ensured that only a thin film of fuzz remained on the top of our heads. I couldn't believe my hair was gone. All of it. For the next several weeks, I was constantly feeling the fuzz with the palm of my hands. In fact, every male Soldier couldn't resist this strange feeling on their palms and continued feeling their hair for days. Still, we were all totally unprepared for what awaited us the next day.

The following morning, I experienced transportation on a "cattle car", which was really a tractor-trailer used to transport troops around the post. Inside this car, about fifty Soldiers were crammed in, making it even hotter that blistering summer day. After about an hour in this painful "cattle car", we pulled up in front of Company A, 3rd Battalion, 1st Basic Combat Training Brigade. This company, called "Alpha Three One" (A-3-1), was located at the base of "Tank Hill", a popular site for running up and down a hill during the morning physical training (PT). I wore my white tee-shirt, olive drab pants, and black combat boots for PT each

---

World War II. She was discharged from the Army in November 1945, she entered Columbia University, completed her baccalaureate degree in 1949 and her masters degree in June 1950. Thereafter, she was commissioned as a second lieutenant in the United States Army Reserve in 1950, she reentered active duty as a first lieutenant in May 1952. She retired on 31 December 1972 and was recalled on active duty to write the WAC history in February 1974. She reverted to retired status on 31 December 1982. *"During its thirty-six years, the WAC was the means of entry for women into the rank and file of the Army. It created a tradition of dedicated service, high standards, and loyal teamwork in every command. Its directors, officers, NCOs, and enlisted women had a spirit of mutual esteem, cooperation, and affection for each other that grew as the Corps did, and, as long as they and their successors live, that spirit will be preserved."*

morning, which was the last year that Soldiers ran in combat boots for training[610].

Figure 24. Me and My Drill Sergeant.
Photo taken at USO club near Fort Jackson (August 1981)[611].

Immediately upon arrival, I met my two tough-acting drill sergeants, Staff Sergeants Weiss and Morris. They introduced themselves as the hardest sergeants on the base, assigned to us because we were the worst Soldiers there. I assumed they found

---

[610] Committee on Defense Women's Health Research 1995; Anderson, J.H. 1997; and Jones et.al. 1988.
[611] This USO club used to be on the corner of Laurel and Park in Columbia, South Carolina. The club relocated to the airport where it serves all military families flying through the area.

out that they were a wild group of Soldiers at the reception station, having nightly pillow fights and shaving cream fights. I was now a member of the second platoon. The female Soldiers were in the third platoon, sleeping on the same floor as me, with a wooden barrier in the hallway separating us.

During the next couple of months, I learned Drill and Ceremony (D&C). This started with stationary movements for a few days, such as "attention", "left face", "right face", and "about face". This was very tedious, with repetition throughout the entire day. Those recruits who had problems knowing the difference between left and right were required to hold a rock in their left hand so that they understood that "left" meant the side that the rock was on. Because it was very hot and humid that summer, with temperatures approaching 100° F every day, many Soldiers were passing out. I came very close a few weeks later when we were marching to the rifle ranges. For the entire summer, there was no transportation to the ranges; so, we continued practicing our D&C skills by marching everywhere throughout the summer.

After the drill sergeants were satisfied with our progress, they began teaching non-stationary techniques such as "forward march", column left march", "column right march", and "counter-column march". To ensure that we kept in step, military cadences were called, such as "left", "left", "left right", and so on with the foot hitting the ground when the word was mentioned. Then, they introduced us to more advanced cadences with more than just two words, which were somewhat musical. These were fondly called "Jodies", named in honor of a mythical civilian named "Jody," whose luxurious lifestyle involved remaining at home instead of joining the military. Jody also lacked the desirable attributes of military men, being neither brave nor squared-away; but, he'd take advantage of our absence by staying at home, driving our car, and making love to our sweetheart. An example was the following:

> *Ain't no use in going home*
> *Jody's got your girl and gone*

Ain't no use in lookin' back
Jody's got your Cadillac

Ain't no use in feeling blue
Jody's got your sister too

Besides long hours of military instruction, we learned important Army knowledge, such as military customs and courtesies. We learned about the differences between commissioned and non-commissioned officers, along with the differences in addressing each. Many hours were spent perfecting our hand salute. Also, we memorized the three General Orders (for Sentries). I can still recite them today, more than three decades later, living the intent of each beyond that of guard duty – respectively never quitting, doing my best, and communicating effectively with others.

1. *I will guard everything within the limits of my post and quit my post only when properly relieved.*

2. *I will obey my special orders and perform all my duties in a military manner.*

3. *I will report violations of my special orders, emergencies, and anything not covered in my instructions to the commander of the relief.*

One day that first week of training, one of our drill sergeants directed us to meet him in the training field for "Police Call". My grandfather was a military policeman when he served during World War II; so, I mistakenly thought that this had something to do with law enforcement. And, I was wrong! Instead, we were instructed on how to "Police the Ground", which meant to pick up anything that wasn't grass and put it in our hands or pockets as we crossed the field in a line from one side to the other. So, every day, it meant getting my hands dirty by primarily picking up cigarette butts, even though I didn't smoke. Back then, smoking was encouraged, especially when the drill sergeants regularly yelled out the smoking command throughout the day during breaks. "Smoke 'em if you got 'em". It wasn't until 1997 when smoking was prohibited in Federal buildings, including Army buildings[612]. No one can really appreciate a "Police Call" until they have actually served in the military.

Another new military duty that I learned was spending an entire day performing Kitchen Police (KP) duties, which included all tedious chores in the mess hall, such as washing the dishes, scrubbing the pots, sweeping & mopping floors, wiping down tables, and serving food on the chow line. KP duty was very tedious and it didn't relieve me from my training since I did this all day long from before until after the regular mess hall hours, in addition to dealing with the large volumes of unpleasant food wastes. Yuk! Today's Soldiers don't have the opportunity to experience this KP duty since the mess halls, now called dining facilities, are operated by civilian contractors, leaving the Soldiers more time for their Soldier duties.

Communications between female and male Soldiers was highly discouraged. The drill sergeants frequently informed everyone that anyone caught talking with each other will be punished. But, these threats didn't prevent us from communicating with each other. We became very proficient at passing handwritten messages while returning mess hall dishes after each meal. We even wrote letters via US Mail, not realizing that our drill instructors read the return addresses before handing our mail to us – they knew we were communicating with each other. While avoiding additional duties Sunday mornings, we attended all religious activities at the Chapel, which included both the Catholic and Protestant services along with Sunday School. Here, I noticed many male and female Soldiers holding hands and talking in the Chapel. The chaplain, excited by the large turnouts for services, didn't inform the sergeants of the romantic activities in the Chapel each Sunday.

Unbeknownst to me, I was participating in a social experiment at Fort Jackson that summer. In 1977, an initial Basic Training test

---

[612] Rutter, 1997. *"The president of the United States, Bill Clinton, has declared a ban on smoking in all federal buildings, but he has backtracked on his plan to prohibit smoking around building entrances and courtyards."*

demonstrated that both men and women could effectively be trained together. As a result, the Army converted the basic training at both Forts McClellan and Jackson to integrate women into the basic training programs with men down to company level[613]. However, in 1982, the gender-integrated training companies were abandoned when reports were received that male performance was declining[614].

While learning Basic Rifle Marksmanship (BRM) training, we marched several days between three and five miles each way to the weapons ranges. I later qualified as a Sharpshooter, hitting 25 of the 40 pop-up targets. Around this time, I was promoted to squad leader. I guess that I failed at avoiding being noticed by my drill sergeants. I held this position for two and half weeks, with the responsibilities for cleaning the latrines every day. Through daily inspections of the latrines, I became proficient in effectively cleaning the showers and toilets, doing it very quickly too. To this day, I really hate cleaning the bathroom.

After the fifth week of training, I received a 12-hour pass for the weekend. Just before I departed the post for some savory greasy pizza, I was promoted to the platoon guide, the person who was in charge of the platoon in the absence of the platoon sergeants. This platoon guide was also responsible for marching the platoon from one place to another. Even though I tried to keep a low profile, I still impressed the drill sergeants with my ability to quickly learn the military skills, passing the periodic tests with better results than the other recruits. So, with no extra pay or benefits, I now had

---

[613] Chapman et al. 1998.
[614] Center for Military Readiness, 2003. In 1997 an independent Defense Department commission headed by former Kansas Senator Nancy Kassebaum Baker, recommended unanimously that co-ed basic training be ended because it was "resulting in less discipline, less unit cohesion, and more distraction from training programs." On the request of Rep. Duncan Hunter (R-CA), and Rep. Roscoe Bartlett (R-MD), the Center for Military Readiness compiled a comprehensive Summary of Relevant Findings and Recommendations. Rep. Bartlett subsequently placed the summary in the Congressional Record on June 11, 2003. (pp. E1223 – E1226)

more responsibilities and more duties, giving me less time for personal stuff, such as sleeping.

The next week involved bivouac training, or living in tents in the field. My company marched to the field in the middle of August. However, we quickly returned back to our barracks the next day because Hurricane Dennis, the second most destructive storm that year was pounding the Carolinas[615]. After the hurricane departed, we returned to the field. I qualified on hand grenades and received field training. The following week, we received training in defensive operations and on several other individual weapons: grenade launcher, light anti-tank weapon, and claymore mine. Afterwards, I received another 12-hour pass. This time, I visited the local USO club. Again, I couldn't resist more pizza. You can never get enough pizza. It has the five major food groups in every bite – bread, meat, dairy, fruit, and vegetable.

Finally, I passed my final PT test and received a first-time pass on all of the military skills tests. Because I did so well on the testing, I received my first ride on a UH-1 Huey helicopter from the field back to the barracks. Most of the other Soldiers, though, had to march the several miles back. Also, my platoon received the *Honor Platoon* for the cycle, making my drill sergeants very happy. In return, we received a graduation party, with alcohol, the weekend before graduation. After I graduated from "boot camp" that summer, I flew home, proudly wearing my uniform.

I was now a Soldier, a member of an important group. Although the US Army is a large bureaucratic group, it's a very professional one with ethical values and the demonstrated ability to remove members who don't live up to its standards, such as Lieutenant William Calley from the *My Lai Massacre* and General Douglas MacArthur from his insubordination of the President[616]. I'm proud to be a member of this group and have willingly risked my life in combat to complete my duties.

---

[615] Longshore 2008, 129.
[616] Oliver 2006 and Dempsey 2010, 18.

The continual confusion, fear and utter bewilderment experienced during this basic training embedded into my mind, which I still remember in vivid clarity decades later. Also, none of us that summer would recognize basic training today where recruits have swapped combat boots with sneakers (easier on the feet), fatigues with gym shorts and tee-shirts. Instead of running in formation, these recruits today run at their own pace, which supposedly challenges the fast Soldiers and avoids injuring the slower ones[617]. No wonder that today I can still run faster than most Soldiers who are half my age.

Groupthink

Groupthink is defined as being rationalized conformity in which group values are both right and good.[618] As such, the group values aren't only expedient but right and good as well. Irving Janis led the initial research on groupthink theory. He defined this as a "quick and easy way to refer to the mode of thinking that persons engage in when concurrence-seeking becomes so dominant in a cohesive ingroup that it tends to override realistic appraisal of alternative courses of action". Groupthink involves mental deterioration and decreased moral judgments as a result of the group pressures. An increased level of pride within the group further causes a higher likelihood of groupthink.

Does this mean that groups are inherently bad? Not at all. In fact, groups help people resolve problems. Many join groups for therapeutic purposes, such as dealing with marital difficulties, substance abuse, employment, and other daily living problems. However, this leads to the "bandwagon" effects, in which members begin believing the popular dominant opinion[619]. Unfortunately, the primary socially negative cost of groupthink is the loss of uniqueness, individual creativity, and independent thinking.

Illustrating some of the problems of groupthink, many scientists readily reference George Orwell's *Nineteen Eighty-Four*, a dark

---

[617] Thompson, 2001.
[618] Whyte 1952. He first coined the term Groupthink.
[619] Perse 2008, 115.

futuristic novel. As portrayed in this book, groups use their own languages to communicate to its members. Orwell was astute to this and coined the concepts of "doublethink" to simultaneously holding and believing contradictory beliefs and "newspeak" containing ideological language. I can easily relate to this. As a member of the US Army, a large organization with millions of members, I frequently used words and phrases that many non-members wouldn't understand. The following paragraph is an example of this representing some of my military experiences.

After becoming a full bird, I became the old man and the Foxtrot November Golf in the 464th Chemical Brigade, even though the top in my company was older than me[620]. While in this unit known for its mop gear, I was authorized a butterbar for my aide, who would square away the fruit salad on my Class A's and Dress Blues, and ensure that I had my douche kit whenever I went on TDY [621]. This aide wouldn't be a ring knocker but could be an eleven bang bang or mud puppy[622]. In my puzzle palace, my G1, G2, G3, and G4 desk jockeys worked for me[623]. Whenever I visited a subordinate unit, there was always chaos but rarely a

---

[620] Full bird is a colonel. Old Man is the commander. Foxtrot November Golf is the fucking new guy. Top is t First Sergeant.
[621] Mop gear refers tochemical warfare clothing from the term: Mission Oriented Protective Posture (MOPP). Butterbar is a second lieutenant. Squared away means having it all together. Fruit salad referse to many ribbons on a uniform. Class A's is the Army dress uniform. Dress blues is the military formal suit. Douche kit refers to a shaving kit. TDY is the acronym for Temporary Duty, or official travel.
[622] Ring knocker is a West Point graduate. Eleven bang bang is an infantryman. Mud puppy is a military policeman.
[623] Puzzle palace means headquarters. Staff officers were identified as "S" for lieutenant and colonel command staff, "G" for general officer command staff, and "J" for joint command staff. The numbers following them represented the type of staff section. Since I commanded in a general officer command billet, my staff was identified at the "G" level. G1 refers to personnel or human resources staff. G2 refers to military intelligence. G3 refers to operations and training. G4 refers to logistics and supplies. Desk jockey means an admin clerk or someone working behind a desk.

Charlie Foxtrot[624]. *Sometimes, though, I would find a gaggle, some gold brickers, and a grab ass situation*[625]. *Afterwards, a lifer noncom would go ape shit over his low-speed high-drag peons and plan a GI party, sometimes giving his half-stepping shamurai warriors instructions about dust bunnies and getting everything dress right dress while adjusting their headspace and timing in the front leaning rest position*[626]. *Sometimes while wearing a brain bucket for cover and my birth control glasses, I would visit my ground pounders out in the boondocks, usually to avoid the dog and pony show and to hear them sing about Jodie*[627]. *While in the field, I would walk several klicks around the area at oh dark thirty to find a fire watch wearing mosquito wings looking for midnight requisitions of pogey bait before returning to the fart sack in their hooch*[628]. *I didn't want my short studs believing I was a starry-eyed jellyfish because I*

---

[624] Chaos is an acronym for the commander has arrived on scene. Charlie Foxtrot means cluster fuck or something really messed up.

[625] Gaggle means mass confusion. Gold bricker is someone dodging responsibility. Grab ass refers to soldiers messing around.

[626] Lifer is a career Soldier. Noncom is short for non-commissioned officer, representing a sergeant. Goning ape shit means being mentally unstable. Low speed and high drag refers to a Soldier who is completely messed up. Peon means a lower ranking person who does not make decisions. GI party refers to cleaning the barracks. Half stepping means doing something half assed. Shamurai warrior is a Soldier who does no real work. Dust bunnies refers to lint under the bunk. Dress right dress means keeping everything lined up and in order. Headspace and timing refers to the individual's knowledge, skills, and abilities. Front leaning rest is the push up position.

[627] Brain bucket is a helmet. Cover refers to a hat, helmet, or something else worn on the head. Birth control glasses are GI issued ugly black plastic glasses, normally issued to basic trainees. Ground pounder means a Soldier. Out in the boondocks refers to in the field. A dog and pony show is something, such as a formal briefing, for senior officers or the public. Jodie is the the guy back home who is worthless and sleeping with the girlfriend.

[628] Klick is one kilometer. Oh dark thirty is sometime really early in the morning. Fire watch refers to night guard duty. Mosquito wings refers to one stripe, or a Private E2. Midnight requisition means stealing from another unit. Pogey bait refers to candy and other junk food snacks. Fart sack is the sleeping bag. Hooch refers to the living quarters, such as tent or barracks.

wanted them to see the re-up pencil pusher[629]. While eating at the DFAC, I sometimes ate with other dopes on a rope drinking their lifer juice talking about their rocks who bolo at the range, usually glad that we had our P38 and John Wayne paper with us[630]. During my career, I pursued UCMJ action against a REMF railroad tracks for smuggling weapons on a freedom bird that didn't go tits up[631]. I even considered giving a big chicken dinner to a senior NCO for a positive result during Operation Golden Flow who thought RHIP, who then ended up on a cattle car to the nearest MCF[632]. After almost thirty years, some of it as a weekend warrior, I heard she who must be obeyed Lima Charlie, put on my civies, popped smoke by taking my POV on a double time to Fort Home to became an ORF[633]. Whiskey Tango Foxtrot, I'm not numb nuts and will put a lid on it[634]. Hooah![635]

---

[629] Short means close to discharge or transfer. Stud is an excellent Soldier. Starry-eyed refers to an officer going out of their way to impress a General by overworking their people. Jellyfish is a superior without a backbone. Re-up means re-enlist and not leave the Army. Pencil pusher is the admin clerk.

[630] DFAC refers to dining facility or other place to eat food. Dope on a rope is an air assault qualified soldier, like myself. Lifer juice is coffee, which I never drank. Rock is a person who is dumb as a rock. Bolo means failing to qualify. P38 is a can opener. John Wayne paper is toilet paper.

[631] UCMJ is the Uniformed Code of Military Justice, which is used to discipline Soldiers. REMF is an acronym for a rear echelon mother fucker Soldier safely in the rear. Railroad tracks is another term for a captain. Freedom bird represents the flight returning to the states. Tits up means the item is broken.

[632] Big chicken dinner is another way to say bad conduct discharge. Operation Golden Flow is the process for collecting urine samples for drug test. RHIP is rank has its privileges. Cattle car is a trailer to transport troops, usually during basic training. MCF is military correctional facility, or military jail.

[633] Weekend warrior is a Reservist or National Guardsman. She who must be obeyed is my wife. Lima Charlie means that I hear you loud and clear. Civies is civilian clothing. Pop smoke means to leave the area in a hurry. POV is my personal automobile (privately owned vehicle). Double time means to do something quickly. Fort Home is my home. ORF is an old retired fart.

[634] Whiskey Tango Foxtrot is another way to say what the fuck. Numb nuts means stupid. Put a lid on it means to stop talking.

[635] Hooah refers to anything and everything except "no." For example, it means: 1. Good copy, solid copy, roger, good or great; message received, understood; 2. Glad to meet you, welcome; 3. I don't know, but will check on it, I haven't the

Most people reading the previous paragraph would think I was writing gobbledygook or some other incomprehensible convoluted language. But, I can assure you that none of this is gibberish without meaning. Almost anyone who spent time in the Army can easily understand this. Without this membership experience, the typical person wouldn't understand much of it. The following is the translation into understandable English.

After becoming a colonel, I became the commander and the new guy in the 464th Chemical Brigade, even though the first sergeant in my company was older than me. While in this unit known for its chemical clothing, I was authorized a second lieutenant for my aide, who would arrange my ribbons on my military business uniform and formal suit and ensure that I had my shaving kit whenever I went on a business trip. This aide would not be a West Point graduate but could be an infantryman or military policeman. In my headquarters, my personnel, military intelligence, operations, and logistics admin clerks worked for me. Whenever I visited a subordinate unit, I was on the scene but rarely saw anything really messed up. Sometimes, though, I would find mass confusion, some dodging responsibilities, and some messing around. Afterwards, a career sergeant would go mentally unstable over his completely messed up Soldiers and plan of cleaning the barracks, sometimes giving his half-assed work-avoiding Soldiers instructions about lint under the beds and getting everything lined up and in order while improving their abilities in the push-up position. Sometimes while wearing a helmet on my head and my ugly plastic black glasses, I would visit my Soldiers out in the field, usually to avoid the formal briefing and to hear them sing about a worthless guy back home sleeping

---

vaguest idea; 4. I'm not listening; 5. That's enough of your drivel--sit down; 6. Stop sniveling; 7. You've got to be kidding; 8. Yes; 9. Thank you; 10. Go to the next [briefing] slide; 11. You have taken the correct action; 12. I don't know what that means, but am too embarrassed to ask for clarification; 13. That's really neat, I want one too; and finally 14. Amen.

with their girls. While in the field, I would walk several kilometers early in the morning to find a private on guard duty who was looking to steal snack food before returning to a sleeping bag in their tent. I didn't want my excellent Soldiers who were about to leave the Army into believing I was a spineless officer trying to impress generals because I wanted these Soldiers to see the re-enlistment clerk. While eating at the dining facility, I sometimes ate with other air assault qualified Soldiers drinking their coffee talking about their dumb Soldiers who failed at the range, usually glad that we had our can opener and toilet paper with us. During my career, I pursued military disciplinary action against a non-combat captain for smuggling weapons on a return flight from combat that didn't break. I even considered giving a bad conduct discharge to a senior sergeant for testing positive on a drug test who thought he could use his rank to get out of this, who then ended up on a troop transport to the nearest military jail. After almost thirty years, some of it as an Army reservist, I heard my wife clearly, put on my civilian clothes, left quickly in my personal car to home to become retired. I'm not stupid, and will stop talking now. Amen.

Psychologists also use the term "groupthink" to describe a group incapable of critically assessing the pros and cons of a decision. Because the group members feel so tightly connected and so cohesive, they prefer to see only one side of an issue. They're easily led by a forceful leader and busy themselves by falling in line behind the boss and kissing up to stay in good favor. They become a mindless, overprotective clique as a group, putting the political goal of squashing dissent above all other matters[636]. Members are discouraged from seeking alternate views and not to "rock the boat" further, usually at risk of being disciplined[637].

Groups engaged in groupthink tend to make faulty decisions when compared to the decisions that could have been reached using a

---

[636] Namie and Namie 2000.
[637] Smith 1992, 308-9

fair, open, and rational decision-making process. They fail to adequately assess their objectives and alternatives, fail to assess the risks, fail to reexamine discarded alternatives after a majority of the group discarded them, fail to seek expert advice, fail to consider any information that doesn't support their position, and fail to make contingency plans in case their decision fails. Symptoms of groupthink include illusions of invulnerability, unquestioned belief in the group's decisions, self-censorship, direct pressure to conform, and members who shield the group from dissenting information[638].

The organized messages that groups communicate reminds me of military psychological operations (PSYOPS). I learned about this through training while stationed at Fort Hood, Texas. This involved identifying and neutralizing Soviet PSYOPS through the John F. Kennedy Special Warfare Center and School, located at Fort Bragg, North Carolina. PSYOPS tasks involve crafting messages that articulate the organizational policies, transmitting them via a variety of media to the intended audience. They can also disrupt, confuse, and protract the adversary's decision-making process. A successful message includes clearly defined objectives, addresses effective situational assessment, uses an effective media technique, and evaluates audience responses[639]. I'm a firm believer that the media has a significant impact upon the effects of popular behavior, including redefining reality[640]. Fortunately, it's against the law for the military to employ PSYOPS against US citizens[641].

We should be fully aware that the most powerful groupthink organization today involves the union of a billion dedicated people with so much passion resulting in the establishment of one great super church that recognizes only one person as its dictatorial spiritual Papal head[642]. Why should we care about this? Just read history. In 391, Christian mobs destroyed the magnificent temple

---

[638] Janis and Mann 1977, 130-131.
[639] See especially Barnett and Lord 1989, and David and McKeldin 2009.
[640] See especially Perse 2008.
[641] 10 USC 167, "Unified Combatant Command for Special Operations Forces".
[642] Walsh 1989, 8.

to Serapis in Alexandria, while burning non-Christian books. Later in 415, another mob murdered Hypatia, the last Pagan scientist of the Alexandrian Library. She was stripped naked, flayed alive with sharp shells, torn from limb to limb and burned[643]. While in 1391, anti-Semitic Christian mobs killed about fifty thousand Jews throughout Spain and Portugal[644].

As part of a group, people tend to feel, think, and act quite differently than if they've been in isolation. They're also readily influenced by suggestions, yet are instinctively hostile to changes. An individual may accept discussions regarding a contradiction of its ideas, while the group won't. As such, groups have authority and intolerance. Also, groups don't tolerate discussions[645]. Contrary to popular belief at the time, mobs weren't mad, not composed of the riffraff, and not criminals. Reasons for the mob actions could be attributed to individuals' needs, motivations, personalities, values and beliefs. In ancient times, these actions were often attributed to evil spirits and religious fanaticism. Today, we have lynch mobs and race riots attributed to deprivations, frustrations, bigotry and crime[646].

Anyone who isn't a part of a Christian organization risks being called a heretic, a savage, a false prophet or an enemy. Whereas, anyone who is a member becomes a horrible traitor and sinner if they ever leave it. All opposing information is attacked and destroyed as soon as possible. Intelligence, passion, or anything else that has the potential to lead the person away from the organization's control, are threats, resulting in members risking brutality and brainwashing. Groupthink prevents us from searching for truth!

---

[643] Hernandez 2009, 93.
[644] Kirsch 2008, 174.
[645] See especially Le Bon 1896.
[646] See especially McPhail 1991.

Charge of the Light Brigade.

The classic example of blind obedience to group decision was the charge of a cavalry brigade led by Lord Cardigan against Russian forces during the Battle of Balaclava on October 25, 1854 in the Crimean War. The charge was the result of miscommunication such that the brigade attempted a much more difficult objective than intended by the higher headquarters commander, Lord Raglan. Blame for this miscommunication remained controversial, as the original order was vague. The charge produced no decisive gains, resulted in very high casualties, and is best remembered as the subject of the poem *The Charge of the Light Brigade* by Alfred, Lord Tennyson. His lines emphasized the valor of the Soldiers in carrying out their orders, even though they knew better. "Theirs but to do and die" was known as the motto of blind obedience[647].

Figure 25. Charge of the Light Brigade.
by Richard Caton Woodville (1894).

Contrary to popular belief, the brigade wasn't completely destroyed, but did suffer terribly, with almost three hundred casualties, including slightly more than one hundred killed[648]. Almost four hundred horses died in the attack[649]. Also there

---

[647] See also Kipling 1890.
[648] Brighton 2004, 185, 294.
[649] Brighton 2004, 294.

weren't six hundred as the poem suggests, but more likely around 660 men[650]. After regrouping, almost two hundred men were still with horses. And, about seventy-five of the men were either unhurt or recovered from the wounds. Public anger wasn't directed because of the number of casualties, but because of their belief that none should have died[651].

Third Reich in Germany.

How could an entire nation submit to the decisions of a few men, or even a single person? Such was the case prevalent in Germany leading up to the Second World War. In 1933, Adolph Hitler became Chancellor of the country, quickly eliminating all opposition. The people idolized him, calling him Führer, or "leader", eventually granting him complete authoritarian power over them[652]. In the midst of the Great Depression, his Third Reich, or Nazi government, restored prosperity and ended mass unemployment. The people's return to prosperity gave Hitler enormous popularity and made his authority unchallenged.

With resources of the state available, the senior leaders convinced civil servants and the police to do what they wanted. Decisions on all matters were reserved solely to these senior leaders, even if it contradicted constitutional powers[653]. Accordingly, many German citizens, primarily civil servants and teachers, aligned themselves with Nazism[654]. Unfortunately, there was no place for women since they were considered property of the state[655].

With absolute authority, the Führer's word was above all other laws. His government wasn't a coordinated, cooperating group, but rather a collection of factions struggling to amass power and gain favor with the Führer. In essence, Hitler became the

---

[650] Brighton 2004, 290.
[651] See especially Crider 2004.
[652] Paxton and Hessler 2012, 281-92.
[653] See especially Evans 2003.
[654] Lee 1998, 7.
[655] Herb and Kaplan 2012, 454.

manufactured myth of a German messiah[656]. There's evidence that he was occasionally compared with Jesus, and revered as God's savior as indicated in a prayer recited by orphans[657]:

> *Führer, my Führer, given me by God, protect and preserve my life for a long time. You saved Germany in time of need. I thank you for my daily bread. Be with me for a long time, do not leave me, Führer, my Führer, my faith, my light, Hail to my Führer!*

Hitler's government promoted Christianity as a militant, non-denominational group that emphasized Christ as an active fighter and anti-Semite who opposed Judaism. Furthermore, it viewed Christianity in terms of creation, good, and God; whereas Judaism was destruction, evil, and Satan[658]. Yet in 1937, all Confessing Church seminaries and teaching was banned. Dissident Protestants were forbidden to attend universities. During Hitler's dictatorship, more than six thousand clergymen, on the charge of treasonable activity, were either imprisoned or executed[659]. Regarding the genocide of the millions of Jews executed in the government's Holocaust, many who condemned them to death were intelligent and educated[660]. Furthermore, a praise given Hitler provides us a haunting reminder of what absolute obedience can do.

> *We do not need intellectual leaders who create new ideas, because the superimposing leader of all desires of youth is Adolph Hitler. Your name, my Führer, is for us everlasting life. He who serves Adolf Hitler, the Führer, serves Germany, and whoever serves Germany, serves God.*

---

[656] Overy 2004, 33-34.
[657] Lepage 2009, 87.
[658] Steigmann-Gall 2003, 22.
[659] Overy 2004, 286-87.
[660] Davies 2009, 64.

Figure 26. Exhumation of Polish Officers from Katyn Massacre.
Excavation of graves containing Polish Generals Mieczysław Smorawiński and Bogusława Bohaterowicza (1943)[661].

Regarding the genocide, groupthink through the Third Reich's inanimate bureaucratic organization minimized the value of individual thought. Important people murdered unimportant people. They did this for ideological reasons of revitalization of the people. Technical reasons involved efficiency for everyone. The therapeutic reason involved the healing of their race[662].

---

[661] Obtained from public domain photo contained in Andrzej Leszek Szcześniak's 1989 Katyń: Tło historyczne, fakty, dokumenty..
[662] Lifton 1986, 496.

The Nazis weren't the only ones during the Second World War involved in senseless murders. The Soviets did something despicable, which they originally blamed on the Nazis. And, this heinous act was dear to my ancestral family. In the Spring of 1940 using German weapons, the Soviets massacred about twenty thousand Polish officers, physicians, engineers, lawyers, and teachers[663]. Thus, about half of the Polish officer corps was executed. Known as the *Katyn Forest Massacre*, the Soviets denied this for decades afterwards until the recent discovery of indisputable evidence[664]. They repeatedly refused accountability for their actions.

Attack on Pearl Harbor.

The World War II attack in Hawaii was a historical example of a poor group decision[665]. Senior US military officers couldn't comprehend the possibility that the Japanese military could travel thousands of miles undetected to attack a US military base. Despite numerous warnings otherwise, the military refused to prepare for a possible attack[666].

A member of Japan's Ministry of War provided the first such warning to a senior State Department official that Japan was planning an attack[667]. Then additional messages throughout the year arrived including numerous amounts during the prior week. The only thing the US didn't know was the exact time of the attack[668] These are the primary reasons behind the poor decision-making culminating in the lack of US preparedness[669].

---

[663] List of victims of this massacre can be found in the document at this website: http://www.katyn.org.au/Lista_Katyn.pdf.
[664] See especially Sanford 2005 and Cienciala et.al. 2007.
[665] See Walsh 1989, 15 and 't Hart 2011, 10.
[666] Ahlstrom and Bruton 2009, 285.
[667] Victor 2007, 35.
[668] Victor 2007, 66.
[669] Kowert 2002, 97.

Kamikaze.

Suicidal group members was a very dangerous concept. An example involved the Kamikaze warriors within the Japanese military during World War II. Most popular were the aviators; yet, this included crash boats and frogmen[670]. Although these warriors sacrificed their lives, their actions were mostly a tactical nuisance rather than a strategic serious threat. What motivated them to do this? One can look to their culture to find answers. They followed the *bushidō* code of patriotism and loyalty above all else, making it shameful for warriors not to be loyal to the emperor[671]. Furthermore, Japanese taken prisoner suffered a label of shame[672]. The tradition of death instead of defeat, capture, and perceived shame was deeply entrenched in Japanese military culture.

Even the German Luftwaffe flew suicidal missions towards the end of the war. We have evidence that about thirty-five pilots signed a suicide pact and died destroying two Soviet bridges across the River Oder in April 1945[673]. Today, there are similar groups with suicidal members, many associated with the Islam religion. Though this religion clearly prohibits Muslims killing themselves and noncombatant civilians[674]. However, many Muslims support the Islamic requirement of a jihad against infidel regimes not behaving according to their interpretations of God's laws[675]. Still, many Muslim suicide warriors have a strong religious motive behind their actions, believing they will be rewarded for their self-sacrifice with a guaranteed automatic place in Heaven, where they will own a multitude of virgins and servants[676].

Bay of Pigs.

The Bay of Pigs invasion was another classic example of groupthink. It was an unsuccessful covert paramilitary operation,

---

[670] Zaloga 2011, 4.
[671] Ohnuki-Tierney 2002, 118.
[672] Gruhl 2007, 190.
[673] Goeschel 2009, 147-48.
[674] Hafez 2007, 125.
[675] Hafez 2007, 70.
[676] Dutton 2007, 154.

launched in April 1961, to invade southern Cuba. Its purpose was to remove Fidel Castro[677]. The planners displayed symptoms of groupthink, which included symptoms of bad decision-making. The group lost sight of its objective, becoming more focused upon the invasion plan details, failing to develop contingencies. It avoided information that conflicted with their initial preferences. The end result was a lethal fiasco[678]. Cuban forces killed over one hundred of the nearly fifteen hundred US forces and captured almost twelve hundred, along with enormous piles of military weapons. In spite of that, the Cubans suffered about sixteen hundred deaths[679].

The biggest problem involved what the US wanted the Cuban Army to do and how to persuade them to do it. Failure to recognize this problem resulted in significant overconfidence and misunderstanding of military capabilities[680]. In 1961, CIA inspector general Lyman B. Kirkpatrick, authored a report *Survey of the Cuban Operation*, which remained classified Top Secret until 1996. This report highlighted problems in understanding capabilities, poor communications, unrealistic assessments, lack of required resources, and no contingency plans[681].

Watergate Scandal.

Towards the end of the Vietnam War, there were individuals at the senior level of the US Government operating with blind group first tendencies[682]. This involved President Nixon's staff deciding to cover-up their involvement in the hotel break-in[683].

The cover-up was meant to avoid potential negative political consequences resulting from the Democratic party's headquarters

---

[677] See especially Pfeiffer 1984, Quesada 2009 and Gleijeses 1995.
[678] Forsyth 2010, 341.
[679] Jones 2008, 122. See also Central Intelligence Agency 2011 site. This site contains the CIA Inspector General's report on this operation, with over seven hundred documents, much of which was originally classified top secret.
[680] Warner 1998.
[681] Kirkpatrick 1961, 143-45.
[682] See especially Anderson 2007.
[683] Forsyth 2010, 337.

being burglarized. This included obstructing the Federal Bureau of Investigation (FBI) and concealing the involvement of senior Government officials. Ironically, the cover-up and details of the break-in were tape-recorded. Members of this group focused more upon wanting to be part of the cohesive inner circle of power[684].

Hostage Rescue in Iran.

Another military example of groupthink involved the attempt to end the Iran hostage crisis by rescuing fifty-three Americans held captive at the US Embassy in Tehran, Iran in April 1980. The failure of Operation Eagle Claw and its humiliating public debacle damaged American prestige worldwide. And, it was a key cause behind President Carter's 1980 presidential election defeat[685].

Morality was Carter's first principle in the guidelines for shaping foreign policy, which overshadowed all other operational concerns. The operation, though, was a feasible plan that represented a good chance for mission success. Yet, the unity of command was nonexistent. A single commander should have been identified. The group's structure definitely influenced its decision-making, especially since the Secretary of State was excluded from the final decision[686]. The component commanders were unwilling to adjust the plan towards accomplishing its mission, even though it had limited room for adaptability and flexibility. The military's "stovepipe" culture of restricting communications between organizations, and the lack of trust and confidence between commanders influenced this inflexibility[687]. Thus, the various services failed to work together cohesively.

Retired Chief of Naval Operations Admiral James L. Holloway, III, led the official investigation in 1980 into the causes of the failure. The *Holloway Report* primarily cited deficiencies in mission planning, command and control, and inter-service operability. Furthermore, insulation of this group from other

---

[684] 't Hart and Kroon 1997, 107.
[685] 't Hart and Kroon 1997, 109 and see especially Kyle 1995..
[686] 't Hart and Kroon 1997, 131.
[687] See especially Holzworth 1997.

people with information, allowed them to make decisions in a vacuum and unchecked from external controls[688]. Ultimately, eight people died.

Figure 27. Space Shuttle Challenger Crewmember Remains.
NASA photo of remains transferring from 7 hearse vehicles to a MAC C-141 plane at the Kennedy Space Center's Shuttle Landing Facility for transport to Dover Air Force Base, Delaware. (30 August 1988.)[689].

Challenger Launch.

Another problem with groups involved its decision-making capability. The Space Shuttle Challenger disaster in 1988 was a lethal example of groupthink or poor group decisions. Because of the difficulty in identifying one crucial decision-making group for the Challenger incident, this wasn't a classical groupthink situation because the participants didn't consist of a cohesive small group of decision-makers[690]. Instead, it involved more than thirty individuals who didn't all know each other and were insulated from others within the organization. And, the decisions were guided by norms and rules regarding how to conduct technical discussions[691]. Yet, the group disregarded facts and made a poor decision for lift-off even though they knew about the problems.

---

[688] 't Hart and Kroon 1997, 114.
[689] The STS-51L crew consisted of: Mike Smith; Dick Scobee; Ron McNair; Ellison S. Onizuka; Greg Jarvis; Judy Resnik; and Sharon Christa McAuliffe.
[690] 't Hart 2011, 63.
[691] Vaughan 1996, 525 note 41.

The actual physical cause of the accident was the failure of the pressure seal in the aft (or rear) field joint of the right Solid Rocket Booster. This seal was highly sensitive to temperature effects, reusability, and dynamic loading[692]. As for the real root cause, the authoritarian group leaders suppressed the minority dissent[693]. The group members assumed their collective decisions were correct and that the dissenters were unethical and immoral[694]. NASA was very self-confident and concerned about its public image, which encouraged suppression of conflicting information, leading to a one-sided consensus on decisions involved in the launching of Challenger[695].

Outcome, nevertheless, was the loss of seven astronauts, NASA's credibility, and a nearly three-year cessation in the shuttle program. This event also served as current studies involving safety, ethics, and communications. It was important to me personally since the US Army nominated me as an astronaut candidate in 1991; and, this could have happened to me at a later point in time, such as the February 2003 Space Shuttle Columbia disaster.

Christian Groupthink.

Christian organizations aren't immune from groupthink. God doesn't shield churches from making poor decisions, even if all of its members pray about it. Why do I believe this? Just look at the two examples I provide below, a modern one and an ancient one.

PTL.

Religious organizations focus upon maintaining the group, often at the detriment of the decision-making, detracting people from critically speaking about the group[696]. An example of this involved the PTL, or "Praise The Lord", group. Founder of this group, Jim Bakker, began his television ministry on Pat Robertson's *700 Club*. The program began as a local television broadcast in a converted

---

[692] Rogers 1986.
[693] Esser and Lindoerfer 1989.
[694] Ahlstrom and.Bruton 2009, 285
[695] De Dreu and Van de Vliert 1997, 11.
[696] Redd 2007, 173.

Charlotte, North Carolina, furniture store, hosted by Jim and his wife, Tammy Faye Bakker. In 1974, Bakker and his staff built what became known as the PTL Television Network, a worldwide Christian satellite cable television network[697]. The program featured many well-known ministers and Christian recording artists[698].

Nothing wrong with that. But, because of his involvement in a highly publicized financial and sexual scandal, Bakker resigned in 1987 turning the cable network, the Heritage USA complex and all ministry assets over to fellow televangelist Jerry Falwell. This attracted national media attention from its discovery of the excessive wealthy lifestyle, the alleged misappropriation of ministry funds, especially details of a sexual encounter between Bakker and Hahn[699].

Lesson is that religious groups should embrace and follow pristine business and leadership practices consistent with their beliefs[700]. Unfortunately, the decisions of the PTL organization were reflections of Bakker's controlling and aggressive leadership[701].

Crucifixion of Jesus.

Groupthink was also involved in the construction of the Tower of Babel, complaints about Moses during the Exodus, and rejection of Caleb and Joshua's faith leading to victory[702]. Groupthink decisions usually overrided evidence[703]. The crucifixion of Jesus was the ultimate religious biblical decision. Religious leaders orchestrated the national rejection of the long-awaited Messiah[704]. In the crowds before Pontius Pilate, the people demanded the release of Barabbas, a murderer, instead[705]. Although disciples

---

[697] Later named The Inspirational Network.
[698] Kyle 2006, 245-46.
[699] Redd 2007, 175.
[700] Redd 2007, 160.
[701] Redd 2007, 141.
[702] French 2012, 5.
[703] Davies 2009, 64-66.
[704] Walsh 1989, 8.
[705] Mark 15:7-11.

Paul and James were probably not susceptible to this groupthink, they couldn't stop it[706].

Crucifixion, done in five stages, was a very painful and cruel death sentence. The first two stages involved flogging and public humiliation. Then, the person was forced to carry a heavy cross while fastened to it. Unlike popular belief, Jesus was probably completely naked on the cross, adding to His humiliation. The last stage involved dying. The Roman process required that the person die a long, lingering death on the cross, with the body later left to rot. However, because of Jewish laws of Deuteronomy 21, bodies of crucifixion victims had to be removed and buried by dark of the same day, normally in a communal garbage dump. This usually required the breaking of legs to expedite the process. Confirmation of death was done by piercing the side of the body and forcing the blood to run out of the heart[707].

Although listed a groupthink issue, there were many scholars who couldn't find external evidence to substantiate a Jewish or Roman custom for granting pardons to prisoners on the eve of Passover[708]. Even the four Gospel accounts of this event were inconsistent. If there was a custom that allowed the Roman governor to release a condemn man, such as Barabbas, there was nothing to prevent the ruling governor from also releasing Jesus under the same custom.

Christians.

There are millions of Americans who call themselves Christians, many who rarely attend church, including on Christmas[709]. They would rather put up a Christmas tree with decorations or even attend a party than go to church. Why should they? It's hard to insist that they keep Christmas Holy when churches close that day[710]. About nine out of ten Protestant pastors planned holding services on Christmas Day 2011. Furthermore, about two out of

---

[706] Strobel 2007, 143.
[707] Phelan 2009, 168-9
[708] Winter 1974, 131.
[709] Boorstein 2011.
[710] Gibson 2011.

three Americans believed that the most enjoyable things they did during the Christmas season had nothing to do with Jesus' birth[711]. Spirituality was a small part of many Christian's lives. They just thought of Christmas and Easter, with the rest of the year not important to them. We can probably find similar attitudes throughout the world.

Figure 28. Give us Barabbas.
Illustrations from volume 9 of *The Bible and its Story Taught by One Thousand Picture Lessons*, edited by Charles F. Horne and Julius A. Bewer (1910).

This should concern us because about a third of the world population is Christian, totaling over two billion[712]. Many of them believe they're Christian only because they say they're Christian taking into consideration no other criteria for this faith, while others believe they are Christians because they inherited it from their family[713]. Still others believe that they're members of God's only church and that all others are Heathens, even though they

---

[711] Turner 2011.
[712] Gordon Conwell Theological Seminary 2011.
[713] Gulley 2010, 7.

worship Jesus and are obedient to God[714]. Basically, many Christians think they serve God, even though they actually fail to serve Him by loving His people.

We have mounting evidence that intelligent, educated, and caring Christians unwittingly create problems, such as hypocrisy, bigotry, materialism, and persecution of others[715]. They also prefer to judge others, instead of accepting, loving, and supporting them. Pride and self-love cause many Christians serious problems. Most Christians like to tell other people how to behave while acting as if they never do anything wrong. They also seem to focus only on a few moral issues, namely abortion and gay marriage, seemingly to the exclusion of more important issues, such as justice and care for the poor. Maybe, it's because we usually don't feel good unless we serve ourselves. And, we love to complain to others, especially about how evil someone is for hurting us, along with condemning others, such as homosexuals and people with AIDS [716]. They simply don't put the principles of Jesus into practice[717].

The biggest problems I see is that we are plagued with many hypocritical Christians, especially those who love to brag about their faith and do good works as a way to disguise their disrespect towards God[718]. They're really Infidels[719]. A Christian hypocrite is someone who professes to be a Christian but doesn't practice the teachings of Jesus. Many Christians, instead, continually repeat their sins and seek forgiveness from God[720].

Hypocrite (υποκριτης), or variations of it, appear about twenty times in the New Testament. Often it's Jesus calling people hypocrites[721]. "You hypocrites!" is a recurring phrase[722]. The

---

[714] Gulley 2010, 1-2.
[715] See especially Willis 1978.
[716] Montgomery 2008, 84, 88, and 112.
[717] Spiegel 2000, 133.
[718] Woolton 1851, 24-25 and 44.
[719] Mason 1810, 576.
[720] Muverengwi 2011, 21.
[721]Such as, Matthew 6:2-5, 16; 7:5; 15:7; 22:18; 23:13-29; 24:51; Mark 7:6; Luke 6:42; 12:56; and 13:15

hypocrites care more about their reputation with others instead of how God thinks of them. Paul describes hypocritical Christians as falsely displaying an image of righteousness instead of actually being righteous[723]. As such, they portray a false image to others. I know that everyone falls short of their own standards from time to time, which includes telling a small lie. We're human, who lie, cheat, and steal just like everyone else in the world. But, hypocrisy isn't doing wrong things; it's claiming to be something we're not[724]. The Christian hypocrite is a non-believer, since he's only pretending to follow Jesus' teachings.

Forced to wear the scarlet letter of an adulterer, Hester in Hawthorne's *Scarlet Letter* struggled for dignity in the face of lust and guilt. The religious leaders of the community preached strict adherence to Christian dogma, demanding her to be branded with a scarlet letter. These leaders, acting as God on Judgment Day, sentenced her to isolation in a small Christian community unwilling to forgive her sin as God might have. The people hypocritically advocated a firm biblical belief yet practiced unchristian acts of intolerance. When she appeared in town, the ruthless Christians shunned her, staring directly at the scarlet as if she were the evil product of the Devil.

The most recent example of hypocrisy was Ted Haggard, who rabidly preached against homosexual practice, while he himself was involved in it on a routine basis. He was founder and former pastor of the New Life Church in Colorado Springs, Colorado; a founder of the Association of Life-Giving Churches; and was leader of the National Association of Evangelicals (NAE) from 2003 until November 2006[725].

No one is perfect and all are dependent on Jesus for redemption, salvation and growth in spiritual maturity[726]. My advice is that

---

[722] Such as Matthew 7:5, 15:7 and Luke 12:56.
[723] 2 Timothy 3:5 and Murverengwi 2011, 10.
[724] Wright 2010, 153.
[725] Cooperman 2006.
[726] Romans 3:23-24.

Christians shouldn't act hypocritically, lest they provide critics with a flimsy reason to reject the gospel message[727]. Furthermore, hypocrisy in the church isn't a good reason to dismiss Christianity. For example hypocritical behavior on a large scale, such as the Inquisition, didn't invalidate Christianity[728].

We should also be aware of the Media Elite, or narrow-minded elitism in the media that slants the news to their beliefs. This involves coverage of issues that they want to publish, and avoids those that contradict their beliefs, even if they have to distort the truth[729]. Jesus instructed His followers to worship in truth[730]. We should seek it out and use it, not hide it under the carpet or feign ignorance because we believe everything we are told. The truth is more than just a simple saying. Regrettably, complex Christian ideas are reduced to bumper stickers, such as those listed in Table 21. But, faith isn't about displaying those bumper stickers either.

Jesus spoke against giving to the poor, praying in public, and fasting solely to be recognized by others[731]. He wasn't for supporting the church while neglecting mercy to others[732]. Furthermore, compassion to others should be given, not earned.

Christians should also improve their skills and abilities to act. They can't rely upon prayer alone to improve their abilities. This reminds me of a story that Defense Secretary Leon Panetta often told about a rabbi and a priest who went to a boxing match together. While there, they discussed each other's religion. Just before the match started, one of the boxers made the sign of the cross. The rabbi asked the priest what that meant. The priest replied that it doesn't mean anything if he can't fight[733]. Many Christians pray for lots of things too. In most cases, it doesn't mean anything either unless they do something about it.

---

[727] Velarde 2009.
[728] McDowell and Stewart 1986.
[729] See especially Goldberg 2003.
[730] John 4:23-24.
[731] Matthew 6:2.
[732] Matthew 23:23.
[733] 2011.

Table 21. Christian Bumper Stickers

God helps those who help themselves.	Take a friend to Heaven!
God is a republican (or democrat or liberal).	The Big Bang theory. And God said 'Pulleth my Finger.'
Believe in God and you shall prosper.	One Nation under God!
Did you thank God today?	WWJD?
Even Darwin KNOWS God created earth (now).	Interface with God: jesus@heaven.net
Exercise daily – walk with the Lord!	God answers knee-mail.
CAUTION! Non-exposure to the Son will cause burning.	Open your Heart, open your Mind, open your Bible!
Don't blame God for the things that people do.	JESUS Don't Leave Earth Without Him.
God's last name is not damnit!	Got Jesus?
God's Love is Big Enough for All of Us.	STUFF TO DO: Pray, Vote, Buy More Ammo!
God's not dead, he's still alive, he's my co-pilot.	Tithe if you love Jesus! Anyone can honk.
God gives and forgives, Man gets and forgets!	As long as there are tests, there will be Prayer in school.
God is. Any questions?	The Christian Right is neither.
God says it, I believe it, That settles it.	The 10 Commandments are not multiple choice.
God is too big to fit into just one religion.	Caution! In case of rapture, this car will swerve.
God spoke, and BANG! It happened!	Keep your eyes on the cross.
Jesus is the reason for the season!	1 Cross + 3 Nails = 4 Given.
If going to Church makes you a Christian, does going into a garage make you a car?	Stop using Jesus as an Excuse!
	Christians make great lovers.

The ideal Christian member has excellent interpersonal skills, has the tendency to share with others, cares for others, is happy and positive, welcomes feedback, is dependable, and possesses integrity. Jesus didn't excluded people with little to no status. He preferred those who possessed grace, gratitude, and faithfulness[734]. Likewise, we should hate sin and love ALL people. People who hate confirm to me that they don't have Jesus in them[735].

Christians who act as if they are better than everyone else are certainly not living by the creeds of Christianity, and may not even be Christians at all. Christianity says that all people are sinners, and none can be righteous on the basis of their own behavior. Jesus said that we shouldn't act like we're better than others, especially to get noticed. Such a "Holier-than-thou" attitude is strongly condemned in the Bible. The focus of Christianity should be on the relationship with Jesus, not on just following a bunch of rules. What is the goal for many American Christians: Kingdom of Heaven or American prosperity? Which one would you choose? Normally, you can only pursue one, not both.

Devil Made Me Do It

Even when Christians know the right things to do, many won't do them. Sadly, they refuse to be held accountable for their decisions and actions. Worse still is that they play the "blame game" and blame others for their actions, focusing upon an enemy such as the devil. This reminds me of the *Flip Wilson Show* in the 1970s and his portrayal of the very popular fictional character Geraldine Jones. She was a sassy African-American woman in a miniskirt who defended her actions with "the devil made me do it" lame excuse, which became a popular phrase back then[736]. Why not? The Bible was full of information about the Devil. He created problems, tempted us, discredited the work of Jesus, possessed

---

[734] Gulley 2010, 65).
[735] Montgomery 2008, 217.
[736] Lomax 2008, 30-33.

people, and deceived us[737]. As such, it's easy to blame the Devil. It's in the Bible, so it must be true.

It's easier to pass responsibility for our actions onto someone else. It's not my fault. It's somebody else's. In the first story of the Bible, Adam told God that Eve made him do it. Then, Eve said the Devil made her do it. I guess we can call this the Original Blame. Although it may provide us instant relief by blaming someone else, it usually doesn't last long since it has a tendency to return back to us. We're much better off if we take responsibility for our actions even if it's bad and ugly initially[738].

This brings us to the popular folklore of Dr. Faust, an arrogant scholar who sold his soul to the Devil in exchange for power and knowledge[739]. He was highly educated, deeply pious, and possessed exemplary virtue.[740] While pursuing knowledge, though, he lost his faith. With more power and knowledge from the Devil, Faust accomplished little or nothing of value. Today, "Faust" has become associated with powerful people whose pride and arrogance led to their downfall. They made unwise deals for worldly power or knowledge at the expense of their own soul.

In fact, there are many tales throughout history about people who made pacts with the Devil. One of the oldest versions known was the tale of *Theophilus of Adana*. He was a sixth century cleric who made a deal to gain an ecclesiastical position. As the oldest story of a pact with the Devil, this was probably the original inspiration behind the Faust legend[741]. Yet, there's a similar story from the third century involving salvation and revocation of the deal[742]. Cyprian of Antioch was a sorcerer who made a deal with several demons to injure another person, Justina. After several

---

[737] Genesis 3:15, Matthew 4:11, 16:23, John 13:27, Acts 5:3, and Revelation 20:3,
[738] Kunst 2011.
[739] See Bevington and Rasmussen, 1993; Goethe 1870; and Marlowe 1604.
[740] Herdt 2008, 138-146.
[741] Palmer and More 1966, 58-77.
[742] Palmer and More 1966, 41-58.

unsuccessful attempts to hurt her, Cyprian made the sign of the cross and freed himself from the Devil[743].

My book wouldn't be complete if I neglected to include a Faustian story from my ancestral home. This was a Polish tale of Pan Twardowski who lived in Kraków during the sixteenth century. He sold his soul in exchange for great knowledge and magical powers. Attempting to outwit the Devil, he designed a special clause in the contract limiting when his soul can be taken to Hell. This was only during his voluntary visit to Rome, a place Twardowski never intended to voluntarily visit. But deals with the Devil are never foolproof. Using a legal loophole, the Devil took him to the moon instead, where he remains today[744].

Besides folklore stories about fictional characters, we have examples of real people claiming the Devil was responsible for them. In 1638, the Massachusetts Bay Colony executed Dorothy Talbye for murdering her three-year-old daughter. In her defense, she claimed she did it at the Devil's direction. During the trial, she described stories about hearing the God's voice (or some other supernatural being). Nevertheless, the court declared that, she actually killed her daughter, even while possessed by the Devil[745]. Although evil existed on earth, proving that the Devil was responsible for human actions was easier done in the movies than in American courts today. Fortunately, the courts tend to believed that people were responsible for their own actions. Imagine that!

Next, you might wonder if people ever claimed that "God made me do it" for their criminal trial defense. Unbelievably, we just need to read the paper today to find an example. In the widely publicized media coverage of the Florida shooting death of Trayvon Martin in February 2012, defendant George Zimmerman claimed no responsibility because God made him do it[746].

---

[743] Meier 1908. Both were later martyred for their Christian faith.
[744] See especially Schamschula 1992.
[745] Felt 1827, 109 and 117.
[746] Goralka 2012.

Likewise, many people rely upon God's miraculous interventions to avoid responsibility for their actions[747]. I saw much of this in the Middle East with people telling me "In sha'Allah", which was the Muslim word for "God willing"[748]. They believe that nothing happened unless God (or Allah) willed it. I saw new buildings falling apart because they wouldn't do maintenance, fearing that they would anger Allah's will to destroy the buildings. I saw emergency respondents refused to provide essential medical care to allow Allah time to take His people if it was His will. Why do anything when you can do nothing and have Allah do everything for you? Christians also have a similar phrase, "If the Lord should will" (Ἐὰν ὁ κύριος θέλῃ), in the New Testament about people not being absolutely sure about the future[749]. But, for Christians, this really meant that we didn't know the future, not that we couldn't control or influence it. Otherwise, we needed to do the best we can whenever we can and take responsibility for our actions.

Claiming responsibility for our actions is easy. Actually taking responsibility and doing something about it is difficult. It involves more than just words. If we attempt to remedy a wrong-doing against another by saying to the other person "I'm sorry", the apology won't work. Just saying these two powerful words isn't enough. They aren't magical words that absolve us completely of our misdeeds. Let me describe something I learned during my days as a practicing Catholic. We had a wonderful prayer that said most of what was expected. It's the *Act of Contrition*. I know that there are many versions of this, but I like the following simple one[750].

> *My God, I am sorry for my sins with all my heart. In choosing to do wrong and failing to do good, I have sinned against you whom I should love above all things. I firmly intend, with your help, to do penance, to sin no more, and to avoid whatever leads me to sin. Our Savior Jesus*

---

[747] Saranam 2005, 40.
[748] Yahya 2002, 13.
[749] James 4:13-15.
[750] Finnegan 2000, 361.

Christ suffered and died for us. In His name, my God, have mercy. Amen.

This prayer required us to do penance, do no more wrong, and avoid wrong-doing situations. However, this prayer missed an important element – atonement. I know that many Christians believe in universal or unlimited atonement of Jesus' death on the cross[751]. I don't believe in this. Call me a heathen then for believing that we don't have unlimited permission to commit wrong-doings without consequences. Atonement of a wrong-doing must include the stages of penance, restitution, and reconciliation[752]. This includes correcting the wrong or injury, such as replacing the loss of material[753]. If we stole something from someone, we're still accountable to provide restitution of this loss to the other person. I've not found one person who would look the other way when someone stole something from them. Everyone I know is always willing to call the police to find the thief, retrieve their stolen things, and punish the thief. Restitution was also required for defamation of character, which was a statement to someone else that false information was true. My point was that if we're truly sorry, we must admit the wrong doing, provide restitution for any losses, and avoid doing future wrongs. Just saying "I'm sorry" isn't enough.

The Church

The church helps many Christians live in a fallen world of the flesh and the Heaven-oriented world of the soul. It shouldn't be just a building and it shouldn't be an exclusive group either. The exclusivity of not inviting just anybody to church isn't Christ-like and reeks of hypocrisy. Jesus in several parables about the lost sheep and the lost coin implied that He was more concerned about the estranged individuals[754]. Christians should be the church, not

---

[751] See especially Kent 1907.
[752] Kent 1907 and Berman 1983, 182.
[753] Hardon 1981, 168.
[754] Luke 15.

just go to church. That's what Jesus said when he defined it as two or more gathered in His name[755].

I have a problem with a church that has its main mission aimed at preferential treatment of rich, attractive, influential, and gifted people. Instead, it should be more concerned with its people's spiritual growth instead of administering an ancient museum[756]. The church shouldn't be about a group with the intent of growing in size. Instead, it should compensate for its inferior capabilities because generally the weaker side fights harder, willing to incur losses that would be unacceptable to the other side[757]. An example included the American rebels during the Revolutionary War against a stronger British empire. Religious leaders should take head to placing too much focus upon perfecting the church's capabilities since it can cause the church to lose sight of its purpose[758].

I'm concerned that many churches were more focused upon their survival, preferring to risk the lives of its followers. An example of my concern involved the *Copernicus Effect*, which was based upon Nicolaus Copernicus. He was a sixteenth century astronomer declared a heretic by the Catholic Church for saying that the Sun, not the Earth, was the center of the Universe. His crime involved seeking the truth by updating an ancient, yet universally rejected, idea of Pythagoreans, Aristachus, and other Greek astronomers[759]. Originally condemned by the church as a heretic and buried in an unmarked grave, he was recently reburied by Polish priests as a hero[760]. We continue having problems with the patriarchal, hierarchal, celibate-constrained, cloistered world of the Catholic Church with its anti-carnal outlook today. It's no wonder that we have numerous clergy sexual abuse scandals.

---

[755] Matthew 18:20.
[756] Gulley 2010, 99.
[757] Record 2005, 17.
[758] Record 2005, 27.
[759] Finocchiaro 2010, 22.
[760] Gera 2010.

As a Catholic, I'm torn being choosing my own path of following the teachings of Jesus with the best possible information or mindlessly following the unquestionable pontiff edicts based entirely on religious concepts from the Dark Ages and which ignore a raging epidemic of priesthood pedophilia sworn to protect God's children. This same Church of mine seems to be more focused upon promoting its bans on contraception, abortion, and human sexuality. What's worse, they want to attack American nuns who focus instead upon doing good for the less fortunate, who take their commitments serious in aiding the sick, nurturing the poor, and teaching children[761].

Some people claim that all groups are evil; self-serving, self-preserving, and self-loving[762]. Since churches are groups, they, too, are evil. Although many churches do evil things, I don't support this theory since they also do good things. For example, in response to Hurricane Katrina, many churches around American supported the victims. More to the point, why did it take a natural disaster to bring out the Christ in Christians? We should also understand that a compassionless Christian is no Christian at all.

Regrettably, many Christians support the church's shame-based culture of manipulation, embarrassment, and disgrace to get what they want, which is to gain followers, power, influence, and obedience. The best of them tend to support their manipulation using biblical citations to indicate that God is also ashamed of the religious misconduct of its reluctant followers[763]. This amounts to nothing more than fear-based religion.

We have problems when Christian groups exploit Scriptures to deny basic human rights. Their theological rigidity and faith exclusion is dangerous, especially if it wants us to believe that Jesus actually came to save us from a mean, jealous, vengeful God[764]. Furthermore, they tend to profess the superiority of its

---

[761] Thomasson 2012.
[762] Campbell 1995.
[763] Gulley 2010, 35.
[764] Bell 2011.

followers, thus creating much harm upon humanity[765]. But, how do we find the truth to stop this? Let me tell you that seeking the truth in the church is difficult. Recently, a United Methodist pastor was removed from his post in North Carolina for endorsing the controversial new best seller, *Love Wins: A Book About Heaven, Hell, and the Fate of Every Person Who Ever Lived*[766]. Although this denomination doesn't have a particular belief about Heaven and Hell, the pastor's articulation about doctrine contrary to its church's belief led to his removal.

Some have characterized the church, or religious group, in one of seven ways using the *Seven Churches of Revelation*[767]. These would be Ephesus forsaking its first love, Smyrna suffering persecution, Pergamum needing to repent, Thyatira having a false leader, Sardis falling asleep, Philadelphia enduring patiently, and Laodicea having lukewarm faith. Many consider Philadelphia the best church in the group since they followed the teaching of Jesus and were obedient to God. However, that wasn't enough. A Christian must never rest on his laurels, or accomplishments, no matter what the situation[768]. We must continue to follow the teachings, doing more good than harm. Yet, Smyrna was the one that receives no criticism since they suffered worldly punishment for following the true teachings of Jesus[769].

In April 2012, I received a letter in the mail from Saint Matthew's Church containing a paper copy of a *Prayer Rug*. Not just any prayer rug, but a folded paper prayer rug with a huge picture of a purple Jesus donning his crown of thorns and a teardrop rolling down his cheek. The message promised me riches from God, but only after I prayed for it, using Scriptures to make it seem legitimate. I'll add that this letter contained numerous testimonies; so, it must be true. I can have anything my heart desires. I just

---

[765] Saranam 2005, xxxi.
[766] Meacham 2011 and Hahn 2011.
[767] Revelation 2:1 to 3:22. These are also known as the Seven Churches of the Apocalypse and the Seven Churches of Asia (not the entire continent, but the Roman providence of Asia).
[768] Barclay 2007, 72-77.
[769] Barclay 2007, 22-28.

needed to return the rug along with a hefty donation. Praise the Lord and be sure to pass the collection plate!

By now, you should realize that I'd question this request without hesitation. A good investigator always searches for the source documents first, which I did. And, do you know what I discovered? There is no real Saint Matthews Church. Instead, this is nothing more than Reverend James Eugene Ewing's attempt to extort money from unsuspecting poor people throughout the country[770]. This so-called church uses a sophisticated software program to target the poorest zip codes in the US – yes, I live in one of those poor communities. And, how much do they make? Millions every month[771]! Not bad for a phony church.

To these con artists, the Bible is just a tool for extracting funds from unsuspecting Christians. While thieves use guns, they use Scripture to steal from us. Don't fall for this scam by sending them any money. This is nothing more than a big time scam. These con artists will use anything, such as fake gold coins, miracle water, and communion wafers, along with other numerous gimmicks to prey on you. And, they'll ask you to conceal your donations by telling you to keep this private, especially from family members who might have some better sense.

If He intended to create a church, Jesus did a very poor job because He provided no clear guidance about it. What we have today evolved over two thousand years, many churches using a fear of Christianity to either inspire confidence or terrify compliance. But, is the church today what Jesus wanted? I propose that the church should be measured by its deeds or the hearts of its members, not by the number or wealth of the members[772].

---

[770] Malisow 2007.
[771] Branstetter 2007.
[772] Davis 1934.

Conclusion.

The need to be part of a group allows someone to easily cross the line of being good to being evil[773]. That's a serious risk anyone takes when joining a Christian group. Based upon the Stanford Prison Experiment in 1971, a transformation of human character can result from environmental effects. The basic need to belong and associate with others allows one to conform to the new norms of any group. Joining a Christian groups should result in our changing to a better person who follows Jesus' teachings. Otherwise, we risk forfeiting our soul while we erroneously believe we're gaining not only the whole world but admittance to Heaven[774].

More to the point, much of Christian theology is framed in terms of redeeming humankind from its willful moral failures, with its focus primarily upon the salvation of humans. I don't believe that God created the rest of the animal kingdom for our amusement. God took notice when a sparrow falls and cherishes all creation[775]. What if there's other intelligent life within the universe? What if we're not the pinnacle of God's creation? What if the Christian story wasn't the final chapter of God's plan for the world?

Christianity plays a major role in shaping our behavior. Its history, culture, and traditions are integral parts of society. They are important in shaping perceptions and influencing mindsets[776]. Unfortunately, autocratic Christian groups rely upon its members' silence to maintain its power. Changes in these groups begin with the individuals. Fortunately today, Christians demanding changes are becoming loud and unrelenting. They're everywhere, in the pews, in the public, and in the families[777]. If it doesn't make sense, you, too, should speak up and question it.

---

[773] Zimbardo 2007, 258
[774] Matthew 16:26-27.
[775] Matthew 10:28-31.
[776] Bingham 2006, 61.
[777] Bonavoglia 2012.

I remember watching *Lord, Save Us from Your Followers*, a 2008 documentary about the collision of faith and culture that attempts to answer why the Gospel of Love is dividing America[778]. One of the main findings in this film is that many Christians follow the "Gospel of Being Right" instead of the "Gospel of Love". Which one do you follow? Your soul depends on your answer.

References

Ahlstrom, D. and Bruton, G.D. (2009). *International Management: Strategy and Culture in the Emerging World*. Mason, Oh.: South-Western Cengage Learning.

Allport, G.W. (1950). *The Individual and His Religion: A Psychological Interpretation*. New York: Macmillan.

Anderson, D. (2007). *Watergate: Scandal in the White House*. Minneapolis, Minn.: Compass Point Books.

Anderson, J.H. (1997, 6 November). "Boot Camp or Summer Camp? Restoring Rigorous Standards to Basic Training," *The Heritage Foundation*. Backgrounder #1147.

Asch, S.E. (1951). "Effects of Group Pressure Upon the Modification and Distortion of Judgment. In *Groups, Leadership and Men: Research in Human Relations*, edited by Harold S. Guetzkow, 177-90. Research sponsored by the Human Relations and Morale Branch of the Office of Naval Research from 1945-50. Pittsburgh, Penn.: Carnegie Press

Barclay, W. (2007). *Letters to the Seven Churches*. Louisville, Ky.: Westminster John Knox Press.

Barnett, F. and Lord, C. (eds.) (1989). *Political Warfare and Psychological Operations: Rethinking the US Approach*. Washington: National Defense University Press.

Bartov, O. (1992). *Hitler's Army:Soldiers, Nazis, and War in the Third Reich*. Oxford: Oxford University Press.

Bell, R. (2011). *Love Wins: A Book About Heaven, Hell, and the Fate of Every Person Who Ever*. New York: HarperCollins.

Bellafaire, J.A. (2005). *The Women's Army Corps: A Commemoration of World War II Service*. Center for Military History Publication 72-15. Washington: Government Printing Office.

Berman, H.J. (1983). *Law and Revolution: The Formation of the Western Legal Tradition*. Cambridge, Mass.: Harvard University Press.

---

[778] Merchant 2008.

Bevington, D. and Rasmussen, E. (1993). *Dr. Faustus A- and B-texts (1604, 1616): Christopher Marlowe and His Collaborator and Revisers.* Manchester, U.K.: Manchester University Press.

Bingham, R.L. (2006, autumn). "Bridging the Religious Divide." *Parameters. Journal of the US Army War College.* 36: 50-66. http://www.carlisle.army.mil/usawc/parameters/Articles/06autumn/bingham.pdf. Accessed 27 November 2011.

Bonavoglia, A. (2012). "American Nuns: Guilty as Charged?" *The Nation.* (May 21). http://www.thenation.com/article/167986/american-nuns-guilty-charged. Accessed 25 June 2012.

Boorstein, M. (2011, 23 December). "No Church, It's Christmas." *Washington Post.* http://www.washingtonpost.com/blogs/under-god/post/no-church-its-Christmas/2011/12/23/gIQAKdLmDP_blog.html. Accessed 28 January 2012.

Branstetter, Z. (2007, 13 May). "Prayers, cash flow into Tulsa." *Tulsa World.* http://www.tulsaworld.com/news/article.aspx?articleID=070513_238_A1_hWatc18175. Accessed 30 September 2012.

Brighton, T. (2004). *Hell Riders: The True Story of the Charge of the Light Brigade.* New York: Henry Holt and Company.

Brown, R.M. (2011). "America's Army in the Global Fracture." *Army.* 61(12): 22-24. http://www.ausa.org/publications/armymagazine/Archive/2011/12/Documents/FC_Brown_1211.pdf. Accessed 17 December 2011.

Campbell, W.D. (1995). "A Personal Struggle for Soul Freedom," Christian Ethics Today: 1(4): 15. http://www.christianethicstoday.com/cet/cet/cetjournal.pdf. Accessed 29 September 2012.

Cawthorne, N. (2004). *Alexander the Great.* London: Haus Publishing.

Center for Military Readiness. (2003, May). *Army Gender-Integrated Basic Training (GIBT), Summary of Relevant Findings and Recommendations: 1993 – 2002.* Washington, D.C.: US Government Printing Office. http://www.cmrlink.org/cmrnotes/gibtsp01.pdf. Accessed 25 June 2012.

Central Intelligence Agency. (2011). *Bay of Pigs: Freedom of Information Act.* (updated August 2) Washington, D.C.: US Government Printing Office. http://www.foia.cia.gov/bay_of_pigs.asp. Accessed 29 June 2012.

Chapman, A.W.; Lilly, C.J.; Romjue, J.L.; and Canedy, S. (1998). *Prepare the Army for War: A Historical Overview of the Army Training and Doctrine Command, 1973-1998.* Washington, D.C.: US Government Printing Office.

Cienciala, A.M.; Lebedeva, N.S.; and Materski, W. (eds.). (2007). *Katyn: A Crime Without Punishment*. New Haven, Conn.: Yale University Press.

Committee on Defense Women's Health Research. (1995). *Recommendations for Research on the Health of Military Women: Bibliographies, Institute of Medicine*. Washington: National Academy Press.

Congregation for the Doctrine of the Faith. (2012, 18 April). *Doctrinal Assessment of the Leadership Conference of Women Religious*. Citta del Vaticano. http://www.vatican.va/roman_curia/congregations/cfaith/documents/rc_con_cfaith_doc_20120418_assessment-lcwr_en.html. Accessed 25 June 2012.

Cooperman, A. (2006, 4 November). "Minister Admits to Buying Drugs and Massage." *The Washington Post*. http://www.washingtonpost.com/wp-dyn/content/article/2006/11/03/AR2006110301617.html. Accessed 30 September 2012.

Crider, L.W. (ed.). (2004). *In Search of the Light Brigade: A Biographical Dictionary of the Members of the Five Original Regiments of the Light Brigade from Jan 1, 1834 to Mar 31, 1856*. Surrey, U.K.: Biddles.

Daly, S. and Kaplan, D. (2012, 6 June). "Talented 'Liar': TV Phenom's War-Injury Tale." *New York Post*. http://www.nypost.com/p/news/national/talented_liar_dEG81EH8MkLd30jbOGfx8I. Accessed 28 July 2012.

David, G.J. and McKeldin, T.R. (eds.) (2009). *Ideas As Weapons: Influence and Perception in Modern Warfare*. Washington: Potomac Books.

Davies, D.T. (2009). *The Calling (What the Lord Intended)*. Maitland, Fl.: Xulon Press.

Davis, E. (1934). *Lovers of Life: An Epic Biography of Soul*. New York: The Baker and Taylor Company.

De Dreu, C.K. and Van de Vliert, E. (1997). "Introduction: Using Conflict in Organizations." In *Using Conflict in Organizations*, edited by Carsten K. De Dreu and Evert Van de Vliert. London: SAGE Publications. 1-22.

Dempsey, J.K. (2010). *Our Army: Soldiers, Politics, and American Civil-Military Relations*. Princeton, N.J.: Princeton University Press.

de Zavala, A.G.; Cichocka, A.; Eidelson, R.; and Jayawickreme, N. (2009). "Collective Narcissism and its Social Consequences." *Journal of Personality and Social Psychology*. 97(6): 1074-96. http://eprints.mdx.ac.uk/4252/1/Golec_collectivenarcissism.pdf. Accessed 29 September 2012.

Dutton, D.G. (2007). *The Psychology of Genocide, Massacres, and Extreme Violence: Why 'Normal' People Come to Commit Atrocities.* Westport, Conn.: Praeger.
Esser, J.K. and Lindoerfer, J.S. (1989). "Groupthink and the Space Shuttle Challenger Accident: Toward a Quantitative Case Analysis." *Journal of Behavioral Decision Making* 2 (3): 167-77.
Evans, R.J. (2003). *The Coming Of The Third Reich.* New York: Penguin Books.
Felt, J.B. (1827). *The Annals of Salem: From Its First Settlement.* Salem, Mass.: W.& S.B. Ives.
Finnegan, S. (2000). *The Book of Catholic Prayer: Prayers for Every Day and All Occasions.* Chicago: Loyola Press.
Finocchiaro, M.A. (2010). *Defending Copernicus and Galileo: Critical Reasoning in the Two Affairs.* New York: Springer.
Forsyth, D.R. (2010). *Group Dynamics.* Belmont, Calif.: Wadsworth, Cengage Learning.
French, B. (2012). *Why Christians Must Be Right.* Bloomington, Ind.: Westbow.
Gera, V. (2010, 22 May). "Astronomer Copernicus to be Reburied as Hero." *The Seattle Times.* http://seattletimes.nwsource.com/html/nationworld/2011926368_apeupolandcopernicusreburied.html. Accessed 12 August 2012.
Gibson, D. (2011, 23 December). "No Church This Sunday – It's Christmas." *The Wall Street Journal.* http://online.wsj.com/article/SB10001424052970204464404577112630659721286.html. Accessed 28 January 2012.
Gleijeses, P. (1995, February). "Ships in the Night: The CIA, the White House and the Bay of Pigs," *Journal of Latin American Studies*, 27: 37-42.
Goeschel, C. (2009). *Suicide in Nazi Germany.* Oxford: Oxford University Press.
Goethe, J.W. (1870). *Faust.* Original 1808 in German. Translated by Bayard Taylor. Cleveland, Oh.: World Publishing. http://www.gutenberg.org/files/14591/14591-h/14591-h.htm. Accessed 31 May 2012.
Golding, W. (1954). *Lord of the Flies.* London: Faber and Faber.
Goralka, J. (2012, 24 July). "George Zimmerman's defense: God made me do it." *Washington Times.* http://communities.washingtontimes.com/neighborhood/end-day/2012/jul/24/george-zimmermans-defense-god-made-me-do-it/. Accessed 7 October 2012.

Gordon Conwell Theological Seminary. (2011, January). "Status of Global Mission, 2011, in Context of 20th and 21st Centuries." http://www.gordonconwell.edu/resources/documents/StatusOfGlobalMission.pdf. Accessed 1 October 2011.

Gruhl, W. (2007). *Imperial Japan's World War Two, 1931-1945.* New Brunswick, N.J.: Transaction Publishers.

Gulley, P. (2010). *If the Church Were Christian: Rediscovery the Values of Jesus.* New York: HarperCollins Publishers.

Hafez, M.M. (2007). Suicide Bombers in Iraq: The Strategy and Ideology of Martyrdom. Washington: United States Institute of Peace.

Hahn, H. (2011, 25 March). "Post on Hell Lands Pastor in Hot Water." *United Methodist News Service.* http://www.umc.org/site/apps/nlnet/content3.aspx?c=lwL4KnN1LtH&b=5259669&ct=9260313. Accessed 6 October 2012.

Hanna, E. (1911). "The Sacrament of Penance." *The Catholic Encyclopedia.* 11. New York: Robert Appleton Company. http://www.newadvent.org/cathen/11618c.htm. Accessed 28 July 2012.

Hardon, J. (1981). *Catholic Catechism: A Contemporary Catechism of the Teachings of the Catholic Church.* New York: Doubleday.

Hasel, M.G. (1998). *Domination and Resistance: Egyptian Military Activity in the Southern Levant, ca 1300 – 1185 BC.* Leiden, The Netherlands: Koninklijke Brill NV.

Hawthorne, N. (1850). *The Scarlet Letter.* Boston, Mass.: Ticknor, Reed & Fields. http://www.gutenberg.org/cache/epub/ 33/pg33.html. Accessed 1 September 2012.

Henderson, W.D. (1985). *Cohesion: The Human Element in Combat.* Leadership and Societal Influence in the Armies of the Soviet Union, the United States, North Vietnam, and Israel. Washington, D.C.: US Government Printing Office. http://www.au.af.mil/au/awc/awcgate/ndu/cohesion/. Accessed 17 December 2011.

Herb, G.H. and Kaplan, D.H. (eds.) (2008). *Nations and Nationalism: A Global Historical Overview: A Global Historical Overview.* Volume 2 (1880-1945). Santa Barbara, Calif.: ABC-CLIO.

Herdt, J.A. (2008). *Putting on Virtue: The Legacy of the Splendid Vices.* Chicago: University of Chicago Press.

Hernandez, D. (2009). *The Greatest Story Ever Forged (Curse of the Christ Myth).* Pittsburgh, Penn.: Red Lead Press.

Hollander, E.P. and Hunt, R.G. (eds). (1963). *Current Perspectives in Social Psychology.* New York: Oxford Press.

Holzworth, C.E. (1997). "Operation Eagle Claw: A Catalyst for Change in the American Military." Masters Thesis. US Marine Corps Command and Staff College. http://www.globalsecurity.org/military/library/report/1997/Holzworth.htm. Accessed 15 September 2012.

James, L. (1994). *The Rise and Fall of the British Empire*. New York: St. Martin's Press.

Janis, I.L. (1971). "Groupthink." *Psychology Today*. 5(6): 43-46 and 74-76.

Janis, I.L. and Mann, L. (1977). *Decision making: a psychological analysis of conflict, choice, and commitment*. New York: Free Press

Johns, J.H.; Bickel, M.D.; Blades, A.C.; Creel, J.B.; Gatling, W.S.; Hinkle, J.M.; Kindred, J.D.; and Stocks, S.E. (1984). *Cohesion in the US Military*. Defense Management Study Group on Military Cohesion. AD-A140 828. Washington, D.C.: National Defense University Press. http://www.dtic.mil/cgi-bin/GetTRDoc?Location=U2&doc=GetTRDoc.pdf&AD=ADA140828. Accessed 10 December 2011.

Jones B.H., Manikowski J.A., Harris J.A., Dziados J.E., Norton S., Ewart T., and Vogel J.A. (1988). "Incidence of and Risk Factors for Injury and Illness Among Male and Female Army Basic Trainees." *Technical Report T19-88*. Natick, Mass.: US Army Research Institute of Environmental Medicine.

Jones, H. (2008). *Bay of Pigs*. New York: Oxford University Press.

Kelly, C. (2009). *The End of Empire: Attila the Hun & the Fall of Rome*. New York: W.W. Norton & Company.

Kent, W. (1907). "Doctrine of the Atonement." *The Catholic Encyclopedia*. 2. New York: Robert Appleton Company. http://www.newadvent.org/cathen/02055a.htm. Accessed 28 July 2012.

Keppie, L.J.F. (1998). *The Making of the Roman Army: From Republic to Empire*. London: Routledge.

Kipling, R. (1890, 28 April). "The Last of the Light Brigade." *St. James' Gazette* (London). http://www.kipling.org.uk/poems_brigade.htm. Accessed 15 September 2012.

Kirkpatrick, L.B. (1961, October). "Inspector General's Survey of the Cuban Operation." Central Intelligence Agency. http://www.gwu.edu/~nsarchiv/NSAEBB/ciacase/EXF.pdf. Accessed 29 June 2012.

Kirsch, K. (2008). *The Grand Inquisitor's Manual: A History of Terror in the Name of God*. New York: HarperCollins.

Kowert, P.A. (2002). *Groupthink Or Deadlock: When Do Leaders Learn from Their Advisors?* Albany, N.Y.: State University of New York Press.

Kunst, J. (2011, 18 October). "Projection 101: The Devil Made Me Do It! How to take responsibility and stop the madness!" *Psychology Today.* http://www.psychologytoday.com/blog/headshrinkers-guide-the-galaxy/201110/projection-101-the-devil-made-me-do-it. Accessed 5 October 2012.

Kyle, J.H. (1995). *The Guts to Try: The Untold Story of the Iran Hostage Rescue Mission by the On-Scene Desert Commander.* New York: Ballantine Publishing.

Kyle, R.G. (2006). *Evangelicalism: An Americanized Christianity.* New Brunswick, N.J.: Transaction Publishers.

Le Bon, G. (1896). *The Crowd: A Study of the Popular Mind.* French original in 1895. Translated by unknown. http://www.gutenberg.org/dirs/etext96/tcrwd10.txt. Accessed 11 August 2012.

Lee, S.J. (1998). *Hitler and Nazi Germany.* London: Routledge.

Lepage, J. (2009). *Hitler Youth, 1922-1945: An Illustrated History.* Jefferson, N.C.: McFarland & Company.

Lifton, R.J. (1986). *The Nazi Doctors: Medical Killing and the Psychology of Genocide.* London: Macmillan.

Lomax, S.S. (2008). *Did the Devil Make Me Do It?* Bloomington, Ind.: AuthorHouse.

Longshore, D. (2008). *Encyclopedia of Hurricanes, Typhoons, and Cyclones.* New York: Facts on File.

Malisow, C. (2007, 22 March). "Saint Matthew's Churches, Inc.: Christians send in money for prayer requests which may just go up in smoke." *Houston Press.* http://www.houstonpress.com/2007-03-22/news/saint-matthew-s-churches-inc/. Accessed 30 September 2012.

Marlowe, C. (1604). *The Tragical History of Doctor Faustus.* http://www.gutenberg.org/files/779/779-h/779-h.htm. Accessed 6 October 2012.

Mason, J.M. (1810). "Concession of Infidels." *The Christian's Magazine.* 3 (10): 574-76.

McDowell, J. and Stewart, D. (1986). *Answers to Tough Questions Skeptics Ask About the Christian Faith.* Carol Stream, Il..: Tyndale House Publishers.

McPhail, C. (1991). *The Myth of the Madding Crowd.* Hawthorne, N.Y.: Aldine-DeGruyter.

Meacham, J. (2011, 14 April). "Pastor Rob Bell: What if Hell Doesn't Exist?" *Time Magazine*. http://www.time.com/time/magazine/article/0,9171,2065289,00.html. Accessed 29 September 2012.

Meier, G. (1908). "Sts. Cyprian and Justina." *The Catholic Encyclopedia*. New York: Robert Appleton Company. http://www.newadvent.org/cathen/04583a.htm. Accessed 5 October 2012.

Merchant, D. (2008). *Lord, Save Us from Your Followers.*. http://www.imdb.com/title/tt1237900/. Accessed 29 September 2012.

Montgomery, D. (2008). *A Membership Guide to the Body of Christ*. Mustang, Ok.: Tate Publishing.

Morden, B.J. (1990). *The Women's Army Corps, 1945 – 1978*. Center of Military History. Washington: Government Printing Office.

Muverengwi, P. (2011). *The Faces of Hypocrisy in the Christian Church*. Bloomington, Ind.:AuthorHouse.

Namie, G. and Namie, R. (2000). *The Bully at Work: What You Can Do to Stop the Hurt and Reclaim Your Dignity on the Job*. Naperville, Ill.: Sourcebooks.

Ohnuki-Tierney, E. (2002). *Kamikaze, Cherry Blossoms, and Nationalisms: The Militarization of Aesthetics in Japanese History*. Chicago: University of Chicago Press.

Oliver, K. (2006). *The My Lai Massacre in American History and Memory*. Manchester, U.K.: Manchester University Press.

Orwell, G. (1949). *Nineteen Eighty-Four*. London: Secker and Warbung.

Overy, R.J. (2004). *The Dictators: Hitler's Germany and Stalin's Russia*. New York: W.W. Norton & Company.

Palmer, P.M. and More, R.P. (1966). *The Sources of the Faust Tradition: From Simon Magus to Lessing*. New York: Octagon Books.

Panetta, L.E. (2011). "Willing to Make That Fight." *Army*. 61(12): 35-38. This is an October 12, 2011 speech to the AUSA Annual Meeting. http://www.defense.gov/speeches/speech.aspx?speechid=1621. Accessed 17 December 2011.

Parker, S. (2006). "Measuring Faith Development." *Journal of Psychology and Theology*. 34(4): 337-348.

Paxton, R.O. and Hessler, J. (2012). *Europe in the Twentieth Century*. 5th Ed. Boston, Mass.: Wadsworth.

Perse, E.M. (2008). *Media Effects and Society*. Mahwah, N.J.: Lawrence Erlbaum Associates.

Pfeiffer, J.B. (1984, 9 November). "The Taylor Committee Investigation of The Bay of Pigs." Central Intelligence Agency report.

http://www.foia.cia.gov/bay-of-pigs/bop-vol4.pdf. Accessed 14 September 2012.

Phelan, G.L. (2009). *Crucifixion and the Death Cry of Jesus Christ*. Maitland, Fl.: Xulon Press.

Quesada, A. (2009). *The Bay of Pigs: Cuba 1961*. Oxford: Osprey Publishing.

Redd, S.E. (2007). "Lived Experiences, Televangelism, and American Media: Lessons Learned from Individuals' Reflections and Media Accounts about the PTL Scandal. " Ph.D. Dissertation. Regent University.

Rogers, W.P. (Chair). (1986). "Report of the Presidential Commission on the Space Shuttle Challenger Accident." http://science.ksc.nasa.gov/shuttle/missions/51-l/docs/rogers-commission/table-of-contents.html. Accessed 30 June 2012.

Rutter, T. (1997, 16 August). "United States Bans Smoking on Federal Property." *British Medical Journal* 315:383-388.

Sanford, G. (2005). *Katyn and the Soviet Massacre of 1940 Truth, Justice and Memory*. New York: Routledge.

Saranam, S. (2005). *God Without Religion: Questioning Centuries of Accepted Truths*. East Ellijay, Ga.: The Pranayama Institute.

Schamschula, W. (1992). "Pan Twardowski: The Polish Variant of the Faust Legend in Slavic Literatures – A Study in Motif History." In *California Slavic Studies*, edited by Henrik Birnbaum, Thomas Eekman, and Hugh McLean. 14: 209-231. Berkeley, Calif.: University of California Press.

Sekunda, N. (1992). *The Persian Army 560-330 BC*. Oxford, U.K.: Osprey Publishing.

Smith, D.K. (1992). *Creating Understanding: A Handbook for Christian Communication Across Cultural Landscapes*. Grand Rapids, Mich.: Zondervans.

Spiegel, J.S. (2000). *Hypocrisy: Moral Fraud and Other Vices*. Ada, Mich.: Baker Books.

Steigmann-Gall, R. (2003). *The Holy Reich: Nazi Conceptions of Christianity, 1919-1945*. Cambridge: Cambridge University Press.

Strobel, L. (2007). *The Case for the Real Jesus: A Journalist Investigates Current Attacks on the Identity of Christ*. Grand Rapids, Mich.: Zondervan.

't Hart, P. (2011). *Beyond Groupthink: Political Group Dynamics and Foreign Policy-Making*. Ann Arbor, Mich.: University of Michigan Press.

't Hart, P. and Kroon, M.B.R. (1997). "Groupthink in Government: Pathologies of Small-Group Decision Making," in *Handbook of Administrative Communication*, edited by J. Garnett and A. Kouzmin. New York: Marcel Dekker.

The Telegraph. (2011, 28 September). "Saudi woman to be lashed for driving car." http://www.telegraph.co.uk/news/worldnews/middleeast/saudiarabia/8793145/Saudi-woman-to-be-lashed-for-driving-car.html. Accessed 28 January 2012.

Tennyson, A. (1854, 9 December). "The Charge of the Light Brigade." *The Examiner*. http://www.gutenberg.org/files/18909/18909-h/18909-h.htm#The_Charge_of_the_Light_Brigade. Accessed 16 September 2012.

Thomasson, D.K. (2012, 21 June). "Catholics Challenged With Nuns Under Siege." *Scripps Howard News Service..*

Thompson, M. (2001, 24 June). "Boot Camp Goes Soft." *Time*.

Turnbull, S. (2003). *Genghis Khan & the Mongol Conquests 1190-1400*. Oxford: Osprey Publishing.

Turner, C. (2011, 29 November). "Research: Pastors plan to host Christmas services despite busyness of Christmas Day." *LifeWay Research*. http://www.lifeway.com/Article/LifeWay-Research-Pastors-plan-to-host-Christmas-services-despite-busyness-of-Christmas-Day. Accessed 28 January 2012.

Unknown (1592). *The Historie of the Damnable Life, and Deserved Death of Doctor Iohn Faustus*. Original 1587 in German as *The History of Dr. Johann Fausten*. Translated by P.F. Gent.

van Wormer, K. and Besthorn, F.H. (2011). *Human Behavior and the Social Environment, Macro Level:Groups, Communities, and Organizations*. 2nd Ed. Oxford: Oxford University Press.

Vaughan, D. (1996). *The Challenger Launch Decision: Risky Technology, Culture and Deviance at NASA*. Chicago: University of Chicago Press

Velarde, R. (2009). "What About Hypocrites in the Church?" *Focus on the Family*. http://www.focusonthefamily.com/faith/becoming_a_christian/is_christ_the_only_way/what_about_hypocrites_in_the_church.aspx. Accessed 1 July 2012.

Victor, G. (2007). *The Pearl Harbor Myth: Rethinking the Unthinkable*. Dulles, Va.: Potomac Books.

Walsh, H.E. (1989). *Groupthink*. Rapidan, Va.: Hartland Publications.

Warner, M. (1998, winter). "The CIA's Internal Probe of the Bay of Pigs Affair: Lessons Unlearned." *Studies in Intellegence*. Central Intelligence Agency. 40: 93-101. Washington, D.C.: US Government Printing Office. https://www.cia.gov/library/

center-for-the-study-of-intelligence/csi-publications/csi-studies/studies/winter98_99/art08.html. Accessed 29 June 2012.
Whyte, W.H. Jr. (1952). "Groupthink." *Fortune.* 45 (March): 114-17, 42, and 46.
Wickham, C. (2005). *Framing the Early Middle Ages:Europe and the Mediterranean, 400-800.* Oxford: Oxford University Press.
Willis, M. (1978). "Hypocrisy in Christians." *Truth Magazine.* 22 (17): 275-77. http://www.truthmagazine.com/archives/volume22/TM022147. Accessed 1 July 2012.
Winter, P. (1974). *On the Trial of Jesus.* 2nd Ed. Berlin: Walter de Gruyter & Company.
Witte, E.H. (1996). "The Extended Group Situation Theory (EGST): Explaining the Amount of Change." In *Understanding Group Behavior: Volume 1: Consensual Action By Small Groups*, edited by E.H. Witte and J.H Davis. Pp. 253-292. Mahwah, N.J.: Lawrence Erlbaum Associates.
Wong, F.A. (2012). "Revised Stolen Valor Act Would Stand Up." *The American Legion Magazine.* 173 (2): 8.
Woolton, J. (1851). *The Christian Manual; or, of the Life and Manners of True Christians.* Cambridge: The University Press.
Wright, B.R. (2010). *Christians are Hate-Filled Hypocrites ... and Other Lies You've Been Told.* Bloomington, Minn.: Bethany House Publishers.
Xyrichis, A. and Ream, E. (2008). "Teamwork: A Concept Analysis." *Journal of Advanced Nursing.* 61(2): 232-241.
Yahya, H. (2002). *Let's Learn Our Islam.* London: Ta-Ha Publishers.
Zaloga, S.J. (2011). *Kamikaze: Japanese Special Attack Weapons 1944-45.* Oxford, U.K.: Osprey Publishing.
Zimbardo, P. (2007). *The Lucifer Effect: Understanding How Good People Turn Evil.* New York: Random House.

Chapter 7. Additional Christian Controversies

> *Many devout Christians aggressively oppose religious controversies. Disagreement, debate, and division over religious issues are deplorable and, in their judgment, contrary to the spirit of Jesus and detrimental to His cause. Hence, they tend to avoid discussions, meetings, literature, and issues which would likely cause controversial opinions. Yet, every meaningful Christian truth is controversial. The truth stings and angers people. It's every Christian's duty to seek the truth, especially when it involves controversy.*

Although I only fully discussed five controversies in this book, I have many more that we could encounter. Although not much is discussed about each, I provide several of them below with some background information to assist you in your future self-learning and self-assessment of these contemporary issues.

Controversial 'What If' Questions

What if we discover that a previously perceived truth was incorrect, would we totally throw everything away and not believe anything more about the subject? When I studied chemistry in college, I completely understood the basic principles of general chemistry and the scientific principles taught from my Freshman level classes. This ranged from the ideal gas laws to the fundamental chemical reactions. However, when I studied more advanced concepts of chemistry later, I understood that nothing completely adhered to these simple general principles. There were non-ideal models for several different situations. In other words, there was a different application of chemical observations depending upon the situation at hand. I had to relearn chemistry with this additional information. With that in mind, would my beliefs in Christianity collapse if some of the information involving changed? The following are several "what if" questions, that if were true, would definitely shake up the beliefs of most Christians.

Was Jesus a Jew and not a modern-defined Christian?

During the time of Jesus, there were two separate Jewish nations, Judea (יהודה) and Galilee (הגליל). As written in the Gospels, He was a resident of Nazareth (נָצְרַת) in Galilee[779]. He was also a descent of the Tribe of Judah (יְהוּדָה). As such, he was ethnically a Jew (יְהוּדִים), coming from the tribe from which the term "Jew" was named[780]. As for following the Jewish religion, he publically observed their traditions. He wore tzitzit (ציצית) on His clothing, as commanded in the Torah[781]. Honoring the Jewish ceremonies, He observed Passover (פֶּסַח)[782], Succot (סָכּוֹת)[783], and Hanukah (חֲנֻכָּה)[784]. He affirmed the Torah (תּוֹרָה) and the Prophets[785]. Regularly attending synagogue, He taught in the Jewish Temple in Jerusalem (יְרוּשָׁלַיִם), where other Jews respected His teachings[786]. In fact, people were forbidden from the Jewish Temple if they weren't Jews[787]. With these facts and indisputable evidence, you can logically conclude that Jesus was a faithful practicing Jew.

Now, was Jesus a Christian is my next question? According to the Merriam Webster dictionary, a Christian is someone who professes belief in the teachings of Jesus. Jesus does indeed meet this definition[788]. However, there's another definition of a Christian, which involves being a member of one of the Churches worshipping Jesus. I'm not sure that He meets this other definition, especially for many of today's Christian organizations and denominations. Which definition of a Christian describes you?

Before you answer this question, let me tell you about several Christian organizations that believe I'm NOT a Christian and don't

---

[779] Matthew 26:69 and John 7:41.
[780] Matthew 1:1 and Hebrews 7:14.
[781] In the Torah: Numbers 15:38 and Deuteronomy 22:12. In the Gospels: Matthew 14:36 and Luke 8:44.
[782] John 2:13.
[783] John 7:2-10. This is otherwise known as the Feast of the Tabernacles.
[784] John 10:22. This is also known as the Festival of Lights.
[785] Matthew 5:17.
[786] Luke 4:15-16 and 21:37.
[787] Acts 21:28-30.
[788] Website: http://www.merriam-webster.com/dictionary/christian.

believe what most Christians believe. Most Christian publishers, for that matter, fall into that group and would NEVER print this book. They, like other groups, have a *Statement of Faith* that requires its Christian members (or authors) to believe in the truthfulness and authority of the Scriptures, both the Old and New Testament. They want us to believe that it's without error in everything it says. I don't believe this since the evidence, and even common sense, would suggest otherwise. If they truly believe their own *Statement of Faith*, then they must be living the life of a hypocrite. To illustrate my point, many of the laws in the Bible require killing anyone who violates many of its dictates, such as adultery and worshipping differently. Most people who profess following these misguided statements don't seek the killing of others. So, I guess, that they just pick and choose which Scriptures to follow. The Bible, also, can be used to justify the killing of everyone, including you.

Jesus wouldn't advocate the killing of everyone. I do realize that is what God did with the Great Flood, while saving Noah and his family[789]. But, Jesus wouldn't do that; and, He wouldn't support their *Statement of Faith* either. How do I know that? The evidence I offer is found in the *Sermon on the Mount* in which he told His followers that, "You have heard that it was said .... But I say to you ...."[790]. Through this, His teachings violated the traditional political and religious patriarchal order, as demonstrated in Gospels. He aggressively challenged the legalistic and unreasonable requirements imposed by the religious leaders, using the Scriptures as His source[791]. I firmly believe that Jesus would never become a modern, Bible-thumping, hypocritical, self-righteous Christian.

Was Jesus just a man and not a god?

Who was Jesus? Was he a God, a man, a symbol, or a prophet? Many of the religions, such as Buddhism and Islam, have tried to convince others that a historical person was divine as a way to

---

[789] Genesis 6-9.
[790] Matthew 5:20-48.
[791] Mark 12:38-40.

suggest that their teachings were absolute. People have the tendency to respond favorably to a god who comes to them in human form using humanly understandable terms.

The source used in answering this question should begin with the Gospels. Jesus claims to have existed before Abraham[792]. He claimed that God sent Him to save the world[793]. The same could be said of Pierre Basile, an unknown boy who killed Richard the Lionhearted[794]. Later, Richard's brother John signed the *Magna Carta*, the basis of people's freedom against absolute monarchies[795]. Jesus claimed that He and God were one[796]. This doesn't necessarily mean that Jesus claimed to be a god, but that He did good works, just like God. He claimed to be a Teacher and Lord[797], along with being the Good Shepherd[798]. Other religious leaders claimed to be a teacher of God's words and expected to be obeyed, just like a lord. Jesus claimed to be "the way, the truth, and the life"[799] and "the bread of life"[800]. He also claimed to give His followers eternal life[801]. I prefer to believe that His claims represented His teachings about God's love. In another set of Scriptures, Jesus claimed to represent everyone, especially the hungry, thirsty, poor, unclothed, sick, and imprisoned[802]. Jesus claimed to be the Son of God[803], which is really not that big of a claim since the Old Testament portrayed God as everyone's Father. Jesus claimed that those who don't believe that He came from Heaven and in His Words would die[804]. If you believe this strictly, you would believe that anyone who lived and died before His time would have been condemned to eternity in Hell. I don't believe

---

[792] John 8:56-58.
[793] John 12:44-46.
[794] Barber 1999, 155-56.
[795] Holt 1992, 3.
[796] John 10:30-33.
[797] John 13:13.
[798] John 10:10-15.
[799] John 14:6-9.
[800] John 6:32-35.
[801] John 6:40 and 10:27-28.
[802] Matthew 25:31-46.
[803] John 5:22-23.
[804] John 8:23-24.

that this was the intent of His statement. Nowhere in this does Jesus state He was a god and needed to be worshipped.

However, He claimed to forgive sins, which only a god can do[805]. And, He claimed to rise after being dead for three days[806]. Now for the biggest claim in the Gospel is that of John 3:16-18. This wasn't a claim made specifically by Jesus, but that of the author's description of Jesus' purpose. Jesus did claim that anyone who follows His teachings of love will spend eternity with God[807].

Furthermore, Jesus tried to bring God closer to people by revealing Him in simple and clearly understandable terms. He didn't try to make himself a god for followers to worship – at least I couldn't find any mention of this in any of the Gospels[808]. Jesus never mentioned creating another religion. Furthermore, I couldn't find anything in the Bible about Jesus glorifying and elevating Himself. Instead, I read about His humility, modesty and selflessness[809]. If He was a god, He would have preferred we followed His teachings, not worshipped Him as a god.

Was Jesus married and did He have children?

Is it important to our faith that Jesus was unmarried and had no children? Likewise, is it important to our faith that he was a virgin and had no sexual relationship with a woman? There are many theories recently that suggest the possibility that Jesus was married.

Recently discovered evidence, a small piece of ancient papyrus called the *Gospel of Jesus' Wife*, suggests that many Christians in the second century believed that He was married[810]. Although this doesn't conclusively prove that Jesus had a wife, it does suggest that the early Christians didn't lose their faith while believing He married and had sexual relations with a woman.

---

[805] Matthew 9:6-8.
[806] Mark 9:31.
[807] John 14:21-23.
[808] Schilpp 1938, 181-183.
[809] Gulley 2010, 19 and 25.
[810] King 2013.

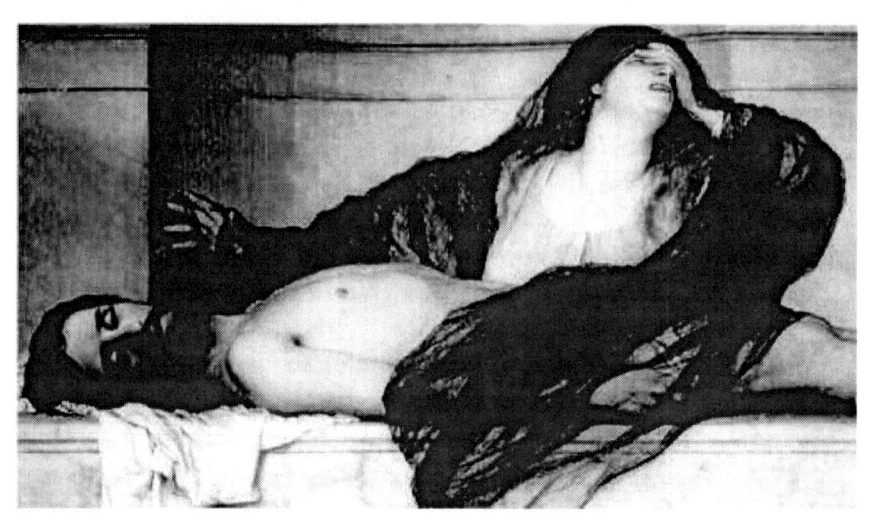

Figure 29. Lamentations of Mary Magdalene on the Body of Christ. by Arnold Böcklin (1868).

One such possibility for a wife was Mary Magdalene, who was from an unknown village of Magdala. There were no records of this village ever existing. Instead, Magdalene might be a play on the word Migdal, which refers to a tower that Shepherds used to watch their flocks. So, this might be another way of saying "Mary the Great". If this wasn't His mother, the Virgin Mary, then it would refer to some other woman who was great in the eyes of Jesus. Mary Magdalene was also the one in the tomb scene calling Jesus "my lord" and "rabboni", which were titles that a Jewish wife used to address her rabbi husband. And, she demanded access to His body from the gardener, which was appropriate for the deceased next of kin to do. Maybe this person was His wife[811]. Just because the Bible doesn't directly mention that He had a wife doesn't mean He didn't. Even though there was no evidence in the Bible or elsewhere, Christian leaders in the second century declared Mary Magdalene a whore. As a result, the two key women in Jesus' life were declared either a mythical perpetual virgin or a whore damned for all eternity by Christian leaders hundreds of years after His departure from this world.

---

[811] Spong 2005, 107.

Does God love Heathens and Atheists?

Fundamentalist Christians talk about the teachings of Jesus, but prefer going back to the dark ages of Israel when the Abrahamic God destroyed entire cities and entire nations in fits of genocidal rage, along with ordering the rape of women and slavery. According to them, God has many enemies, those judge to spend eternity in Hell. These include foreigners, heretics, homosexuals, dismissed wives, drunken sons, disobedient slaves, and anyone not doing His will (at least according to someone else's interpretation of His will)[812]. And they claim the source of their information is the Bible, which is definitely one of the World's most dangerous books, giving one the authority to kill[813].

If you believe those hellfire-and-brimstone preachers, all of those godless Heathens are a serious danger to everyone. Why not? In a recent study, people would prefer to trust a rapist over that of an Atheist[814]. Maybe, the typical Christian believes all Heathens are racists, such as members of Nazism, white-supremacy, and other hate groups. How would Jesus treat them? He would love them, even the racists. I doubt He would support or agree with them. And, whatever we do to the least of our neighbors, we do to Jesus[815]. Even the Good Samaritan was a Heathen and Atheist, and was definitely better than the religious leaders.

In the story of Cain and Abel, we have the biblical story of the first murder. What would have happened if God accepted both sacrifices to promote cooperation between the shepherd and the farmer? Would Cain have killed Abel? Instead, we have the example of a violent competition in which God repeatedly plays favorites, such as giving blessings to one person instead of another[816]. In another biblical story, we have Esau questioning why his father, Isaac, had only one blessing, the one he was tricked into

---

[812] See especially Hoffman 2006.
[813] See especially Collins 2003.
[814] Gervais et.al. 2011.
[815] Matthew 25:40.
[816] See especially Schwartz 1998. Regina Schartz is, an English professor at Northwestern University in Chicago

giving to Jacob[817]. I prefer to interpret these stories as discussions of human intolerance and violence rather than about God and His hate for others. Conversely, Jesus' teachings reveal to us that God prefers compromise and love over hateful competition.

Wasn't the message of Jesus about love, especially love of one's neighbors? Did He not provide us this in His parable about the *Good Samaritan*? Which is better, a kind group of Atheists or a hateful group of Christians? I know several Atheists who have been very kind to others, even loving fellow humans (i.e. some have setup scholarships to help students in need).

Figure 30. Inferno 22.
by Gustave Doré (1857).

Is Hell merely a separation from God?

What is Hell? And, where do I find the truth about this? Like most Christian questions, the best place to begin is the Bible, which tells us that Hell is a place of flaming fire. For instance, the sexually immoral and perverse residents of Sodom and Gomorrah

---

[817] Genesis 27:38.

suffered punishment of eternal fire[818]. Also in the Bible, we are reminded that people were advised to cut off their body parts if those parts offended God, else they too would be sent into a fire that never quenches[819]. And in Revelation, we read about the lake of fire and brimstone (ואש גפרית) where souls are tormented forever[820]. For centuries, Christian leaders have used these Scriptures as vivid descriptions of judgment and eternal damnation to encourage repentance and control behavior.

Hell is mentioned over fifty times in the King James Version of 1611[821]. Yet, does this word have the same meaning each time mentioned? For example in the Old Testament, Sheol (שְׁאוֹל Š'ôl) was the original word used in place of the word Hell, but described the location where souls were kept until the *Day of Judgment* as written in Revelation 20:12-15. Its actual translation meant "grave" or "pit". Thus, this isn't the fiery place of eternity. In the New Testament, written mostly in Greek, we find the word Hades (Ἅδου), which meant temporary place of the unsaved after death. Another word for Hell was mentioned in 2 Peter 2:4, Tartarus (Τάρταρος), which meant the place of the underworld, that was even lower than Hades. Jesus also described this place using Gehenna (γέεννα), which referenced the smoldering Gehenna Valley near the base of Mount Zion[822]. In other words, Hell was a place no one wanted to go.

Who goes to Hell and who makes that Final Judgment? If you're to believe Bible-thumping preachers with their hell-fire and damnation sermons, it would be those people who don't believe in their views and are unwilling to repent of their sins. On the other hand, if God were to separate the unrepentant on this world, what will happen to the uncreated souls who are never born[823]? I prefer to have God make this judgment of my life, not someone using Scripture to coerce me do something they want me to do.

---

[818] Jude 1:7.
[819] Mark 9:43.
[820] 20:10-14.
[821] Vinsten 2010, 28.
[822] This also meant the Valley of Hinnom.
[823] See especially Davies and Evans 1998.

But once in Hell, how long do souls stay? Many Christian leaders throughout history suggest that this would be forever. Yet, the words they use from the Bible could represent a different length of time, even though they are used for meaning eternity. In the Old Testament, we can find the Hebrew word Olam (עוֹלָם) when describing Sheol. This adjective meant a time of unknown duration[824]. Definitely not eternity. While in the New Testament, we can find the Greek words Aion (αἰών), meaning age, and Aionios (αἰώνιος), relating to an age. None of these words conclusively refer to an eternity in Hell.

Aside from the Bible, much of our understanding of Hell comes from literature. For example, Dante used the biblical destruction of Sodom and Gomorrah by fire and brimstone[825]. He then added descriptions from the medieval condemnations of citizens of Cahors, a city in southern France[826]. Another example comes from English Puritan preacher Thomas Vincent, who was known for his "Fire and Brimstone" preaching methods, informing people that Jesus only loved true Christians[827]. As an eyewitness of the Great Fire of London, he authored the 1670 book *Fire and Brimstone in Hell, to Burn the Wicked*.

What about the idea that Hell is a separation from God? Who came up with that idea? Let me begin my discussion with the popular American evangelist Billy Graham who had several things to say about Hell in 1970. This place "means separation from God. We are separated from his light, from his fellowship. That is going to be Hell"[828]. Almost twenty-five years later, he maintained his statement that "Hell is death to the spirit, death to the soul, separation from God"[829].

---

[824] Bennet 1800, 44.
[825] Genesis 19:24-25.
[826] The Church declared it a sin for bankers charging excessive or abusive interest on their loans, and Cahors was infamous for having bankers doing this.
[827] Charles 2008, 93 and Thiselton 2011.
[828] Ostling and Graham 1993.
[829] Graham 1970, 81.

Additional Christian Controversies

As head of the largest Christian church, Pope John Paul II on July 28, 1999, in his weekly address to approximately 8,500 people, spoke that "The images of Hell that Sacred Scripture presents to us must be correctly interpreted. They show the complete frustration and emptiness of life without God. Rather than a place, Hell indicates the state of those who freely and definitively separate themselves from God, the source of all life and joy. ... This state of definitive self-exclusion from communion with God and the blessed is called 'Hell' .... Damnation consists precisely in definitive separation from God".

But, can these two global modern Christian leaders be wrong that Hell is a separation from God? Disputing this separation idea are a few biblical verses. In Psalms 139:8, we read that God is present with souls in Hell. Found in Revelation is a verse implying that souls tormented by fire in Hell is done in the presence of Jesus[830]. Yet these two verses contradict others in the Bible, such as 2 Thessalonians 1:9, which says punishment is an eternity spent away from Jesus. We can even find information about Hell in the Sermon on the Mount in which Jesus discussed five messages that reflect final punishment as separation from Him, not suffering from fire and brimstone[831].

I'm not going to tell you that Hell is a separation from God or that it's a fiery pit for all of eternity[832]. I don't know. I haven't been to the real one, just to some places in this mortal world that come close. I can tell you that it's difficult to reconcile the contradictory verses of the Bible. Most controversies are difficult to resolve. Jesus certainly didn't evade discussing Hell. He devoted a great deal of discussion to the reality of eternal punishment and the importance of avoiding it. We just need to figure out how we're going to reconcile Hell with God's love for us. Many others propose answers for this and try to convince us that Hell is probably a free choice, not a penalty judgment. The prospect of eternal torment is irreconcilable with God's love.

---

[830] 14:10.
[831] See especially Fudge and Peterson 2000.
[832] Additional views about Hell can be found in Walvoord 2010.

For me, I prefer to think of Hell as separation from God, the source of all love, joy, peace, and light[833]. This punishment is much worse than spending an eternity in a dark pit with fire and brimstone.

Can souls be saved after death?

When you die, where do you go? Do you have just two places, Heaven or Hell? Or are there other places, such as Purgatory and Sheol? We hear many sermons about these places and what it takes to get there. Many of these sermons lead us to believe that our place for eternity is determined by what we do during the finite time we spend alive on this World, whether we are here for 1 minute or 100 years. Are we to believe that we can be judged to spend eternity in Hell for something that happened during 1 minute of our life without consideration of the other 1.5 billion other minutes in a 50-year old person's lifespan? As the topic of this section implies, can we repent and be saved after death?

One of my favorite movies is Mel Brooks' 1991 comedy, *Defending Your Life*, portraying people immediately after death going to court in the afterlife to prove their worth. It contains a profound and powerful question – what's the real meaning of life and can you learn it after you die[834]? I don't know if this is true; yet, some evangelical theologians indicate the possibility of postmortem conversions, giving souls future chances for salvation after death. This is really a post-death purification process to more fully atone for offenses against God[835].

Postmortem conversion isn't a new concept for Christianity. For example, Purgatory is a postmortem probation[836]. And, it has been part of the Catholic theology since the Council of Trent in 1546[837].

---

[833] Buenting 2010, 96.
[834] Books 1991.
[835] Taylor 1998, 8.
[836] See especially Walls 2012.
[837] Hanna 1911. The decree of the Council of Trent (Session 25) defined: "Whereas the Catholic Church, instructed by the Holy Ghost, has from the Sacred Scriptures and the ancient tradition of the Fathers taught in Councils and very recently in this Ecumenical synod that there is a purgatory, and that the

Yet, the belief in Purgatory is becoming less believable as Christians believe in total forgiveness, so why should there be a delay in getting into Heaven[838]?

Bombarding our minds are messages of religious fads, pious fancies, boasted piety, supernatural spells, religious creeds, and power[839]. None of these will alter our existence after death. Instead, we should pay more attention to religious spirituality and to deeds that help relieve human pains such as hunger and sickness. Then, we should let the afterlife take care of itself.

Should you kill to prevent the killings of others?

The real question remains, is it morally allowable to employ force in the protection and preservation of values[840]? We can apply the same type of principles behind military ethics to that of Christian ethics. *Jus ad bellum* involves justification of action and *jus in bello* involves the limitation of those actions[841]. For me, the use of force is justified to protect the innocent, to recover something wrongly taken, to punish evil, and to defend again a wrongful attack. However, in my opinion, punishing evil is one that is extremely hard to justify. For example, how do we define evil? And, what is the correct use of force for the punishment? Do you become judge, jury, and executioner for this offense? Is it right to punish someone because they believe something different than you? Is it necessary to kill a person in order to save the person? Was the defeat of Nazism in World War II commensurate with the loss of 55 million lives[842]? Objection to violence, war, and killing can be linked to an idealistic vision of world community, which doesn't exist today.

---

souls therein are helped by the suffrages of the faithful, but principally by the acceptable Sacrifice of the Altar; the Holy Synod enjoins on the Bishops that they diligently endeavor to have the sound doctrine of the Fathers in Councils regarding purgatory everywhere taught and preached, held and believed by the faithful."
[838] Taylor 1998, 9-10.
[839] Schlipp 1938, 3-4.
[840] Johnson 1985, 13.
[841] Johnson 1985, 14.
[842] Coffey, 1983.

As a military leader, I had to possess the capability of influencing the environment to the benefit of my military organization[843]. I was also expected to fully understand that statements of values alone had little impact upon the organizational culture. Instead, changing the culture involved the leaders' climate and their effective use of resource allocation and reward criteria. In changing this culture, I had to be ethically competent in addition to being technically and tactically competent.

Unfortunately, this was easier said than accomplished since the complexities of the current world today poses several challenges to the military leader's ethical decision-making, similar to those affecting peace officers. For example, Desert Storm promoted force protection as a requirement in subsequent conflicts, which resulted in a problem of determining whether force protection or that protection of innocents should have priority in the actions[844]. Regarding this dilemma, I was trained to consider the *Doctrine of Double Effect*, which involved legitimacy, effect, intent, and proportionality of the action[845]. In essence, the use of force shouldn't be based upon expediency and efficiency without considering the moral requirement to minimize risk to innocents.

Unfortunately, current society has a higher value placed upon self-related activities and personal choice, in lieu of service to others[846]. A person saying that he has nothing worth dying for is the same as him having nothing worth living for. As such, to improve my ability to influence my environment, I studied the historical examples of strategic leaders failing to establish an ethical climate, especially those that resulted in national scandals. Some of these examples included King Henry II, President Nixon, and President Reagan in which the conditions that fostered unethical climate included frustrations, misguided loyalties, and gamesmanship[847].

---

[843] Magee 1998.
[844] Carlino 2002.
[845] Carlino 2002.
[846] Toner 1996.
[847] Shepard 1992.

During my military career, especially while in command of thousands of Soldiers, I was totally responsible for establishing and maintaining the ethical culture and moral climate. In this complex world, I based my decisions upon the particular situation, the tasks to be done, and the characteristics in my organization[848]. I analyzed this culture by asking myself answers to four questions: who's in charge, how do I view people, how do I expect others to act, and what are my expectations of how people interact with one another[849]. I understood that changing culture depended upon how leaders measured and controlled the organization, including both their role modeling (teaching and coaching) processes and reward allocation.

Using Augustine's view, there's no moral difference between a state, representing many people, and that of a gang of thugs, representing few people. This view laid the foundation for the justification for warfare, otherwise known as the *Just War Theory*[850]. *Just War* concepts involve a balance between two competing principles: the taking of a human life as evil and the protection of innocent humans through the taking of a life. When dealing with *Just War*, I applied several mechanisms to guide my moral decision-making, such as international and national laws[851]. *Jus ad bellum* (reasons for going to war) were typically done for defense of territorial integrity or sovereignty of the state, not fighting for a universal humanity. This had several elements: just cause, legitimate authority, public declaration, just intent, proportionality, last resort, and reasonable hope of success. However, most wars that the US fights didn't involve national sovereignty or territorial integrity; instead, we fought for national interests and values. For example, Desert Storm was a classic Westphalian story of restoring Kuwaiti sovereignty with a happy ending, however being tainted by others as being done for economic purposes or for American national interests of oil. The

---

[848] Schein 1996.
[849] Stroup 1996.
[850] Cook 2000.
[851] Cook 2001.

jus in bello (conduct during war) involved discrimination (who can be attacked) and proportionality (how they can be attacked). The military was obligated to conduct itself in a professional manner in war, but wasn't responsible for the moral reasons for going to war.

When dealing with others, such as my Soldiers and civilian leaders, I applied a method to understand and assess my ethical development, and learned to apply the Kohlberg stages of ethical development for this application[852]. This model had six levels: 1) reward and punishment, 2) instrumental process, 3) peer group, 4) societal expectations, 5) social contract, and 6) universal moral principle. Examples of famous people who had reached level six included Gandhi and Martin Luther King, Jr. This method was applicable today to provide a framework to assist leaders in assessing the ethical development of others. Understanding the ethical perspective of others improved the leader's decision-making. Caution should be noted, however, that this method didn't assess the actions of people; rather, it addressed their motives.

Being a unique professional as a military leader, I had an obligation to act ethically. As such, I supported the three elements of the military profession: expertise, responsibility, and corporateness[853]. First, the military leader was an expert with the management of violence, based upon education and experience. Second, he was responsible to society for its security, similar to the client of every professional being society. Finally, similar to a license allowing a professional engineer to practice in his profession, the military officer had his commission for his legal right, granting it corporateness through entrance to the group. Sometimes a conflict between personal and professional integrity occurred, such as a trial lawyer defending a guilty person in court. In the end, professionals stop being such when they went beyond their service function to society.

---

[852] Cook 1999.
[853] Huntington 1957.

As mentioned previously, many Americans use relativism ethics, or the belief that "what is best for me" is morally good[854]. However, the moral obligation of the Soldier is to defend society, even if to his death. In essence, morality is not a science; whereas, the leaders should rely upon their core values in judging each situation separately. The Army has repeatedly demonstrated enduring principles and characteristics, such as subordination to civil authorities and respect for human rights[855]. This indicates that the military leader's characteristics of being a professional are: service focus, expert knowledge, unique culture and professional ethos. To be successful as Christians, we must be self-aware, understanding the environment and ourselves, while being adaptive with the ability to recognize and react to changes.

Is lying allowable to follow the teachings of Jesus?

In the Bible, we have an example of God punishing people for lying, specifically that of Ananias and his wife, Sapphira[856]. This married couple donated the sales of their land to the apostle Peter, claiming it to be the entire amount of the sales. They withheld part of the proceeds and lied about it solely for selfish reasons. Their crime was that they were withholding money from God and trying to impress the other early Christians with a lie.

Yet, the Bible also contained several examples of "righteous lying"[857]. The first example was that of Rahib, who hid the spies that Joshua sent into Jericho[858]. She also lied to government officials about the spies, protecting them from execution. Her faith and "righteous lying" spared her life when others in Jericho perished[859]. Although her lying was wrong, it was consequently praised in the Scriptures. The second example was that of Elisha

---

[854] Snider et al 1999.
[855] US Army 2001.
[856] Acts 4-5.
[857] I'll use this term of "righteous lying" to mean not telling the truth or intentionally withholding information completely for righteous reasons, such as saving people from execution. This also means that the individual doing the "righteous lying" isn't doing it for personal gain.
[858] Joshua 6.
[859] Hebrews 11:31 and James 2:25.

lying to blinded charioteers, directing them to the king of Israel instead of the king of Syria. God supported this lie by temporarily blinding the charioteers[860]. The next example was that of Jael, wife of Hebar the Kenite[861]. Not only did she lie to Sisera, captain of the Canaanite army, by promising him safety, she killed him while he slept. She was later described as the heroine who delivered Israel from the troops of king Jabin[862].

Not only does the Bible have examples of people lying on their own initiative, it has examples of God directing people to lie. For example, He commanded Moses to lie to the Pharaoh, while he was asking permission to worship three days in the wilderness[863]. Next, we have God telling Samuel to take an offering to Him to Bethlehem to deceive Saul. Actually, the real reason was for Samuel to anoint David as king[864].

Next, we have examples of God Himself lying to His people. The Bible described God deceiving a prophet and also sending strong delusions to His people to believe a lie[865]. What about Jesus? There was an example of Him lying too. His lie involved His response to His brothers' request to attend a feast at the Tabernacle with them. Jesus told them that He wasn't going to attend the feast. But, after they departed, He went anyways to the feast, but in secret[866].

Personally, I'm a strong believer in telling the truth every time in every situation[867]. However, I also believe in exceptions to this. This is similar to the arguments that Augustine made on lying and against lying[868]. I believe the real test to determine whether to lie involves who benefits from it. If you benefit from it, I recommend

---

[860] 2 Kings 6:18-20.
[861] Judges 4.
[862] Judges 5:23-27.
[863] Exodus 3:18.
[864] 1 Samuel 16:2.
[865] Ezekiel 14:9 and 2 Thessalonians 2:8-12.
[866] John 7:2-10.
[867] See especially Komp 1998 and Nyberg 1995.
[868] Augusting 1887a and 1887b.

Additional Christian Controversies

against lying. If someone does and you don't, then lying might be acceptable. Likewise, I firmly believe it's completely selfish to use the truth like a sledgehammer, especially if spoken in anger or retaliation. A historical example involves Dietrich Bonhoeffer, a Christian leader who lied to Nazi officials and saved the lives of many Jews[869]. Bonhoeffer was later executed by hanging for strongly opposing the Nazi euthanasia programs and the genocide of Jews[870].

A personal example involving lying happened when I taught at the US Military Academy (USMA). Its Honor Code was very simple. "A cadet will not lie, cheat, steal, or tolerate those who do"[871]. Even though it's simple and clear, they have classes and seminars to discuss what is and isn't a lie. I attended several of these to hear discussions about specific examples, such as whether speeding while driving is a violation of this code. The one discussion that caught my interest was a story that a fellow chemistry instructor shared with his cadets. He admitted that he lied to a Soldier while he was on duty in the field and he'd do it again. He then went on to explain the story of that Soldier trying to contact his wife from the field. He hadn't spoken to her in over a week and needed to ask her something about their plans when he returned home. He asked this instructor, who was working in the headquarters tactical operations center at that time if he'd received a message from his wife. This military officer intentionally lied to him and responded with "no". You see, earlier that day he received a message from the post chaplain that his wife died; and, he was on his way to meet him in the field to break the bad news. Since this military officer didn't benefit from lying and that telling the truth would have created more personal emotional trauma without the appropriate support network available, he felt it the correct moral thing to lie[872]. This military officer was highly regarded by the cadets since not only did he graduate from the Academy, he was both the captain of

---

[869] Brauch 2009, 54.
[870] Plant 2004, 1. Died on 9 April 1945 in Flossenbürg.
[871] Offstein 2006, 30.
[872] This is considered a lie of omission for leaving out other known information.

football team and first captain (top cadet) when he attended there. So, his words of advice were very credible. It depends!

Can you have sex without always committing a sin?

Bees do it. Birds do it. Humans do it. Ever since the beginning of time. These pure, raw, animal-like acts of sex have historically been done for two main reasons – procreation and enjoyment. Sex as a method to demonstrate love is another reason for this. This spiritual nurturing of each other is what I call love making. It's also true that sex is one of the two primary drives of humans, the other being hunger[873]. This section isn't about the mechanical aspects of sex, but the emotional, spiritual, and religious parts.

When is it morally and legal acceptable for you to have sex with someone else? Legally and religiously, sex is generally allowed only within the confines of marriage. But, what is marriage? Is it the union of consenting adults? Does it have to be with a member of the opposite gender? Is it a permanent un-revocable union? These are just some of the many questions we have.

In a very basic form, marriage is both a socially and religious legitimate sexual union that begins with a public announcement, such as a wedding. These marital partners should be of sound mind, of majority age and legally released from any previous marriages. Marriage is also an implicit contract that assumes the willingness of the partners to share intimate sexual and reproductive privileges. And, it provides the protective, affective, socialization, economic, and educational needs for their children.

The Old Testament described sexual ethics using purity and property[874]. Purity was physical in nature, and property involved the patriarchal culture of the ancient Hebrew society. Elsewhere in the Old Testament, we find violent sexual images of violated

---

[873] See especially Hite 2003.
[874] See especially Countryman 2007 and Weems 1995. Many of the purity laws can be found in Leviticus 11-26. Patriarchal laws can be found throughout Exodus and Deuteronomy.

women, especially in the stories of Hosea, Jeremiah, and Ezekiel[875]. Even the patriarchs, Abraham, Isaac, Jacob, Joseph, and David, had multiple wives, possession of many symbolizing great wealth.

On the other hand, much of the New Testament described sexual sins as those acts that harm others or were based upon selfish reasons. There were several exceptions in this as well. For example with homosexual acts, Paul described them as unclean and dishonorable[876]. I disagree with this because Christians should affirm them, not as a matter of condescension or generosity, but in compliance with the teachings of Jesus to love everyone, with no exceptions[877]. As for women's rights, Paul continued to advocate the patriarchal property rights over them[878].

Paul in several of this writings condemned sexual desire and promoted passionless sex within the marriage. Maybe, the real problem for Paul wasn't the desire, but the lack of sexual control[879]. Jewish literature between 200 BCE and 200 CE rarely included anything about condemnation of sexual desire, instead dealing with sexual immorality and excessive desire[880].

Maybe this was why Christianity generally associated sex with evil, sin, and the Fall of man[881]. Rules were added against sexual intercourse through translation multiple translations of the ancient texts[882]. Early Christians adopted the Greek philosophies, altering them to avoid sex at all costs. Christian churches were more interested in their legalism instead of compassion, being more preoccupied with governance and authority, than with the

---

[875] In Hosea 3:1-2, God directed him to marry a promiscuous woman of ill-repute. In Jeremiah 8:10, God directs giving the wives of some men to others. In Jeremiah 13:22, the rape of women is justified. In Ezekiel 18:6 and 22:10, sex with a woman during her period is not allowed.
[876] Romans 1:18-32.
[877] Countryman 2007, 282.
[878] 1 Corinthians 5:1.
[879] See especially Goldman 1991.
[880] Edward 2007, 16.
[881] Foucault 1985, 14 and 1986, 170.
[882] Gaca 2003, 17. In Greek, this was written as πορνεία.

individual's spiritual vitality[883]. It's no wonder that the Church had a stifling grip on repressive sexual morality[884].

Figure 31. The Birth of Venus.
by William-Adolphe Bouguereau (1879).

After reading the Gospels, we can discover large inconsistencies between the Jesus in these four books and that in Christianity today. The Gospel Jesus was unusually kind, open-minded, accepting and understanding of everyone, even those trying to find their sexuality, even having prostitutes in his company and risking

---

[883] Moore 1998, 243.
[884] Burrus 2007, 6.

His reputation by saving a woman condemned to certain death for adultery. This Jesus was also intimate, emotional, and physically, expressive. In contrast, the Bible-thumping preacher today often describes a Jesus who is inhumanely pure, uncompassionate, and asexual[885]. If sex was considered sinful, how could we have a pure God born through this act? Could this be the reason He needed a miraculous virgin birth?

Through moralism and neurotic obsessions, many Christians with clouded judgment try to avoid all sexual temptations[886]. From a mythological perspective, they fear Aphrodite, the classic Greek sex goddess, who rose from the sea naked appearing in garments of temptation[887]. I refer to this as avoiding Epicurean sex, which means to avoid delighting in the touches, smells, sights and sounds of bodies pleasuring each other. This Epicurean sex is also associated with love, peace, and friendship[888]. What could be so wrong with that?

These obsessed Christians probably limited their understanding of sex to just the physical aspects of sexual intercourse and used hostile crude words such as "screw' and "fuck", indicating men's military-related conquest of women. This included using derogatory terms, such as "slut", "tramp", and "whore", for women who enjoyed having sex with others. Furthermore, men who enjoyed having sex were treated quite the opposite, receiving positive socially-acceptable terms such as "Casanova", "ladies-man", "playboy", and "stud". These people were obviously missing the nurturing acts involved in love making, while at the same time degrading women[889].

Let me try to explain a problem that obsessed people miss when trying to view sex from these pious dictates. I'll do this by using three characters in Nathaniel Hawthorne's *The Scarlet Letter*. The

---

[885] Moore 1998, 68.
[886] Moore 1998, 165.
[887] Cyrino 2010, 14, 62-63, 87, 92, 105, 139,
[888] Moore 1998, 282.
[889] Spong 2005, 73.

first was Hester Prynne, who embraced sex fully and accepted the consequences, living life as though nothing had happened. The second was Arthur Dimmesdale, her lover and a Christian leader, who hid his sin and tried to maintain an ordinary life with a troubled heart. The last was Roger Chillingworth, her husband, who was a wounded and betrayed avenger, more interested in hurting others. Which one of these followed the teachings of Jesus – the loving adulterer, the unrepentant pious Christian leader, or the harmful, betrayed avenger?

What about societal changes since biblical times? Has anything changed that would affect sexual morals? Let me remind you that the increase in women's rights during the early twentieth century increased the need for birth control. The development of the Pill in the 1960s resulted in a sexual revolution. Most protestant religions conformed its faith to these, while the Roman Catholic Church and others unwillingly refused to change. Nevertheless, many Catholics do use birth control, ignoring the Papal teachings[890].

Compared to two thousand years ago, we don't support slavery, we have equalities between men and women, and we no longer are dependent upon a large household for economic support[891]. So, why should we use the Bible as the ultimate rulebook for sex? Apparently, most Americans living in a Christian nation don't since they willingly violate the biblical standards for sex[892].

However, in a recent survey of American Christians, about half of all Protestants found it morally acceptable for unmarried men and women not only to have sexual fantasies, but to cohabitate. I found it even more interesting to see that about two-thirds of Catholics found these sexual behaviors morally acceptable[893].

Is sex really the biggest threat to Christianity? Foucault, in his highly referenced study on human sexuality, poised the question of

---

[890] Spong 2005, 47.
[891] Loader 2010, 125.
[892] Hite 2003 and Ellens 2006, 4.
[893] Barna Group 2003.

why sex was considered to be a sin, causing us to repress our natural desires[894]. For me, there are several kinds of forbidden sex, which include incest, pedophilia, necrophilia, bestiality, adultery, and rape. Consensual sex between two adults in love isn't one of them.

From a physical perspective, we typically treat sexual problems as mechanical problems. As a chemical engineer, I can view sex as part of a mechanical body containing a series of chemicals, pumps, and plumbing. Yet, lovemaking, to me, is a ritual that allows the spirit to make human activities magically effective. It requires art, attention to details, and a devoted imagination[895].

Sex is more than procreation and pleasure; it's the physical intimacy between two people[896]. Mind, body, emotions, spirit are connected through it. This is clearly the case in the *Song of Solomon*, an intimate loving relationship between a king and the Pharaoh's daughter. As a gift from God, sex can be wonderfully sensuous, highly erotic, playful, romantic, and powerfully passionate. How can any God-fearing person believe otherwise? Contrary to popular belief, sex wasn't the original sin. It was the original blessing[897].

Are women equal to men?

Do you believe in a God who condemns half of the human race, women, to a subservient second-class role? In the last hundred years, women have received the right to vote in the US, been elected to Congress, held senior level Government positions, and served as CEOs of Fortune 100 companies. However, several Christian churches won't change their archaic position on women. Bishop Spong commented that, "pious, all-male Roman Catholic Church leaders, clothed in their ecclesiastical dresses, [pronounce]

---

[894] 1978, 1985 and 1986. He died in 1984, leaving unfinished his fourth volume on the history of sexuality of Christianity, supposedly to be titled Confessions of the Flesh.
[895] Moore 1998, 11.
[896] See especially Davidson 2007.
[897] Genesis 1: 26-29.

in the name of a God called "Father," what a woman can and cannot do with her body"[898].

The ideal woman was the Virgin Mary. Women were either to remain virginal and serve as nuns or bear children by losing virgin purity. Mary didn't become the Virgin Mother until Matthew wrote about it in the Gospel, later becoming a creed in the third or fourth century[899]. In fact, Mary became a perpetual Virgin, even though she continued to bear children with Joseph.

Adding to Mary's myth, Pope Pius IX on December 8, 1854, declared her own birth was an *Immaculate Conception*. This was a special attempt to prove that Jesus was without sin. This was in response to the scientists, at that time, proving that women had eggs and supplied half of the creation of all human life. This meant that Mary supplied half of Jesus' genetic makeup; and, since she was born of Adam's life line and carried sin, Jesus would have been born a sinner unless Mary was born sinless in an *Immaculate Conception*. Then, on November 1, 1950, Pope Pius XII decreed that Mary didn't die, but ascended into Heaven since only sinful people can experience death. These Papal decrees de-sexed Mary and dehumanized her, thus remaining faithful in the Church's second-rate sexist treatment of women[900].

The Bible was also written by men within a male-controlled world. Women were blamed for everything, starting with sin. Men had excuses for everything involving women. If they raped women, it was because the women had tempted them with provocative clothing. If men abused them, it was because women deserved it. If they divorced women, it was because they gave men displeasure[901]. In ancient history, women were considered second-class citizens. Physically, they were weaker than men; so, it was assumed that men were better, with examples in Table 22[902].

---

[898] Spong 2005, 80-81.
[899] Spong 2005, 83.
[900] Spong 2005, 85.
[901] Spong 2005, 87.
[902] Spong 2005, 72.

Table 22. Women as Weaker Sex in Ancient Documents

Document	Description
Plato's *The Republic*	Socrates asked his older brother, Glaucon, "And can you mention any pursuit of mankind in which the male sex has not all these gifts and qualities in a higher degree than the female?"[903]?
Oeconomicus	Another Socratic dialogue, Xenophon wrote, "The ideal woman should see as little as possible, hear as little as possible, and ask as little as possible"[904].
Hindu, Code 5:148 of the *Law of Manus*	Dictated that women, "As a child, she must remain under her father's control; as a young woman, under her husband's; and when her husband is dead, under her sons. She must never seek to live independently"[905]. Also according to Code 5:158, women must be devoted to a single husband and remain celibate as a widow.
Buddhist prayers	Includes asking for male rebirth[906].
Jewish prayer	Offers thanks to God, "Blessed art Thou, O Lord our God, King of the Universe, who has not made me a heathen ... or a woman"[907].
Koran	Stated that a woman's worth is considered that of half a man[908].

The Bible contained several Scriptures that were terrible for women. In Genesis 2:18-23, the first woman, Eve, was created so that man wouldn't be alone and that he'd have a helper. She wasn't created separate from Adam, but was derived from a part of

---

[903] The quote was usually written as "Do you know anything at all practiced among mankind, in which in all these respects, the male sex is not far better than the female?"
[904] The actual quote in my translation was written as "What proficiency was she likely to bring with her, when she was not quite fifteen at the time she wedded me, and during the whole prior period of her life had been most carefully brought up to see and hear as little as possible, and to ask the fewest questions."
[905] Manu 2004, 96. Manu was the mythical first king of the Earth.
[906] Faure 2003, 112.
[907] Payne 2009, 84.
[908] Bhutto 1998.

him. Later, in Genesis 19:6-8, Lot offered two of his virgin daughters to be gang-raped by a mob of people in Sodom for their evening's entertainment. This was done without asking the girls what they wanted. God then judged this man to be righteous and worthy of deliverance from destruction[909]. Finally, in 1 Corinthians 11:8-9, it's written that man wasn't created for a woman. Instead, she was created for him.

Today, we have cultures that continue to treat women as objects. Senior officials in the *Majlis al-Ifta' al-A'ala*, Saudi Arabia's highest religious council, said allowing women to drive would inevitably lead to "no more virgins". They justified their comments by referring to other Muslim countries where women were allowed to drive. They told their followers that allowing women to drive would increase prostitution, pornography, homosexuality, and divorce. This county was also the only place in the world where women are prohibited from driving with corporal punishment for violating the ban[910]. Shaima Jastaniya received ten lashes for persistently flouting the driving ban[911]. Furthermore, under Saudi Arabia's strict Islamic laws, women required a male guardian's permission to work or travel abroad. What concerns me was that many Christian males also wanted the same treatment for women, using the Bible as its justification source. Yet, in my opinion, male and female dictate biological functions, not human worth or divine value[912].

Can you break rules to follow the teachings of Jesus?

As I mentioned before, I prefer to view the Bible as God's love story to us. It shouldn't be taken as a rule book of immutable laws. Yet, many Christians today live by its numerous set of moral laws that have little similarities to the teachings of Jesus[913]. Table 23

---

[909] Later, these two daughters slept with their righteous father and become pregnant. Their sons: Moab becomes the father of the Moabites, and Ammon becomes father of the Ammonites.
[910] Bloxham 2011.
[911] Tomlinson 2011.
[912] See Galatians 3:28.
[913] Gulley 2010, 60.

Additional Christian Controversies

contains several biblical rules that many today don't follow. Some of them even contradict the teaching of Jesus.

Table 23. Biblical Rules I Refuse to Follow

Scripture	Biblical Rule
Leviticus 19:19	Don't wear clothes made of several fabrics.
Leviticus 19:27	Don't cut your hair nor shave.
Leviticus 20:9	Kill anyone who curses their parents.
Leviticus 20:10	Kill anyone committing adultery.
Leviticus 21:9	Burn to death any prostitute who is the daughter of a priest.
Leviticus 21:17-18	The blind and lame can't go to God's altar.
Leviticus 24:14-16	Kill anyone who curses God.
Deuteronomy 13:6-10	Kill anyone who suggests worshipping another god.
Deuteronomy 13:12-15	Destroy cities and everything in it if they worship a different god.
Deuteronomy 17:2-7	Kill anyone with a different religion.

Some laws and rules are obsolete, such as the ones previously listed above. They're completely outdated that they have no validity[914]. So, why do we have Christian leaders and other educated Christians telling us that this Bible is error-free and contains God's words to us? If they don't followed these obsolete rules, why not?

Don't get me wrong. Laws are generally good for society, especially those that prevent theft and harm to others. But in many

---

[914] Peczenik 2009, 22.

states there are laws still in effect that ban something no sane person would ever do. Although no one really enforces them, the fact remains that they are still laws[915].

When considering Christian rules, we should consider avoiding harm to others as more important than compliance with religious laws such that a greater good can be done by breaking these rules[916]. Even within the Bible, we had people breaking the rules. For example, the book of Ruth broke the rules in the Old Testament. It was a story about two unescorted women, with the men taking a background role[917]. Jesus was also known for breaking the rules, such as working on the Sabbath so that he could help others[918]. He didn't eliminate the rules; he just transformed them to support His teachings. To put it another way, we must keep the spirit of the law, not just the letter. Today, I'd rather focus upon determining the difference between right and wrong by how much harm or good it does[919].

---

[915] McGlynn 2011. Although I didn't confirm these laws with the statutes in each state, I'll list some examples of interesting civil laws: 1. Missouri, it's illegal to drive with an uncaged bear; 2. In Maine, it's illegal to have Christmas decorations up after January fourteenth; 3. In New Jersey, it's illegal to wear a bulletproof vest while committing a murder; 4. In Nevada, it's illegal for a man to buy drinks for more than three people at a time; 5. In Wisconsin, it's illegal to serve butter substitutes in state prisons; 6. In New Jersey, once convicted of drunk driving you may never again have personalized plates; 7. In North Dakota, beer and pretzels can't be served at the same time in any bar or restaurant; 8. In Alaska, waking a sleeping bear for a photo opportunity is strictly forbidden; 9. In Connecticut, a pickle isn't officially a pickle unless it bounces; 10. In South Carolina, you must be eighteen to play a pinball machine; 11. In Michigan, anyone over twelve may own a hand gun as long as they haven't committed a felony; 12. In Idaho, it's illegal for a man to give his sweetheart a box of candy weighing more than fifty pounds; 13. In North Carolina, bingo games can't last more than five hours; 14. In Connecticut, it's illegal to walk across a street on your hands; 15. In Louisiana, there's a five hundred dollar fine for instructing a pizza delivery man to deliver pizza to a friend unknowingly; 16. In Ohio, it's illegal to get a fish drunk; and my favorite is, 17. In Arizona, it's illegal to own more than two dildos.
[916] Gulley 2010, 80.
[917] James 2008.
[918] Luke 6:1-4. Matthew 12:1-8.
[919] Loader 2010, 125.

Additional Christian Controversies 311

Can fame, fortune and power be both good and bad?

Imagine if you were a medieval king or queen with the fame, fortune, and power over everything in your kingdom. You'd be the most famous person in the kingdom with use of all of the luxuries available at the time. Of course, the power you had would be absolute over your subjects. This was what most people wanted back then. And, they were willing to do anything to obtain it, such as lie, cheat, steal, and even kill. But, exactly, what would they've received? They'd live in a large unventilated building with no central heating and air conditioning. Most likely, there would be neither running water nor indoor plumbing. Entertainment would be provided by royal musicians, jesters, and actors. Decisions for running and protecting the kingdom would be based upon slow hand-carried messages. Medicine and dentistry would be very primitive. Life would be very harsh compared to our modern living.

Now fast forward several centuries and imagine living an average life in America. Our typical life style is much better than that of medieval or ancient royalty. We live in comfortable homes with running water, not to mention hot water and indoor plumbing. With television and radios, entertainment from movies, music, and games are readily available. With the Internet, we have near-instant access to global information in addition to local events. Fame is made possible with the cell phones, Facebook, You Tube, and Twitter. The quality of life is much better, too, with fresh foods from around the world, freezers to keep food fresh for long periods, and advanced healthcare to provide and extend our quality of life. The list is endless. Still, most people feel that they have limited fame, fortune, and power today. They want more!

Regrettably, many people with the desire to gain fame, fortune, and power for their own selfish benefit have no concern about what it takes to obtain it. Their main concern would be the speed and cost. Everything to them is fair, provided they don't get caught and pay a penalty. Using cut-throat competition, poverty wages, and unsanitary conditions to obtain one's desires would be allowable [920]. Nevertheless, is this really good if they lose their souls in the process? It's even more tragic when we see many Christians intentionally worshipping the Golden Calf of worldly success [921].

Who do we idolize? Just look at the magazines in the stores, such as *People Magazine* and *The National Enquirer*, along with the television shows, such as *Who Wants to Marry a Millionaire* and the many so-called "reality" television shows, such as *Keeping Up With the Kardashians,* or MTV's *Jersey Shore.* Sports figures are also highly paid and revered, while America's teachers are disrespected daily in our classrooms, not to mention poorly compensated. The message is very clear. We receive messages that celebrities of fame, fortune, and power are the successful ones in life. Instead, we should be looking to people who are willing to risk life, limb, and reputation to help others [922]. The unsung helpful people are my heroes.

Reading history, we can easily find examples of people who were successful in obtaining significant amounts of fame, fortune, and power. Yet, they probably lost their souls and eternal fate along the way. My list of infamous examples include Adolf Hitler with his Final Solution of Jewish genocide [923], Genghis Khan with his destructive genocidal conquests throughout Asia [924], Marcus Junius Brutus with his assassination of Julius Caesar [925], Osama Bin Laden with his support of global terrorism causing the deaths of thousands [926], and Vlad the Impaler with his sadistic pleasure in torturing to death as many as one hundred thousand people [927].

---

[920] Schilpp 1938, 57-58.
[921] Schilpp 1938, 62.
[922] See especially Salkin 2008.
[923] Kershaw 2008, 277 , 668-99 and 685.
[924] See especially de Hartog 2004. Genghis Khan was known to have destroyed entire towns, creating considerable damage and destruction everywhere. For example, about three-fourths of the Iranians were killed, which is more than ten million.
[925] See especially Canfora 2007.
[926] See especially Scheuer 2011.
[927] See especially Trow 2004. Vlad III, Prince of Wallachia, was the inspirational source of the Dracula stories.

As for wealth, many of today's richest people have given much of their wealth for the benefit of others through their philanthropic gifts. The following three wealthy people have given in excess of $10 billion: Warren Buffett for healthcare, extreme poverty, education, and access to information technology; Bill Gates for education, AIDS prevention, and sanitation; and Li Ka-shing for education and healthcare[928]. But, is this enough? These people should be commended for this effort; but, like Jesus, I regard our unknown heroes who have given more of themselves as doing more than these wealthy people. Jesus provided us two messages regarding wealth. In one, He told us that it's easier for a camel to go through the eye of a needle than for a rich person to enter God's Kingdom[929]. In another, God preferred small offerings from the poor over that of extravagant ones from the rich[930]

Ironically, through several centuries of acquisitions from its members, the churches themselves own property, invest funds, and employ labor. In fact, many of its practices have been no better than those which the Church condemns in the secular world. Yet, its members always hears that the Church needs more and more money. For example, the Catholic Church is the biggest financial power and property owner today. If I had to take a guess at the total worth of this church with its numerous priceless artworks, prime real estate and other holdings, I would say that they have more than $1 trillion in assets. This makes the Pope the head of the wealthiest empire in the world. Yet many people would question why can't this Church spend some of its available resources on its poor? But, it does. It's also the largest provider of health care, education, and charity throughout the world. And, the Pope, along with its other church leaders, takes a vow of poverty, meaning everything they own belongs to the Church. Its priceless art is held without consideration of selling for humanity to enjoy. And, its land and buildings are held as places of worship. But,

---

[928] See especially Hockfield 2011.
[929] Matthew 19:16-30, which is known as the Rich and the Kingdom of God lesson.
[930] Mark 12:41-44 and Luke 21:1-4, which is known as the Widow's Mite lesson.

does a Christian church require this, being a museum and having elaborate places of worship? Would Jesus advocate not helping its poor if it had resources available to do otherwise? Why should someone feel entitled to worship Jesus in a cathedral? From personal experience, I found it better to worship in a school gymnasium, in a tent, and even in a foxhole.

Although not popular and rarely recognized are those unknown heroes, such as fire fighters, peace officers, military service-members, emergency medical technicians, and teachers. Yes, I could even talk about the *Medal of Honor* and the recipients' demonstrated willingness to make the ultimate sacrifice for others. In fact, a good friend of mine in Indiana was awarded this medal for heroism in Vietnam and won't talk about him out of respect for his privacy. But, I'll provide you four examples in Table 24 of people within the last century who did something similar and weren't eligible for this honor.

In the words of Victor Hugo, author of *Les Misérables*, "For many deeds are performed in petty combats. .... Life, misfortune, isolation, abandonment, poverty, are the fields of battle which have their heroes; obscure heroes, who are, sometimes, grander than the heroes who win renown"[931].

Table 24. Recent Heroic Individuals.

Person	Description
Anuradha Koirala	Founder of the Maita Nepal and called the "Angel of Mercy"[932] by Prince Charles, spent several years working to prevent human trafficking and sexual exploitation in Nepal. Her work included raiding brothels, educating people and providing a safe haven for thousands of Nepalese women and girls[933]. For her work, she was honored as the 2010 CNN *Hero of the Year*.

---

[931] 1887, 651-652.
[932] This is the same title also given to Mother Teresa of Calcutta.
[933] Joshi 2004, 248.

Table 24. Recent Heroic Individuals (continued).

Person	Description
Liviu Librescu	A Holocaust survivor and celebrated expert in composite structures and aeroelsaticity with prestigious awards, taught engineering classes at Virginia Polytechnic Institute and State University. In April 2007, Seung-Hui Cho killed thirty-two people in a deadly shooting rampage on campus. Dr. Librescu, at 76 years old, held the door of his classroom shut to allow most of his twenty-three students the time to escape to safety. While holding the door, Cho shot Dr. Librescu five times, killing him[934]. From the words of Jesus, there is no greater love than that of someone making the ultimate sacrifice for someone else[935]. How ironic for someone to survive the Holocaust, only to be killed in a senseless massacre more than sixty years later.
Irena Sendler	A twenty-something year old, risked her life numerous times in Nazi-occupied Poland. While forging documents and frequently entering the Warsaw ghetto, she helped smuggle thousands of children from the ghetto into safety, ultimately placing them in convents, orphanages, and Polish families[936]. Thousands of women owe their lives to her.
Harriet Tubman	An African American woman who helped about seventy slaves move north to freedom during thirteen trips on the Underground Railroad during the Civil War[937]. Later in life, she promoted women's suffrage.

Would Jesus drink, dance, and party?

Would the perfect, sinless Man create and drink alcohol? And, would He dance and party? We have heard about His first miracle

---

[934] See especially Moynihan 2007. The massacre took place on the date of the Holocaust Remembrance Day (Yom HaShoah). Minal Panchal, a graduate student, was the only student of his killed.
[935] John 15:13.
[936] See especially Mieszkowska 2011.
[937] See especially McGowan and Kashatus 2011.

of changing water into wine at the wedding in Cana[938]. Elsewhere in the Gospels, we discover others accusing Jesus of being a drunk[939]. He even spoke of wine in His teachings, such as putting new wine only in new containers[940]. Finally, we have Jesus drinking communion wine at the Last Supper[941]. So, on the surface, we have evidence that Jesus often drank an alcoholic beverage.

What about the culture? Was drinking acceptable, or was there an abstinence of alcohol advocated by the religious and society leaders at the time? Jesus definitely lived in a society in which wine was identified as a divine blessing that made the heart glad, limited by the dangers of excess or drunkenness[942]. An Old Testament verse mentioned celebrating to God with alcohol and another mentioned there's nothing better than eating, drinking, and being merry[943].

There are many scholars today who would argue that Jesus' first miracle didn't involve changing water into alcoholic wine, but just fresh grape juice. I don't believe them. There were no methods available during Jesus' time to preserve grape juice and prevent it from fermenting into alcoholic wine, such as freezing the grapes. In fact, there were no Hebrew or Greek words for non-alcoholic grape juice. So, if you harvested the grapes and stored them, fermentation process would occur naturally, resulting in alcoholic wine. This scientific process hasn't changed[944].

Still, these alcohol prohibitionists today plead their case, using the Bible as their source. They cite Jesus mentioning not drinking fruit of the vine until the kingdom of God comes[945]. Maybe, He really meant not celebrating with alcohol until that joyful day arrives. These scholars would lead us to believe that alcohol is intoxicating

---

[938] John 2:1-11.
[939] Matthew 11:16-19 and Luke 7:31-35.
[940] Luke 5:37-38; Mark 2:22.
[941] Matthew 26:26-29, Mark 14:22-25, and Luke 22:14-23.
[942] McGrath 2004, 16.
[943] Deuteronomy 14:24-26 and Ecclesiastes 8:15.
[944] Brown 2011, 25.
[945] Luke 22:18 and Matthew 26:29.

and will destroy people's lives, leading us to believe that complete abstinence of alcohol is a divine imperative[946].

Figure 32. Marriage at Cana.
by Tintoretto (1561).

For me, drinking alcohol in moderation is one more way to enjoy God's gifts, one of life's pleasures. Instead of abstinence, Jesus warned us against drunkenness[947]. I learned that abuse of alcohol or anything else to the point of impairing your judgment is a serious sin. Taking the extreme of prohibiting all alcohol is even more dangerous than actually abusing it, leading Christians to improper judgment and abusive treatment of others.

What about dancing and partying? The Old Testament was full of references associated with dancing[948]. Psalms contained a couple of verses identifying dancing as a way of praising God[949]. Women

---

[946] Bacchiocchi 1989, chapter 5: Jesus and Wine
[947] Luke 21:34.
[948] Judges 11:34 gives an example of the daughter of one of the Israeli judges dancing. Judges 21:19-23 provided additional example of women dancing.
[949] Psalms 149:3 and 150:4.

danced to celebrate God's deliverance of them from Egypt after crossing the Red Sea[950]. Also, women danced in celebration of King David's victories, in addition to David dancing before the Arc of the Covenant[951]. Solomon also wrote that there was a time for dancing[952]. And, the prophet Jeremiah foretold a time when dancing would joyously result from God's work[953].

However, the Bible contained other examples indicating times with dancing weren't appropriate. Leading the example were Israelis dancing around the golden calf while Moses was on Mount Sinai receiving the Ten Commandments[954]. After watching his step-daughter Salome dancing, Herod Antipater granted her anything she wanted, which cost John the Baptist his head[955]. Furthermore, though, I couldn't find any direct mention within the New Testament of Jesus, His apostles, or of Christians dancing. Nevertheless, it appears to me that Jesus would party on occasion with sinners and the dirtiest of the dirty. I can't imagine Him being so pious and fearful of having fun that He wouldn't drink, party, and dance. More importantly, even if He wouldn't, I seriously doubt that He'll hold it against me if I did.

Can pursuing salvation result in not getting it?

We all have a finite time to live. And, we know it. We wonder what existence will be like when we die, especially after hearing stories of good people going to Heaven and bad people going to Hell. Yet, the criteria for entrance to Heaven, or salvation, differs widely from one group to another. So, what's the truth? How do we get into Heaven? Does salvation mean being rescued from sin and going to Heaven when we die? Or, is it taking a lifelong journey towards love as Jesus taught? Should we see ourselves as wretched sinners deserving damnation instead; or, should we see

---

[950] Exodus 15:20-21.
[951] 1 Samuel 18:6 and 2 Samuel 6:14-16.
[952] Ecclesiastes 3:4.
[953] Jeremiah 31:13.
[954] Exodus 32:19.
[955] Matthew 14:3-11 and Mark 6:17-29.

Additional Christian Controversies

ourselves as cherished and valued with much potential[956]? For that matter, why would God reward finite acts in a finite time with infinite heavenly or hellish consequences[957]?

Unfortunately, we hear allegations from religious leaders that salvation is only for a select few Christians. People who refuse or neglect to be born again will spend their eternal future in Hell[958]. This salvation must be done while alive; afterwards, it's too late[959]. Furthermore, many conservative Christians believe it their obligation to point out to others what will and or won't lead them astray and risk salvation. Many times this isn't polite. In fact, it's part of a preacher's job to warn his people about false religions, meaning religions other than the preacher's. It's as though these leaders are trying to sell us a celestial life insurance policy[960]. However, their "Holier than thou" attitude repulses people in their salvation attempts[961]. This "save thyself" message would be nothing more than a perversion of Jesus' message in offering salvation to others for the sole purpose of securing their own.

Complicating the process of trying to convince others about salvation in the United States was a lack of social cohesion[962]. Although significant sacrifices were made with heroic responses by emergency personnel in times of disaster including renewed interest in community service, Americans participating in volunteering or support activities remains low[963]. Many Christian groups throughout history sent missionaries throughout the world to send their "good news" message about salvation. With all good intentions, these missionaries provided physical, mental, social, and economic support to the poor. Unfortunately, they were accompanied by merchants, who were very interested in exploiting

---

[956] Gulley 2010, 44.
[957] Saranam 2005, 60.
[958] Revelation 20:11-15.
[959] 2 Corinthians 6:2.
[960] Schilpp 1938, 101-102.
[961] Schilpp 1938, 34.
[962] Putnam 2000
[963] Putnam 2003.

and robbing them[964]. As a result, these people began associating Christianity with exploitation.

It's very difficult for poor, unemployed people, many suffering from oppressive brutal violence, to be concerned with salvation, especially when they're fighting daily to live yet another day. That's why Jesus was very interested in helping people who were living a miserable destitute life. People needed their physical needs met before they started to worry about their spiritual needs.

Many Christians, unfortunately, believe that the quality and sincerity of their worship will be the sole thing that determines their eternal destination[965]. Why not? Christian leaders, along with their members, use judgment and creedal compliance as ways to control members. In essence, they control other Christians with righteousness instead of love.

Rob Bell, author of a recent best-selling book about sin, salvation, and judgment, believed that the Jesus story was about God's love, peace, forgiveness, and joy for everyone, not for just a select few with the rest of us forever being tormented in Hell[966]. His book inspired the April 25, 2011, *Time Magazine* cover, "What if There's No Hell". In response, many prominent religious leaders criticized Bell's book. For example, R. Albert Mohler, Jr., president of the Southern Baptist Theological Seminary stated that his book was "theologically disastrous". I doubt that these religious leaders can justify what the churches did during the Middle Ages, when forgiveness and salvation were given in exchange for sums of money, resulting in great wealth for churches.

Jesus promised salvation to everyone, including to the poor, social outcasts, and sinners, not just a select few. Definitely, not to the pious religious elite. Take away Hell and you take away the biggest

---

[964] Schilpp 1938, 115.
[965] Gulley 2010, 12.
[966] 2011, preface. He is the pastor of Mars Hill Bible Church in Grand Rapids, Michigan, my childhood hometown.

Additional Christian Controversies

sanction a church has against people. Who determines if someone goes to Hell anyways, God or man through the Church? Jesus taught us that anyone trying to save their lives shall lose it[967]. He even demonstrated this on the cross by not saving His own life, while being ridiculed by a sneering mob. This was especially true for the Christians today who try everything to save themselves from Hell, only to lose their soul along the way[968].

I like to think about salvation using the Parable of the Sheep and the Goats[969]. In this parable, the sheep were good and goats weren't, even though they didn't know why. The sheep, following the teachings of Jesus, served the lowly because they cared, not because they wanted salvation. The goats didn't. It's sad that many Christians serve God to earn salvation instead of doing it because they loved doing it.

Can Christians judge another in the name of God?

Bible-thumping "Holier than thou" pious Christians have been judging others for centuries. And, they'll continue to judge others in the name of God. But, is this something God, or even Jesus, advocates? In the Bible, we can definitely find reference to judging fairly and righteously[970]. But do we really understand what this means?

I firmly believe that God will judge a person's actions and motives, but will always hold out the chance for repentance. Christians, on the other hand, are never given the right nor the responsibility of eternally judgment. Only God can make the judgment of eternal destiny. Christians are incapable of correctly weighing action, motives, opportunities, and don't know all things about any individual: God alone is capable to do so[971]. He's omnipotent. Humans aren't.

---

[967] Matthew 10:39 and 16:25; Mark 8:35; Luke 9:24 and 17:33.
[968] Matthew 27:42.
[969] Matthew 25:31-46.
[970] Matthew 7:1-6 and John 7:24.
[971] Hebrews 10:30, Romans 14:10, and James 4:11-12.

Figure 33. Last Judgment.
Laatste Oordeel (1558) by Pieter Bruegel the Elder.

Furthermore, Jesus spoke harshly about the pious religious leaders, all good men who frequently performed good deeds. These priests, scribes, and Pharisees were rebuked because of their harsh judgments of others with censure and rebuke[972]. Unfortunately, many Christians today believe that condemnation of others was God-ordained. But why would this be wrong in the eyes of Jesus? Many Christian organizations insisted that they're divinely inspired and not prone to error; yet, they tended to overlook their own greed, racism, sexism, sexual abuse, and infighting[973]. They simply didn't have the moral compass to pass judgment upon others.

So, what would be wrong with this? During Jesus' time, the sick were believed to be condemned by God and were forced to leave. His interaction with these people was highly discouraged. Examples of despicable people included Zacchaeus who was

---

[972] Matthew 23:1-39.
[973] See especially Boyd 2005.

judged by men for becoming rich as a tax collector, but wasn't judged the same way by Jesus[974]. It wasn't his long list of good deeds that Jesus favored, but that he admitted his sinful faults and tried to repent those faults through deeds[975]. This was very similar to the Parable of the *Pharisee and the Tax Collector*[976]. Many Christians prayed like the Pharisee in that they judged one another by finding fault and sin in others. Although the Pharisee was a good man and tried his best to serve God, he wasn't perfectly good[977]. Judging someone else in the name of God wasn't acceptable.

Yet, as Christians, we're taught that we're God's children who deserve to be punished for our sins. We're fallen sinners banished from His presence needing divine wrath. The Church, then, was the unique way to offer forgiveness and rescue us hopeless, lost sinners. And, if you didn't repent and asked for forgiveness, then you were punished. Christians throughout history had the belief that if they could discipline their own children, then they could discipline child-like adults, such as slaves and women. Today, many Christian groups forced members to leave their group, through excommunication, shunning or some other form of isolation practice, for violating their religious rules. These rules included the clothes we wore, the music we listened to, the words we spoke, and even the movie we watched[978]. We don't use Inquisition techniques today, such as burning or torturing our heretics. We have a much more modern way of dealing with them. Instead of throwing stones at them, we launch a propaganda campaign against them, making them an outcast in society, or at least from our group. We had better follow the rules, or face the consequences of their judgment[979].

---

[974] Luke 19:1-10.
[975] Capon 2002, 416.
[976] Luke 18:9-14.
[977] Capon 2002, 341.
[978] Gulley 2010, 107. The Quakers have dis-fellowshipped members for adding buttons and collars to their clothes.
[979] Schilpp 1938, 16.

Maybe, we're just prone to judging others for our own failures. Why not? Much of our time is occupied with celebrities, athletes, and sex, instead of hard work. And when we fail to do something or we want something without much work, we quickly call a lawyer to sue anyone blocking our way. And, it makes us feel good to blame someone else instead of being motivated to achieve it with hard work[980].

The Bible contains many stories about violence, bloodshed, and other criminal behavior. It also contains the story of God's love for us. Judging others based upon a violent story or a love story will be the same way that God judges us. Llily-livered, pansy-assed, bleeding-heart, wishy-washy, America-hating, namby-pamby Christian judgments don't adhere to the teachings of Jesus. In other words, misinterpreting the Bible to condemn others is "Scriptural Malpractice". Don't do it!

Can loving another violate the teachings of Jesus?

Jesus was asked to define God's law in a simple manner. He answered by describing the greatest commandment to love. He never advocated strict compliance with religious doctrine or policies. Yet, can everything done in the name of love support the teachings of Jesus? If you love Him, you will obey His commands, and the biggest command is to love one another[981]. But, I suggest that there are limits to this.

We have crimes of passion, or love, which includes suicide, jealousy, vengeance, and even murder[982]. Don't get me wrong. Crimes of love aren't all the same. Sometimes it involves an obsessive desire to do what your loved ones want no matter the cost. In essence, these people lack the ability to tell their loved ones "no" after being told "if you love me, you will …"

An example of this happened between two rich Texans over a hundred years ago. Lena Sneed left her husband John and asked

---

[980] Thomas 2011.
[981] John 14:23.
[982] See especially Proal 1905.

for a divorce to be with Albert Boyce, Jr. To prevent the divorce, John had her committed to an asylum with a diagnosis of moral insanity. In response, Boyce rescued her. She was quickly found, caught, and returned from Canada back to Texas where she was re-committed to the asylum. Shortly afterwards in a vengeful state-of- mind, Sneed murdered defenseless Boyce and his father. He avoided convictions both times since these were declared justifiable homicides, or obligation to safeguard his honor[983]. Was this really the love of a person or, the love of an object of possession? Nonetheless, Sneed murdered a couple of people.

Two more recent events included Wanda Holloway who hired a hit man to murder the young girl who competed against her daughter, Shanna, in high school. She was known as the *Texas Cheerleading Murdering Mom* in a scandal immortalized in two movies[984]. Next, we have teenagers Tyler Witt and Steven Colver who were in love. In the name of this love in 2009, they both murdered Joanne Witt, Tyler's mother[985].

Be cautious of anyone commanding you to do something hateful to prove you love them. That demonstrates control over you, not love of you.

Probing Questions

Jesus taught by asking His followers controversial questions[986]. In fact, He created several paradoxes to address controversial issues. As an example, He posed several statements that confused His followers, such as telling them that the first shall be last, leaders should become servants, and those who save their lives will lose it[987]. Jesus understood the importance of probing our beliefs if we want to establish the credibility of information[988]. Questioning long-standing dogma should be encouraged instead of being used

---

[983] See especially Neal 2011.
[984] Lang and Mascia 2012.
[985] Breuer 2011.
[986] Matthew 21:28-45; and Luke 10:25-37.
[987] Schilpp 1938, 6.
[988] See especially Fadem 2010.

as evidence for punishment[989]. As such, I felt it important enough to provide you the following additional questions for your further study and discussion.

1. Which is the best basis to understand Christian religion: 1) human thoughts and ideas; 2) moral and ethical considerations; or 3) world order, harmony, and balance[990]? Why?

2. Friedrich Schleiermacher, in his book *On the Social Element in Religion*, stated that "the sum total of religion is to feel that, in its highest unity, all that moves us in feeling is one; to feel that whatever is single and particular is only possible by means of this unity; to feel, that is to say, that our being and living is a being and living in and through God"[991]. Does this conflict with your thoughts on Christianity and its beliefs? Why?

3. Some say that a controversy is a bad sign for the truth. Do you agree with this? Why[992]?

4. Can someone be a Christian who doesn't attend a Christian church? Is Christian church membership required for all Christians[993]?

5. Is humanism separate from theism? If so, is one more important than the other for a Christian[994]?

6. Can science explain miracles? Can science explain life after death[995]?

---

[989] In his book, *Jesus Religion*, Louis Charles presents a logical argument, revealing the insanity that has been created by Christian theology. Learn some of the historical facts surrounding the creation of Christianity and the Bible, as well as Louis' personal experiences of searching for the truth behind fearful Christian teachings.
[990] Capps 1995, 9.
[991] 1893, 43. This was part of his second speech about the nature of religion.
[992] Beach 2002, 4.
[993] Beach 2002, 22 and Black 1910, 145.
[994] Beach 2002, 35.

7. What are the scientific arguments for or against the existence of God? Of Jesus and his miracles and teachings[996]?

8. Can you be a Christian if you don't believe that Jesus is the divine Son of God[997]?

9. Is it important to understand secular philosophies in order to effectively understand Christianity?

10. Is intellectual reason the enemy of authority, faith, hope, and love? What are the arguments for or against Martin Luther's assessment that reason is the "Devil's whore"? What are the arguments for or against Aquinas saying that "to impugn human reason is to impugn God"[998]?

11. Can we have truth without knowledge of scientifically proven facts[999]? Is science important to understand Christianity?

12. Does Christian faith require emotional trust, intellectual belief, and conscious obedience[1000]?

13. What are the arguments supporting the thesis that Christians' reasons are really rationalizations? Why do we have brilliant rational unbelievers[1001]?

14. What are some of the key miracles described in the Bible? What are the arguments to reject them as factual events? Are these miracles crucial to the Christian faith[1002]?

---

[995] Ward 2008, 83 and 134.
[996] Ward 2008, 216.
[997] Black 1910, 73.
[998] Kreeft and Tacelli 1994, 11.
[999] Kreeft and Tacelli 1994, 26.
[1000] Kreeft and Tacelli 1994, 27.
[1001] Kreeft and Tacelli 1994, 28.
[1002] Abbott 1885, 625.

15. Christianity can be defined as the religious truths involving Jesus. What are those basic truths, and what are the sources of these truths[1003]? Can you describe the credibility of these sources[1004]?

16. Christmas is the day we celebrate the birth of Jesus. There's no known document that proves that He was born in late December; but, it's highly unlikely. I've read several sources that suggest his real birth is in late September, indicating that the conception occurred in late December. Do you believe that the early Christian leaders chose December 25th to celebrate His birthday to counter pagan festivals involving the Winter solstice? Is knowledge of His exact birth date important to the Christian faith[1005]?

17. There are no accurate records, even within the gospels, that provide us an accurate chronology of the life of Jesus. Is knowledge of His correct biography important to the Christian faith[1006]?

18. Where is the first place you look for help in your search to understand Christianity? For some people, the last place is the Church – why do you think this happens[1007]?

19. If our knowledge of Christianity is based upon selective information, is truth compromised? What are the implications of selectivity for the Christian faith? How should a Christian leader select information and facts to teach others about Christianity? Should they withhold information?

20. Can an omnipotent being create a rock too heavy for itself to lift? Can God not do what is logically impossible and that the

---

[1003] I suggest reading Brown 2011 for some interesting thoughts.
[1004] Abbott 1885, 185-86.
[1005] Abbott 1885, 187-88.
[1006] Abbott 1885, 510.
[1007] McLaren 1999, 209.

Additional Christian Controversies 329

existence of some greater good, such as free will, may not be obtainable by God without the existence of evil[1008]?

21. Why does God grant us free will? If He knows how we will decide when he creates us, then how can there be free will?

22. The existence of evil seems to be incompatible with the existence of an omnipotent, omniscient, and morally perfect God. Epicurus asked the following, "Either God wants to abolish evil, and cannot; or he can, but does not want to. If he wants to, but cannot, he is impotent. If he can, but does not want to, he is wicked. If God can abolish evil, and God really wants to do it, why is there evil in the world"[1009]?

23. Did Jesus create Christianity; or, did it create Him[1010]?

Conclusion.

We can easily find information on several sides of controversies. Finding the truth about them is much harder. I've provided you with dozens of them throughout this book; yet, haven't touched the surface of the numerous ones not mentioned. This includes such topics as abortion, evolution versus creationism, homosexuality, perfection of Jesus, and eternal virginity of Mary. People can only "pursue the truth about God and not possess it", as many religious zealots claim[1011].

Maybe the real problem is one of semantics, or some other issue of communication. Blocking knowledge of this truth is the pious attitude among much of Christians today. Furthermore, authoritarian Christian leaders have an "I can't be wrong" attitude in dealing with their followers. Some of them have quickly excommunicated members for challenging their teachings, telling others that those members rebelled against God. These people shouldn't stop us in seeking the truth through honest debate of

---

[1008] Beebe 2003.
[1009] Haught 1996. This book contains the quote from Epicurus.
[1010] See especially Charles 2008.
[1011] Saranam 2005, xxii.

controversies, especially if it's done based upon fact, not upon half-truths, rumors, or opinions.

I hope that I've provided you additional insight into Christianity. There are many things we don't know about this theology. I, for sure, don't have all of the questions. And, as an imperfect human, I definitely don't have all the answers either. But, I'm still willing to learn and have an open mind to understand the desires of God. I'm not going to ignore reality; and I'm not always going to bow down to public sentiment. I'm a Christian, not because I belong to any Church, but because I believe in and strive to follow the teachings of Jesus. Belief in Jesus, as a Christian, should lead us to emulate Him, and to doing good in this world. His message to me is more important than His being God's Messenger.

After several years of research, reading hundreds of references, assessing empirical evidence, understanding history, I wrote this book containing about one hundred-thousand words and numerous footnotes. Accordingly, can I summarize the truth that we seek into just a few words? Through all of my work, I can honestly and logically summarize this into three words that I know to be the absolute truth.

God loves you.

References

Abbott, L. (ed.). (1885). A Dictionary of Religious Knowledge, for Popular and Professional Use. New York: Harper & Brothers Publishers.

Augustine (1887a). "Against Lying." Original 395 in Latin. Translated by H. Browne from *Nicene and Post-Nicene Fathers, First Series*, Vol. 3. Edited by Philip Schaff. Buffalo, N.Y.: Christian Literature Publishing Co. Revised and edited for New Advent by Kevin Knight. http://www.newadvent.org/fathers/ 1313.htm. Accessed 26 August 2012.

Augustine (1887b). "On Lying." Original 395 in Latin. Translated by H. Browne from *Nicene and Post-Nicene Fathers, First Series*, Vol. 3. Edited by Philip Schaff. Buffalo, N.Y.: Christian Literature Publishing Co. Revised and edited for New Advent by

Kevin Knight. http://www.newadvent.org/fathers/1312.htm. Accessed 26 August 2012.

Bacchiocchi, S. (1989). *Wine in the Bible: A Biblical Study on the Use of Alcoholic Beverages*. Vol. 8 of Biblical Perspectives Series. Berrien Springs, Mich.: Biblical Perspectives.

Barber, R. (1999). *The Companion Guide to Gascony and the Dordorgne*. Suffolk, U.K: St Edmundsbury Press.

Barna Group. (2003, 3 November). "Morality Continues to Decay." http://www.barna.org/barna-update/article/5-barna-update/129-morality-continues-to-decay. Accessed 1 September 2012.

Beach, G.K. (2002). *Questions for the Religious Journey: Finding Your Own Path*. Boston, Mass.: Skinner House Books.

Beebe, J.R. (2003, 17 August) "Logical Problem of Evil," *Internet Encyclopedia of Philosophy*. http://www.iep.utm.edu/evil-log/. Accessed 15 March 2011.

Bell, R. (2011). *Love Wins: A Book About Heaven, Hell, and the Fate of Every Person Who Ever Lived*. New York: HarperCollins.

Bennet, G. (1800). *Olam Haneshamoth: or, a View of the Intermediate State*. London: B. Scott.

Bhutto, B. (1998). "Politics and the Muslim Woman." In *Liberal Islam: A Source Book*, edited by Charles Kurzman. Oxford: Oxford University Press. 12: 107-111.

Black, S.C. (1910). *Plain Answers to Religious Questions Modern Men are Asking*. Philadelphia, Penns.: Westminster Press.

Bloxham, A. (2011). "Allowing women drivers in Saudi Arabia will be 'end of virginity'." *The Telegraph*. http://www.telegraph.co.uk/motoring/news/8930168/Allowing-women-drivers-in-Saudi-Arabia-will-be-end-of-virginity.html. Accessed 28 January 2012.

Boyd, G.A. (2005). *The Myth of a Christian Nation: How the Quest for Political Power Is Destroying the Church*. Grand Rapids, Mich.: Zondervan.

Brauch, M.T. (2009). Abusing Scripture: The Consequences of Misreading the Bible. Downers Grove, Ill.: InterVarsity Press.

Breuer, H. (2011, 15 August). "Tylar Witt & Boyfriend Sentenced for Murdering Her Mother." *People*. http://www.people.com/peoplearticle/0,,20518413,00.html. Accessed 16 September 2012.

Brooks, A. (director). (1991). *Defending Your Life*. Film. http://www.imdb.com/title/tt0101698/. Accessed 2 September 2012.

Brown, S. (2011). *Jesus Drank, Judas Repented and God Divorced His Bride*. 2nd Ed. Cupertino, Calif.: Happy About.

Buenting, J. (2010). *The Problem of Hell: A Philosophical Anthology*. Surrey, U.K.: Ashgate Publishing.

Burrus, V. (2007). *The Sex Lives of Saints: An Erotics of Ancient Hagiography*. Philadelphia, Penn.: University of Pennsylvania Press.

Canfora, L. (2007). *Julius Caesar: The Life and Times of the People's Dictator*. Original Italian in 1999. Translated by M. Hill and K. Windle. Berkeley and Los Angelos: University of California Press.

Capon, R.F. (2002). *Kingdom, Grace, Judgment: Paradox, Outrage, and Vindication in the Parables of Jesus*. Grand Rapids, Mich.: Eerdmans Publishing.

Capps, W.H. (1995). *Religious Studies: The Making of a Disciple*. Minneapolis, Minn.: Augsburg Fortress.

Carlino, M.A. (2002, spring). "Moral Limits of Strategic Attack." *Parameters*. Journal of the US Army War College. 32: 15-29. http://www.carlisle.army.mil/USAWC/parameters/Articles/02spring/carlino.htm. Accessed 25 August 2012.

Charles, L. (2008) *Jesus Religion: A Critical Examination of Christian Insanity*. Massillon, Oh.: Angels & Ghosts.

CNN. (2010, 22 November). "Woman fighting sex slavery named CNN Hero of the Year." http://www.cnn.com/2010/LIVING/11/21/cnnheroes.hero.of.year/index.html. Accessed 7 September 2012.

Coffey, J.W. (1983). "The American Bishops on War and Peace." *Parameters*. Journal of the US Army War College. 13(12): 30-38. http://www.carlisle.army.mil/USAWC/parameters/Articles/1983/coffey.htm. Accessed 25 August 2012.

Collins, J.J. (2003). "The Zeal of Phinehas: The Bible and the Legitimation of Violence". *Journal of Biblical Literature*. 122(1): 3-21.

Cook, M.L. (2001). "Ethical Issues in War: an Overview." In *Selected Readings, Course 501*, Vol. 1. Carlisle Barracks, PA: US Army War College. July/August. 142-153.

Cook, M.L. (2000, spring). "Moral Foundations of Military Service." *Parameters*. 30: 129-141. http://www.carlisle.army.mil/USAWC/parameters/Articles/00spring/cook.htm. Accessed 25 August 2012.

Cook, M.L. (1999). "Moral Reasoning as a Strategic Leader Competency." In *Selected Readings, Course 501*, Volume 1. Carlisle Barracks, PA: US Army War College. August, 183-188

Countryman, L.W. (2007). *Dirt, Greed, and Sex: Sexual Ethics in the New Testament and Their Implications for Today.* 2nd ed. Minneapolis, Minn.: Fortress.

Cyrino, M.S. (2010). *Aphrodite.* Abingdon, Oh.: Routlege.

Dante (Durante degli Alighieri). (1867). *The Divine Comedy: The Vision of Paradise, Purgatory, and Hell.* Italian original ca. 1308-1321. Translated by Henry W. Longfellow. Leipzig, Ger.: Bernhard Tauchnitz.

Davidson, R.M. (2007). *Flame of Yahweh: Sexuality in the Old Testament.* Peabody, Mass.: Hendrickson.

Davies, B. and Evans, G.R. (eds). (1998). *Anselm of Canterbury: The Major Works.* Oxford: Oxford University Press.

de Hartog, L. (2004). *Genghis Khan: Conqueror of the World.* New York: Tauris Parke.

Edward, E.J. (2007). *Paul and Ancient Views of Sexual Desire: Paul's Sexual Ethics in 1 Thessalonians 4, 1 Corinthians 7 and Romans 1.* Library of New Testament Studies 354. New York: T&T Clark.

Ellens, J.H. (2006). *Sex in the Bible: A New Consideration.* Westport, Ct.: Praeger.

Fadem, T.J. (2010). *How to Ask the Best Probing Questions.* Upper Saddle River, N.J.: Pearson Education.

Faure, B. (2003). *The Power of Denial: Buddhism, Purity and Gender.*

Foucault, M. (1978). *The History of Sexuality: An Introduction.* Original French in 1977. Vol 1. New York: Random House.

Foucault, M. (1985). *The History of Sexuality: The Use of Pleasure.* Original French in 1984. Vol 2. New York: Random House.

Foucault, M. (1986). *The History of Sexuality: The Care of the Self.* Original French in 1984. Vol 3. New York: Random House.

Fudge, E.W. and Peterson, R.A. (2000). *Two Views of Hell: A Biblical and Theological Dialogue.* Downers Grove, ill.: InterVarsity Press.

Gaca, K.L. (2003). *The Making of Fornication: Eros, Ethics, and Political Reform in Greek Philosophy and Early Christianity.* Berkeley, Calif.: University of California Press.

Gervais, W.M.; Shariff, A.F.; and Norenzayan, A. (2011). "Do You Believe in Atheists? Distrust is Central to Anti-Atheist Prejudice." *Journal of Personality and Social Psychology.* 101(6): 1189-1206. http://www2.psych.ubc.ca/~will/Gervais%20et%20al-%20Atheist%20Distrust.pdf. Accessed 2 September 2012.

Goldman, A.L. (1991, 2 February). "Was St. Paul Gay? Claim Stirs Fury." *The New York Times.* http://www.nytimes.com/1991/02/02/nyregion/was-st-paul-gay-claim-stirs-fury.html. Accessed 20 August 2011.

Graham, B. (1970). *The Challenge: Sermons from Madison Square Garden.* Kingswood, England: World's Work.

Gulley, P. (2010). *If the Church Were Christian: Rediscovery the Values of Jesus.* New York: HarperCollins Publishers.

Hanna, E. (1911). "Purgatory". *The Catholic Encyclopedia.* New York: Robert Appleton Company. http://www.newadvent.org/cathen/12575a.htm. Accessed 2 September 2012.

Haught, J.A. (1996). *2000 Years of Disbelief: Famous People with the Courage to Doubt.* New York: Prometheus Books.

Hawthorne, N. (1850). *The Scarlet Letter.* Boston, Mass.: Ticknor, Reed & Fields. http://www.gutenberg.org/cache/epub/33/pg33.html. Accessed 1 September 2012.

Hite, S. (2003). *The Hite Report: A Nationwide Study of Female Sexuality.* New York: Seven Stories Press.

Hockfield, V. (2011). *A Guide to Philanthropy and the Top Five Philanthropists, Including Warren Buffett, Bill Gates and Howard Hughes.* Baldwin City, Kans.: Webster's Digital Services.

Hoffman, R.J. (2006). The Just War and Jihad: Violence in Judaism, Christianity, and Islam. Amherst, N.Y.: Prometheus Books.

Holt, J.C. (1992). Magna Carta. Cambridge: Cambridge University Press.

Hugo, V. (1887). *Les Misérables.* Original French in 1862. Translated by Isabel F. Hapgood. New York: Thomas Y. Crowell.

Huntington, S.P. (1957). *The Soldier and the State: The Theory and Politics of Civil-Military Relations.* Cambridge, MA: The Belknap Press of Harvard University.

James, C.C. (2008). *The Gospel of Ruth: Loving God Enough to Break the Rules.* Grand Rapids, Mich.: Zondervan.

John Paul II. (1999, 28 July). General Audience. http://www.vatican.va/holy_father/john_paul_ii/audiences/1999/documents/hf_jp-ii_aud_28071999_en.html. Accessed 3 September 2012.

Johnson, J.T. (1985, Spring). "Threats, Values, and Defense: Does Defense of Values by Force Remain a Moral Possibility?" *Parameters.* Journal of the US Army War College. 15(1): 13.

Joshi, S. (2004). "'Cheli-Beti' Discourses of Trafficking and Constructions of Gender, Citizenship and Nation in Modern Nepal." In *Sexual Sites, Seminal Attitudes: Sexualities,*

Masculinities and Culture in South Asia, edited by S. Srivastava. London: Sage Publications.

Kant, I. (1930) 'Ethical Duties Toward Others: Truthfulness,' in Lectures on Ethics, London: Methuen.

Kant, I. (1898) 'On the Supposed Right to Tell Lies From Benevolent Motives,' in Kant's Critique of Practical Reason and Other Works of the Theory of Ethics, London: Longmans, Green & Company, appendix 1.

Kershaw, I. (2008). *Hitler: A Biography*. New York: W.W. Norton & Company.

King, K.L. (2013). "Jesus said to them, 'My wife ..': A New Coptic Gospel Papyrus." Accepted draft. *Harvard Theological Review*. http://www.hds.harvard.edu/sites/hds.harvard.edu/ files/attachments/faculty-research/research-projects/the-gospel-of-jesuss-wife/ 29865/King_JesusSaidToThem_draft_0920.pdf. Accessed 22 September 2012.

Komp, D.M. (1998) *Anatomy of a Lie*, Grand Rapids, Michigan: Zondervan.

Kreeft, P. and Tacelli, R.K. (1994). *Handbook of Christian Apologetics: Hundreds of Answers to Crucial Questions*. Downers Grove, Ill.: InterVarsity Press.

Lang, A. and Mascia, K. (2012, 20 February). "The Texas Cheerleader Case: A Daughter's Painful Journey." *People*. http://www.people.com/people/archive/article/0,,20571464,00.ht ml. Accessed 15 September 2012.

Loader, W. (2010). *Sexuality in the New Testament: Understanding the Key Texts*. London: Society for Promoting Christian Knowledge.

Magee, R.R. (Ed.) (1998). *Strategic Leadership Primer*. Carlisle Barracks, Penn.: US Army War College (Department of Command, Leadership, and Management). Washington: Government Printing Office.

Manu. (2004). *Manusmruti*. Original Sanskrit in circa 1500 BCE. Translated by Patrick Olivelle in *The Law Code of Manus*. Oxford World's Classics. Oxford: Oxford University Press.

McGlynn, K. (2011, 25 May). "17 Ridiculous Laws Still on the Books in the U.S." *Huffington Post*. http://www. huffingtonpost.com/2010/03/02/17-ridiculous-laws-still_n_ 481379.html#s71645&title=In_Missouri_It. Accessed 26 August 2012.

McGowan, J.A. and Kashatus, W.C. (2011). *Harriet Tubman: A Biography*. Santa Barbara, Calif.: ABC-CLIO.

McGrath, J. (2004). "A Glutton and a Drunkard": What Would Jesus Drink?" In *Religion & Alcohol: Sobering Thoughts*, edited by C.K. Robertson. New York: Peter Lang Publishing.

McLaren, B.D. (1999). Finding Faith: A Self-Discovery Guide for Your Spiritual Quest. Grand Rapids, Mich.: Zondervan.

Mieszkowska, A. (2011). *Irena Sendler: Mother of the Children of the Holocaust.* Santa Barbara, Calif.: Praeger.

Moore, T. (1998). *The Soul of Sex: Cultivating Life as an Act of Love.* New York: HarperPerennial[1012].

Moynihan, C. (2007, 19 April). "Professor's Violent Death Came Where He Sought Peace." *The New York Times.* http://www.nytimes.com/2007/04/19/us/19professor.html?_r=1&ref=liviulibrescu. Accessed 7 September 2012.

Neal, B. (2011). *Vengeance Is Mine: The Scandalous Love Triangle That Triggered the Boyce-Sneed Feud.* Denton, Tx.: University of North Texas Press.

Nyberg, D. (1995). *The Varnished Truth.* Chicago: University of Chicago Press.

Offstein, E.H. (2006). *Stand Your Ground: Building Honorable Leaders the West Point Way.* Westport, Conn.: Greenwood Publishing Group.

Ostling, R.N. and Graham, B. (1993, 15 November). "Of Angels, Devils and Messages From God," *Time Magazine.* http://www.time.com/time/magazine/article/0,9171,979587,00.html. Accessed 3 September 2012.

Payne, P.B. (2009). *Man and Woman, One in Christ: An Exegetical and Theological Study of Paul's Letters.* Grand Rapids, Mich.: Zondervans.

Peczenik, A. (2009). *On Law and Reason.* Law and Philosophy Library 8. Dordrecht, Netherlands: Springer Science + Business Media.

Plant, S. (2004). *Bonhoeffer.* London: Continuum.

Plato. (1894). *The Republic.* Original Greek in 380 BCE. Translated by Benjamin Jowett and finished by Lewis Campbell. http://www.gutenberg.org/files/1497/1497-h/1497-h.htm. Accessed 31 August 2012.

Proal, L. (1905). *Passion and Criminality: a Legal and Literary Study.* Original French in 1901. Translated by A.R. Allinson. London: The Emperial Press.

[1012] Dr. Moore is psychotherapist who lived as a monk in a Catholic religious order for more than ten years. He taught at Southern Methodist University.

Putnam, R.D. (2000). *Bowling Alone: The Collapse and Revival of American Community*. New York: Simon and Schuster.

Putnam, R.D. (2003) "Bowling Together," in Dionne, E.J.Jr; Drogosz, K.M.; and Litan, R.E.; *United We Serve: National Service and the Future of Citizenship*. Washington: Brookings Institution Press. p 13-19.

Salkin, J.K. (2008). *Righteous Gentiles in the Hebrew Bible: Ancient Role Models for Sacred Relationships*. Woodstock, Vt.: Jewish Lights Publishing.

Saranam, S. (2005). *God Without Religion: Questioning Centuries of Accepted Truths*. East Ellijay, Ga.: The Pranayama Institute.

Schein, E.H. (1996) "Leadership and Organizational Culture" In *The Leader of the Future: New Visions, Strategies, and Practices for the Next Era*. San Francisco, Calif.: Jossey-Bass.

Scheuer, M. (2011). *Osama Bin Laden*. New York: Oxford University Press.

Schilpp, P.A. (1938). *The Quest for Religious Realism: Some Paradoxes of Religion*. New York: Harper & Brothers Publishers. The Mendenhall lectures, seventeenth series, delivered at DePauw University.

Schleiermacher, F. (1893). *On Religion: Speeches to its Cultured Despisers*. Original German in 1799. Translated by John Oman. London: K. Paul, Trench, Trubner & Co. http://www.ccel.org/ccel/schleiermach/religion.toc.html. Accessed 25 August 2012.

Schwartz, R.M. (1998). *The Curse of Cain The Violent Legacy of Monotheism*. Chicago: University of Chicago Press.

Schwartz, R.M. (2006, June). "Holy Terror". *Society of Biblical Literature Forum*. http://sbl-site.org/publications/article.aspx?articleId=161. Accessed 3 September 2012.

Shepard, J.E., Jr. (1992) "Thomas Becket, Ollie North and You." In *Military Leadership*. San Francisco, CA: Westview.

Snider, D.M.; Nagl, J.A.; and Pfaff, T. (1999). *Army Professionalism, The Military Ethic, and Officership in the 21st Century Leaders*. Carlisle Barracks, PA: US Army War College (Strategic Studies Institute).

Spong, J.S. (2005). *The Sins of Scripture: Exposing the Bible's Texts of Hate to Reveal the God of Love*. New York: Harper Collins Publishing.

Stroup, T.G. (1996). "Leadership and Organizational Culture: Actions Speak Louder than Words." *Military Review*. 76(1): 44-49.

Taylor, M.J. (1998). *Purgatory*. Huntington, Ind.: Our Sunday Visitor Publishing.

Thiselton, A.C. (2011). *1 & 2 Thessalonians Through the Centuries*. West Sussex, U.K.: Blackwell Publishing.

Thomas, C. (2011, 12 October). "Punishing Success Won't Breed Pioneers." Commentary. *Naples Daily News*, 5B.

Tomlinson, H. (2011, 16 November)."Pardon no bar to Saudi Arabia flogging." *The Australian*. http://www.theaustralian.com.au/news/world/pardon-no-bar-to-saudi-arabia-flogging/story-e6frg6so-1226195990330. Accessed 28 January 2012.

Toner, J.H. (1996). "Gallant Atavism: The Military Ethic in an Age of Nihilism." *Airpower Journal*. 10(2): 13-22. http://www.airpower.au.af.mil/airchronicles/apj/apj96/sum96/toner1.pdf. Accessed 25 August 2012.

Trow, M.J. (2004). *Vlad the Impaler: In Search of the Real Dracula*. Charleston, S.C.: History Press.

US Army (2001). *The Army*. Army Field Manual 1. The Army, Department of the Army. Washington, DC: US Government Printing Office

Vinsten, L. (2010). *Hell is a Real Place! The Salvation is in the Living Jesus Christ*. Bloomington, Ind.: Xlibris Publishing.

Vincent, T. (1670). *Fire and Brimstone in Hell to Burn the Wicked*. London: George Calvert and Samuel Sprint.

Walls, J.L. (2012). *Purgatory: The Logic of Total Transformation: The Logic of Total Transformation*. Oxford: Oxford University Press.

Walvoord, J.F. (2010). *Four Views on Hell*. Grand Rapids, Mich.: Zondervan.

Ward, K. (2008). *The Big Questions in Science and Religion*. West Conshohocken, Penn.: Templeton Foundation Press.

Weems, R.J. (1995). *Battered Love: Marriage, Sex, and Violence in the Hebrew Prophets*. Minneapolis, Minn.: Fortress Press.

Xenophon (1897). *Oeconomicus*. Original Greek in 370 BCE. Translated by H.G. Dakyns. London: Macmillan and Company. http://www.gutenberg.org/files/1173/1173-h/1173-h.htm. Accessed 31 August 2012.

Abbreviations

AD	Anno Domini
AIDS	Acquired Immunodeficiency Syndrome
AWOL	Absent Without Leave
BC	Before Christ
BCE	Before Common Era
BRM	Basic Rifle Marksmanship
CARM	Christian Apologetics & Research Ministry
CE	Common Era
CEO	Chief Executive Officer
CIA	Central Intelligence Agency
CNN	Cable News Network
CQ	Charge of Quarters
D&C	Drill and Ceremony (ie military marching)
DFAC	Dining Facility (military)
DWP	Democratic Workers Party
EC-PATR	Ecumenical Patriarch (of Constantinople)
FBI	Federal Bureau of Investigation
GI	Government Issue
ILC	International Lutheran Council
KP	Kitchen Police (ie military kitchen duties)
MCF	Military Correction Facility (ie jail)
NAE	National Association of Evangelicals
NASA	National Aeronautics and Space Administration
NCO	Non-Commissioned Officer
NT	New Testament
OIC	Officer in Charge
OT	Old Testament
PCA	Redeemer Presbyterian Church
PCUSA	Presbyterian Church USA
POV	Privately Owned Vehicle
PSYOPS	Psychological Operations (military)
PT	Physical Training
PTL	Praise The Lord (organization)
PTSD	Post-traumatic Stress Disorder
ROTC	Reserve Officers' Training Corps
THREATCON	Threat Condition
TDY	Temporary Duty (official travel)
TV	Television

UCMJ	Uniform Code of Military Justice
UMC	United Methodist Church
US	United States
USMA	US Military Academy (West Point, NY)
USO	United Service Organization (military)
VUCA	Volatile, Uncertain, Complex, and Ambiguous
VX	O-ethyl S-[2-(diisopropylamino)ethyl] methylphosphonothioate [a WMD nerve agent]
WAC	Women's Army Corps
WMD	Weapons of Mass Destruction
WWII	World War II
WWJD	What Would Jesus Do?

ΘΣ	God (nominative Greek)
ΙΣ	Jesus (nominative Greek)
ΚΣ	Lord (nominative Greek)
𝔓	papyri codice symbol (followed by a superscript)

Index

Authors, Artists, Groups and Key People

700 Club, 252

Abanes, R., 96, 147
Abbott, L., 327, 328, 330
Ackerman, H. and Wylie, M., 76, 79
Ackoff, R.L., 6, 30
Ackroyd, P.R. and Evans, C.F., 87, 147
Adamantius, O., 62
Ader, C., 22
Adrian Room, 147
Aeschylus, 42, 79
Aesop, 111, 147
Africanus, 43
Agamben, G., 44, 79
Agnostics, 24, 25
Ahlstrom, D. and Bruton, G.D., 247, 252, 270
Alamo Christian Ministries, 160
Alamo, T., 160, 210
Aland, K. and Aland, B., 110, 147
Alcock, J., 22
Alexander the Great, 225, 271
Algernon, S., 111, 147
Allen, P.L., 18, 30
Allport, G.W., 222, 270
Amish, 168, 209, 215
Andersen, C.P., 204, 206
Anderson, D., 249, 270
Anderson, J.H., 229, 270
Aphrodite, 303, 333
Applewhite, M., 161
Aquinas, T., 71, 84, 327
Aramaic, 87, 90, 91, 106, 107
Arendzen, J., 96, 147
Aristachus, 265
Aristotle, 37, 39, 40, 79
Army Civilian Study Panel, 190, 206
Army Science Board, 122

Asch, S.E., 224, 270
Asinof, E., 159, 206
Athanasius, 93, 147
Athenian Empire, 3, 6
Attila, 225, 275
Augustine, 37, 41, 62, 75, 79, 113, 116, 148, 155, 295, 298, 330
Aune, D.E., 102, 147, 150
Aurelius, M., 41, 44, 79, 82, 178
Austen, J., 124, 153, 154
Austin, M.M., 61, 79

Bacchiocchi, S., 317, 331
Bacon, F., 111, 148
Bagozzi, R.P.; Dholakia, U.M.; and Basuroy, S., 43, 79
Baker, B., 22, 30
Bakker, J., 162, 252, 253
Bakker, T.F., 253
Balk, A.P., 206, 207
Barabbas, 6, 136, 253, 254, 255
Barber, R., 284, 331
Barclay, W., 267, 270
Barnes, R., 170, 207
Barnett, F. and Lord, C., 241, 270
Barrett, D.B. and Johnson, T.M., 148, 193, 199, 200, 201, 207
Bartov, O., 226, 270
Baruch, 91, 151
Basile, P., 284
Beach, G.K., 326, 331
Bearak, B., 161, 207
Bechtel, F., 91, 148
Beck, J. and Friedwald, W., 76, 79
Becker, C.H., 59, 79
Bede, 123, 148
Beduhn, J.D., 113, 148
Beebe, J.R., 329, 331
Bell, A.G., 22
Bell, R., 266, 270, 320, 331
Bellafaire, J.A., 227, 270

Benigni, U., 110, 148
Benner, E., 186, 207
Bennet, G., 290, 331
Ben-Sasson, H.H., 117, 148
Bent, W., 162, 206
Berman, H.J., 264, 270
Bernhard, A.E., 96, 148
Betts, R.K., 187, 207
Bevington, D. and Rasmussen, E., 261, 271
Bhutto, B., 307, 331
Bihl, M., 116, 148
Bingham, R.L., 269, 271
Black, D.A., 107, 148
Black, S.C., 326, 327, 331
Blackman, R.H. and Utzinger, J.M., 39, 79
Bloxham, A., 308, 331
Böcklin, A., 286
Bohaterowicza, B., 246
Bohr, N.H.D., 10, 30, 33
Bonavoglia, A., 269, 271
Bonhoeffer, D., 128, 299, 336
Boorstein, M., 254, 271
Borek, D.; Lovett, D.; and Towns, E., 193, 194, 196, 197, 207
Borzello, A., 169, 207
Bouguereau, W.A., 192, 302
Bowler, P.J., 22, 30
Boyd, G.A., 322, 331
Bradlaugh, C., 91, 92, 148
Bradley, O.N., 191, 207
Branstetter, Z., 268, 271
Brauch, M.T., 128, 148, 299, 331
Bredfeldt, G., 185, 208
Bréhier, L., 69, 79
Brennan, J.G., 42, 79
Breuer, H., 325, 331
Brighton, T., 243, 271
Briner, B. and Pritchard, R., 206, 208
Brinkley, B., 101, 149
Brontë sisters, 124, 152
Brooks, A., 331
Brotzman, E.R., 107, 149
Brown, A.W., 22

Brown, D., 96, 149
Brown, R.M., 222, 223, 271, 316
Brown, S., 328, 331
Browne, S. and Harrison, L., 173, 208
Bruce, F.F., 93, 149
Buckingham, C.T., 38, 80
Buenting, J., 292, 332
Buffett, W., 313, 334
Burchardus, J., 180, 208
Burgon, J.W., 135, 136, 137, 138, 149
Burns, L.C., 141, 149
Burrus, V., 302, 332
Burton, J.G., 46, 80
Buxton, C., 186
Bwire, R., 170, 208

Cain and Abel, 287, 337
Calley, W., 186, 234
Callick, R., 172, 208
Calvin, J., 202, 208
Campbell, A.; Whitehead, J.; and Finkelstein, S., 191, 208
Campbell, W.D., 266, 271
Camping, H., 162-64, 208, 214, 215
Canfora, L., 312, 332
Cannon, L., 159, 208
Capill, G., 164, 214
Capon, R.F., 323, 332
Capps, W.H., 326, 332
Carlin, G., 3
Carlino, M.A., 294, 332
Catholic, 2, 41, 50, 61, 69, 73, 75, 76, 84, 89, 93, 99, 114, 145, 159, 169, 171, 172, 173, 176, 180, 182, 194, 209, 232, 263, 265, 266, 273, 274, 279, 292, 304, 305, 313
Cawthorne, N., 225, 271
Center for Military Readiness, 233, 271
Central Intelligence Agency, 118, 149, 249, 271, 275, 277, 279

Index 343

Chapman, A.W.; Lilly, C.J.; Romjue, J.L.; and Canedy, S., 233, 271
Charles, L., 290, 326, 329, 332
Chatterjee, P., 159, 208
Christian Identity, 173, 174, 214
Chrysostom, J., 62
Church, F.P., 53, 80
Churchill, W., 184, 211
Cicero, M.T., 27, 37, 43, 80
Cienciala, A.M.; Lebedeva, N.S.; and Materski, W., 247, 272
Clark, M., 24, 30
Clemens, T.F., 62
Coates, G.W., 195, 209
Coffey, J.W., 293, 332
Coker, C., 45, 49, 80
Collins, J.J., 287, 332
Collins, K.J., 7, 30
Columbus, 22, 34
Comfort, P., 107, 110, 149
Committee on Defense Women's Health Research, 229, 272
Congregation for the Doctrine of the Faith, 272
Cook, M.L., 295, 296, 332
Cooperman, A., 257, 272
Copernicus, 265, 273
Crusades, 69, 79, 84
Countryman, L.W., 300, 301, 333
Crider, L.W., 244, 272
Crouch, T., 22, 30
Culpeper, J., 140, 149, 152
Curran, T., 204, 209
Custer, G., 22, 30
Cutbirth, J., 170, 209
Cyprian and Justina (saints), 261, 277
Cyril of Jerusalem, 75, 80
Cyrino, M.S., 303, 333

da Rocha, J.J., 64
Daigneault, A. and Sangalli, A., 31
Dalton, J., 7, 31
Daly, S. and Kaplan, D., 223, 272
Daniel (person), 101, 198

Dante, 71, 80, 179, 290, 333
Daraul, A., 172, 209
Darwin, C., 6, 22
Darwin, E., 22
Dasgupta, S., 59, 80
David, 90, 101, 126, 127, 131, 132, 133, 196, 298, 301, 318
David, G.J. and McKeldin, T.R., 241, 272
Davidson, J., 107, 149
Davidson, R.M., 305, 333
Davies, B. and Evans, G.R., 289, 333
Davies, D.T., 245, 253, 272
Davis, E., 268, 272
Davy, H., 22
Dawkins, R., 4, 19, 21, 23, 31
Dawson, C., 60, 61, 62, 69, 80
De Dreu, C.K. and Van de Vliert, E., 252, 272
de Hartog, L., 312, 333
de Moleyns, F., 22
de Zavala, A.G.; Cichocka, A.; Eidelson, R.; and Jayawickreme, N., 225, 272
DeConick, A.D., 102, 149
Defoe, D., 123, 150
Democratic Workers Party, 172
Dempsey, J.K., 234, 272
Denison, J.C., 91, 150
Descartes, 37, 41, 45, 80
Dewey, J., 40, 81
Di Mambro, J., 165
Dickens, C., 1, 4, 124, 155
Dillon, W.S., 119, 150
Dimont, M.I., 128, 150
Doré, G., 72, 179, 196, 288
Dörner, D., 187, 209
Doyle, T.P.; Sipe, A.W.R.; and Wall, P.J., 159, 209
Dracula, 312, 338
Draper, J.A., 93, 150
Driver, J., 40, 81
Drum, W., 91, 150
Duling, D.C., 101, 150
Dumas, A., 195, 209

Dupries, L.E., 70
Dutton, D.G., 248, 273

Eastwood, C., 19, 31
Ebbinghaus, H., 13
Eckholm, E., 168, 209
Edgar, S., 108, 150
Edison, T., 22
Edward, E.J., 301, 333
Ehrman, B.D., 102, 126, 150
Einstein, A., 9, 10, 21, 31, 33
Eiriksson, L., 22
Eisenhower, D., 184, 216, 217, 218
Ellens, J.H., 304, 333
Elliot, J.K., 95, 110, 150
Epictetus, 37, 42, 44, 81
Epicurus, 37, 39, 40, 45, 81, 329
Esser, J.K. and Lindoerfer, J.S., 252, 273
Estes, R., 62, 81
Evans, C.A., 126, 150
Evans, C.S., 28, 31
Evans, J.E. and Maunder, E., 10, 31
Evans, M., 40, 41, 81
Evans, R.J., 244, 273
Ewing, J.E., 268

Fadem, T.J., 325, 333
Falwell, J., 253
Fantus, C., 174, 209
Fara, P., 22, 32
Faure, B., 307, 333
Felt, J.B., 262, 273
Finkelstein, S. et. al., 29, 32
Finnegan, S., 263, 273
Finocchiaro, M.A., 265, 273
Fladager, B., 171, 209
Flammarion, C., 11
Fleischmann, R., 124, 150
Fokkelman, J.P., 139, 151
Fonda, J., 204, 206, 209, 211
Foote, G.W. and Wheeler, J.M., 176, 210
Forbes, G.W., 202, 210
Forsyth, D.R., 249, 273
Foucault, M., 301, 304, 333

Fowler, J., 222
Franklin, B., 111, 151
French, B., 253, 273
French, S.E., 38, 81
Friedman, H.H., 193, 194, 196, 197, 210
Friedman, M., 43, 44, 81
Fudge, E.W. and Peterson, R.A., 291, 333
Fuerbringher, O., 6, 32
Fundamentalist Church of Jesus Christ of Latter Day Saints, 165

Gaca, K.L., 301, 333
Galileo, 6, 273
Gandhi, 185
Gandi, 296
Gassmann, G.; Howard, D.H.; and Oldenburg, M.W., 145, 151
Gates, B., 313, 334
Genghis Khan, 225, 279, 312, 333
Gera, V., 265, 273
Gervais, W.M.; Shariff, A.F.; and Norenzayan, A., 287, 333
Gesta Matthiæ, 94
Giannet, S.M., 54, 56, 57, 81
Gibbon, E., 69, 81
Gibson, D., 254, 273
Gigot, F., 91, 151, 210
Gleijeses, P., 249, 273
Goeschel, C., 248, 273
Goethe, J.W., 261, 273
Goldberg, B., 210, 258
Golding, W., 223, 273
Goldman, A.L., 334
Goleman, D.; Boyatzis, R.; and McKee, A., 159, 210
Goralka, J., 262, 273
Gordon Conwell Theological Seminary, 88, 151, 255, 274
Gordon, D.R., 39, 81
Gould, S.J., 20, 32
Goya, F., 66
Graham, B., 290, 334, 336
Graver, S., 124, 151
Gray, C., 22, 32

Index   **345**

Gray, E., 22
Grayling, A.C., 141, 151
Greenleaf, R.K. and Spears, L.C., 192, 210
Gregory the Great, 71, 82
Gruber, H., 173, 174, 210
Gruhl, W., 248, 274
Gulley, P., 5, 30, 32, 75, 82, 113, 126, 143, 147, 151, 255, 260, 265, 266, 274, 285, 308, 310, 319, 320, 323, 334

Hadot, P., 41, 82
Hafez, M.M., 248, 274
Haggard, T., 257
Hahn, J., 162, 253
Hahn, P., 93, 151, 267
Hale, M.F., 165
Halliburton, 159, 208
Hanna, E., 274, 292, 334
Haraburda, S.S., 12, 13, 25, 27, 32, 211
Hardon, J., 264, 274
Harkness, G.E., 37, 38, 49, 59, 73, 74, 75, 82
Harris, S.L., 102, 151
Hasel, M.G., 225, 274
Hassett, M., 199, 211
Haught, J.A., 329, 334
Hawthorne, N., 257, 274, 303, 334
Hayes, J.H. and Holladay, C.R., 142, 151
Hayward, S.F., 184, 211
Heathens, 75, 219, 255, 287
Heaven's Gate, 172, 207, 211
Heine, R.E., 109, 151
Henderson, W.D., 221, 223, 274
Herb, G.H. and Kaplan, D.H., 244, 274
Herdt, J.A., 261, 274
Hernandez, D., 242, 274
Herod Antipater, 318
Herpolsheimer, 50, 51, 53
Hexham, I.; Poewe, K., 161, 211
Hibernians, 173, 213
Hick, J., 57, 82

Hills, N.D., 180, 211
Hite, S., 300, 304, 334
Hitler, A., 184, 244, 245, 276, 277, 312, 335
Hobbes, T., 49, 82
Hockfield, V., 313, 334
Hoffman, R.J., 287, 334
Hollander, E.P. and Hunt, R.G., 221, 274
Hollmann, W.B., 140, 151
Holloway, J.L., III, 250
Holowchak, M.A., 41, 82
Holt, J.C., 23, 32, 284, 334
Holzer, H.M. and Holzer, E., 204, 211
Holzworth, C.E., 250, 275
Horne, C.F. and Bewer, J.A., 255
Hubble, E.P., 32
Hughes D., 33
Hughes, D., 18
Hugo, V., 314, 334
Huntington, S.P., 296, 334
Hyde, D., 141, 152
Hylton, H., 166, 211
Hypatia, 242

Illuminati, 173, 174, 210
Infidels, 256, 276
Isen, A.M. and Shalker, T.E, 43, 82

Jacobs, L., 101, 152
James, C.C., 310, 334
James, L., 226, 275
James, M.R., 152
Janis, I.L., 235, 275
Janis, I.L. and Mann, L., 241, 275
Jastaniya, S., 279, 308, 338
Jeffs, W., 165, 211, 217
Jesus, 3, 5, 21, 24, 27, 28, 32, 37, 38, 49-59, 73, 74, 78-89, 96-102, 107, 109-10, 119, 126-38, 144-52, 159, 161, 170, 175, 176, 191, 193, 199- 208, 217, 219, 224, 245, 253-69, 274, 278, 280-91, 298, 301, 306-38
Ji-sook, B., 172, 211

Joan of Arc, 67, 68
John (person), 92, 100, 102
John Paul II, 291, 334
John the Baptist, 318
Johns, J.H.; Bickel, M.D.; Blades, A.C.; Creel, J.B.; Gatling, W.S.; Hinkle, J.M.; Kindred, J.D.; and Stocks, S.E., 221, 223, 275
Johnson, J.T., 293, 334
Johnson, K.D., 77, 82
Johnson, T.M., 152
Jones B.H., Manikowski J.A., Harris J.A., Dziados J.E., Norton S., Ewart T., and Vogel J.A., 229, 275
Jones, H., 249, 275
Jones, J., 166, 167
Joseph, 194, 301
Joshi, S., 314, 334
Joshua (person), 90, 195, 253, 297
Jost, L., 197, 211
Jouret, L., 165
Judas, 64, 127, 133, 135, 154, 199, 331
Julius Caesar, 24, 312, 332

Kamm, W., 167
Kant, I., 37, 39, 41, 335
Ka-shing, L., 313
Kataribabo, D., 169
Keane, B., 125, 152
Keith, C., 138, 152
Keller, T., 97, 152
Kelly, C., 225, 275
Kempis, T., 41
Kennedy, J.F., 241
Kennedy, R.F., 42, 82
Kent, W., 53, 264, 275
Kenyon, F.G., 137, 152
Kenyon, K.S., 124, 152
Keppie, L.J.F., 225, 275
Kershaw, I., 312, 335
Kibweteere, J., 169
King, K.L., 285, 335
King, M.L. Jr., 42, 82, 185, 202, 211, 215, 296

King, P.J. and Stager, L.E., 118, 152
Kington, T., 170, 211
Kipling, R., 243, 275
Kirkpatrick, F.G., 146, 152
Kirkpatrick, L.B., 249, 275
Kirsch, J.P., 63, 83, 93, 152, 176, 178, 212
Kirsch, K., 242, 275
Klenke, K., 184, 212
Knights of Malta, 173, 174
Knights Templar, 165, 173, 174, 179, 213
Koester, H., 93, 152
Koirala, A., 314
Komp, D.M., 298, 335
Koppel, G., 124, 153
Köstenberger, A.J. and Kruger, M.J., 110, 153
Kowert, P.A., 247, 276
Krasner, S.D., 70, 83
Kreeft, P. and Tacelli, R.K., 327, 335
Ku Klux Klan, 214
Kunst, J., 261, 276
Kurst-Swanger, K., 171, 212
Kyle, J.H., 250, 276
Kyle, R.G., 253, 276

Lacey, M. and Malkin, E., 168, 212
Lalich, J., 172, 173, 212
Lamarck, J., 22
Lamont-Brown, R., 22, 33
Lang, A. and Mascia, K., 325, 335
Laurens, J.P., 177
Lazarus, 55
Le Bon, G., 242, 276
Lee, S.J., 244, 276
Legionaries of Christ, 168
Lenepveu, J.E., 68
Lepage, J., 245, 276
Lewis, J.R., 165, 212
Lewis, P.; Kuhnert, K.; and Maginnis, R., 183, 186, 212
Liberman, A., 139, 153
Librescu, L., 315, 336

Index

Lifton, R.J., 246, 276
Lincoln, A., 71, 83, 185, 217
Lindbergh, C., 22
Lippy, C.H., 18, 33
Lipsius, J., 41
Loader, W., 304, 310, 335
Logan, F.D., 178, 212
Lomax, S.S., 260, 276
Longshore, D., 234, 276
Lord Our Righteousness Church, 162
Lose, D., 113, 153
Loughlin, J., 176, 180, 212
Luftwaffe, 248
Luke (person), 101, 200
Łukowski, P., 141, 153
Lussier, E., 118, 153
Luther, M., 7, 33, 72, 73, 83, 145, 181, 327
Lutheran, 41, 145, 151
Lyons, H., 168, 214

MacCaffrey, J., 179, 181, 212
Machiavelli, 76, 186, 207
Maciel, M., 168, 212
Madison, J., 29, 33
Magee, R.R., 294, 335
Maita Nepal, 314
Majlis al-Ifta' al-A'ala, 308
Malisow, C., 268, 276
Manchester, W., 180, 212
Mann, H., 177, 178, 213
Manns, F., 115, 116, 117, 118, 153
Manu, 307, 335
Marin, R. and Chong, T., 76, 83
Marlowe, C., 261, 271, 276
Martin, R.P., 128, 153
martyr, 42, 62, 94, 99, 100, 148, 199, 200, 201
Mary Magdalene, 286
Masaccio, 198
Maseko, A.N., 144, 153
Mason, G.A., 73, 83
Mason, J.M., 256, 276
Matthew (person), 98, 101, 306
Maupertius, P.L., 22

Maxwell, J.C., 10, 33
Mayans, 164
McCarthy, J., 186, 210
McDermott, J.J., 101, 153
McDonald, L.M., 88, 153
McDowell, J. and Stewart, D., 258, 276
McFaul, J., 174, 213
McGlynn, K., 310, 335
McGowan, J.A. and Kashatus, W.C., 315, 335
McGrath, J., 316, 336
McKenna, S., 65, 83
McLaren, B.D., 328, 336
McPhail, C., 242, 276
Meacham, J., 267, 277
Mead, F.S., 144, 153
Media Elite, 210, 258
Mehra, J., 11, 33
Meier, G., 277
Melendez, B., 76, 83
Merchant, D., 270, 277
Methodist, 2, 144, 146, 155, 156, 267, 274, 361
Metzger, B.M., 93, 96, 107, 153
Mieszkowska, A., 315, 336
Miller, F.P.; Vandome, A.F.; and McBrewster, J., 70, 83
Milton, J., 111, 123, 153
Mizell, L.R. Jr., 162, 213
Moeller, C., 174, 213
Mohler, R.A. Jr., 320
Monter, E.W., 67, 83
Montgomery, D., 256, 260, 277
Moore, R.L., 187, 213
Moore, T., 302, 303, 305, 336
Morden, B.J., 227, 277
Moses, 85, 90, 94, 101, 195, 209, 218, 253, 298, 318
Moskos, C.C.; Williams, J.A.; and Segal, D.R., 45, 49, 83
Mother Teresa, 184, 314
Movement for the Restoration of the Ten Commandments of God, 169, 172, 215
Moynihan, C., 315, 336

Mozhaiski, A., 22
Mulder, W., 180, 213
Mullet, S., 168, 215
Munkácsy, M., 23
Munoz, O., 171, 213
Murphy, A., 16
Murphy, D.E., 169, 213
Murray, D., 146, 154
Muslim, 2, 25, 69, 160, 205, 248, 263, 308, 331
Muverengwi, P., 213, 256, 277
Mwerinde, C., 164, 169
Myrer, A., 45, 84

Nagel, T., 24, 33
Namie, G. and Namie, R., 240, 277
Napoleon, 187
Neal, B., 325, 336
Nelson, C., 169, 214
Nelson, S.; Smith, M.; and Walker, N., 167, 214
Newton, I., 10, 21
Nicene Council, 95
Niebuhr, R., 41, 84
Niemöller, M., 128
Nobili, A., 170
Nyberg, D., 298, 336

Oeconomicus, 307, 338
Oestereich, T., 178, 214
Office of the Inspector General, 159, 214
Offstein, E.H., 299, 336
Ohnuki-Tierney, E., 248, 277
Olcott, H.S., 59, 84
Oliver, K., 234, 277
Olson, R.E., 143, 154
Oltean, D., 164, 214
Order of St. Charbel, 167
Order of the Solar Temple, 165, 172, 209, 212
Orr, J., 126, 154
Orthodox, 73, 93, 145, 171
Orwell, G., 125, 154, 220, 235, 236, 277
Osama Bin Laden, 312, 337

Ott, M., 181, 214
Overton, J.H., 146, 154
Overy, R.J., 245, 277

Pagels, E. and King, K.L., 96, 154
Paine, T., 124, 154
Palmer, P.M. and More, R.P., 261, 277
Pan Twardowski, 262
Panetta, L.E., 258, 277
Pape, J.M., 183, 214
Parker, S., 222, 277
Parks, R., 185
Patterson, K.; Grenny, J.; Maxfield, D.; McMillan, R.; and Switzler, A., 182, 214
Patzia, A.G., 136, 137, 154
Paul, 59, 72, 92, 95, 98, 101, 254, 257, 301, 333, 334, 336
Paxton, R.O. and Hessler, J., 244, 277
Payne, P.B., 307, 336
Peczenik, A., 309, 336
Pegis, A.C., 71, 84
Peoples Temple, 166, 172, 214
Perse, E.M., 235, 241, 277
Peter (person), 64, 75, 92, 94, 98, 102, 198, 297
Pfeiffer, J.B., 249, 277
Phelan, G.L., 254, 278
Phelps, F., 170, 171, 209
Phillips, D.T., 185, 215
Phillips, J.P., 69, 84
Pieter Bruegel the Elder, 322
Plaisted, D.A., 69, 84
Plant, S., 299, 336
Plato, 40, 336
Poe, T.M., 223
Polelle, M.R., 185, 215
Pontius Pilate, 21, 100, 253
Poovey, M., 124, 154
Pope, H., 91, 154
Porter, H.D., 171, 209
Praise The Lord (PTL), 162, 252, 253, 278
Presbyterian, 97, 145, 152

Index

Proal, L., 324, 336
Putnam, R.D., 319, 337
Pythagoreans, 265

Quarles, C.L., 174, 214
Quesada, A., 249, 278

Randolf, S. and Phillips, H., 22, 34
Ratzinger, J., 173, 215
Record, J., 215, 265
Redd, S.E., 252, 253, 278
Rees, J.C., 185, 215
Reid, G., 93, 94, 154
Reimink, T., 163, 215
Repin, I., 52
Rey, A.R., 163, 215
Rhodes, R., 143, 154
Richard the Lionhearted, 284
Riding, A., 167, 215
Robertson, P., 164, 252
Robinson, E., 127, 154
Robinson, J.M., 127, 154
Rogers, W.P., 252, 278
Rudolph, 50
Russell, J.B., 8, 34, 67, 84
Ruth, 90, 310, 334
Rutherford, E., 10, 34
Rutter, T., 232, 278
Ryden, B.S., 9, 34
Ryne, L., 22, 34

Saint Matthew's Churches, Inc., 267, 268, 276
Salembier, L., 145, 154, 180, 215
Salkin, J.K., 312, 337
Sanford, G., 247, 278
Santa Claus, 49, 50, 51, 52, 53, 58, 80
Santayana, G., 3, 4
Santucci, J., 169, 215
Saranam, S., 78, 84, 263, 267, 278, 319, 329, 337
Saul, 130, 196, 298
Schacter, D., 13
Schaff, P., 62, 73, 84
Schaff, P. and Henry W., 62, 63, 84

Schamschula, W., 262, 278
Scheeres, J., 172, 215
Schein, E.H., 295, 337
Scheuer, M., 312, 337
Schilpp, P.A., 6, 7, 12, 18, 19, 26, 34, 285, 312, 319, 320, 323, 325, 337
Schleiermacher, F., 326, 337
Schnackenburg, R., 58, 84
Schrödinger, E., 11, 34
Schwartz, R.M., 287, 337
Second Infantry Division, Korean War Veterans Association, 19, 34
Sedgwick, F., 139, 154
Sekunda, N., 225, 278
Sendler, I., 315, 336
Seneca, 37, 40, 43, 44, 69, 78, 83, 84, 94, 95
Seok, J.M., 171
Shahan, T., 179, 215
Shay, J.S., 38, 85
Sheeran, T.J. and Seewer, J., 168, 215
Shelley, M., 124, 154, 155
Shepard, J.E., Jr., 294, 337
Simon, B., 8, 35
Simpson, D.A., 35
Sister Mary Elephant, 76, 83
Sisters of Charity of Saint Elizabeth, 76, 85
Slater, M., 124, 155
slavery, 18, 37, 77, 88, 117, 130, 185, 194, 201, 287, 304, 332
Slick, M., 89, 136, 155
Smith, D.K., 240, 278
Smith, E.J. et.al., 10, 35
Smith, J.E., 184, 216
Smith, R.M., 108, 155
Smithsonian National Air and Space Museum, 22, 35
Smorawiński, M., 246
Sneddon, C.R., 108, 155
Sneed, J., 324, 336
Snider, D.M.; Nagl, J.A.; and Pfaff, T., 297, 337

Snowden, D.J. and Boone, M.E., 185, 216
Socrates, 6, 35, 307
Solzhenitsyn, A.I., 78, 85
Sorley, L., 185, 216
Souvay, C., 91, 155
Spahn, M., 69, 85
Spiegel, J.S., 256, 278
Spinney, F.C., 2, 4
Spong, J.S., 77, 85, 87, 96, 106, 127, 128, 129, 142, 155, 172, 175, 216, 286, 303, 304, 305, 306, 337
Spring, H., 45, 85
Starry, D.A., 184, 189, 216
Steigmann-Gall, R., 245, 278
Steinmetz, S., 139, 155
Stern, G., 139, 155
Stevens, J., 164, 216
Stevenson, M., 164, 216
Stock, B., 116, 155
Stockdale, J.B., 42, 43, 79, 85
Stone, I.F., 6, 35
Stowers, S.K., 55, 85
Stradivari, A., 14
Strobel, L., 254, 278
Stroup, T.G., 295, 337
Super, C.W., 139, 155
Swift, J., 123, 156

't Hart, P., 247, 251, 278
't Hart, P. and Kroon, M.B.R., 250, 251, 279
Talbye, D., 262
Talmud, 98
Tamar, 1
Taylor, C., 41, 85
Taylor, M.J., 292, 293, 338
Tennyson, A., 243, 279
Tertullianus, 62
Texas Cheerleading Murdering Mom, 325
Theodoret of Cyrus, 62
Theophilus of Adana, 261
Third Reich, 226, 244, 270, 273, 278

Thiselton, A.C., 290, 338
Thomas, C., 324, 338
Thomasson, D.K., 266, 279
Thompson, M., 235, 279
Thomson, D., 14
Thomson, J.J., 7, 35
Tintoretto, 317
Tissot, J., 57, 194
Tomkins, S., 146, 156
Tomlinson, H., 308, 338
Toner, J.H., 294, 338
Trow, M.J., 312, 338
Trujillo, A., 170, 216
Trumble, A., 138, 156
Tubman, H., 315, 335
Turnbull, S., 226, 279
Turner, C., 255, 279
Turner, M.P., 163, 216
Tusser, T., 111, 156

Ulmer, W.F. Jr., 47, 187, 216

Vacandard, E., 35, 61, 64, 65, 66, 67, 85
Van Allsburg, C., 50, 85
Van Voorst, R.E., 113, 156
van Wormer, K. and Besthorn, F.H., 222, 279
Vander Heeren, A., 107, 156
Vaticana, 75, 85
Vaughan, D., 251, 279
Velarde, R., 258, 279
Verkamp, B.J., 70, 86
Vermès, G., 202, 217
Victor, G., 247, 279
Vincent, T., 290, 338
Vinsten, L., 289, 338
Virgin Mary, 169, 286, 306
Virkler, H.A. and Ayayo, K.G., 114, 156
von Templern, V., 175

Wagner, D., 166, 217
Wake, W., 95, 97, 156
Walker, W., 145, 156
Walls, J.L., 292, 338

Index 351

Walsh, H.E., 241, 247, 253, 279
Walt Disney, 185
Walvoord, J.F., 291, 338
Walzer, M., 41, 86
Ward, K., 327, 338
Warner, M., 249, 279
Washington, G., 185, 215
Webber, G., 168, 217
Weber, N., 180, 217
Weems, R.J., 300, 338
Weigley, R.F., 184, 217
Wesley, J., 7, 30, 111, 146, 154, 156
Westboro Baptist Church, 170, 171
Westenholz, J.G., 1, 4
Wheat, C.E., 186, 217
Whitehead, G., 22
Whyte, W.H. Jr., 235, 280
Wicca, 2, 89, 205
Wickham, C., 225, 280
Wierzbicka, A., 139, 156
Wijnants, J., 203
Wilgoren, J., 165, 217
Wilkes, C.G., 191, 217
Wilkes, D.E. Jr., 177, 217
Williams, F. J.; Pederson, W.D.; and Marsala, V.J., 185, 217
Williams, P., 185, 197, 218
Williamson, T., 141, 156
Willis, M., 256, 280
Wilmore, J.C., 171
Wilson, C.W.; Warren, C.; Morrison, W.; and Stanley, A.P., 116, 156

Winter, P., 254, 280
Witt, T., 325, 331
Witte, E.H., 222, 280
Wittgenstein, L., 125, 141, 151, 157
Wolach, D.M., 141, 157
Wollstonecraft, M., 124, 154, 157
Wong, F.A., 223, 280
Woodville, R.C., 243
Woolfe, L., 193, 196, 218
Woolton, J., 256, 280
Working Lady Nuns of Nazareth House, 170
Wright Brothers, 22, 34
Wright, B.R., 257, 280
Wukovits, J. and Clark, W.K., 184, 218

Xenophon, 307, 338
Xyrichis, A. and Ream, E., 223, 280

Yahya, H., 263, 280
Yo Yo Ma, 14
Yoder, J.H., 58, 86

Zaloga, S.J., 248, 280
Zimbardo, P., 269, 280
Zimmerman, G., 262, 273
Zuckerman, P., 143, 157
Zylstra, S.E., 138, 157

Books and Films

Agamemnon, The, 42, 79
America's Got Talent, 223
Animal Farm, 125, 154
Arc of the Covenant, 318

Beowulf, 123, 156
Bugs Bunny, 76

Charlie Brown Christmas, 76, 83
Count of Monte Cristo, The, 195, 209

Defending Your Life, 292, 331
Divine Comedy, 71, 80, 333
Drummer Boy, 50

Economist, The, 24, 31

Fame is the Spur, 44, 85
Faust, 261, 271, 273, 276, 277, 278, 279
Frankenstein (or, The Modern Prometheus), 124, 155

Gulliver's Travels, 123, 156

Heartbreak Ridge, 19

It's the Great Pumpkin, Charlie Brown, 76, 83

Jersey Shore, 312
Jessica Hahn Bares It All, 162

Keeping Up With the Kardashians, 312

Law of Manus, 307, 335
Les Misérables, 314, 334
Lord of the Flies, 223, 273
Lord, Save Us from Your Followers, 270, 277

Magna Carta, 284, 334
Marquis of Queensburg Rules, 186

Nineteen Eighty-Four, 125, 154, 235, 277

On the Social Element in Religion, 326, 337
Once an Eagle, 45, 84

Paradise Lost, 111, 123, 153
Paradise Regained, 123, 154
Polar Express, The, 53, 85

Rights of Man, 124, 154
Republic, The, 307, 336
Road Runner, The, 76
Robinson Crusoe, 123, 150

Scarlet Letter, 257, 274, 303, 334
Star Trek, 9, 39, 79

Vindication of the Rights of Women, A., 124, 157

Wizard of Oz, 16
Yes, Virginia, there is a Santa, 53

Canonical and non-Canonical Scriptures

Acts, 6, 92, 133-34, 178, 198, 205, 261, 282, 297
Acts and Martyr, 94
Acts of Andrew, 94
Acts of Bartholomew, 94
Acts of John, 94
Acts of Matthew, 94
Acts of Paul, 94
Acts of Paul and Thecla, 94, 95, 100
Acts of Peter, 94
Acts of Peter and Paul, 94
Acts of Philip, 94
Acts of Simon and Jude, 94
Acts of Thomas, 94

Adam and Eve, book, 98
Amos, 91
Apocalypse of Abraham, 94
Apocalypse of Baruch, 94
Apocalypse of Daniel, 94
Apocalypse of Mary, 94
Apocalypse of Paul, 94
Apocalypses of Peter, 94
Apocrypha, 93-95, 99, 150, 152, 154-55
Ascension of Isaias, 94
Assumption of Moses, 94

1 Chronicles, 8, 90, 131

Index

2 Chronicles, 90
Codex Vaticanus, 110, 148
Colossians, 92
1 Corinthians, 92, 127, 131-35, 308, 333
2 Corinthians, 92, 132, 206, 319
Correspondence of Paul and Seneca, 94

Daniel, 91, 98, 198
Deuteronomy, 1, 49, 56, 90, 97, 130, 131, 254, 282, 300, 309, 316

Ecclesiastes, 90, 132, 135, 316, 318
Enoch, book, 98
Ephesians, 92
Epistle of Jeremiah, 99
Epistle of Peter to James the Less, 94
Epistles of Ignatius, 99
Epistles of Jesus Christ and Abgarus, King of Edessa, 99
Epistles of Paul to the Corinthians, 94
Epistles of the Blessed Virgin, 94
Esdras, 94
Esther, 90
Exodus, 1, 56, 90, 97, 130, 131, 195, 253, 298, 300, 318
Ezekiel, 91, 131, 134, 298, 301
Ezra, 90

First Epistle of Clement to the Corinthians, 98

Galatians, 92, 132, 134
General Epistle of Barnabas, 98
Genesis, 1, 90, 97, 131, 134, 193, 261, 288, 305, 307
Gospel according to the Egyptians, 94
Gospel according to the Hebrews, 94
Gospel of Bartholomew, 94
Gospel of Gamaliel, 94
Gospel of Jesus' Wife, 285, 335
Gospel of Nicodemus, 94, 100
Gospel of Peter, 94
Gospel of Philip, 94
Gospel of the Birth of Mary, 98
Gospel of the Infancy, 94
Gospel of The Infancy, 99
Gospel of the Twelve Apostles, 94
Gospel of Thomas, 94

Habakkuk, 91
Haggai, 91
Hebrews, 92, 132, 134, 135
Henoch, 94
Hosea, 91, 301

Infancy Gospel of James, 94
Isaiah, 8, 39, 91, 109, 111, 113, 132

James, 92, 112, 132, 133, 134, 263, 297, 321
Jannes and Mambres, 94
Jasher, book, 99
Jeremiah, 56, 90, 91, 98, 301, 318
Job, 42, 82, 90, 132, 133, 135
Joel, 91
John, 21, 54, 64, 71, 92, 102, 110, 127, 131-34, 137-38, 144, 146, 149, 152, 192, 193, 206, 258, 261, 282, 284, 285, 298, 315-16, 321, 324
1 John, 92, 193
2 John, 92
3 John, 92
Jonah, 91
Joshua, 90, 99, 132, 195
Jubilees, 94
Jude, 92, 289
Judges, 90, 298, 317
Judicium Petri, 94
Judith, book, 90, 99, 154

1 Kings, 90, 131, 197
2 Kings, 90, 131, 298
Koran, 98, 99, 307

Lamentations, 91
Latin Vulgate, 108
Legend of Abgar, 94
Letter of Herod to Pilate the
    Governor, 98
Letter of Lentulus, 94
Letter of Pilate to Herod, 98
Letter of the Smyrnaeans, 100
Leviticus, 56, 90, 97, 130, 131,
    300, 309
Luke, 6, 55, 92, 101, 110, 113, 117,
    127, 130-35, 175, 202, 208, 210,
    256, 264, 282, 310, 313, 316,
    317, 321, 323, 325

1,2,3,4 Maccabees (Machabees),
    90, 94, 99
Malachi, 91
Mark, 54, 55, 56, 92, 101, 110, 127,
    130, 133-37, 164, 175, 205, 208,
    253, 256, 283, 285, 289, 313,
    316, 321
Matthew, 55, 56, 57, 58, 64, 75, 85,
    92, 101, 109-13, 127, 132-38,
    203, 205, 206, 208, 256, 258,
    261, 265, 269, 282-87, 310, 313,
    316, 318, 321, 322, 325
Micah, 91
Minor Pilate Apocrypha, 94

Nahum, 91
Narrative of Joseph of Arimathea,
    94
Nehemiah, 56, 90
Nomina Sacra, 110
Numbers, 1, 90, 97, 195, 282

Obadiah, 91
Odes of Solomon, 90, 100

Pentateuch, 90, 101, 153
Pericope Adulterae, 137
1 Peter, 92, 111, 132
2 Peter, 92, 134, 135, 289
Philemon, 92
Philippians, 92, 134, 206

Prayer of Azarias, 98
Prayer of Manasseh, 100
Prayer of Manasses, 94
Preaching of Paul, 94
Preaching of Peter, 94
Prophecy of Baruch, 98
Proverbs, 90, 111, 114, 132, 133
Psalms, 61, 90, 101, 317
Psalms of Solomon, 94, 100

Report of Pilate to Augustus
    Caesar, 100
Report of Pilate to the Emperor, 94
Revelation, 92, 102, 135, 261, 267,
    289, 291, 319
Romans, 92, 134, 205, 333

1 Samuel, 90, 130, 132, 196, 298,
    318
2 Samuel, 90, 99, 128, 131, 197,
    318
Secrets of Enoch, book, 98
Secrets of Henoch, 94
Septuagint, 107, 156
Shepherd of Hermas, 98
Sibylline Oracles, 94
Solomon, 90, 94, 100, 197, 305,
    318
Song of Solomon, 90, 305
Susanna, book, 101

Teaching of Addai, 94
Testaments of the Twelve
    Patriarchs, 94, 101
Testamentum Domini Nostri Jesu,
1 Thessalonians, 92, 333, 338
2 Thessalonians, 92, 291, 298, 338
1 Timothy, 73, 92, 111, 134
2 Timothy, 92, 102, 132, 94
Titus, 92
Tobias, 90, 101, 150
Tobit, book, 101
Transitus Mariæ, 94

Wisdom of Jesus, Son of Sirach,
    90, 99

Wisdom of Solomon, 100

Zechariah, 91, 127

Zephaniah, 91

Subjects

abortion, 73, 87, 256, 266, 329
Act of Contrition, 263
adultery, 72, 87, 117, 176, 178, 192, 283, 303, 305, 309
amelioration, 140
anti-Semitism, 128
Atheism, 19, 23, 25, 35, 157, 205, 287, 288, 333
atonement, 264, 275

Banquet of Chestnuts, 180
Bay of Pigs, 248, 271, 273, 275, 277, 279
bestiality, 305
bigotry, 95, 206, 219, 242, 256
Black Sox Scandal, 159
bride price, 1
Buddhism, 25, 59, 283, 307, 333
bushidō, 248

Cadaver Synod, 177, 217
Calvinism, 41, 93
Catechism, 75, 85, 274
Charge of the Light Brigade, 243, 271, 272, 275, 279
Christmas, 50, 53, 125, 152, 254, 271, 273, 279, 310, 328
codicology, 110
cold fusion, 8, 35
creationism, 21, 23, 329
crucifixion, 100, 198, 253, 254, 278

dittography, 136, 137
divorce, 117, 306, 308, 325

evolution, 20, 21, 22, 23, 30, 32, 37, 161, 329
exhibitionism, 87

Facebook, 54, 311
Final Judgment, 289
fission, 136
flat earth, 8, 34
Freemasonry, 173, 174, 210
fusion, 136

generalization (error), 140
genocide, 77, 201, 245, 246, 273, 276, 299, 312
Gnosticism, 96, 147, 152
Good Samaritan, 55, 202, 203, 205, 206, 287, 288
Great Depression, 244
groupthink, 223, 235, 240-54, 273-80
Greek, 42, 79, 80, 81, 87, 90, 92, 98-100, 106, 107, 110, 127, 136-38, 145, 147, 148, 150, 153-55, 265, 289, 290, 301, 303, 316, 333, 336, 338

haplography, 137
hate, 50, 85, 128, 155, 202, 209, 216, 260, 280, 287, 288, 325, 337
Heaven, 1, 43, 50, 53, 110, 111, 131, 161, 169, 248, 259, 260, 264, 267,-70, 284, 292, 293, 306, 318, 331
Hebrew, 6, 87, 90, 91, 99, 101, 106, 107, 109, 290, 300, 316, 337, 338
Hell, 1, 30, 55, 80, 111, 124, 179, 262, 267, 270, 274, 277, 284, 287-92, 318, 320-33, 338
Hellenistic, 61, 79, 102
hermeneutics, 114, 156
Hinduism, 25, 59, 143, 307

homophony, 137
homosexual, 87, 88, 161, 182, 256, 257, 287, 301, 308, 329
Honor Code, 299, 336
Holocaust, 128, 171, 245, 315, 336
Hurricane Dennis, 234
Hurricane Katrina, 266
hypocrisy, 56, 83, 206, 213, 219, 256, 257, 258, 264, 277-78, 280

incest, 88, 178, 305
Inquisition, 18, 35, 66, 67, 68, 69, 70, 73, 85, 258, 323
Iran Hostage Rescue, 250, 276
Inquisition, 18, 35, 66, 67, 68, 69, 70, 73, 85, 258, 323
Iran Hostage Rescue, 250, 276

Judah, 1
Judaism, 59, 102, 205, 245, 334
jus ad bellum, 293, 295
jus in bello, 293, 296
Just War Theory, 295

Kamikaze, 248, 277, 280
Katyn Forest Massacre, 246, 247, 272, 278

Little Big Horn, 22
love, 2, 54, 55-58, 74, 85- 88, 103, 105, 110-13, 130, 132, 137, 147, 155, 193, 206, 216, 219, 256-70, 284-91, 300-3, 308, 315, 318, 320, 321, 324, 325, 327, 330, 331, 336-38
luminiferous aether, 10

Martian Canals, 10
Medal of Honor, 19, 314
metathesis, 137
Michigan, 50, 103, 104, 164, 226, 227, 310, 320
minuscule script, 110
moralism, 77, 303
murder, 6, 83, 88, 128, 165, 167, 171, 173, 176, 178, 201, 208, 209, 213, 224, 242, 246-47, 253, 262, 287, 324-25, 331
My Lai Massacre, 234, 277

necrophilia, 305

Operation Eagle Claw, 250, 275

paleography, 107, 110, 149, 153
papyrus, 107, 110, 112, 138, 285, 335
Pearl Harbor, 120, 247, 279
pedophilia, 266, 305
pejoration, 140
persecution, 58, 60, 65, 174, 219, 256, 267
philanthropy, 168, 313, 334
phrenology, 9, 35
polygamy, 88, 131
pornography, 308
PSYOPS, 241
Purgatory, 292, 293, 333, 334, 338

rape, 14, 88, 207, 287, 305, 306
rapture, 162, 163, 216, 259

sacred prostitution, 1
semantics, 156, 329
Seven Deadly Sins, 71, 73, 74
Seven Virtues, 71, 73, 74
sex, 4, 30, 77, 126, 152, 161, 164, 167-69, 188, 209, 210, 214, 285, 300-5, 324, 332-36
Siege of Jerusalem, 117
sorcery, 67
Sorites Paradox, 141, 149, 152, 157
Space Shuttle Challenger, 251, 252, 273, 278, 279
Space Shuttle Columbia, 252
specialization (error), 140
static universe, 8, 31
stoic, 40, 41, 42, 44, 45, 48, 55, 81, 82, 85

Tailhook, 159, 214, 217
Texas, 46, 203, 241, 325, 335

Index

torture, 6, 66, 67, 70, 88, 201
Twitter, 311

uncial script, 110, 135
Underground Railroad, 315
Utopia, 125

vengeance, 132, 195, 324, 325, 336
Venus, 302
Vulcan Planet, 9

war, 16, 19, 22, 69, 80, 88, 100, 117, 128, 184, 193, 207, 216, 226, 231, 247, 248, 265, 270, 274, 293, 295, 332, 334
Watergate Scandal, 249, 270
Weapons of Mass Destruction, 122, 125, 183
wisdom, 1, 3, 5, 6, 13, 28, 30, 41, 90, 99, 100, 114, 132, 151, 196, 197, 215, 218
witch, 16, 67, 83

About the Author

The author earned a Bachelor's Degree in Chemistry from Central Michigan University, along with a Masters and a Doctorate Degree in Chemical Engineering from Michigan State University. Colonel Scott S. Haraburda served in the US Army, rising through the ranks to command the 472nd Chemical Battalion and later command the 464th Chemical Brigade. He also taught chemistry at West Point, ran the Army Science Board in the Pentagon, provided logistics in Kuwait, and graduated from the Army War College. He retired from the US Army in 2010, earning the Legion of Merit for distinguished service.

In his civilian experience, Dr. Haraburda worked as an engineer for Bayer Corporation and General Electric; the Deputy Site Project Manager for the Newport Chemical Agent Disposal Facility in Indiana, where he helped to successfully destroy the facility's entire VX nerve-agent stockpile; and the Director of Manufacturing & Engineering for the Crane Army Ammunition Activity in Indiana. Dr. Haraburda was awarded two US patents and has authored numerous technical and management articles. He is also a Registered Professional Engineer in the State of Indiana. In 2009, he received the Alan Rankin Award as member of the Terre Haute Children's Museum's Board of Directors for outstanding community leadership. In 2011, he was inducted into the Central Michigan University ROTC Hall of Fame.

Dr. Haraburda spent several years teaching Sunday school classes in various non-denominational Christian churches (& chapels), including the United Methodist Church. He also served one year as the Sunday School Superintendent while he was teaching at West Point. During his military service as a battalion commander and brigade commander, he was responsible for the supporting and maintaining the religious needs of thousands of Soldiers.

Scott and his wife, Marie, are a team with a small writing company nestled in the wooded hills of southern Indiana.